Folklore
and Literature

*SUNY series in Latin American and
Iberian Thought and Culture*

Jorge J. E. Gracia, Editor

Folklore *and Literature*

Studies in the Portuguese, Brazilian, Sephardic, and Hispanic Oral Traditions

Manuel da Costa Fontes

State University of New York Press

Published by
State University of New York Press, Albany

For information, address State University of New York
Press, State University Plaza, Albany, N.Y., 12246

Production by Diane Ganeles
Marketing by Fran Keneston

Library of Congress Cataloging-in-Publication Data

Fontes, Manuel da Costa.
    Folklore and literature : studies in the Portuguese, Brazilian,
Sephardic, and Hispanic oral traditions / Manuel da Costa Fontes.
        p.   cn. — (SUNY series in Latin American and Iberian thought
and culture)
    Includes bibliographical references (p.   –   ) and index.
    1. Literature and folklore—Portugal.   2. Literature and folklore—
Spain.   3. Literature and folklore—Brazil.   4. Folk literature,
Portuguese—History and criticism.   5. Folk literature, Spanish—
History and criticism.   I. Title.   II. Series.
    GR238F65   2000
    398'.0946—dc21   99–39443
                                                                  CIP

10 9 8 7 6 5 4 3 2 1

To Bráulio do Nascimento
Vice-President of the Brazilian National Folklore
Commission (UNESCO)

and

Luiz Antonio Barreto
Secretary of Education, State of Sergipe

Contents

vii

Contents

Introduction

People sang and told stories to each other since time immemorial, developing an oral, folk literature long before the appearance of written literature. Since love is a basic human emotion, it stands to reason that the first songs must have been lyrical, but people also sang narrative poems in which they perpetuated, for example, the memory of their heroes and important events. In prose, they developed sacred myths about their gods, the creation of the world, and the origins of human beings, along with secular legends which, although also regarded as true, were set in a less remote past and included supernatural creatures such as fairies, elves, werewolves, witches, and vampires.[1] They created incantations to protect themselves from evil and from various illnesses, and to mollify the powers of nature. Besides singing, in moments of leisure people also entertained themselves with imaginative, fictional prose narratives known as folktales. They tested their wits with riddles and embellished their speech with sayings and proverbs that condensed nuggets of wisdom acquired over the centuries. These love songs, narrative poems, myths, legends, incantations, folktales, riddles, and proverbs were orally transmitted from generation to generation. Communities continued to enrich their repertoires with new materials of their own invention, but they also borrowed from neighbors who, in turn, had acquired much of what they knew from others. When writing was eventually invented, these oral, traditional songs and stories began to be written down, forming the basis of a literature which, in time, would become increasingly learned.

In the Iberian Peninsula, the earliest native literary manifestations, the eleventh-century *jarchas*, were short women's songs of two,

1

three, or four lines written in Mozarabic, the Latin-derived vernacular spoken by the Christian inhabitants of Andaluzia who lived under the domination of the Arabic-speaking invaders. These songs, which survived thanks to their use at the end of learned *muwashahah* written in Arabic but also in Hebrew, have much in common with the Galician-Portuguese *cantigas de amigo* that began to be written down during the thirteenth century. A young lady sings about her lover who is sometimes absent on a voyage, often confiding in her mother and sisters. Although similar Castilian *villancicos* did not begin to be written down until the fifteenth century, there is no doubt that they are much older. In turn, these *jarchas, cantigas de amigo,* and *villancicos* parallel the *chansons de femme* of neighboring France (Frenk 1978, 21–37), not to mention the Anglo-Saxon women's songs and the German Frauenlieder. Thus, they constitute indigenous, Iberian folk songs, and a manifestation of a pan-European type of folk poetry as well.

According to Ramón Menéndez Pidal and to many other scholars, the Castilian epic derives from the heroic songs brought into the Iberian Peninsula by Germanic invaders. It was orally composed by anonymous poets, and, rather than having a fixed form, it existed in variants, changing from singer to singer and even from performance to performance. When first created, these epics reflected faithfully the historical events that they perpetuated; most of the fictitious elements that they included were added over time, as those events were gradually forgotten. Although a group of scholars dispute the Germanic origins and the faithful historical character of these poems (Deyermond 1995, 48–49), everyone agrees that, at one time, they represented another type of folk poetry (Deyermond 1972; 1980, 65).

The medieval epics that have come down to us are the *Cantar de Mio Cid,* the *Poema de Fernán González,* the incomplete *Mocedades de Rodrigo,* and a fragment of *Roncesvalles*; others, such as *Los Siete Infantes de Lara* and *Sancho II y el cerco de Zamora,* were prosified in chronicles, which included them because they were considered historical. The chronicles also testify to the existence of numerous historical legends (see Castillo 1967), some of which may have been versified and turned into epics (Deyermond 1995, 62–137), though others probably were not. There always have been legends and, as Alan Deyermond pointed out, "en cada época hay tradiciones y anécdotas seudohistoriográficas que nunca llegan a tener forma poética" (there exist in every period traditions and pseudohistorical stories that are never put into verse; 1995, 56). Naturally, religious legends abounded, and there were also many other types of legends.

Minstrels chanted the lengthy epics in courts, castles, and public squares, and their listeners often retained particularly appealing passages that they began to sing separately, thus transforming them into ballads. In Spain, there were also Carolingian ballads, which derived from the French epics that minstrels also sang throughout the country. Historical ballads about important events were created, and a large corpus of pan-European ballads dealing with universal aspects of human existence made its way across the Pyrenees.[2] Many of these ballads were compiled and published during the fifteenth and sixteenth centuries, thus being transformed from oral folk poetry into written literature. Numerous writers used them in their works, at the same time creating new, learned ballads of their own.

Folktales began to be written down early in the twelfth century, starting with Pedro Alfonso's *Disciplina clericalis* (ca. 1106) or the Scholar's guide. There followed numerous collections of *exempla*, which used folktales to entertain but also to teach moral lessons. Many of these stories were of ancient Indo-European origins, existing in many languages, as they still exist today in an area that extends all the way from India to Europe, but others were of Eastern origin, being introduced into Iberia by the Moslem invasion (711 A.D.). Some eventually made their way into other European countries (see M. J. Lacarra 1989, 9–85). In addition to the medieval collections of *exempla*, in Spain and Portugal the folktale continued to be compiled during the Renaissance by individuals such as Juan Timoneda[3] and Gonçalo Fernandes Trancoso (1974), playing an important role in the picaresque novel and in the works of numerous writers, including Gil Vicente (see, e.g., Viegas Guerreiro 1981) and Miguel de Cervantes Saavedra.[4]

Medieval and Renaissance writers also demonstrated great interest in popular proverbs, often including them in poetic and prose works as early as the thirteenth century (O'Kane 1959; Deyermond 1980, 250). Iñigo López de Mendoza, marquis of Santillana, collected them in the fifteenth century (Santillana 1987), and, during the Renaissance, his example was followed by compilers such as Juan de Mal Lara (1996) and Gonzalo Correas (1924). Numerous writers continued to include them in their works.[5]

Except for the epic, all of these genres still exist in the modern pan-Iberian traditions, which often supplement our knowledge of the past through their preservation of materials that failed to reach print. *Cantigas de amigo* have been recorded in Portugal,[6] and in her splendid corpus of the popular Hispanic lyric between the fifteenth and seventeenth centuries, Margit Frenk (1987, 1992) often lists modern parallels of various types of early songs. Numerous legends from Spain, Portugal, and the Americas have been published, often as appendixes to tale collections, and a brilliant, prolific young Spaniard, José Manuel Pedrosa,[7] has recently discovered that many of the early historical legends still exist in various parts of Spain.[8] The modern ballad tradition of Spain, Portugal, their overseas extensions, and the Sephardim is no doubt the richest in the world,[9] and often supplements our knowledge of the early tradition thanks to its preservation of text-types that did not reach print in the past or versions that include crucial details absent from their early congeners. Since some of these ballads derive from lost epic poems, they also contribute to our knowledge of the epic tradition of the Middle Ages.[10] Many of the modern Spanish folktales indexed by Ralph Steele Boggs (1930) and by Julio Camarena and Maxime Chevalier (1995, 1997) appear in the works of early writers; some of these folktales, which also exist in the oral tradition of the Sephardim (Haboucha 1992) and the Americas (Hansen 1957; Robe 1973), supplement our knowledge of the early tradition and early literature as well.[11]

First and foremost, writers used folklore in their works because of the oral origins of written literature. Since during the Middle Ages and the Renaissance most people were illiterate, books were often read out loud in front of audiences, and writers wished to appeal to as many listeners as possible. The oral tradition, which conveys folk literature from generation to generation through the spoken voice rather than through a written text, was still familiar to everyone, not just to the illiterate or semiliterate rural masses who now preserve it best. Since the distinction between oral and written literature was less pronounced than it is today, learned authors readily incorporated folk literature into their works, often through allusions that would be instantly recognized by contemporary audiences. Conversely, some writers imitated the popular style so well that the folk occasionally accepted as their own some of the poems that these authors had written. There are many examples of this reciprocal borrowing in Portugal and Spain. Most people are no longer familiar with the oral tradition, however. As a result, our understanding of medieval and Renaissance literature is frequently diminished.

Because early writers contributed to the development of folk literature with materials of their own creation, it is often difficult to determine whether a particular poem or story is of learned or folk origins (see Rosenberg 1991 and Bottigheimer's 1993 review of the former's work). Even a story that appears with variants in the works of several authors as well as in the modern tradition, bearing important earmarks of oral transmission, may have been originally learned. A folk item could also be refashioned in one way or another by a learned writer and subsequently become traditional in its new form. In the last analysis, most arguments in favor of learned or folk origins are ultimately futile. The purpose of this book is not to engage in such a discussion, but to bring together several article-length studies in which, over the years, I have shown, especially from a Luso-Brazilian perspective, that a familiarity with modern folktales, ballads, and lyric poetry can often shed light on medieval and Renaissance Iberian literature. All of these studies have been updated; several were conflated, supplemented, and completely rewritten. My title was inspired by one of Frenk's pathfinding works on the early lyric, *Entre folklore y literatura: Lírica hispánica antigua* (1971).

Chapter 1, "*Puputiriru*: An Eastern Folktale from the *Disciplina clericalis*," begins by examining the "Dream-Bread Story," an Eastern folktale that entered into Iberia with the Moslem invasion (711 A.D.) and that became very popular in Europe thanks to its inclusion in Pedro Alfonso's learned *Disciplina clericalis* (1106). Versions of this story are still told in Portugal, Spain, Brazil, and elsewhere. Because "bread" used to be a popular metaphor for female genitalia, the folk adapted the story in a pornographic way. This metamorphosis appeared, with variants, in a learned fifteenth-century French rondeau, and in works by Philippe de Vigneulles (1515), François Rabelais (1532), and Nicolas de Troyes (ca. 1536). Timoneda published one Spanish version (1564). The two modern Portuguese folk versions, which are much closer to the bawdy French renditions, suggest that the story also existed in Portugal during the sixteenth century and that Timoneda felt compelled to tone down his literary adaptation considerably.

Chapter 2, "On Alfonso X's 'Interrupted' Encounter with a *soldadeira*," reinterprets the satiric "Fui eu poer a mão noutro dia," a *cantiga d'escarnho* written in Galician-Portuguese by Alfonso X of Castile (thirteenth century). In this poem, the poet describes his encounter with a prostitute on a Friday, at 3:00 P.M. She asks him to stop, because it is the day and hour when Christ died. Scholars believe that the poem then focuses on the suffering caused by coitus interruptus, but folklore enabled me to clarify the meaning of the text's metaphors, showing that there is no interruption. Since the poem is really a pun (i.e., no "meat" on Fridays), it is also wrong to confuse the poetic voice with the king's, as some critics have done.

Chapter 3, "Martínez de Toledo's 'Nightmare' and the Courtly and Oral Traditions," attempts to decipher the short, highly debated retraction that Alfonso Martínez de Toledo added to his misogynistic *Corbacho* (1438) because of the highly negative reaction that it provoked. Modern folklore enabled me to settle the debate, showing that he wrote his retraction in jest. By drawing metaphors from the oral tradition and from the courtly code, Martínez de Toledo reaffirms what he had written in his book, implying that ladies who practice courtly love are no better than prostitutes.

Chapter 4 focuses on "Knitting and Sewing Metaphors and a Maiden's Honor in *La Celestina*." In *Celestina* (1499), Fernando de Rojas tells the story of two young lovers, Calisto and Melibea, who are brought together by an old procuress, Celestina. While portraying Celestina's corruption of Melibea, Rojas brings together a series of weaving metaphors—*thread, yarn balls, needles, pins, sewing,* and *stitches*—that he links to a maiden's "honor." Two modern Portuguese folk stories and a Brazilian chapbook that bring all of these terms together contribute to document their metaphoric character, and suggest that the author drew them from the folk tradition.

Chapter 5, *"El idólatra de María*: An Anti-Christian Jewish Ballad?" scrutinizes a poem which, although absent from the early collections, is no doubt of medieval origin, thus supplementing our knowledge of the early tradition. *El idólatra* exists in the Portuguese, Galician, Castilian, Catalan, and Sephardic traditions. Because of the Virgin's uncharacteristic refusal to assist a drowning sailor, it seemed that the ballad was originally composed by a Jew as an anti-Christian poem. As I demonstrate, however, the Virgin's refusal to help the sailor came about because of a contamination with *El marinero al agua*, a folk ballad whose shipwrecked protagonist drowns (and, therefore, cannot be saved). *El idólatra* is based on two learned medieval Christian ideas: Mary in her roles as guide of the ship of faith and patroness of mariners. Thus, the ballad was originally composed as a learned Christian poem, being subsequently accepted by the folk; it acquired its strong anti-Christian character among the Sephardim after their expulsion from Spain (1492).

Chapter 6, "Gil Vicente's *Remando Vão Remadores* and *Barca Bela*," shows that the beautiful ballad that Vicente, a Portuguese playwright who also wrote in Spanish, wrote to open his *Auto da Barca do Purgatório* (1517), *Remando Vão Remadores*, rearranges the narrative elements in *Barca Bela*, a modern Portuguese and Brazilian folk ballad. In its turn, *Barca Bela* constitutes a religious adaptation of the Castilian *El conde Arnaldos*, first written down by J. Rodríguez del Padrón (ca. 1440). Vicente's utilization of *Barca Bela* suggests that it was already part of the oral folk tradition at the beginning of the sixteenth century. This chapter also shows how a learned writer can adapt something of popular character in order to create a new, highly original poem.

Chapter 7 examines "The Oral Transmission of *Flérida*." Vicente concluded his *Tragicomedia de don Duardos* (1525) with a ballad about the elopement of the English protagonist, Don Duardos, and the Bizantine princess Flérida. Known as *Flérida*, this ballad exists in Portuguese, Spanish, and Judeo-Spanish, but each tradition preserves it in a unique manner, viewing the elopement of the princess in its own special way.

Chapter 8, "Three New Ballads Derived from *Don Duardos*," shows how two new ballads, *Lizarda* (Azores, Madeira, Brazil) and *O Hortelão das Flores* (Beira Alta and Beira Baixa), combine *Flérida* with different portions of the play in order to explain why Flérida's elopement comes about. A third ballad, the Sephardic *El falso hortelano*, invents a continuation, showing how misfortunate Flérida was afterward, because, being a very conservative community, the Sephardim wanted to discourage notions of romantic love on the part of their daughters. Thus, this chapter examines how the oral tradition incorporated these metamorphoses of the work of a learned author, creating a new poem inspired by Vicente's play as well.[12]

In sum, this book shows how some modern ballads and folktales supplement our knowledge of the early oral tradition and early literature. Although they were "lost," in the sense that they were not included in collections of *exempla* and in the medieval and sixteenth-century compilations known as *cancioneros* and *romanceros*, it is possible to demonstrate that they go back to the Middle Ages and to the Renaissance. Some are exclusively Portuguese and Brazilian today, thus pointing to the conservatism of the Luso-Brazilian tradition. I also prove that the modern oral tradition enhances our understanding of early literature in several ways. Besides documenting how writers such as Rojas, Vicente, and Timoneda adapted and used folklore in their works, the book demonstrates how modern folklore enables us to understand crucial passages of early works whose learned authors took for granted a familiarity with the oral tradition, thus enabling us to restore those passages to their intended meaning. In addition, I show how the folk accepted and adapted some originally learned works, transmitting them orally to the present. As far as I know, this book, which also studies the vicissitudes of oral transmission in detail, is the first one exclusively dedicated to the relationship between folklore and literature in a Luso-Brazilian context, taking into account the pan-Hispanic traditions as well.

Except for Samuel G. Armistead's translation of *Aqueya panadera* (see chap. 1n7), the English translations are mine. In Portuguese, Spanish, Catalan, and Judeo-Spanish ballads, the present and the past (preterit and imperfect tenses) often alternate. Since it would have been very awkward to render this literally in English, I opted for only one tense, choosing the one that prevailed in each poem.

This book has benefited from the help of numerous friends. Samuel G. Armistead has given me much valuable advice over the years, and came to my rescue with rare, hard-to-find items. Diego Catalán and Ana Valenciano sent me copies of all the versions of several ballads at the Menéndez Pidal Archive, enabling me to make the chapters on *Flérida* and *Don Duardos* more thorough and complete. I am also indebted to Diego Catalán for permission to edit and publish the Sephardic versions of *Flérida* and *El falso hortelano* in two appendixes (B and D). José Joaquim Dias Marques, Radd Ehrman, E. Michael Gerli, Maria Eugenia Lacarra, Francisco Márquez Villanueva, Yakov Malkiel, Randolph D. Pope, Joseph T. Snow, Mercedes Vaquero, and Louise Vasvari read drafts of some of the articles on which this book is based, offering valuable advice in the process. Harriet Goldberg and Arthur L.-Askins came to my rescue on two critical occasions. I would also like to acknowledge the help of four colleagues from my department, Rosa Comisso, Luis Hermosilla, Françoise Massardier-Kenney, and Greg Shreve. Another colleague, Richard M. Berrong, read a draft of this book, offering many invaluable suggestions. The numerous friends who, over the years, have sent me their publications and materials that helped with various phases of this project include Luiz Antonio Barreto, Jesús Antonio Cid, Giuseppe Di Stefano, Pere Ferré, Luis Estepa, Margit Frenk, Maria Aliete Galhoz, William H. González, Israel J. Katz, John E. Keller, Bráulio do Nascimento, José Manuel Pedrosa, João David Pinto-Correia, Flor Salazar, Jackson da Silva Lima, Pedro da Silveira, and Maximiano Trapero. I would like to express my heartfelt gratitude to all of them, and to the Research Council, Kent State University, for the Research Appointment that enabled me to dedicate the spring of 1997 to this project. The chairperson of my department, Rick M. Newton, has been unwavering in his encouragement of research, and supported my request for a leave-of-absence under difficult circumstances. Finally, I would like to thank my family for their patience and understanding during the many hours that it took me to complete this book.

1

Puputiriru: An Eastern Folktale from the *Disciplina clericalis*

In the winter of 1978, while collecting ballads among Portuguese immigrants in New England (see NI), my wife and I were unable to travel for several days because of the harshness of the weather. Fortunately, this apparent mishap did not result in a waste of our time, for it gave us the opportunity to conduct extensive interviews in Taunton, Massachusetts, with Guilherme Alexandre da Silveira, a septuagenarian from the island of Flores, Azores, who knew many folktales.[1] Mr. Silveira, who had never learned how to read and write, favored the lengthy folktale—many of his stories took more than thirty minutes to record—but he also knew some relatively shorter jokes and anecdotes. One of these was enigmatically entitled *Puputiriru*. Embarrassed by the presence of two ladies,[2] Mr. Silveira felt obliged to replace two key words with common, easily deciphered gestures.

The story can be summarized as follows: A priest who has never been with a woman before wants to have sex. One day he sees a beautiful prostitute who is new in town and she invites him in, proposing a bet. If he is able to answer three questions correctly, she will sleep with him and give him a certain sum; otherwise, he will have to pay her an equal sum and she will not have to go to bed with him. When the priest agrees, the girl tells him to come back at 8:00 P.M. sharp. The poor man can hardly wait for the appointed hour. Meanwhile, the prostitute makes the same bet with a navy captain, telling him to come back at 8:10 P.M. Later on a soldier comes by and, seeing that he has money, she makes the same bet with him, instructing him to come at 8:15 P.M. The priest arrives and she tells

9

him to wait on a sofa, because she has work to do in the kitchen. When the captain enters, she tells him to wait with the priest. The priest is extremely embarrassed. After the sailor comes in, the prostitute asks the priest: "Father, what is the most beautiful thing that there is?" "My cassock," he replies. She starts laughing and asks: "And the most handsome thing?" "Me, for I am a good-looking man, and I work very hard to save souls." "And what is the puputiriru?" "The sound the sexton makes when he rings the church bells." She replies with a guffaw and tells him that he has lost the bet.

The captain's turn comes next. "What is the most beautiful thing?" "Me, for I am a navy captain. Look at these insignia." "Do you think you scare me? And what is the most handsome thing?" "When I get my troops ready for battle in order to kill women like you." "Do you think you scare me? And what is the puputiriru?" "It's the sound the bullets make when I tell them to fire on you." The prostitute says that he has lost.

The captain then tells the soldier that he will be promoted if he is able to answer her questions. She asks him: "What is the most beautiful thing?" "Your bosom" [lit., *altars*]. "And the most handsome thing?" "Your pretty [pussy]." "And what is the puputiriru?" "I have got it right here." She takes the soldier to bed. Besides sleeping with her and winning the money, he also earns a promotion.[3]

There is some confusion about the different branches of the armed forces. A navy captain is not likely to promote a soldier, who belongs to the army. The character is really a sailor, for at one point he says that his ship is about to leave. The priest and the captain's replies reflect their respective professions. In a way, the three protagonists may be said to represent the three estates, nobility, clergy, and commoners, for the nobility were often associated with arms, while sailors were usually drawn from the masses. The captain and the priest also stand for the distinction between arms and letters.[4] The winner is the lowest in social status. Obviously, the presence of a priest need not be taken as a sign of anticlericalism. Bawdy stories involving the clergy, especially priests, are frequent in Catholic countries, for people are naturally inclined to poke fun at figures in positions of authority (see Legman 1962, 201; Thompson 1946, 212; Aarne and Thompson 1973, 486–507 [nos. 1725–1849*]).

While recording this story, I had no idea that it boasted a truly ancient, venerable Oriental ancestry. Its first known version seems to be the one found in a Buddhist book written at least three centuries before Christ. A partridge, a monkey, and an elephant live in a great banyan-tree and decide to choose the eldest of the three as their leader. Each of them says what is the oldest thing that he can remember. The partridge wins by claiming that the tree on which they live sprang from the seed of a fruit that it had eaten a long time ago (Baum 1917, 379).

The animals in this fable were eventually replaced by human characters. A Persian text from the thirteenth century transforms the protagonists into three traveling companions, a Moslem, a Christian, and a Jew. According to a later Arabic variant, it is Jesus, Peter, and Judas who travel from Rome to Jerusalem. In each of these versions, the traveling companions decide that the one who has the best dream will eat the food that is left (a cake, a goose) all by himself, but the third one—the Jew and Judas in these instances—gets up while the other two are asleep, and eats it (381–82).

This story seems to have made its way to Europe thanks to the Moslem invasion of Spain in 711. It appears for the first time in the *Disciplina clericalis* or the Scholar's guide of Pedro Alfonso, a Spanish Jew who converted to Christianity in 1106. Two burghers and a peasant on their way to Mecca share their food, but there comes a time when they are left with only enough flour to make a small loaf of bread. Hoping to cheat the peasant out of his share, the burghers propose that the one who has the best dream should eat the whole loaf. Realizing what they are up to, the peasant gets up and eats the bread. Then one of the burghers wakes up and says that he dreamed that two angels had taken him before God. The other burgher dreamed that two angels had taken him to hell. They wake up the peasant, who pretends to be asleep. Since he had seen that one of his companions had gone to Heaven and the other one to hell, he had gotten up and eaten the bread, for he had thought that they would never return (1980, 75–76 [Span. trans.], 132–33 [Lat. orig.]).

This story has been translated into English as follows:

> Once there were two city men and a countryman who were going to Mecca on a pilgrimage. They ate together until they came near Mecca, where their provisions gave out, and they had nothing left but a little flour with which they could make one small loaf.
>
> The city men, seeing this, said to each other, "We have little bread and our companion eats much; we should think how we can get his share of the bread and eat it by ourselves."
>
> They all three agreed to the following plan: that they would make the loaf and bake it; and while it was cooking, they would go to sleep, and whoever had the most extravagant dream should have the bread for himself. The city dwellers said this as a trick because they

thought the countryman was stupid enough to believe such ruses. They made the loaf, put it on the fire, and then lay down to sleep.

The countryman, aware of the trick, took the half-baked loaf from the fire while his companions were sleeping, ate it, and lay down again.

One of the city dwellers, as if frightened by a dream, awoke and called to his companion. The second city dweller said, "What is the matter?"

And the first said, "I had a wonderful dream: it seemed that two angels opened the gates of Heaven, took me up, and led me before God."

His companion said to him, "This dream is wonderful, but I dreamed that with two angels leading me and opening the earth, I was taken to hell."

The peasant heard all this and still pretended to be asleep; but the deceitful city men, who had already been deceived, called the countryman to wake up. And he, slyly, as if he were frightened, answered, "Who is calling me?"

They said, "We, your companions."

And he said, "Have you returned already?"

And they said, "Where did we go, that we should return?"

And the rustic said, "I dreamed that two angels took one of you and opened the gates of Heaven and took him before God; then two other angels took the other and opened the earth and took him to hell. When I saw these things, I thought that neither of you would ever return, and I got up and ate the bread."   (Keller and Jones 1969, 78–80)

The precise sources of the *Disciplina clericalis* will probably never be established. The book could have existed in an Eastern language, for Alfonso states that God inspired him to translate it into Latin, but some scholars believe that he used various sources, either written or oral (see Lacarra's introd. to the ed. cited, 23). The book became extremely popular throughout Europe. It has been found in Spain, France, Italy, England, Belgium, Germany, Switzerland, Holland, and Sweden, in whole or in part, in more that sixty manuscripts dating from the twelfth to the fifteenth centuries. There were also many early translations of the *Disciplina clericalis* into the vernacular languages of Europe and, between the thirteenth and nineteenth centuries, the Three-Dream or Dream-Bread Story was incorporated into numerous other works as well (Baum 1917,

383–99). Since such stories were widely used in sermons during the twelfth and thirteenth centuries, the narrative probably passed into the oral tradition at a very early date. As Paul Franklin Baum surmises, "the literary and oral propagation of course went on at one and the same time; and for every written instance we have of it, we may be sure there were a dozen or a score of oral repetitions" (399).

The story has been collected in France, Italy, Holland, Germany, Iceland, Hungary, Russia and other Slavic countries, the United States and Canada, and elsewhere (Aarne and Thompson 1973, no. 1626). In France and Italy, the character who outwits his companions is either a Gascon or a Sicilian, members of two groups that have been stereotyped as being particularly clever in those countries. In England, the winner is usually Irish (Baum 1917, 401–3). In one American version, the protagonists are three hobos, an Italian, a Mexican, and an American; the Mexican wins the prize, which is now a stolen chicken (Botkin 1957, 51–52). A versified American rendition replaces the bread with a piece of baloney, and two Irishmen are outwitted by a Jew:

> Two Irishmen and a Hebrew one day
>   Went out for recreation.
> They took enough provisions along
>   To spend a week's vacation.
> One night they got lost in the woods;
>   The night was dark and lonely.
> At last the food they had gave out,
>   Except a piece of baloney.
> As one of them took up a knife,
>   I said, "It's no use carving,
> For if we share this piece of baloney,
>   It won't keep us from starving."
> So I suggested we all go to sleep,
>   And so did Maloney.
> And the one that had the best of dreams
>   Wins the piece of baloney.
> The following morn we all got up,
>   It was quarter after seven.
> One of them said: "I had a dream,
>   I died and went to Heaven;
> St. Peter met me at the gate,
>   Riding on a pony.
> I guess that dream couldn't be beat,
>   So that wins the piece of baloney."
> The other one said: "I too had a dream;
>   I died and went to Heaven;

St. Peter met me at the gate,
   Stuck out his hand, and said, 'Hello, Maloney!,'
I guess that dream couldn't be beat,
   So that wins the piece of baloney."
The Hebrew said: "It's true, my friend,
   That you were sleeping.
The reason why I know it is
   'Cause I was peeping.
I saw you both go up in Heaven;
   And, believe me, I was lonely;
I thought you would never come back again,
   So I got up and ate the baloney."
         (Botkin 1944, 452–53)

This story has also been collected in Spain (Boggs 1930, no. 1626); Spanish America (Robe 1973, no. 1626; Hansen 1957, no. 1626); and Brazil (Barroso 1949, 347 [= Câmara Cascudo n.d., 307–8]; Câmara Cascudo 1922, 245; 1955, 30; Fernandes 1970, 206). One of the Brazilian variants (Câmara Cascudo 1922, 245) recalls the Arabic version mentioned earlier, for it also has Jesus, St. Peter, and Judas as protagonists. In another Brazilian rendition, the contestants are a Jesuit, a Dominican, and a Capuchin (Torres 1922, *apud* Câmara Cascudo 1955, 30). According to Câmara Cascudo (1955, 32), Leite de Vasconcellos published a version in Portugal, but I have been unable to find it; unfortunately, it was not included in the two posthumous volumes of his monumental tale collection (1963–66).

The Brazilian version that follows is similar to the American ones in the sense that the protagonists also represent ethnic groups that came to that country as immigrants. While a Spaniard and a Japanese sleep, an Italian gets up and eats the small loaf of maize bread that a miserly woman had given them:

   Um espanhol, um italiano e um japonês viajavam juntos, uma vez, por uma estrada.

   Então, em certa altura da viagem, estavam os três já mortos de fome e bateram numa casa e pediram alguma coisa para comer.

   E a mulher de lá, que era muito miserável, só deu pra eles uma broa pequenininha.

   Então eles pegaram a broa, foram em baixo de uma árvore e viram que o negócio estava ruim mesmo: aquela broa não dava para matar a fome nem de um, quanto mais de três!

Daí, um deles resolveu uma coisa: iriam os três dormir. Aquele que sonhasse que tinha viajado mais longe do que o outro era o que comeria a broa.

E então os três dormiram e acordaram depois.

O espanhol disse:

—Eu sonhei que fui prò Céu!

E o japonês:

—E eu sonhei que fui prò Inferno, que é mais longe do que o Céu! Até me lembro que passei no Céu e vi você lá, de longe.

E o italiano, então:

—Pois olhem. Eu não fui pra lugar nenhum; eu fiquei acordado. E como vocês estavam demorando pra chegar da viagem, eu peguei e comi a broa.

(Fernandes 1970, 206)

(A Spaniard, an Italian, and a Japanese were once traveling together on a road. Then, at one point, the three were very hungry, knocked at the door of a house, and asked for something to eat. The woman, who was very stingy, only gave them a small loaf of maize bread. They took the bread, sat under a tree, and realized that the situation was really bad. The loaf was not enough for one, much less for three. For that reason, one of them made a decision. The three ought to go to sleep, and the one who traveled the farthest in a dream would be the one to eat the bread. They went to sleep and woke up. The Spaniard said: "I dreamed that I went to heaven!" The Japanese: "And I dreamed that I went to hell, which is even farther. In fact, I remember passing Heaven, and saw you there, from afar." The Italian: "Well, look, I did not go anywhere. I stayed awake and, since you were taking so long to come back, I took the bread and ate it.")

The Portuguese text recorded by Mr. Silveira in Massachusetts, however, offers a completely different perspective on the story. The three protagonists no longer travel together,[5] the dream has been replaced by three questions, and the stakes have been raised, for the winner's reward consists of much more than a mere loaf of bread or some other sort of sustenance: sex with a whore.

This surprising substitution was triggered by the metaphoric value of the words "bread" and "baker-girl," which, during the Middle Ages and the Renaissance, also meant "vagina" and "prostitute." Note the following song from the *Libro de Buen Amor* (1330, 1343), in which Juan Ruiz, the archpriest of Hita, complains about losing Cruz, a baker-girl whose favors he sought, to Ferrant Garçía, whom he had sent to speak with her on his behalf. The treacherous García had eaten her sweetest bread:

115	*Mis ojos no verán luz*	My eyes will not behold the light
	pues perdido he a Cruz.	for I have lost my Cross.
116	Cruz cruzada, panadera,	The crossed Cross, a baker-girl,
	tomé por entendedera,	I chose as a mistress
	tomé senda por carrera	and took a trail instead of a road
	como faz el andaluz.	just like an Andaluzian.
117	Coidando que la avría,	Thinking that she would be mine
	díxelo a Ferrand Garçía	I told Hernando García
	que troxies' la pletesía	to arrange the affair
	e fuese pleités e duz.	as negotiator and guide.
118	Díxom' que l' plazía de grado,	He said he would be glad to do it
	fízos' de la Cruz privado:	and became intimate with Cross.
	a mí dio rrumiar salvado,	He left me the bran to chew
	él comió el pan más duz.	and ate her sweetest bread.

(Ruiz 1974)[6]

Francisco Márquez Villanueva has brought together a series of passages, ranging from the fifteenth to the twentieth centuries, where the words *pan* (bread) and *panadera* (baker-woman) are used in the same manner (1988), and Samuel G. Armistead recorded in Delacroix, from Joseph Ocampo, one of the last descendants of early Spanish-speaking settlers who still speaks the language of his ancestors, a song that still reflects the same tradition:

3	Aqueya panadera,	That baker-girl,
	que va por ayí,	who's going by there,
	la yamo y la yamo	I call and call to her
	y no quiere venir.	and she doesn't want to come.
	¡Y ay qué panadera	Oh, what a baker-girl
	Y ay qué panaderiya!	and what a little baker-girl!
	El alma me yeva.	She takes away my soul.
4	Aqueya panadera	That baker-girl
	me debe un boyo.	owes me a bun.
	Por no verle la cara,	So I won't have to see her face;
	se lo perdono.	she can keep it.
	¡Y ay qué panadera	Oh, what a baker-girl
	y ay qué panaderiya!	and what a little baker-girl!
	El alma me yeva.	She takes away my soul.

(Armistead 1992, 87)[7]

Because of the metaphoric value attached to the word "bread," then, the short narrative introduced by Pedro Alfonso into Europe in the twelfth century was divided into two different stories. In its complete form, the second, bawdy version, which replaces the original loaf of bread with a woman, was first documented, in France, by Philippe de Vigneulles's *Les cent nouvelles nouvelles* (1515). Three small groups of monks, merchants, and soldiers meet at an inn where some spring chickens (*poussins*) and other types of food are being prepared for supper, but everyone prefers the hens. One of the soldiers suggests that a representative of each group come up with a clever saying, and that the winner divide the chicken with his companions. He begins by stating "qu'il n'y a aujourd'huy soubz le cieulx plus beau umbrage que d'estandart, plus beau coussin que beau ronssin ne clincailles que de harnas" (today there isn't under the heavens a shade more beautiful than that from a banner, a pillow more beautiful than a beautiful nag, or hardware [also "copper"] other than a suit of armor). One of the merchants replies: "il n'y a plus beaulx umbrage que belle maison, plus beau coussin que belle table ne clincailles que de monnoie" (there is no shade more beautiful than a beautiful house, no pillow more beautiful than a beautiful table, or coppers other than money). The representative of the monks surprises everyone with the following: "il n'y a aujourd'hui au monde plus beau umbraige que de courtine, plus beau coussin que de tetine ne clinquailles que de coillons" (there isn't in the world today a shade more beautiful than that from a curtain, a pillow more beautiful than tits, or hardware other than that of testicles). He is declared the winner and divides the hens with the other monks (Vigneulles 1972, 246–50).

The similarity between Vigneulles's story and the modern Portuguese folk joke are clear. Although the prize here is not a vagina, there is an implicit reference to one in the monk's bawdy reply, and the spring chickens that he wins for supper could be taken as metaphors for young girls. The French soldiers, merchants, and monks correspond to the Portuguese priest, captain, and sailor. As noted, the Portuguese characters can be roughly related to the three estates. In the French version, the three groups represent arms, commerce, and letters, as well as the clergy, and the soldiers and merchants' sayings are equally related to their respective professions. Rather than being personified in the figure of a common sailor, the third estate is represented by a merchant. The travel motif that is almost absent in the Portuguese rendition is implicit, since the protagonists meet at an inn. This ties Vigneulles's version more closely to the Dream-Bread Story, where the travel motif is clearly present. The purpose here is to illustrate both the cleverness of the monks and the bawdy life that they lead despite the admonitions of their saintly superior. Note that the *clincailles* (hardware, copper) in the three replies are onomatopeic, for the word clearly imitates the sound associated with it.

Vigneulles's story was already circulating in this form during the Middle Ages. A variant of the third reply was woven into a fifteenth-century rondeau, whose author sees a vagina between two sheets. The unabashed refrain is *Ung con!* (A cunt). Since the vagina has been split from top to bottom by either a hatchet or a sword (an obvious reference to vigorous sexual activity), it emits so much smoke that it is truly astonishing:

Un con sentant le faguenas	A reeking cunt
Vy l'autre jour entre deux draps,	I saw the other day between two bed sheets,
Enveloppé pour la gellée.	wrapped up for the jelly.
Il avoit la fesse avallee	Its ass was hanging down
De force d'aller l'entrepas.	as a result of all the riding.
De vitz il avoit à plains sacz,	It had a sack full of pricks,
De couillons portoit plain carcas,	it had a full quiver of balls,
Et sy crioit à gueulle baye	and it bawled:
Ung con!	A cunt!
Fendu estoit de hault en bas;	It was split from top to bottom,
Mais, par ma foy, je ne sçay pas	but, to be sure, I do not know
Si s'estoit de hache ou d'espee:	whether it was by an ax or a sword
Car il gectoit sy grant fumee	because it threw out such a great smoke
Que c'estoit ung merveilleux cas,	that it was a wondrous thing.
Ung con.	A cunt.
(Schwob 1904, 142)	

The parallelisms with Vigneulles's version are the sheets, which correspond to the curtains, and the quiver full of balls, which are equivalent to testicles in the monk's reply. The cushion of a woman's chest in Vigneulles's variant is represented by the smoke emitted by the vagina. As attested by Rabelais a few years later, the smoke motif was also traditional, even though it was more frequently associated with a woman's breasts.

In *Pantagruel* (1532: chap. 17; 1542: chap. 27), the hero tells his two companions, Epistémon and Panurge, that they have spent too much time talking about food. They should leave at once for "il n'est umbre que d'estandartz, il n'est fumée que de chevaulx et clycquetys que de harnoys" (there is no better shade than from banners, smoke than from horses, and jingling than from armor); Epistémon smiles and says: "Il n'est umbre que de cuisine, fumée que de pastez et clicquetys que de tasses" (There is no better shade than from a kitchen, smoke than from meat pies, and jingling than from cups). Panurge replies: "Il n'est umbre que de courtines, fumée que de tetins [*con* in the 1533 ed.] et clicquetys que de couillons" (There is no better shade than from curtains, smoke than from tits [*cunt* in the 1533 ed.], and jingling than from balls; Rabelais 1912–22, 4: 278). Note that the word used to designate sound (*clycquetys*) has an onomatopeic value here is well.

Like the author of the anonymous fifteenth-century rondeau, who draws elements from the third reply in our story in order to compose his own poem, Rabelais weaves part of of this story into his own work, using the three replies to characterize the valor of Pantagruel, the gluttony of Epistémon, and the sensuality of Panurge (Françon and Frautschi 1957, 1052; Kasprzyk 1963, 65). The author probably thought of this story because his protagonists, besides traveling in Paris, were eating at an inn, three motifs (travel, inn, and food) that already appear in Vigneulles.

To some extent, Rabelais repeats the association with three different classes or estates found in the Portuguese rendition and in Vigneulles's variant. Pantagruel is both a nobleman and a warrior, his tutor Epistémon, although dissociated from the church, is still a man of letters, and Panurge, despite his status as a student, also happens to be a commoner. Note that Pantagruel's statement is related to his own profession as a warrior, and that Epistémon's reply echoes the gluttony traditionally attributed to the clergy.

Our story reappears about four years after the first edition of *Pantagruel* in Nicolas de Troyes's *Grand parangon des nouvelles nouvelles* (ca. 1536), where it is used in an independent form. Three travelers, a nobleman, a merchant, and a Franciscan friar meet at an inn whose keeper, a woman, asks them to eat together. Once finished, the nobleman tells the lady that, since the Franciscan does not have any money, the three should express a wish. The one who, in her opinion, comes up with the best one, will not have to pay. The nobleman begins: "Il n'est que hombre d'estandart, fumée de chevaulx et cliquetis de harnois!" (There is no better shade than from a banner, smoke than from horses, and jingling than from armor!). The merchant continues: "Il n'est que umbre de pot, fumée de pastés et cliquetis de monnoye!" (There is no better shade than from a pot, smoke than from meat pies, and jingling than from coins!). The Franciscan counters: "Il n'est que umbre de courtines, fumée de tetins et cliquetis de fesse[s]!" (There is no better shade than from curtains, smoke than from tits, and jingling than from buttocks!). The lady declares the Franciscan the winner and the other two pay for his meal (Troyes 1970, 63–65).

Once again, the protagonists represent three different arts or estates. Contrary to what some critics thought, there is no direct relationship between the versions of Troyes and Rabelais.[8] The latter did no repeat the story accurately in 1532, since he used only two characters, Pantagruel and Panurge, rather than the requisite three, but he was aware of two traditional alternatives for what was the best smoke. As already noted, in an early edition Rabelais wrote *con*, paralleling the fifteenth-century rondeau, but he replaced it with *tetins* later on.

The variants in all the sayings or replies examined so far indicate that, rather than borrowing from each other, the French authors who used the story were drawing from an oral, living tradition. Troyes is the only one to identify the best sound with that of buttocks. The most important element first documented by his version is the lady-innkeeper who is assigned the role of judge. She is the earliest predecessor of the prostitute found in Mr. Silveira's Portuguese rendition.

The next appearance of our story is in Spain, in 1564, when Juan Timoneda included it in his *Buen aviso y portacuentos*. Three companions, a captain, a muleteer, and a rogue, arrive at an inn owned by a widow who enjoys banter. She informs them that, since there are only a couple of partridges for supper, the one who answers three questions to her satisfaction will eat them with her. She wants them to declare what is the best shade, sight, and sound in this worldly life. The captain: "Sombra de tienda de campo, vista de Españoles, y ruydo de atambores" (Shade of a field tent, sight of Spaniards, and noise of drums); the muleteer: "Sombra de meson, vista de poblado, ruydo de azemilas" (Shade of an inn, sight of a town, and noise of mules); the rogue: "Sombra de pauellon, vista de gentil muger, ruydo de colchones" (Shade of bed canopy, sight of pretty woman, noise of mattresses). Of course, she declares the rogue the winner (1911: 226; 1947: 340–41; 1990: 151–52; rpt. in Chevalier 1978, 20–21).[9]

Timoneda's version is obviously drawn from oral tradition. As shown by the reference to Spaniards in the first reply, the joke is thoroughly Spanish. The bed canopy parallels the French curtains, but the best smoke, which comes from the woman's breast or vagina, has been replaced by the "sight of a pretty woman," and the sound produced by the testicles becomes the noise of mattresses. The absence of the monk and the relative tameness of this reply may reflect the more austere character of Spanish literature, but that is not necessarily the case with the oral tradition of Spain. Official prudery does not always affect popular culture. The term for "mattress," *colchones*, rhymes with the "partridges," *perdigones*, which come at the end of the widow's reply, but so would the Spanish word for "testicles," *cojones*. Timoneda probably preferred the less offensive *colchones*, a choice which, in a way, would seem to make more sense, for mattresses are much more likely to produce a clearly audible sound than testicles.

Although the captain and the muleteer stand for two different occupations, the rogue cannot be said to belong to any particular profession. Consequently, the French representation of the three estates or of arms, commerce, and letters has essentially been eliminated. As shown by the inclusion of a priest in the Portuguese version collected in New England and in a variant from the District of Leiria, however, Iberian renditions must also have included a clergyman at one time.

Since the oldest form of the story in question came to Europe through Spain, its second metamorphosis could well have developed in Iberia. Its licentious character would explain the lack of further written documentation. On the other hand, the more daring character of French literature, the greater number of French versions, and France's central location and consequent role as a center of dissemination suggest that the second form of Alfonso's story originated in that country. But although the weight of the evidence leans toward the French side, the problem of origins still remains unresolved.[10]

Our story reappears in France in July of 1743, in the *Journal de police*. This version is unquestionably oral, for it was provided by an anonymous informant in order to amuse a police officer. Unable to decipher an inscription placed over the fireplace in their room, three travelers, an officer, a merchant, and a monk, ask the lady-innkeeper for help in solving the puzzle. She is very pretty and tells them, smiling, that the one who guesses correctly will get to sleep with her. The inscription reads: "ombre, fumée, trictrac" (shade, smoke, trictrac). The officer tries his luck first: "Ombre de ma cuirasse, fumée de mes pistolets, trictrac de mon épée" (Shade of my breast-plate, smoke of my pistols, trictrac of my sword). The merchant: "Ombre de ma boutique, fumée de ma cuisine, trictrac de mes écus" (Shade of my shop, smoke of my kitchen, trictrac of my crowns). Looking lewdly at the lady, the monk shouts: "Ombre de mon corps, fumée de mon, . . . trictrac de mes. . . . " (Shade of my body, smoke of my, . . . trictrac of my. . . . Clouzot 1915, 287).

The two key words prudishly omitted are not difficult to figure out. "Smoke," *fumée*, is followed by *mon*; it must refer to *con* (vagina), for the usual *tetins* are plural. Since the informant was obviously a man (hence the allusion to the shade of his body rather than to curtains, indicating a top position), the omitted *con* belongs to him only while he is engaged in the act of possessing it. In the fifteenth-century rondeau, we recall, there is an allusion to the great amount of smoke emitted by the vagina in the midst of vigorous sexual activity. At one point, Rabelais also associated the best smoke with a vagina, replacing it with a reference to a woman's breast in a later edition. The *mes* that comes after "trictrac" probably refers to the plural *couillons*, "testicles," which are the part of the anatomy traditionally used to end the third reply in the French tradition. As often happens in that tradition, the protagonists represent three fundamental medieval occupations, arms, commerce, and letters.

The lady-innkeeper in Troyes's version judges the three wishes expressed by her customers, and the one in Timoneda challenges her guests to answer three questions in order to determine which one will eat the remaining two partridges with her. In this last French variant, the inkeeper is much closer to the prostitute in Mr. Silveira's Portuguese rendition, for she promises to go to bed with the guest who deciphers the inscription. Although the variant in question is from 1743, this does not mean that the transformation of the lady-innkeeper from a judge to a woman of easy virtue constitutes a fairly recent development. Since the Azores are a conservative, extremely isolated archaic lateral area within the Portuguese tradition, which is already noted for its overall conservatism, the chances are that the motif is very old.

The only other known Portuguese version was recorded by Michel Giacometti in September 1973, in the District of Leiria. A very rich princess would marry only the man who spoke what she wanted to hear. A priest tries his luck despite his celibate status and tells her: "Ó menina, ó menina, prà minha fortaleza as minhas igrejas; e pra luxo os meus castiçais e para reque-treque os meus sinos!" (Miss, Miss, for fortitude my church, for luxury my candlesticks, and for reque-treque [onomatopoeic nonsense] my church bells!). She rejects him. An army captain tries next: "Ó menina, ó menina, prà minha fortaleza as minhas tropas; e pra luxo a minha espada e reque-treque os meus tambores" (Miss, Miss, for fortitude my troops, for luxury my sword, and for reque-treque my drums). She does not want him either. Then there comes a plain soldier: "Ó menina, pra luxo os meus botões; prà minha fortaleza o meu caralho e reque-treque os meus colhões" (Miss, Miss, for luxury my buttons, for forti-tude my prick, and for reque-treque my balls). She cries out: "És tu que és meu! És tu que és meu!" (You are the one! You are the one! Soromenho and Soromenho 1984–86, 1: 296 [no. 191]).[11]

This Continental Portuguese rendition has evolved considerably, deviating most from the early tradition. The innkeeper has been transformed into a princess, the protagonists are her suitors, the three questions are replaced by sayings designed to please her, and the prize is her hand in marriage.[12] The licentious character of the soldier's words is also present in the first two sayings, for the priest's candle-sticks and church bells and the captain's sword and drums are suscep-tible to equally salacious interpretations. This feature is unique to the version under scrutiny. The variant from Leiria also preserves some early elements. The three protagonists are essentially the same as in the Azorean rendition, thereby representing the three estates; arms and letters are embodied in the first two. The humblest character is also the winner. The third part of his reply is very close to the French tradition, for it retains the reference to the sound of testicles.

As we have seen, this second form of the apparently inoffensive story introduced into Europe by the *Disciplina clericalis* in the twelfth century is known in a total of nine versions, six of which are complete. The other three survive thanks to their partial use in a medieval French rondeau and in *Pantagruel* (2 vars.). The fact that the author of the anonymous rondeau and Rabelais wove part of the story into their own work testifies to its great popularity in France during the Middle Ages and during the Renaissance, providing an-other argument concerning its probable French origins.[13] Including these three partial variants, there are a total of six French versions of the story in question, whereas only three seem to have survived in the Iberian traditions: the one published by Timoneda in 1564, and the two modern Portuguese renditions.

As confirmed by its use of elements from the Spanish and French traditions, the version recorded by Mr. Silveira originated at an early period. Together with the other Portuguese variant, it coin-cides with Timoneda in awarding the prize to a member of the third estate. In this respect, the Iberian versions are closer to the first form of the story as found in the *Disciplina clericalis*, where the peasant outwits the two burghers.

The exclusion of a merchant in all three Iberian renditions may also tell us something about the values that prevailed in Portugal and Spain during the sixteenth and seventeenth centuries. Merchants were held in low esteem because people suspected that they were New Christians descended from Jewish converts. Peasants, on the other hand, were highly regarded, particularly in Spain.[14] The idea was that Jews and their descendants were too smart and too lazy to dedicate themselves to hard, backbreaking farm work, preferring to make a living through commerce and the professions instead. Unhindered by such prejudices, French society developed in a different manner, hence its replacement of the Islamic peasant in the *Disciplina clericalis* by a merchant in order to represent the third estate.

In the French forms of the story, the third saying or reply must identify the best shade, smoke (cushion in Vigneulles), and sound. Timoneda's widow replaces the best smoke with the best sight. In this detail, the Spanish version is much closer to Mr. Silveira's rendition, where the prostitute asks what is the most beautiful thing and the most handsome thing. Despite sharing these three details with Timoneda (award of the prize to a member of the third estate, exclusion of a merchant, and identification of the best sight; note that the first two items are also paralleled in Leiria), however, the Azorean story has much more in common with the French tradition.

In a way, the captain, the priest, and the sailor (soldier in Leiria) stand for the three estates, and the idea of arms and letters is also embodied in the first two. This, we recall, parallels the French tradition, where the three protagonists, a nobleman (or soldiers), a merchant, and a monk represent arms, commerce, and letters, as well as the three estates.

With the exception of Rabelais, where Panurge, who is the lowest in rank of the three protagonists, comes up with the best saying (and there is no prize), in the French version it is a monk who defeats the other contestants. This monk corresponds to the rogue, sailor, and soldier who constitute his Iberian counterparts but, being a clergyman, he also parallels the Portuguese priest, even though the latter is not rewarded with victory. In this context, it is interesting to note that, in the French tradition, the monk is supposed to be poorer and humbler than the merchant who represents the third estate. In the Portuguese versions, on the other hand, the priest is accorded a higher rank.

As we have seen, the lady-innkeeper makes her first appearance in Nicolas de Troyes. Her transformation into a prostitute (a princess in Leiria), we recall, is also closer to the French tradition for, in the version from 1743, she promises to go to bed with the guest who solves the puzzle. This metamorphosis is foreshadowed by

Timoneda. His lady-innkeeper likes to jest with her guests, eliciting a reply that would make other women blush. Proper women would probably avoid such situations because of what they could eventually lead to. Timoneda's innkeeper, however, rewards the rogue with a mere partridge. She does not go as far as the lady in the last French version.

Although this development is first documented in 1743, there is a strong possibility that it goes back to medieval times. As attested in the unabashed sexual activity depicted in the fifteenth-century rondeau, it was not difficult to translate the lewdness in the third reply into real action.

The correct solution to the prostitute's queries—woman's breast, vagina, and penis—is also closer to the French tradition. Curtains, woman's breast, and testicles prevail in three out of five French answers (Vigneulles, final version of *Pantagruel*, Troyes, with the difference that testicles are replaced by buttocks in the last), but there are three references to the vagina (rondeau, early version of *Pantagruel*, 1743), and the fifteenth-century rondeau mentions a sack full of pricks and a quiver full of testicles. Note that the Portuguese version from Leiria also includes a penis in its third saying.

The final answer or saying, however, usually ends with a reference to the sound made by testicles during intercourse. This sound, which is rendered by the onomatopoeic *clincailles* (Vigneulles), *cliquetis* (Rabelais, Troyes), and *trictrac* (1743) of the query, corresponds to the apparently enigmatic Azorean *puputiriru* (*reque-treque* in Leiria). Since *puputiriru* designates the penis rather than the testicles, it embodies two additional levels of humor due to the scatological inference implicit in *pupu* and the repeated shooting suggested by *tiriru*, for it comes from the Portuguese for "shot," *tiro*.

The absence of a merchant, the award of the prize to a commoner rather than to a clergyman, and the identification of the best sight as part of the third reply were undoubtedly traditional in the Peninsula during the sixteenth century, for these features are paralleled in Timoneda's version. On the other hand, there is no question that some early Iberian versions also included several details found in the two modern Portuguese variants. Since those features are shared with the variants that made their way into French literature, their presence in the modern Portuguese tradition cannot be explained in any other fashion. There must have been early Iberian versions that also included a clergyman; the three protagonists represented the three estates as well as arms and letters; some forms of the third saying or reply were as daring as in France, including some sort of onomatopoeic equivalent for the testicles or for the penis; and, in some instances, the winner's reward undoubtedly consisted of more than just a plain meal. Given all of this evidence, there is no question that Timoneda felt obliged to tone down the victor's reply, and there is a strong possibility that he also felt compelled to replace the clergyman with another character.

Although the story studied in this chapter is not documented in Portuguese literature, Mr. Silveira's rendition and the one from Leiria show that it must have been well-known in Portugal as far back as the sixteenth century, perhaps even earlier. The Azorean version is particularly valuable. It shares several details with Timoneda's but, as witnessed by its preservation of a greater number of correspondences with the French tradition, it constitutes an unexpurgated, even older form of the story. In other words, the modern Portuguese version recorded from an illiterate Azorean septuagenarian in Massachusetts has enabled us to shed light on the past, determining, with a fair degree of certainty, what the Iberian tradition that inspired Timoneda must have been like.

Puputiriru is an excellent example of the relationship between folklore and literature as well. Its ultimate source is a fable that was included in a Buddhist book written at least three centuries before the Christian era. Persian and Arabic versions document the transformation of the three animals in the fable into traveling human companions. Notwithstanding their apparent folkloric origins, once written down, these versions may be regarded as literature. The story made its way into Europe thanks to the Moslem invasion of Spain in 711, and Alfonso included it in his *Disciplina clericalis* at the beginning of the twelfth century, without specifying whether his sources were written or oral. Through the *Disciplina clericalis*, the Dream-Bread Story spread throughout Europe, being subsequently exported to the Americas. Because "bread" was a metaphor for the vagina, the story acquired a bawdy character, and the winner's prize was transformed from a loaf of bread into a woman. This metamorphosis, which was first observed in a fifteenth-century French rondeau, was subsequently used by Vigneulles (1515), François Rabelais (1532, 1542), Troyes (ca. 1536), Timoneda (1564), and in the *Journal de police* (1743). It was also recorded in Leiria, Portugal (1973), and from an immigrant from the Azores in Taunton, Massachusetts (1978). Despite their literary character, the early French and Spanish versions point to the folk origins of the story, thus bearing witness to the constant exchange between learned and popular culture, that is, between folklore and literature.

2

On Alfonso X's "Interrupted" Encounter with a *soldadeira*

In the first two verses of one of Alfonso X's *cantigas de escarnho*, the poet states that he had placed his hand on a *soldadeira*'s genitals a few days earlier and then recounts through her what happened by letting her speak in the first person, as if the incident were occurring right then and there. The woman reminds him that the time is not a good one, for the hour is the same as that when Our Lord suffered His Passion. In other words, it was 3:00 in the afternoon. Although the woman does not mention a specific day, it was clearly a Friday, because Christ died on that day at three in the afternoon, and the poem is permeated with references to His Passion. According to Manuel Rodrigues Lapa (1965, 23n), Alexandre Pinheiro Torres (1977, 51n), Joseph T. Snow (1990, 119), and Benjamin Liu (1995, 210–11), the action occurs on Good Friday, but this hypothesis must be discarded. The text fails to mention Good Friday specifically, even though it was such an important day in the Christian calendar and, if Good Friday had been intended, the poem would have been unthinkably heretical. The action could have taken place on any Friday, for Friday was a day of fast on which Christians remembered the Passion and death of Our Lord by abstaining from meat,[1] and fasts were associated with sexual abstinence. Even sexual relations between husband and wife were regarded as sinful on holidays and at certain times of the year, particularly during Lent, which was also a period of fast (Armistead and Silverman 1977, 75–76, and n5; Liu 1995, 210 and n29; Payer 1984, 23–28).[2] Since carnal relations were also discouraged on Friday (Payer 1984, 25–26), what the *soldadeira* is really saying is that, for religious reasons, she can never have sex on Friday, particularly at 3:00 in the afternoon. In other words, no meat of any kind on Fridays. Coming from a prostitute, this refusal is both incredible and obviously funny.

The woman then compares her own passion with Christ's, and concludes by asking Him to remember, when she appears before Him to be judged, how much she herself has suffered.

The poem goes as follows:

Fui eu poer a mão noutro di-	The other day I went to put my hand
a a ũa soldadeira no covon,	in the hole of a camp follower
e disse-m'ela: —Tol-te, arloton,	and she said: "Pull it back, you rascal;
ca non é est' a [ora d'alguen mi	this is not the hour for someone
5 fornigar, u prendeu] Nostro Senhor	to screw me, for it is the one when Our Lord suffered
paixon, mais é-xe de min, pecador,	His Passion, so get away from me, a sinner,
por muito mal que me lh'eu mereci.	for I have offended Him a great deal.
U a vós começastes, entendi	When you started it, I well realized
ben que non era de Deus aquel son,	that the sound was an ungodly one,
10 ca os pontos del no meu coraçon	for its stitches in my heart
se ficaron, de guisa que logu'i	remained, so that right then and there
cuidei morrer, e dix' assi: —Senhor,	I feared to die, and said: Lord,
beeito sejas tu, que sofredor	blessed art thou, who causes me to suffer
me fazes deste marteiro par ti!	this martyrdom for your sake!
15 Quisera-m'eu fogir logo dali,	I wanted to run away from there at once,
e non vos fora muit[o] sen razon,	and not without a very good reason,
com medo de morrer e con al non,	for I feared death, nothing less,
mais non púdi—tan gran coita sofri;	but I couldn't. I suffered much
e dixe logu' enton:—Deus, meu Senhor,	and then said: God, my Lord,
20 esta paixon sofro por teu amor,	this passion I bear for your love,
pola tua, que sofresti por min.	for the sake of your Passion, as you suffered for me.
Nunca, dê-lo dia en que naci,	Never, since the day I was born
fui tan coitada, se Deus me perdon;	have I been in such distress; may God forgive me,
e con pavor, aquesta oraçon	and, terrified, this prayer
25 comecei logo e dixe a Deus assi:	I began, saying to God as follows:
—Fel e azedo bevisti, Senhor,	Bile and vinegar you drank, Lord,
por min, mais muit' est' aquesto peior	for my sake, but this is much worse,
que por ti bevo nen que recebi.	what I drink and receive for you.

E poren, ai, Jesu Cristo, Senhor,	And so, oh Jesus Christ, Lord,
30 en juizo, quando ante ti for,	when I appear before you to be judged,
nembre-ch'esto que por ti padeci!	please remember how I suffered this for you!"

(Rodrigues Lapa 1965, no. 14)[3]

Despite the humor present here, this poem must have been regarded as pornographic, even by thirteenth-century standards, and the references to the Passion are definitely blasphemous, at least according to modern mores. In the words of Pinheiro Torres, "perpassa por toda esta composição um tom herético" (there is a heretical tone throughout this whole poem; 1977, 51n). In spite of recalling the fact that the mixture of religion and eroticism was common in the Goliardic poetry that was so popular throughout Western Europe at the time, Kenneth R. Scholberg identifies the poetic voice with the author's, as if the incident had really happened to the king himself, and concludes that this poem exceeds everything done previously by far: "Pero no creo que haya poesía más atrevida ni más sacrílega que la del Rey Sabio" (I do not believe there is a more daring or sacrilegious song than the one written by Alfonso X, the Wise; 1971, 85).

It is perhaps because of the sacrilege involved that scholars have taken the woman's protest seriously, believing that the poet heeded her words as well, for they have interpreted the last three of the five strophes as an expression of her repentance. Had the sexual act, which apparently began in the second strophe, continued, the *soldadeira*'s playful contrition, combined as it is with comparisons between her physical passion and the Passion of Christ, would be even more blasphemous and therefore unthinkable. This is no doubt what has caused modern scholars to think that the woman decided to put an end to what was happening. To quote Pinheiro Torres once again, she suffers miserably because of her sudden, religiously induced abstinence in the middle of the act, "por não levar o seu 'martírio' até ao fim" (for not being able to carry her "martyrdom" to conclusion; 1977, 51n; see also Rodrigues Lapa 1965, 23n; Snow 1990, 119; Scholberg 1971, 85). There is no hint of coitus interruptus in the poem, however. Thanks to the advances made during the last few years in our understanding of the euphemisms and metaphors used in medieval and Renaissance poetry and prose,[4] some of which have been perpetuated by the modern oral tradition, it is now possible to show that the woman never really puts a stop to the encounter.

Although the poet begins by placing his hand on the *soldadeira*'s genitals (1–2), at another level the hand also represents the phallus.

When the woman orders her customer to take his hand away, she says *é-xe de min*, which also means "pull it out" in the context; so, as the first verse in the second strophe indicates, the sexual act has already begun. As the following example documents, the hand could acquire a phallic connotation,[5] for a woman berates an impotent lover by comparing him to a clock without a hand:

	Es un bravo sin espada,
	    nada;
		He is a brave man without a sword,
		    nothing at all;

225	reloj con pesas sin mano,
	    vano;
		a clock with weights but no hand,
		    worthless;

	y un impotente en el lecho,
	    sin provecho.
		and an impotent man in bed,
		    plain useless.

(Alzieu, Jammes, and Lissorgues 1984, no. 97)

The ungodly sound that the *soldadeira* hears right after (9) confirms this interpretation. Rather than denoting "arroubos de prazer" (outbursts of pleasure; Pinheiro Torres 1977, 51n), the sound refers to the noise made by the testicles as they hit her during intercourse, a sound that also used to be rendered with some sort of onomatopoeic word (see chap. 1, p. 25). As the woman says about her impotent lover in the poem just quoted, the bells that he rings do not make a good (i.e., healthy) sound:

	castrado y casto varón,
	    castrón:
		castrated and chaste male,
		    castrated,

	mal podrá haceros buen son,	can hardly produce a good sound,
180	aunque cascabeles toque.	though he may jingle his little bells.

(Alzieu, Jammes, and Lissorgues 1984, no. 97)

The *soldadeira* then mentions the effect that the stitches that go along with the sound make in her "heart" (10). The word chosen here, *pontos*, was a well-known metaphor used to designate the action of the phallic "needle" with which they were given. This image, which reappears in *La Celestina*, has survived in modern folklore until today (see chap. 4, pp. 58–63). In the first example given in the next selection, a lady who begs her lover for three stitches reaches a pitch (also called *punto*) higher than a bugle. In the second example, a young lady uses the word in an astrological context, while giving instructions to her lover:

	Tres puntos me pide,
	    porque le aprieta,
		She begs me for three stitches,
		    for she is anxious,

	y alcanza más puntos
	    que una corneta.
		and reaches a pitch higher
		    than a bugle.

(Alzieu, Jammes, and Lissorgues 1984, no. 131)

	Si astrología sabéis,	If you know about astrology,
25	antes que me destoquéis,	before taking off my hood,
	suplícoos que me clavéis	I beg you to nail into me
	el punto en el mediodía.	the pointer [stitch] right at midday.

(no. 61)

Just before mentioning the "sound" (9) and the "stitches" (10), the speaker refers to the very moment when the action began: "U a vós começastes" (8), that is, "When you started it" (the *foda*). Since, besides initiating intercourse, the male poet is the one who is responsible for both the concomitant "sound" and "stitches," it does not make any sense to attribute these words and those that follow to him, as done by Rodrigues Lapa in a revised edition (see n3).

The stitches so greatly affect the *soldadeira*'s heart that she thinks she is about to die (12). Here the poet is patting himself on the back, for "death" constituted a metaphor for orgasm "en todas las lenguas europeas, incluso el latín, tanto clásico como medieval" (in all European languages, including both classical and medieval Latin; Whinnom 1981, 35). He is doing a good job, for the woman is about to reach orgasm. In the following poem, a lover who has challenged a lady for a joust refers to his own happy "death" and "resurrection," thus drawing an implicit comparison with the Passion that precedes Christ's death and Resurrection in the process:

	Las lanzas bien correrá	The jouster shall expertly run
	con ánimo el justador,	the lances with courage,
35	y de alcanzar tal favor,	and, having obtained such favor,
	de alegre se morirá.	he will die of happiness.

	Volverá a resucitar	He will resuscitate again
	con su lanza entera y sana;	with his lance whole and healthy;
	su persona muy ufana	full of pride, his person
40	volverá luego a justar.	will return to jousting at once.

(Alzieu, Jammes, and Lissorgues 1984, no. 3)

It is clear that, when the *soldadeira* goes on to bless the Lord for having caused her to suffer such torture for His sake (12–14), the word used, *marteiro*, refers to Christ's Passion as well as to her own pleasure.

Fearing death, she feels like running away right then and there, but is unable to, which makes her suffering even greater (15–18). In other words, her pleasure increases as she feels the orgasm drawing nearer. Then she offers her bereavement to the Lord, saying that she is going through the ordeal for His sake, for He had also suffered for her (19–21). Since she uses the word *paixon* to describe her situation, the *soldadeira* is in fact comparing her own physical pleasure with the Passion of Christ.

Alfonso X was not alone in using Christ's Passion in such a manner. As Matthew Bailey explained in relation to a poem that Juan del Encina dedicated to three women, "la una dueña, la otra beata y la otra donzella" (one a lady, one a devout woman, another a maiden)—which, unfortunately, is too long to be quoted here—the words *apassionado, compassión,* and *passión* refer "not to the abstract suffering of the courtly lover, but rather to lust" (1989, 437). Those same words allude to the Passion as well.

Although Yvonne Jane Tillier documented instances in which courtly poets associated the Passion with the vicissitudes of human love in several ways, she did not take matters this far, even though she quoted a poem written by Carvajales that can also be interpreted in a similar manner:

Paciencia, mi coraçón,	Patience, my heart,
non quieras desesperar,	don't you despair;
que, después de la passión,	after the passion,
viene la resurrectión.	there comes the resurrection.

    (*Cancionero de Estúñiga*, no. 142)

While it is true that, at a literal level, the poet "reassures himself that his own suffering in love will be short lived by reminding himself of the sequence of events, passion followed by resurrection" (Tillier 1985, 71), at another level he is also using the word *passión* in order to refer to the lust that leads to "death" (orgasm) soon to be followed by a "resurrection" (another erection). Thus, the situation here matches the openly erotic poem quoted earlier, where the lover states that he will happily die in the joust in order to be resurrected soon after.

As the king's poem continues, the *soldadeira* emphasizes the fact that she has never seen herself in such agony since the day she was born (22–23). In other words, finding herself in the throes of passion, she believes that she has never had so much pleasure before. Terrified, the woman then begins to pray (24–25). This means that, feeling herself dying—that is, reaching orgasm—she decides to say a last-minute prayer before giving up the ghost, so to speak. In the prayer she states that, since what she is receiving for the Lord's sake is far worse than the bile and vinegar that He drank while on the Cross (26–28), she hopes that He will remember her sacrifice when she appears before Him for judgment (29–31). Now that we understand the context, the meaning of this concluding prayer is clear enough.

The poem, then, begins as a joke. When the *soldadeira* pretends that she cannot have sexual relations at 3:00 in the afternoon on the grounds that it is the hour when Christ died on the Cross, she is really saying that she cannot have meat of any kind on Fridays. The rest of the poem is also a joke. A proper understanding of the metaphors that the poet uses indicates that, contrary to what previous critics thought, there is no coitus interruptus. The interruption is only apparent, which is in itself comical. Though related to the Passion, the expressions of suffering that follow refer to the pleasure that the *soldadeira* feels as she continues to perform the sex act, which is brought to a satisfactory conclusion. She reaches a monumental orgasm in the process. Although the whole poem is blasphemous, at least to many modern readers, it is nevertheless a joke and, therefore, it does not make any sense to suppose that it is autobiographical, as if the incident had really happened to the king. There is no question but that, in this instance, the author and the narrator constitute two different entities, and that the poetic voice is entirely fictitious.

Metaphors played a crucial role in medieval literature and, in many instances, their meaning is no longer clear to us. Their importance cannot be overemphasized, however, for a proper understanding of those metaphors enables us to recover the originally intended meaning of many texts and passages. Since metaphors are a linguistic phenomenon, there is no doubt that they began to be used in daily speech long before making their way into literature.[6] People availed themselves of metaphors especially when dealing with embarrassing subjects that they hesitated to discuss openly, such as sex, replacing the most offensive words with terms used in domestic and farming activities like *sewing*, *spinning* and *weaving*, and *ploughing*. As a result, the substitution of words like "hand" and "stitches" for the phallus and its action during intercourse often acquired a comical effect.

Not all metaphors found in medieval literature had their origin in popular speech, however. One only has to think of the language of courtly love (see chap. 4) to realize that learned individuals invented many new ones of their own. In time, some of those learned metaphors became current among the folk, and this constant interchange between learned and popular culture often makes it impossible to determine whether a particular metaphor was originally folkloric or literary. For example, the use of terms associated with the Passion of Christ and human love in courtly poetry would seem to point to learned origins, but it is also true that, at a time when religion pervaded every aspect of daily life, common people would also have been capable of inventing them. In any case, two key concepts examined in Alfonso's poem, the one regarding the sound (*son*) of testicles and the stitches (*pontos*) made with the phallic needle have been documented in modern folk literature as well.

Many modern readers may wonder how a devout monarch like Alfonso X, who, after all, oversaw the compilation of the *Cantigas de Santa María* and is known to posterity as the Wise King, could have written the poem under scrutiny. Religious parody was very common during the Middle Ages, however. As already mentioned, it pervaded the Goliardic poetry that was popular throughout Western Europe at the time.[7] As for Spain itself, one only has to remember the blasphemous character of Juan Ruiz's "Cruz, cruzada, panadera" (see Vasvari 1983), the irreverent parody of the canonical hours, also included in his *Libro de buen amor* (cc. 372–87), and the blasphemous way in which Carvajales and Juan del Encina equate the Passion of Our Lord with human lust, in order to realize that our medieval forebears were not very troubled about such matters. They were far more earthy than we are, and what seems blasphemous, sacrilegious, and even heretical to us did not exceed the bounds of entertainment and literature to them.[8]

3

Martínez de Toledo's "Nightmare" and the Courtly and Oral Traditions

The realization that a number of apparently innocent words and expressions had hidden sexual connotations has played an important role in the study of early and traditional Hispanic poetry for several years.[1] Edith Rogers (1980) and others also contributed toward an understanding of this type of language in the *Romancero*.[2] Our appreciation of Juan Ruiz's *Libro de buen amor* increased tremendously with Louise O. Vasvari's splendid studies of its equivocal metaphors.[3] Besides discovering that, thanks to this type of language, fifteenth- and early sixteenth-century courtly poetry was not as insipid as previously thought, Keith Whinnom's pathfinding *Poesía amatoria de la época de los Reyes Católicos* (1981) inspired several additional studies on that genre.[4] As far as prose is concerned, the decodification of kindred metaphors led to a reevaluation of crucial passages in works such as *Celestina*,[5] *Lozana andaluza*,[6] and *Lazarillo de Tormes*.[7]

This necessarily brief summary is meant to emphasize the fact that sexual metaphors were not restricted to any particular genre. Since such language abounds in folklore and world literatures, the only logical explanation is that it constitutes a universal phenomenon of folkloric origins.[8] To paraphrase Miguel Garci-Gómez, bashfulness caused our first parents to cover their genitalia with fig leaves. For similar reasons, their descendants, including writers, felt a need to veil references to the sexual organs and to their functions with a less than direct sort of language: "De los órganos y operaciones que conducen a su realización, en el lenguage del buen gusto, no se puede o no se debe hablar, si no es con circunlocuciones y eufemismos, con metominias, metáforas y símbolos" (In tasteful language, one cannot speak about the genitalia and its functions except through circumlocutions, euphemisms, metonymies, metaphors, and symbols; 1989, 7).

Many of those symbols and euphemisms made their way into literature when the dichotomy between learned and popular culture was not as pronounced as today, but writers also invented new ones of their own. During the Middle Ages and the Renaissance, however, the exchange between the common folk and the learned was so frequent that often it is either extremely difficult or impossible to be absolutely certain about the origins of an apparently popular poem (see Frenk 1987, v–vii), and much less the source of a particular symbol or metaphor. In any case, certain key words and expressions, many of which were current in folk literature, meant much more than they said at face value. Writers used them because, being still very close to the common folk—after all, most people could not yet read and write—they were perfectly aware of this.

The fact that those levels of meaning are no longer obvious to modern readers diminishes our understanding of medieval and Renaissance literature considerably. In the pages that follow, I will attempt to show how, together with the euphemistic code characteristic of courtly poetry, both ancient and modern oral tradition helps to clarify an important, heretofore misunderstood part of the *Corbacho*, thus restoring to it its originally intended meaning.

Alfonso Martínez de Toledo's *Arcipreste de Talavera o Corbacho* (1438) is a misogynistic work penned as a reaction against the excesses of courtly love. Having elevated women to the rank of goddesses, courtly love was eventually perceived as a cult that rivaled Christianity, which it parodied, as well as an anti-Christian religion, for it placed women where God Himself ought to be (see Gerli 1976a, 108–21; 1981). To counter this situation, Martínez de Toledo, archpriest of Talavera and chaplain of King John II, in whose court there prevailed "an atmosphere charged with courtly eroticism and almost decadent literary refinement" (Gerli 1976a, 113), ridicules human love and lovers in general. Nevertheless, he focuses especially on "los vicios, tachas e malas condiciones de las malas e viçiosas mugeres" (the vices, blemishes, and evil character of wicked and vicious women), portraying women as being helplessly wicked and diabolic because of their very nature, even though the epigraph of part 2 just quoted also concedes the existence of some good, virtuous women ("las buenas en sus virtudes aprovando" [praising the good ones for their virtue]; 145).[9] Martínez de Toledo aimed to deal a severe blow to courtly love by deflating the romantic image of women, taking them off the pedestal where it had placed them. According to Martínez, women are fickle, hypocritical, untrustworthy and treacherous, lustful, invariably proud, jealous of each other, cruel, and stubborn. In the words of E. Michael Gerli, although the author tries to achieve some balance by criticizing men as well, he concentrates on women because "his first desire was to demythologize the demiurge of the cult of love" (1976a, 117).

It goes without saying that, notwithstanding its frequent humor—some of the *exempla* and portraits used to enliven the lessons are truly funny—such ruthless invective could not possibly be well received by any woman. The queen herself, Doña María (35), and, as indicated by the palinode at the end of the book, the other ladies of the court, were furious. Because this retraction is absent from the only extant manuscript from Martínez de Toledo's lifetime, the Contreras codex (1466), appearing for the first time in the incunabulum of 1498, some scholars have argued that it was not written by the archpriest, who had died in 1468. Since here my main purpose is to examine the language and meaning of the addendum in question, for the sake of convenience I will treat it as being written by Martínez de Toledo. Subsequently I will list the reasons why I favor his authorship.

The archpriest seems to address his "epistle" to those who, either because of their wealth or good looks (*bienes*), have always been lucky in love. He is not as lucky himself, for the ladies no longer favor him: "Aquellos a quien *natura* de sus *bienes* dotó e *amor* siempre quiso dar *favor* e *gozo*, que oyan de su amigo mi breve tal o qual epístola enderezco, a los quales *paz* e *salud* sea otorgada *con amor* de aquellas en cuyo disfavor del todo puesto so" (Let those whom *nature* endowed with its *goods* and to whom *love* always wished to give *favor* and *pleasure* hear from me, their friend, the brief, so and so epistle that I address to them, to whom may *peace* and *health* be granted *with love* by those in whose disfavor I have been wholly placed; 304).[10]

These words mean much more that what they first seem to convey. *Natura*, of course, was often used to designate both the male and female genitalia. In a Golden Age sonnet, an extremely jealous husband guards his honor so zealously that he wakes up with his finger "en la natura de su dama" (in the nature of his lady; Alzieu, Jammes, and Lissorgues 1984, no. 22.10). In another poem, Lucas Gil, a young man who is "pujante de natura" (of powerful nature), shows Teresa de Locía a *basto* (ace of clubs) of respectable proportions as he assaults her (no. 118.9–10; see also Allaigre 1980, 63–74).

Consequently, by referring to *natura* while coupling the favor (*favor*) of the ladies with the pleasure (*gozo*) that they give, the narrator is in fact addressing his "epistle"—note the religious connotation—to his more fortunate, sexually active peers "whom nature endowed with its goods" who, unlike him, have not been ostracized by the ladies. As we shall see later, the archpriest writes in order to seek the advice of those friends. His recourse to this equivocal, comical, deliberately ambiguous language at the beginning of his letter, signals that what follows should not be read only at a literal level.

Since love was the cause of "lovesickness," *mal de amores*, which was regarded as a real illness during the Middle Ages, being seriously dealt with in contemporary medical treatises,[11] the *paz e salud* (peace and health) that Martínez de Toledo hopes that his friends will continue to enjoy, with love, from the ladies whose wrath he himself has incurred, constitutes an allusion to the most efficient remedy for that illness: coitus.

The word *paz* refers to the medieval and Renaissance custom whereby people gave the peace to each other with a kiss on the cheek during Mass, rather than with a handshake, as today. In the *Cantar de Mío Cid*, Muño Gustioz accuses the gluttonous Asur González, the eldest of the Infantes de Carrión, of causing the revulsion of those to whom he offers the peace because he always eats well before going to Mass: "Antes almuerzas / que vayas a oración, // a los que das paz, / fártaslos aderredor" (You always have breakfast before going to say your prayers and you sicken those to whom you give the kiss of peace; 1968, vv. 3384–85). His overindulgence probably gave him bad breath. In Francisco de Quevedo's *Vida del buscón llamado don Pablos*, Alonso Ramplón writes to the protagonist, his nephew Pablos, that his mother has been condemned to be burned as a witch, and that it was said that she kissed a devil on the anus every night with the following words: "Dícese que *daba paz* cada noche a un cabrón en el ojo que no tiene niña" (They say that each night she gave the kiss of peace to a goat in the eye that has no pupil; 1988, 51).

Paz, however, also refers to the peace and lack of torment that comes with sexual satisfaction. Since the ladies have declared war on him, the archpriest no longer enjoys such "peace." The implication, of course, is that, as a result, he is suffering from *mal de amores*.

In this context, the word *salud* is practically synonymous with *paz*. In Francisco Delicado's *Retrato de la Lozana andaluza* (1528), when Lozana and Diomedes fall in love at first sight, Diomedes asks her: "Señora, si no *remediamos* con socorro de médicos sabios, dubdo la *sanidad*, y pues yo voy a Cáliz, suplico a vuestra merced *se venga* conmigo" (Madam, if we do not *apply remedy* with the advice of learned doctors, I fear for my *health*, and, since I am going to Cáliz, I beg your grace *to come* with me; 1985, 182). In other words, Diomedes pretends to be seriously lovesick, and Lozana can restore his health by achieving an orgasm with him. Later on, in a burlesque letter of excommunication against a "cruel maiden" sought from Cupid by a spurned lover, the damsel is referred to as "una cruel doncella de sanidad" (a cruel health maiden; 495). As a prostitute, her job is to alleviate the symptoms of those who suffer from lovesickness, improving their *salud* or *sanidad* in the process. Because of her "cruelty," the "maiden" is not as indiscriminate as she ought to be, betraying her professional responsibilities by turning down one of her prospective customers. Hence the lawsuit.

Given the ironic tone established from the very beginning, there is nothing heretical, at least by former standards, in Martínez de Toledo's reference to those whom he pretends to advise, as if they themselves did not know any better, as "Hermanos en Jesucristo" (Brothers in Christ).[12] He wonders whether he should stand by his work or attempt to regain the favor of women, with words that suggest that his superiors forced him to write the book in the first place: "Hermanos en Jesucristo, yo, pues, *forçado hove de ocupar mi entendimiento en diversas e muchas imaginaciones*, si mejor me sería tal disfavor, haviendo de proseguir lo comiençado, continuado ex propósito, o nuevamente buscar *paz* e *buena concordia* de aquellas que siempre *matan sin cuchillo ni espada* e *tormentan* a quien *quieren* sin que bevan *la toca*" (Brothers in Christ, since *I was forced to occupy my mind with numerous, various fancies*, I wonder if it would be best for me to remain in such disfavor, persisting in what I have begun, *ex proposito*, or once again to seek *peace* and *harmony* from those who always *kill without knife or sword* and *torment* whomever they wish [*love*] without putting them through the *water torture*).[13]

The deliberate ambiguity of the entire passage turns the archpriest's insinuation that he wrote the book against his will, if it is really there, into a very lame excuse. He could also be saying that it was his predicament that forced him to think about possible solutions. The reference to the women with whom he would like to have *paz* and *buena concordia* (peace and harmony) as those who can kill without having to avail themselves of a knife or a sword, and torment whomever they wish, including those they love (the verb *quieren* conveys both meanings), alludes, once again, to sexual intercourse. They could torment and kill without blunt weapons because, being able to inspire love, they caused lovesickness and even death by refusing intercourse, *salud* (health), to their victims. A passage in Fernando de Rojas's *Celestina* (1499) confirms this interpretation. Having enumerated the charms with which *natura* has endowed his beloved Melibea, Calisto concludes: "Estas son sus *armas*; con éstas *mata y vence*" (These are her *weapons*; with these she *kills* and conquers; 1987, 191).

Martínez's allusion to death includes another level of meaning: it refers to another type of demise, the loss of an erection, right after lovemaking. In the parody of Juan del Encina's *Justa de amores* quoted in the previous chapter,[14] the lover boasts to the lady to whom he dedicates his poem that

	Las *lanzas* bien correrá	The jouster shall expertly run
	con ánimo el justador,	the *lances* with courage,
35	y de alcanzar tal favor,	and, having obtained such favor,
	de alegre *se morirá*.	he *will die* of happiness.
	Volverá a *resucitar*	He *will resuscitate* again
	con su lanza entera y sana;	with his lance whole and healthy;
	su persona muy ufana	full of pride, his person
40	volverá luego a justar.	will return to jousting at once.

(Alzieu, Jammes, and Lissorgues 1984, no. 3)

Martínez's utilization of this type of language leaves no doubt as to the type of favor he would like to regain. The expression *sin que bevan la toca* (without them having to drink the water torture) encloses several levels of meaning. Besides designating women while alluding to their hair by referring to their headdress, *toca* lends itself to other types of wordplay because it is a form of the verb *tocar*, "to touch." The word was also used in the sense of *cunnus*: "Señora, *tocar* quería / donde la camisa *os toca*" (Madam, I would like to *touch* where your shift *touches* you; no. 50.27–28). This last meaning is even clearer in a poem where a *galán* takes his *caracol* (snail) to Marta de Coca "para que en su *toca* / le traiga y le cuelgue, / y a fe que se huelgue, / y ande muy lozana" (so that in her *toca* she can carry and hang him and amuse herself in good earnest and be very sprightly; no. 89n.16–19). Within the present context, however, the word refers more specifically to a form of torture inflicted with water filtered through a piece of cloth: "Tormento de *toca*, el que se da en el potro con ciertas medidas de agua, que passa por la *toca*" (*Toca* torture, the one inflicted on people on the rack with certain amounts of water, which is filtered through a *toca*; Covarrubias 1994). The ladies can torment their victims *sin que bevan la toca* (without making them drink the water torture) because they do not even have to touch or torture them physically in order to make them suffer.

Musing that he would have to burn his book (i.e., recant) in order to regain favor with the ladies, the archpriest falls asleep and dreams that "*sobre mí* veía señoras más de mill, que el mundo ya por cierto non las aborresciera por ser de tal gala, *de nombre e renombre famosas*, más de tanto *fermosas*, ya sin par *graciosas* a par que *gentiles. . . .*" (*over me* I saw more than one thousand ladies, whom the world certainly would not detest, because they were of such grace, *famous for their lineages and reputations*, and moreover *beautiful*, unmatched in their *grace* and *kindness* [elegance]).

No matter how we read it, this would seem to be quite a dream. More than one thousand courtly ladies famous for their lineage (*nombre*), renown, beauty, and grace, but perhaps not really so kind or well-mannered (*gentiles*)—or were they?—either attack or place themselves on top (*sobre mí*) of the archpriest.

At first sight, it is baffling that the ladies "en stima *del pie hasta encima* traían esecusiones a manera de *martirio*" (*on top of their feet* were instruments in the style of *torment*), for it is difficult to imagine how they could carry instruments of torture on their feet. However, as shown in the case of Berceo's mother superior who "Pisó por su ventura yerva fuert enconada" (By her fate stepped on a very poisonous weed; 1985, v. 507c), becoming pregnant in the process (see Devoto 1974b and Garci-Gómez 1989), the foot, though used more often to designate the male parts, was also associated with the female genitalia.[15] *Martirio*, which is related to the courtly phenomenon that Tillier labeled "passion poetry," refers to the torment that women inflict by withholding their favors, as well as to the "suffering" (pleasure) of the lover as he or she is about "to die" (reach an orgasm). In Alfonso X's *cantiga d'escarnho* examined in chapter 2, the camp follower enjoys herself so much while having sex that she thinks she will surely die, and praises the Lord for making her suffer such torments for His sake: "Senhor, / beeito sejas tu, que sofredor / me fazes deste *marteiro* par ti!" (Lord, blessed art thou, who causes me to suffer this *martyrdom* for your sake! Rodrigues Lapa 1965, no. 14; Pinheiro Torres 1977, 50). These two meanings of *martirio* cause the reader to wonder what kind of torment the archpriest is about to suffer for having written the book.

Besides exacting revenge with blows from their distaffs and slippers, the ladies pummel him with their fists and pull his hair: "dando los golpes tales de *ruecas* e *chapines*, puños e remesones, qual en penitencia de los males que hize, e aun de mis pecados" (giving me such blows with their *distaffs* and *slippers*, fists, and pulling my hair, as penance for the harm that I caused, and even because of my sins).

Distaffs and shoes have been traditionally associated with the female genitalia. A Golden Age poem opens with the following verses: "Bras quiere hacer / a Juana una güeca, / y ella dábale con la *rueca*" (Bras wishes to give Juana a notch with his spindle, and she hit him over and over with her *distaff*; Alzieu, Jammes, and Lissorgues 1984, no. 45.1–3). Gonzalo Correas collected a related proverb: "Abreme, hilandera de *ruekka*, haréte la güeca" (Open up, woman who spins with a *distaff*; I will give you a notch with my spindle; qtd. in ibid., no. 45n). The modern oral tradition, which perpetuates the ancient connection between sewing, weaving, and sexual activities (see Allaigre 1980, 88–89; Costa Fontes 1984, 1985), also preserves this metaphoric meaning of the distaff. In the Portuguese and Galician versions of *O Cego* (The Blind Man; Span. *El raptor pordiosero* [The Abductor in Beggar's Guise]; RPI, O3; CMP, O3), the mother or grandmother who conspire with an abductor disguised as a blind man advises her daughter or granddaughter to take her distaff along as she shows him the way: "Pega, minha filha, / na roca e no linho, // ensina o caminho / ao pobre ceguinho" (Take, my daughter, the distaff and the flax, and show the way to the poor blind man; TM, no. 567). The implication is clearer in the modern variants of *As Queixas de D. Urraca* (*Las quejas de doña Urraca* [Urraca's Complaint]; RPI, A8). In the early version, the princess threatens her dying father, who has forgotten her in his will, that she will go throughout the land and offer her body to Moors and Christians alike (Nucio 1967, 213–14). In the modern tradition, this threat is replaced by the following words: "—Ê vou-me por aqui abaixo / muito triste e mal fadada; // vou pècurá *roca* e fuso, / que mulhé nã tem outra arma" (I shall go down this road very sad and ill-fated; I will look for a *distaff* [i.e., use my distaff] and spindle, for a woman does not have any other weapon).[16] Finally, in *A Fonte do Salgueirinho* (The Spring of the Willow; RPI, X32), a poem that seems exclusive to the Portuguese and Galician traditions,[17] a mother berates her daughter for breaking her water jug at the fountain because, rather than minding her distaff and reel, she was thinking of a young man instead:

4   —Anda cá, perra traidora,   donde tinhas o sentido?
     Não o tinhas tu na *roca*,   nem tão-pouco no sarilho;
6   tinha-lo naquele mancebo   que d'amores anda contigo.

                          (TM, no. 1185)

(Come here, you treacherous bitch, what were you thinking about?
You were not minding your *distaff* or your reel, but rather that
young man who is courting you.)

The corresponding use of "shoe" in both literature and folklore
has been amply documented by Harry Sieber (1978, 45–58) and by
others (i.e., Garci-Gómez 1989, 19–20), but I would like to present
two modern Portuguese examples. In 1973, I collected in Tracy, California, a riddle that goes as follows: "Em cima de ti estou, / debaixo
de mim te tenho; / estou arrenegando / por te meter o que tenho. —*O
sapato*" (I am on top of you, beneath me I have you, and I am very
anxious to prick you with my business.—*The shoe*).[18] The inference
is the same in a popular quatrain about an encounter between a lady
and a priest in the woods: "Senhora Dona Helena / perdeu um *sapato*, / o padre Francisco / achou-lho no mato" (Lady Helena lost one
shoe and Father Francisco found it in the woods; Leite de Vasconcellos 1975–83, 2: 370). In both instances, the shoe acquires a
metaphoric value paralleling the early tradition.

These examples show that the feet, distaff, and slippers with
which the courtly ladies torment the archpriest in his "nightmare,"
through repeated blows, stand for their vaginas. Given the context,
it is not farfetched to wonder if, while all of this is going on, the
remesones (pulling) that they further punish (or tease him with), do
indeed refer to the to the hair on his head. Whatever the case, the
archpriest does not really feel his book was far off the mark: while
trying to explain to himself the cause of his present predicament, he
contrasts "los males que hize" (the harm I caused) with "mis pecados" (my sins). In other words, the anger his book caused was probably justified, at least in his mind, since he does not seem to count it
among his sins.

The women go on to refer specifically to his book, accusing the
author of gross ingratitude. They remind him of their past favors.
Notwithstanding his advanced age, they claim, he will feel a need for
them again in the future. Such is the fate of old men, even though
they should know better: "Loco atrevido, ¿dó te vino osar de escrevir
ni hablar de aquellas que merescen del mundo la victoria? Have,
have memoria quanto de nos haviste algund tiempo pasado gasajado. Pues no digas aún desta agua no beveré, que a la vejez acos-
tumbra entrar el diablo artero en la cabeza vieja del torpe vil asno"
(You old fool, how dare you write or speak ill of those who merit victory in the world? Remember; remember the time when you used to
receive shelter from us. Never say "from this water I shall not

drink," for in old age the deceitful devil usually gets into the head of the vile, lascivious ass).

As the attack continues, one of the women drags him by the hair, ignoring his pleas for mercy: "merced no valía demandarle *de quedo que conocer* me pluguiese" (it was useless to beg her for mercy, for I could not *move* even though I would have liked *to know her*). These cryptic words indicate that the archpriest is unable to perform (*quedo*), that is, to know her in the biblical sense (*conocer*), even though he would he would like very much to (*pluguiese*). Under such conditions, he cannot defend himself to his or to the ladies' satisfaction.

This is what causes the dream to become a nightmare. Though suffering from *mal de amores*, the archpriest is unable to perform. Since the ladies imply that he is already old, the problem might be related to his age. More probably, however, the archpriest's impotence was due to the violence of the assault by the women. Later, he makes it clear that it was just a temporary difficulty.

As the dream goes on, another woman places her "foot" on his throat in order to asphyxiate him, causing his tongue to stick out more than a hand's breadth: "La segunda quel *pie* me puso en la garganta a fin de me ahogar, que *la lengua* sacar me hazía un palmo" (The second one put her *foot* on my throat in order to asphyxiate me and forced *my tongue* to stick out by a handbreadth). Since the archpriest is unable to perform, these words may embody a suggestion of cunnilingus.

The archpriest's troubles multiply when the other women cover him with blows from their *chapines* (slippers) in such a manner that he cannot see them. The blows fall so rapidly upon him that he fails to glimpse anything else: "las otras no pude devisar, quel golpe de los *chapines* me cerrava la vista" (I was unable to see the others, for the blows from the *slippers* were blinding me). Being a helpless old man, there is really nothing he can do: "las *ruecas* e las *aspas* quebravan *sobre mí* como sobre un *mancebo* que fuera de soldada, que a mi sembrar quedé *más muerto que no bivo*, que *morir* más amava que tal *dolor* passar" (the *distaffs* and *reels* fell *on top of me* as if I were a *young journeyman*, and I felt *more like a dead than a living person*, and would rather *die* than have to suffer such *grief*).

Had he been a young journeyman, he would no doubt have given a better account of himself but, being old, the distraught archpriest was not even able to achieve an erection (*más muerto que no bivo*; *more like a dead than a living person*). His agony is so great that, at that moment, he would rather die than be subject to such grief.

The *aspas* (reels) in the women's arsenal correspond to the *sarilho* (reel) that also goes along with the distaff in the modern *Fonte do Salgueirinho*. The term chosen to express the old man's predicament, *dolor* (woe, grief, pain), encloses yet another level of humor, for it was used to express unsatisfied desire, in courtly (Whinnom 1981, 41) as well as in openly erotic poetry. As the lovesick Calisto asks his servant Sempronio after Melibea spurns him in her "garden," "¿Quál *dolor* puede ser tal, / que se yguale con mi mal?" (What *pain* can be so great as to compare with my grief? Rojas 1987, 91). The metaphor becomes even more transparent in the parody of the priest Juan del Encina's *Justa de amores* (Love joust) previously quoted, where the lover tells his lady "que de mi *dolor* crecido / será la tela el remedio" (for my swollen *pain* / shall the fabric [woman's vagina] serve as a remedy; Alzieu, Jammes, and Lissorgues no. 3.21–22). Consequently, the old man's dolor (pain) lies in the fact that he is unable to muster the kind of dolor (pain) that he would like.

The archpriest's affliction is such that he awakens in a cold sweat, thinking that he had been in the clutches of some extremely cruel women. Having more or less recovered his senses—lo and behold!—he feels something and realizes what the source of his troubles was: "Empero tal o qual mi sentido cobrado, *sentí* e conoscí *el mal* dónde me venía" (Yet, having more or less recovered my senses, *I felt* and knew where *my pain* was coming from). As it turns out, the apparent nightmare was not so terrible after all. Since *mal* (pain, illness) constitutes an abbreviation for *mal de amores* (lovesickness), he awakens with an erection.

Half conscious, he is so startled by what he feels and hardly recognizes, that he wonders whether it is really there, or if it is just a figment of his imagination, a mere dream, or plain vanity on his part: "pero quedé *espantado* e *apenas conociera el que solía*, o si era *verdad* o *sueño* o *vanidad*" (but I was *astonished*, and *barely recognized the thing I used to know*, and wondered whether it was *for real*, *a dream*, or *plain vanity*). Fortunately, the whole episode was nothing but a dream. His suspicions are confirmed because, trembling, he wishes that he could have a real woman next to him right then and there: "temblava, Dios lo sabe, que quisiera tener cabe mí compañía para me consolar" (I trembled so, as God well knows, that I wished to have next to me company to give me solace). Alas, he was all alone, and so he complains: "¡Guay del que duerme solo!" (Woe to the one who sleeps all alone!).

The archpriest then addresses in a more direct manner his fellow men, to whom he was writing. Knowing that they feel as he does—and there is a pun in his double utilization of the word *sentido*, for, in the first instance (see the next section), it refers to the senses—he asks for their advice. Should he continue to suffer for such a motive? "Por ende, pensé, siquisiera, hermanos, por descanso y reposo de mí, de vos comunicar del todo mi trabajo, como a aquellos que siento que havéis tal *sentido*, que me daréis *sentido*, si debo yo *morir penando por tal*" (Finally, I decided, my brothers, at least for the sake of my peace and rest, to inform you of my predicament, for I sense that *you feel as I do*, and that you will advise me whether I ought *to die suffering for such a reason*).

The reason behind the archpriest's suffering, as we know, is the disfavor of the ladies. The words he chooses to pose his question express his predicament in a rather graphic manner, for *penando* encloses a reference to the penis. Encina's *Justa de amores* begins as follows: "Pues por vos crece mi *pena* / quiero, señora, rogaros / que queráis aparejaros / a la justa que se ordena" (Since *my pain* becomes swollen because of you, Madam, I would like to beg you to get ready for the required joust; Alzieu, Jammes, and Lissorgues 1984, no. 3n.1–4). The metaphor is even more evident in a *sátira* where the poet, like the archpriest, juxtaposes the verbs *morir* and *penar*: "Mas por las casadas tiernas / *peno* y *muero* de contino" (For the newly married young ones *I suffer* and *die* continuously; no. 96.24–25).

The fact that the author now places himself on the same footing as his luckier "brothers in Christ," to whom he addresses the "epistle"—he feels just as they do (*sentido*)—confirms that his impotence was but a nightmare. Were that not the case, there would be no point in inquiring whether he ought to continue *morir penando* (to die suffering). Here the metaphor signifies precisely the opposite of what it was intended to convey, for the writer's suffering is caused by the fact that he can no longer "die" while making love. The withdrawal of the angry ladies' favors was so effective that, barred from even the slightest chance to dip his *pena*, he dreamed about it instead.

The archpriest restates the question by asking more explicitly whether he ought to burn his book in order to regain favor with the ladies: "Por ende, hermanos, de dos uno demando, o *paz* haya e perdón final, *bien querencia* de aquellas *so qual manto beví* en esta vida, o que queme el libro que yo he acabado e no perezca. Mas, con arrepentimiento demando perdón dellas, e me lo otorguen o que quede el libro y yo sea mal quisto para mientra biva de tanta linda dama, o que *pena* cruel sea" (Finally, brothers, I ask you one of two things: shall I have *peace*, lasting forgiveness, *affection* from those *under whose cloaks* I have sipped in this life, or shall I burn the book

I have finished so as not to perish? Lastly, with repentance I ask for their forgiveness, and if they do not grant it to me, the book will remain, and I shall be loathed for as long as I live by so many beautiful ladies, no matter how cruel *the penalty* [pain]).

Feeling that a proper reading of this ambiguous passage was important to determine the true intentions of the palinode, Mario Penna (introd. to his 1955 ed. of Martínez's work, xlix) and Christine J. Whitbourn (1970, 59) attempted to clarify it by proposing minor emendations. In Penna's opinion, the author does not speak in earnest; he does not really intend to burn his book. Whitbourn, on the other hand, feels that these words constitute a sincere retraction: "The whole nature and tone of the *demanda* argues that it is a retraction; its logical ending is an acknowledgement of defeat and a gallant apology, not a gesture of defiance" (58).

The truth of the matter is that the deliberate ambiguity of the entire palinode renders the proposed emendations of the passage under scrutiny, minor as they are, unnecessary. Given the metaphoric value of *paz* (peace) and *bien querencia* (affection, goodwill) in the context, the archpriest wants more than just to make peace with the ladies he has angered. That is why he uses the phrase *so qual manto beví*, "under whose cloaks I have sipped," to allude to the "favor" that he had previously enjoyed. The *no perezca* (not perish) at the very end of the query could refer to the book as well as to the archpriest himself because, as he had just stated, the situation had turned his life into a continuous death. The tone of the entire palinode makes it perfectly clear, however, that, although he begs the ladies to forgive him, he does not have any intention to burn (i.e., to recant) his book, no matter the penalty. The penalty (*pena*), of course, consisted of the perpetuation of the interdiction that caused him to *morir penando* (to die suffering).

The repetition of this word while pretending to seek pardon further underscores the burlesque character of the palinode, which the archpriest pursues to the very end. After dating his "epistle," he closes it by bemoaning the fate of the poor man who has to sleep alone with a migraine, and into whose house no distaff enters all year-round: "Pero, ¡guay del cuitado que siempre solo duerme con *dolor de axaqueca* e en su casa *rueca* nunca entra en todo el año! Este es el pejor daño" (But woe to the wretched one who always sleeps alone *with a constant headache* and into whose house *a distaff* fails to enter all year-round! This is the worst injury). The implication, of course, is that such a continuous "headache" could be easily cured by a *rueca*.

Now that we understand what the author has been up to, even the title of the retraction itself acquires a new significance, for, writing in the third person, he pretends to apologize for two different reasons: "demanda perdón si en algo de lo que ha dicho *ha enojado* o *no bien dicho*" (he asks for forgiveness if something he said *has caused anger* or he *has said it poorly*). Besides meaning poorly or offensively said, the expression "no bien dicho" also means "not clearly put." Should there be any doubt concerning the purpose of his book, the palinode that follows will make his intentions perfectly clear. There is no question that it does. Rather than apologize, the writer does precisely the opposite, adding insult to injury.

On the surface, the women depicted here are mean and cruel, just as he said they were throughout the book. At another level, they are even more lustful than those previously portrayed. Since their assault against the poor, apparently defenseless archpriest with their *ruecas* and *chapines* amounts no nothing less than rape, he is in fact calling them lecherous whores. Moreover, the palinode is directed against highborn ladies ("de nombre e renombre famosas"; famous for their lineages and reputations), those who were more likely to frequent courtly circles, to participate in the games of courtly love, and to read and criticize the book that he had written with the specific purpose of attacking that type of love. Thus, the writer responds to the ladies' predictable reaction by telling them, in an even more graphic, though polysemic, euphemistic, and comical manner, what he really thought they were. To make matters worse, Martínez knew perfectly well that, since he was using their own courtly code in combination with some current folk concepts, those ladies were more than likely to understand his meaning. Though an apparent retraction, his palinode is really a form of ridicule. Once decoded, the reader realizes that, rather than repudiate his book, the author reaffirms everything he has written. While pretending to apologize, he does the opposite. Therefore, the feigned palinode is in fact an epilogue.

Because of the ambiguous character of the courtly and folkloric euphemisms used, my analysis may not always have been convincing. Indeed, the retraction can also be read in a straightforward, less problematic manner. On the other hand, Martínez de Toledo's accumulation of so many charged, equivocal terms is unquestionably deliberate. Why else should he have used, within such a short space, so many words and expressions susceptible of more than one interpretation, such as *natura, favor, gozo, paz, salud, buena concordia, bienquerencia,* and *toca*; forms of the verbs *matar, morir,* and *sentir, tormento, martirio, pie, ruecas, chapines, sobre mí, conocer, más muerto que no bivo, dolor, el mal, sentido, morir penando, pena*; and *dolor de axaqueca* for lack of a *rueca*? The euphemistic character of most of these words and expressions has been documented in the erotic literature of the time as well as in folklore; the few that have not been found elsewhere can be attributed to Martínez's prodigious talent and verbal artistry. The purpose of equivocal language, of course, is to provide deniability, but, as the archpriest intended, the accumulation just summarized indicates, just in itself, that his palinode conveys more than what it seems to say.

No matter how it is read, the assault by so many women against the archpriest is extremely funny. On the surface, it is truly comical that the women should fall upon a man with their distaffs and slippers. At another level, it is even more comical that so many beautiful, obviously young women should demand so much of one man, and an old man at that, in such a forward, shamelessly aggressive manner. In other words, besides denouncing courtly love as a cover for lust and the beautiful ladies who participated in it as quenchless whores, the archpriest also ridicules them in the process. Once understood, the whole palinode is unquestionably hilarious. Since the laughter that it provokes diminishes the sting of the insult, it would seem that, rather than causing serious injury to his adversaries, Martínez de Toledo was more interested in eliciting a good laugh. In other words, the whole thing was really a game.

Besides settling the argument about the sincerity of the retraction, the preceding analysis also helps to resolve the dispute concerning its authorship.

Arguing that Martínez himself could not have possibly written such a retraction, Whitbourn provides several reasons that indicate precisely the contrary. One reason why the archpriest could not have written it, she maintains, is that the women in the palinode remind him of past misdemeanors ("Have, have memoria quanto de nos haviste algund tiempo pasado gasajado"; Remember, remember the time when you used to receive shelter from us) to which he alludes on several occasions throughout the book (1970, 59).[19] Although Martínez exaggerates in order to take women off their courtly pedestal, the knowledge that he displays of the female psyche would seem to confirm the accusation, for he certainly knew what he was talking about. A distant, uninvolved observer was not as likely to have gained such knowledge. We also know that in 1427 a rival priest from Toledo, Francisco Fernández, accused him in a letter to Pope Martin V of living with a woman. The accusation was not necessarily true, but, as Gerli points out, "accusations of this nature were not lightly made" (1976a, 21).

Whitbourn's second point is equally weak. In the palinode, the women deal with the archpriest in a manner very similar to Martínez's description of Poverty's treatment of Fortune in part 4. Poverty jumps on top of Fortune and places a foot on her throat in order to choke her, thus causing her tongue to stick out a hand's breadth: "E estando así la Fortuna en tierra como muerta sin sentido alguno, . . . la Pobreza luego saltóle encima e púsole el un pie en la garganta que la quería afogar. . . . E dávale con el pie en la garganta que la lengua le fazía un palmo sacar" (And when Fortune was senseless on the ground, as if dead, . . . Poverty jumped right away on top of her and put a foot on her throat, wishing to asphyxiate her. . . . And she pressed her foot on her throat in such a manner that she caused her tongue to stick out by a handbreadth; 290–91). In the dream, we recall, the first woman who assaults the archpriest does the same to him. This evidence leads Whitbourn to conclude that "the author of the *Demanda*, if it was not Martínez himself, may have derived some of his inspiration from him" (1970, 60). The verbal coincidences are such, however, that it is very difficult to imagine how someone else could have written it.

But there is more. Following Martín de Riquer (see p. 334 of his 1949 ed. of the *Corbacho*), Whitbourn observes that the similarities between the manner used to express the date in the allegory about Poverty and Fortune and the expression of date at the end of the palinode are equally striking (1970, 60). Poverty concludes her sentence against Fortune as follows: "Dada en tierra de Babilonia . . . en el mes de julio, . . . reinante Saturno en la casa de Mercurio, Júpiter estando enfermo de cólica pasión" (Pronounced in the land of Babylon . . . in the month of July, . . . when Saturn reigned in the house of Mercury, because Jupiter was ill with colic pain; 295). The conclusion of the palinode is very similar: "En el año octavo, a diez de Setiembre, fue la presente escriptura, reinante Júpiter en la casa de Venus, estando mal Saturno de dolor de costado" (The present writing took place on 10 September of the eighth year, when Jupiter reigned in the house of Venus, because Saturn was sick with a backache). Once again, it seems difficult to imagine how this could have been written by anyone other than Martínez himself.

Whitbourn goes on to list numerous stylistic similarities between the palinode and the rest of the *Corbacho*, only to conclude that it was probably not written by the archpriest. In her opinion, Martínez contradicts himself by begging women for their forgiveness:

In spite of these similarities to Martínez's work, there are strong arguments against his having been the author of it. If authentic, it would constitute a complete denial of everything Martínez has been at pains to establish in the rest of the work. It shows woman tyrannizing over man, and demanding homage of him; it shows man disposed to render her the homage she desires, and abjectly begging for pity and forgiveness. The tone is arch and gallant and the attitude precisely in accordance with that which the Archpriest has so consistently and painstakingly endeavoured to discredit in his book. The *demanda* has a flippancy and irreverence at variance with the remainder of the work. (1970, 60–61)

As we have seen, however, Martínez's retraction is only apparent, for he reaffirms what he had written, thus adding insult to injury. Although the women make him "suffer," he is far from begging their forgiveness. Even though arch and gallant on the surface, the tone is really coarse and comical.

Finally, what seems to be irreverent to modern readers was taken very lightly during the Middle Ages. Alfonso X's *Cantigas de Santa María* witness the king's devotion to the Virgin; nevertheless, Alfonso X was able to write a *cantiga d'escarnho* where a camp follower compares her *marteiros* during coitus with the Passion of Christ, a convention followed by several other writers for the next three centuries (see Tillier 1985 and chap. 2 of this book). Another archpriest, Juan Ruiz, was capable of including in his book the apparently heretical song about *Cruz cruzada, panadera* (see Vasvari 1983), as well as numerous sexual metaphors (1988–89) and other irreverent poems, such as his parody of the canonical hours (cc. 372–87). Encina authored the previously cited *Justa de amores* where a lover promises his lady that, once "dead," he will soon "resuscitate" in order to go on with the "battle."[20] Yet, both Juan Ruiz (i.e., cc. 20–43) and Encina (1977, nos. 35–40) also composed beautiful, moving poems in honor of the Blessed Mother, who represented purity and chastity. There is no question that, notwithstanding the religiosity of the Middle Ages, our ancestors were not as prudish and sensitive as many of us are about sexual and religious matters.

Whitbourn also objects that, contrary to the rest of the *Corbacho*, the style of the palinode is less than direct (1970, 61). It could not be otherwise, for the archpriest responds to his detractors by confronting them on their terms. He uses their courtly language, laced with popular metaphors that have persisted until modern times—distaff, shoe, foot, and lovesickness (*mal* for *mal de amores*)—in order to ridicule them while telling them what he thinks they are. In other words, Martínez's defense of his book constitutes a counterattack in which he further diminishes his adversaries by using as a weapon the linguistic code that was so dear to them. Hence his recourse to an apparently indirect style. Although there were some exceptions—Juan Alfonso de Baena included in his *Cancionero* (ca. 1444) a brutal, salacious poem by Villasandino that constitutes a good example (1966, no. 104)—it simply was not good form to say such things in a direct manner.

There are additional reasons to favor Martínez's authorship. As Erich Von Richtoften demonstrated, the archpriest was inspired by Andreas Capellanus's *De amore libri tres*, which has been translated as The art of courtly love: "Alfonso Martínez follows Book III of the *Art of Courtly Love*, the 'Rejection of Love,' as a source for the first and second parts of his work, copying entire passages of it, with some slight changes, almost word for word."[21] Capellanus advocates courtly love in parts 1 and 2 of *De amore*, rejecting it in part 3 (1960, 187–212). Martínez follows him in parts 1 and 2 of his book, where he does precisely the opposite. Parts 3 and 4 of the *Corbacho* seek their inspiration elsewhere (see Gerli 1976a, 55–62), but Martínez's apparent retraction is probably based on *The Art of Courtly Love*. Andreas seems to recant what he proposes throughout his book, and Martínez does exactly the same.[22]

Martínez de Toledo died in 1468 (see Gerli 1977). The only surviving copy of his book made during his lifetime is Alfonso de Contreras's codex, which dates from 1466, and the palinode appeared for the first time in the first printed edition, published thirty years after the death of the archpriest (1498). This is what led to the controversy concerning his authorship. Von Richthofen surmises that Martínez could have written the palinode after 1466, or even earlier; its absence from the Contreras codex could be explained by the existence of another manuscript tradition (1941, 464, n1).

Von Richthofen's first hypothesis makes more sense, for, in the palinode itself, the archpriest declares himself to be an old man. This does not necessarily mean that he wrote it after 1466, when he was already sixty-eight years old, but chances are that he was well beyond his middle years.

Unfortunately, all kinds of speculation are possible here. Since, at the time, books circulated in manuscript, those who possessed copies could have failed to add the palinode because they ignored its existence or simply did not take the trouble to do so. A few people could also have disliked the tone of Martínez's reaction. Thus, the palinode could even have been written in 1438 or soon after. On the

other hand, Martínez declares himself already old in the palinode itself. Here, it is possible to argue that his self-avowed old age and his
mischievous hint at the impotence expected in a man's later years
were a mere ruse, a literary device designed to emphasize the cruelty and voracious lechery of his courtly detractors. After all, in the
palinode Martínez uses almost the same language found in part 4 of
the *Corbacho* on two occasions. This could be taken as an indication
that he wrote it when the book was still fresh on his mind.

Other hypotheses could be ventured regarding the date of the
palinode, but it is pointless to do so. What really matters is its authorship, and the evidence that Martínez wrote it is so overwhelm-
ing that it is difficult to imagine how anyone can argue against it.

Although the palinode is not very kind to the ladies, Martínez's
contemporaries did not necessarily regard it as cruel, mean-spirited
invective. In all probability, the feigned retraction also seemed hilarious to them, the work of a good-humored, irrepressibly cheerful
man more bent on having a good laugh than on harming anyone. If
the latter had been his purpose, he would have used a less comical,
more direct kind of language.

To conclude: Having served as chaplain to John II and Henry IV,
Martínez was thoroughly familiar with the language of courtly love,
which he used as an effective, comical weapon, turning their own
code against his detractors. He also used some folkloric metaphors,
thus combining both learned and popular culture. Gerli was on the
mark when he concluded that "the first impression evoked by the
passage may contain implications not yet fathomed by its critics"
(1976a, 33), and that "Irony seems to be the key to its interpretation"
(34).

4

Knitting and Sewing Metaphors and a Maiden's Honor in *La Celestina*

As Samuel G. Armistead has repeatedly shown, contemporary folklore, especially the *Romancero*, may provide valuable lessons for the understanding of medieval literature. The modern oral tradition often preserves ballads omitted from the early *cancioneros*, *pliegos sueltos*, and *romanceros*; records extensive text types previously documented only through allusions or short quotations; and shelters versions of ballads which, though printed in early times, retain crucial details absent from their early congeners.[1] Consequently, modern balladry often enables scholars to gain a better understanding of the past.

Maxime Chevalier (1975, 1978) and others have shown that this is also true of the folktale, a genre which, besides its accepted importance in medieval Spanish literature, continued to play a central role in Golden Age texts as well. It is clear that folktales possessed greater currency in the Middle Ages and the Renaissance than they do today. They were still familiar to everyone, not just to the untutored or semilettered rural masses who now preserve them best. Since the barrier between oral and written literature was in the past less pronounced than it is today, learned authors incorporated folktales into their works in several ways. They adapted the versions that they knew to a variety of situations by (1) transcribing them as a whole; (2) weaving them intertextually into their works, often evoking them only in part; (3) using them as a frame for episodes of their own invention; or (4) on occasion merely alluding to them by naming a character or repeating a key expression without further development or elaboration.

These writers also used legends, proverbs, riddles, popular lyrics, and other folk genres in their works. They assumed that their audience was familiar with those folk materials, and that even brief allusions to them would be instantly recognized. This situation is, however, no longer true because of the gulf that now exists between learned and popular culture. As a result, our understanding of early literature may be frequently diminished in the absence of folklore.

Upon occasion, however, the modern oral tradition permits us to bridge this gap, since it can preserve variants of the folk materials that inspired medieval and Renaissance writers. My purpose here is to demonstrate the value of modern folklore to the understanding of early literature through two Portuguese folk jests that also serve as the basis for a Brazilian chapbook, a related conundrum, and an etiologic joke that bring together terms that help to explain the meaning of *hilado* (yarn) and other key words used by Fernando de Rojas in *La Celestina* (1499).

Besides serving as an excuse to enter the homes of the maidens that she, as a professional procuress, seeks to bring into her fold, the *hilado* sold by Celestina has several additional levels of meaning. As Alan Deyermond has shown, it is related to the images of hunting, trapping, and captivity and, since the devil conjured into it by the old bawd passes, symbolically, into Melibea's waistband and into the chain with which a grateful Calisto rewards Celestina, the *hilado* is at the center of an evil magic circle that connects and influences everyone who comes in contact with these objects, leading them to untimely, unnatural deaths. Even Celestina herself is not immune to the power of her own spell (Deyermond 1977, 1978).

Rosario Ferré has also unraveled several new levels of meaning for this *hilado* and for related words. She shows that *hilado* also constitutes a metaphor for *cupiditas*, both as a "tejido de lujuria" (fabric of lust) and as a "tejido de codicia" (fabric of greed), being textually and metaphorically woven into the fabric of *La Celestina* as a whole: "El hilado como metáfora matriz es . . . ante todo un tejido de 'cupiditas', del cual depende (en el sentido de des-enlazarse o des-envolverse) el discurso de la obra" (The yarn as the chief metaphor is . . . first and foremost a fabric of *cupiditas*, from which depends [in the sense of unraveling and development] the discourse of the work; R. Ferré 1983, 4). Finally, Otis Handy has presented us with a splendid reading of "The Rhetorical and Psychological Defloration of Melibea," showing through a perceptive interpretation of the language used that Melibea is "suffering from a burning fire for Calisto which can only be extinguished by the act of love" (1983, 21) and that "she is not a victim, but a willing, eager participant in *loco amor*" (25).

The folkloric and literary evidence that follows will further support Ferré and Handy's findings, demonstrating even more graphically that *hilado* and the metaphors associated with it also represent lust.

The first folk story, which I recorded in Toronto, Canada, on 29 December 1976, was told by Francisco Machado de Castro, a sixty-two-year-old immigrant from the island of Terceira, Azores:

O Bocage era muito de casa do senhô rei. E agora o senhô rei tinha uma filha, e agora a filha, a mãe dizia à filha:

—Tu nunca deixes homes nenhum te tocá-te. Porque se tu deixares um home tocá-te, tu perdes logo a tua honra. Nunca te deixes home nenhum te tocá.

O Bocage, sabido, muito batido, e sabia dessas coisas. Ele um dia sai a cavalo e ela a esperá-lo no lugá ond'ele passava. E diz . . . E ela vai, chega lá. A saí a cavalo. E ele vai, chega ò pé dela, e toca-le nũa perna.

Diz ela assim:

—Ah, pá, Bocage, tu nã me toques, porqu'a minha mãe diz que quando os homes me toco, as mulheres pèrdie logo a honra!

Diz ele:

— Ê vou-te dá um ponto num lugá, que tu nunca mais perdes a tua honra.

Já sabe, ela, coitada, muito contente. Tamém era meia ignorante. E desce p'ao chão, e ele deu-le o ponto. Ela gostou do sê ponto.

Chega a casa e diz à mãe:

—Ah, minha mãe! Quero dizê a minha mãe qu'ê que nã perco mais a minha honra!

Diz a mãe:

—Ah, minha filha, coma foi?

—Ah, minha mãe, muito bem. O Bocage deu-me um ponto, qu'eu 'tou muito contente e muito satisfeita.

Diz agora ela:

—Mas então porque é qu'ele nã te deu mais?

—Ah, minha mãe, ele nã me deu mais porque diz que nã tinha mais linhas.

Mas tinha um rapazinho a vê isto tudo. Diz o rapaz desta maneira:

—Ele quando te 'tava a dá o ponto tinha dois novelos deste tamanho? [*Gesto com os punhos fechados.*]

(Bocage used to visit the king's house a lot. The king had a daughter, and her mother used to say to her: "Never let any man touch you. If you allow it, you will lose your honor right away. Never let any man touch you." Bocage, who was cunning and very experienced, knew a lot about those things. One day he went horseback riding and saw her waiting for him. He went next to her and touched her on the leg. She said: "Bocage, don't you touch me; my mother says that, when men do that, women lose their honor right away!" He replied: "I'm going to give you a stitch in a certain spot, so that you will never have to worry about losing your honor." The poor girl, you know, was very happy with this. She was kind of stupid. She laid on the ground, and he gave her the stitch. She liked it. When she arrived home, she said to her mother: "Oh, Mom, I want you to know that I will never have to worry about losing my honor!" The mother: "What happened, daughter?" "Mother, no problem. Bocage gave me a stitch, and I'm very happy and satisfied with it." The mother then said: "Then why didn't he give you more?" "Mother, he said that he had run out of yarn." A little boy who was listening to this said as follows: "When he was giving you that stitch, did he happen to have a couple of yarn balls about this size?" (*Gesture with clenched fists.*)

This story had not been previously recorded, perhaps because of the reluctance of field investigators to publish materials that could be branded as obscene (see Armistead and Silverman 1979, 107–8). As we shall see, however, Mr. Castro's version probably goes far back in time. Thanks to the isolation in which the inhabitants of the Azores have lived since their ancestors settled that archipelago during the fifteenth century, those islands constitute a conservative, lateral area within the Portuguese tradition. During subsequent fieldwork in Toronto, I was able to collect a second variant of this story from another archaic lateral area, the province of Trás-os-Montes. It was recorded on 11 June 1984, by the fifty-three-year-old Albertina Esteves, from Quinta dos Garabatos, Duas Igrejas (Miranda do Douro). When I asked her if she knew any stories about "dois novelos e uma agulha" (two yarn balls and a needle), she replied that she remembered two. The first one goes as follows:

Isso era duma vez um pai que tinha uma filha. O pai tinha uma filha e disse pra i-ela, diz:

—Olha, Maria, eu tenho que dar uma voltinha, e tu, minha filha, tenho medo que perdas a honra.

—Não, meu pai, eu não perdo a honra—diz.

—Olha, tu foste criada com muita estima, muito inocente. Tu não sabes qu'o mundo é de marotos. Portanto, eu saio, mas tu ficas em casa. Não saias com ninguém.

—'Tá bem, pai. Não saio.

Mas ela tinha um primo que gostava dela. E diz-l'o primo, diz:

—Ó Maria! 'Tás à janela! Antão, 'tás tanto tempo à janela! Antão teu pai não te chama pa dentro?—porqu'antes nunca ia pà janela.

—O meu pai não 'tá em casa.

—Antão vem passear comigo.

—Ah, isso é que eu não vou.

—Mas porquê?

—Porque posso perder a honra.

—Não, Maria, não perdes. Olha, e antão, se tens assim tanto medo, eu arranjo isso. Olha, eu posso-te coser a honra, que depois ela já nunca se perde.

—Oh, então 'tá bem!

Pronto. Foram e coseram a honra.

Depois da honra está cosida passearam, passearam até que calhou. Pronto.

Lá vem à noite pra casa. Quando veio pra casa, o pai já lá 'tava.

—Onde foste, Maria? Ó desgraçada, o que é que tu fizeste?

—Ó pai, não s'aflija, que eu não perdi a honra.

—Como é que tu dizes? Que não perdest'a honra?

—Não perdi, pai—disse—, porqu'olha: o primo coseu-a bem cosida. E eu ainda queria que me desse mais pontos, mas ele não quis. Que disse que tinha acabado o fio. Mas não acabou, pai—disse, pondo as duas mãos fechadas juntas. Disse:—Porque ele ficou com dois novelos assim, e também vi a agulha.

(Once upon a time there was a father and daughter. The father said to her: "Look, Maria, I've got to go somewhere, and I'm afraid you will lose your honor, daughter." "I won't lose it," she says. "Look, you were raised with much care, and you're very innocent. You do not know that the world is full of rascals. When I go, make sure you stay in the house. Don't go out with anyone." "O.K., Dad. I won't." But there was a cousin who liked her, and he said: "Maria, you have been for so long at the window! How come your father has not called you back inside?" (She never used to go to the window.) "My dad isn't home." "Then let's go for a stroll." "No, I won't." "Why not?" "I could lose my honor." "No, Maria, you won't. Look, if you are so scared, I can fix that. I can sew it up for you, and you will never lose it." "Oh, that's great!" Fine and dandy. They went for a stroll and sewed up the honor. When Maria returned home, at night, her father was already back. "Where did you go, Maria? What have you done, you wretched creature?" "Don't worry, Dad. I haven't lost my honor." "What are you saying? You have not lost your honor?" "I didn't, Dad. My cousin sewed it up real good. I wanted a few more stitches, but he said he had run out of yarn. But he really hadn't," she said, clenching her fists together, "because he had two yarn balls like this, and I also saw his needle.")

In these two stories,[2] a concerned parent (in one a mother who happens to be the queen; in the second, a father) worries about the preservation of a daughter's *honor*, warning her to avoid compromising situations (e.g., allowing a man to place his hand upon her leg and leaving the house alone). In both cases, naturally, the girl does exactly the opposite of what she is told: in the first story, the princess goes horseback riding and chances upon Bocage (a late eighteenth-century Portuguese poet transformed into a folk figure, similar to the Spanish trickster Quevedo, and to whom many off-color jokes are attributed by popular tradition).[3] As she dismounts, Bocage places his hand on her leg. In the second tale, after some hesitation, the young lady eventually accepts a cousin's invitation to leave her house and go for a walk. When both women protest that they do not wish to lose their honor, they are reassured by the masculine protagonists that, with a stitch or two, their virtue can be restored in such a way that they need not worry about losing it again. And so they agree to some *pontos* (stitches) which are administered with an *agulha* (needle) and *linhas* or *fio* (thread). Later, when the two young women explain to their parents what had happened, they declare they had enjoyed the stitching so much that they in fact begged for more *pontos*. The two men protested, however, claiming that they had exhausted the supply of thread that they normally carried rolled in their *novelos* (yarn balls).

While attending a conference in Brazil (Aracaju, State of Sergipe), I asked Bráulio do Nascimento, whose knows the oral tradition of his country better than anyone,[4] if he knew variants of this story. The reply was affirmative. Besides telling me that it was an international tale-type (Aarne and Thompson 1973, no. 1542**, *The Maiden's Honor*), he recommended that I speak with a common friend, Jackson da Silva Lima. The day after, the latter brought me a photocopy of *O Costureiro de Honra*, a chapbook written by Adam Fialho (n.d). As Silva Lima informed me, Adam Fialho is the pseudonym of Manoel d'Almeida Filho, an author of popular chapbooks from Paraíba who lived in Aracaju, where he died, for more than sixty years. Written in heptassyllabic sextets, the chapbook tells the story of a farming couple, João and Sofia, who lived in the backlands with their three daughters. The oldest and prettiest, Marina, was seventeen years old, and the other two, Marta and Maria, were sixteen and fifteen, respectively. Since they did not have any neighbors and did not know any boys, they were very innocent but, nevertheless, their parents took great precautions. The poor girls "só caminhavam peadas / para as honras não caírem / entre o mudar das passadas" (only walked with shackles, to keep their honor from falling between steps; 4), and, when visitors showed up unexpectedly,

Os pais atendiam tudo	The parents would take care of everything
com as três filhas sentadas,	while their three daughters sat,
para que ninguém soubesse	so no one would know
que elas estavam peadas.	that they wore shackles.

(Fialho n.d., 5)

One day the mother fell ill and the couple had to travel far, leaving the girls alone for a few days. It was then that Afonso, a young cattle buyer, showed up and asked the girls for lodging. Upon discovering why they walked so awkwardly he offered them his services, stating that he was a professional seamster and that he was engaged in sewing the honor of the maidens who lived in the backlands so that they could run about "sem medo da perdição" (without fear of perdition; 10). Very happy, the girls accepted the offer immediately, and Afonso let them know that it would be necessary for him to spend a night with each of them in order to do the job well. The oldest girl, Marina, was the first one. As we can see, the poem is based on the Portuguese joke, for it uses the same euphemisms:

Com a *agulha* apontada,	With his *needle* pointed,
pronta para iniciar,	ready to begin the job,
já com a *linha* enfiada,	the *yarn* already threaded
os *novelos* no lugar,	and the *skeins* in place,
pelas ourelas da *honra*	on the rims of her *honor*
começou a *costurar*. (16)	he then began to *sew*.

Very happy, Marta does not want Afonso to stop sewing. In the Portuguese jokes, the hero protests that he is running out of thread, but Afonso gives a more complete reply ("A linha se derreteu, / os novelos encolheram, / a agulha amoleceu" [The yarn has melted; the skeins shrank; the needle went soft; 18]), and rests for a little while in order to be able to continue afterward. On the second and third nights, he does the same with the other two sisters. When their parents return, the three girls run to hug them and let them know what happened. Nine months later, each girl gives them a grandson.

Despite its brevity, this summary suffices to show that *O Costureiro de Honra* is based on the Portuguese story. In Brazil, the story served as inspiration for a popular chapbook, being thus adapted, and in a richer and more developed manner, to a literary genre of semipopular character.[5]

The central motif of these three versions is J86, which was documented in China: *Rocks falling together and thread entering needle's eye suggest sexual intercourse: hence its beginning.* This motif is also indexed as Z186: *Symbolism: Needle and thread—sexual intercourse* (Thompson 1955–58).

Most of these metaphors or euphemisms reappear in a conundrum and in an etiologic joke that I have also collected.[6] Like the Chinese motif, however, the conundrum explicitly adds the image of knitting. Whereas a baby's cape is made with one yarn ball and two needles, the baby is made the other way around—two yarn balls and one needle. I recorded it in 1977, while doing fieldwork in the island of São Jorge, Azores (see SJ), from the sixty-eight-year-old José Bento de Ramos:

—Que diferença há entre o bébé e a capa que veste?

—A diferença que há é que a capa é feita com um novelo e duas agulhas. O bébé deve ser o contrário: dois novelos e uma agulha.

(What's the difference between a baby and the clothes he wears? The clothes are made with a yarn ball and two needles. With the baby, it must be the other way around: two yarn balls and a needle.)

Whereas knitting is the central image in this conundrum, the etiologic joke, which Albertina Esteves recorded in Toronto right after telling her version of the folk story, emphasizes sewing. It purports to explain the main anatomic differences between the sexes:

—Não sabe a diferença que há, porque é que os homens são diferentes das mulheres? Porque toda a gente, Deus quando fez, foi co'a barriga rota. O homem e a mulhere.

Depois, antão o homem e a mulher viviam tristes, porque tinham qu'andar sempre a pegar das tripas co'as mãos.

E depois Nosso Senhor deu-l'antão um novelo e uma agulha pra coserem a barriga.

A mulher, como era mais perfeita, deu o ponto mais miudinho, e acabou-l'o fio. Acabou-s'o fio antes d'acabá de coser a barriga. O homem era mais trapalhão, deu os pontos mais largos. Olhe: segurou o fio, segurou o novelo, segurou a agulha, e ficou-le tudo por ali.

(Don't you know why men are different from women? Because God made everyone with his belly torn. Both men and women. They were very sad, for they had to hold their intestines in with their hands. Then Our Lord gave them a yarn ball and a needle for them to sew up their bellies. Being neater, the woman made small stitches and ran out of yarn. She ran out of yarn before the job was done. Being clumsier, the man made larger stitches. Look: he sewed up the yarn, the yarn ball, the needle, and left everything hanging there.)

In *La Celestina*, Rojas also uses euphemisms similar to those found in the two folk stories, the conundrum, and the etiologic joke. At the end of Celestina's first interview with Melibea on behalf of Calisto, her ailing client who suffers from a grievous "toothache"—a euphemism for unrelenting sexual desire (West 1979; Herrero 1986)—the old bawd asks the girl for her girdle (rope belt), believed to have touched all the holy relics in Rome and Jerusalem (Rojas 1987, 164), and for a prayer. Melibea is so angry when she first hears Calisto's name—he had already approached her—that she threatens Celestina. Nevertheless, Melibea gives her the girdle; needing more time to write down the prayer, she instructs Celestina to return very secretly for it the day after (168).

Besides its hypothetical curative properties, Melibea's girdle also represents her chastity (West 1979, 136; Dunn 1975, 414; Costa Fontes 1990–91, 23), and the request for the prayer, which still exists in the oral tradition (Costa Fontes 1995a, 97n2), is truly ironic, since it is a folk spell for real, not metaphoric toothaches.[7] As I have stated elsewhere, "With such veiled language, Celestina is in fact telling Melibea the truth, and Melibea understands it perfectly well" (Costa Fontes 1995a, 97–98). That is why, fearing her mother's interference, Melibea asks Celestina to return very secretly for the prayer the next day (see also Herrero 1986, 136).

It is during Celestina's second interview with Melibea, in which this type of veiled language also abounds, that we find a series of metaphors that coincide with the Portuguese folk stories and with the Brazilian chapbook. Feeling ill, Melibea sends her maid, Lucrecia, to fetch Celestina right away, and the girl explains that her mistress "se siente muy fatigada de desmayos y de dolor del coraçón" (feels very tired with swoons and pain in the heart; Rojas 1987, 237; all the citations that follow are from this ed.). Celestina rushes to Melibea's house and sprinkles her speech with a series of references to *agujas* (needles) and *puntos* (stitches) as she explains the remedy for the wound opened in her heart by her recently born love for Calisto. Although the harsh stitches hurt the wound, Melibea must allow Celestina to reveal the tip of her healing needle if she is to be cured: "Señora, no tengas por nuevo ser más fuerte de sofrir al herido la ardiente trementina y los ásperos *puntos* que lastiman *lo llagado, doblan la passión,* que no la primera lisión, que dio sobre sano. Pues si tú quieres ser sana y que te descubra la punta de mi sotil *aguja* sin temor, haz para tus manos y pies una ligadura de sosiego . . . y verás obrar a la antigua maestra destas *llagas*" (Madam, do not be surprised to find out that it is more difficult for a wounded person to bear the burning turpentine and the harsh *stitches,* which hurt the *wound* and *double the passion,* than the very first lesion, which struck when you were still whole. If you wish to regain your health and for me to reveal the tip of my subtle *needle* without fear, then make for your hands and feet a bond of tranquillity . . . and you will see the old expert of such *wounds* at work; 242).

As Rosario Ferré and Handy realized, the needle is indeed a phallic symbol (R. Ferré 1983, 12), and the stitches are a euphemism for the action of the penis during coitus (Handy 1983, 21–22). Handy interprets "la ardiente trementina" (burning turpentine) as orgasmic fluid, "los ásperos puntos" (harsh stitches) as the breaking of the hymen (21–22), and *llaga* (wound) as suffering or love (18). In fact, the *llaga* is also a euphemism for the vagina, whose passion will be doubled by the stitches that will simultaneously cure its desire. The use of *llaga* in this context borders on sacrilege, for that word also brings to mind the wounds of Christ.

To ensure her victory, Celestina presses on, embroidering her speech with additional references to the *aguja* and *puntos* that can cure Melibea: "Señora, este es otro y segundo *punto,* el qual si tú con tu mal sofrimiento no consientes, poco aprovechará mi venida, y si como prometiste lo sufres, tú quedarás *sana* y sin deubda, y Calisto sin quexa y *pagado.* Primero te avisé de mi cura y desta invisible *aguja* que *sin llegar a ti sientes en sólo mentarla mi boca*" (Madam, this is another, second *stitch,* and if you do not bear it, my visit will be of little use to you. But if you bear it as you promised, you will be *healed* and cured, and Calisto will be without complaint and *satisfied.* I warned you right away about my remedy and this invisible *needle*, which *you feel as soon as I mention it, even though it has not yet touched you*; 243).

Celestina's insistence on the curative power of sewing is meant to arouse the young Melibea, who seems readily affected, not to say pricked, by the invisible needle invoked by the old bawd; so much so that Celestina observes an immediate reaction to her words. The terms *sana* (healed) and *pagado* (satisfied) refer to the postcoital satisfaction that Melibea and Calisto will feel after they have sex. The invisibility of the needle that has such an effect on Melibea certainly "provides further evidence that what transpires here is a psychic seduction with a clear physical subtext" (Handy 1983, 23). Melibea's ability to feel this needle despite its invisibility—just picture the facial expression that caused Celestina to utter the words in question—is of course indicative of her strong arousal. Note also the double meaning of Celestina's last three words. Through such veiled language, Celestina is suggesting that, should Melibea accept the remedy prescribed by her, she would be instantly "cured" of her affliction, leaving Calisto free of his ailment and satisfied in the process. The terms *needle* and *stitch*, then, possessed for Rojas the same meaning that they have in the Luso-Brazilian stories.

When Melibea tells Celestina not to mention Calisto's name, the old bawd also says to her: "Sufre, señora, con paciencia, que es el primer *punto* y principal. No se quiebre, si no, todo nuestro trabajo es perdido. *Tu llaga es grande*, tiene necessidad de áspera cura; y lo *duro* con *duro* se ablanda más efficazmente" (Please bear it with patience, Madam, for this is the first and most important *stitch*. If it breaks, all our work is lost. *Your wound is big*, requires a harsh remedy, and a *harsh* wound responds better to something *hard*; 243).

We already know what Celestina means by *punto* and *llaga*. According to Handy, the first *duro* denotes the pangs of love, and the second one is another phallic reference (1983, 22). Indeed, the word *duro*, which means "hard," seems to refer to an erection, as confirmed by a somewhat cryptic burlesque version of the ballad *A Volta do Navegante* (*La vuelta del navegante* [The Mariner's Return]; RPI, I9; CMP I8) that I collected in São Jorge (Azores) in 1977:

—Deus 'teja com minhas tias,	"May God be with my aunts
sentadinhas a fiar.	as they sit spinning."
—Deus venha com o sobrinho,	"May God come with my nephew
com a sua verga tesa.	and his hard rod."
5 —A senhora dá-me licença?	"May I have your permission,
	Ma'am?

Quem na toma é cabeludo	The one who takes it is hairy
no seu rapado.	in the bare area."
—Meta o senhor,	"Please stick in, Mister,
que 'tá destapado.	for it is uncovered.
10 e sente o mole no *duro*	Sit what is soft on what is *hard*,
e diga-me se quer	and tell me if you would rather
do branco do cu	have something from the whiteness of the ass
ou do alvo d'entre as pernas.	or from the target between the legs."

(SJ, no. 224)

Earlier in the interview, Celestina had already made it clear that it was physical desire, rather than love, which had caused Melibea's predicament. When Melibea told her that she suspected that the cause of her pain had been Celestina's request for the prayer on Calisto's behalf, the procuress countered that Calisto was not the real cause for her suffering: "¿Cómo, señora, tan mal hombre es aquél, tan mal nombre es el suyo que en sólo ser nombrado trae consigo ponçoña su sonido? No creas que sea éssa la causa de tu sentimiento, antes otra que yo barrunto; y pues que ansí es, si tú licencia me das, yo, señora, te la diré" (How can he be such a bad man and have such a bad reputation that the very sound of his name is poisonous to you? Don't you imagine that to be the cause of your suffering? I suspect another, and since I am right, I will tell you what it is, Madam, if you give me permission; 241).

Since here there is no spiritual love involved—Celestina's tone is too coarse for that—, Melibea's predicament consists of simple lust. Calisto, who, like Melibea, suffers from the same illness, plays a somewhat mechanical role in the affair. He is the medicine, providing Celestina with the *aguja* and *puntos* needed to treat Melibea's *llaga*. This treatment, of course, will also heal his grievous "toothache." Thus, both Calisto and Melibea are Celestina's patients, while the old bawd, in addition to her role as intermediary, also plays the role of "doctor." Melibea explicitly refers to her as such, while coyly wondering why the old bawd needs her permission to cure her: "De licencia tienes tú necessidad para me dar la salud? ¿Quál *médico* jamás pidió tal seguro para curar al paciente?" (You need permission to give me health? Has a *doctor* ever needed such assurance in order to cure a patient? ibid.).

In fact, Celestina is more than a mere doctor. She is also a surgeon, and her insistence on the curative power of sewing is related to the fact that, as already stated, love was regarded as a real illness during the Middle Ages. In the medical treatises of the time, "Médico tras médico discute solemnemente la causa de la enfermedad (inflamación del cerebro por el deseo insatisfecho), la diagnosis (por los mismos síntomas que presentan Arnalte, Leriano y Calisto), el pronóstico (en general se restablece el enfermo con el tiempo aunque hay casos desesperados en los que el mal puede ser mortífero) y el remedio" (Doctor after doctor discusses solemnly the cause of the illness [inflammation of the brain due to unsatisfied desire], the diagnosis [through the same symptoms as those exhibited by Arnalte, Leriano, and Calisto], the prognosis [the sick person usually recovers in time, even though there are bad cases in which the illness can be deadly], and the remedy; Whinnom 1979, 13–14; see also Shipley 1975).

During her second interview with Melibea, then, Celestina assumes the role of doctor; Melibea and Calisto are her patients. This interpretation is reinforced by the medical use of needles and stitches and frequent references to illnesses, remedies, cures, and doctors throughout the interview:

> Celestina: Pero para yo dar mediante Dios congrua y saludable *melezina* es necessario saber de ti tres cosas. . . . Por ende cumple que al *médico* como al confesor se hable toda verdad abiertamente. (But for me to find you, with God's help, a suitable and healthy *remedy*, you must tell me three things. . . . For that reason, it is necessary to tell the whole truth frankly to the *doctor*, as to the confessor; 240)

> Melibea: Mi *mal* es de coraçón, la yzquierda teta es su aposentamiento; tiende sus rayos a todas partes. (My *illness* is of the heart; the left breast is its seat; it irradiates everywhere; 241)

> Celestina: sabe que no ay cosa más contraria en las grandes *curas* delante los animosos çurujanos que los flacos coraçones, los quales con su gran lástima, con sus dolorosas hablas, con sus sentibles meneos, ponen temor al *enfermo*, hazen que desconfíe de la salud, y al *médico* enojan y turban, y la turbación altera la mano, rige sin orden la aguja. (I want you to know that nothing hinders great *cures* for bold *surgeons* more than the fainthearted, who, with their great pity, their sorrowful words, their pained wriggling, cause the *ill person* to fear and doubt that there is a cure, and so anger and hamper the *doctor* so that his hand is affected and he cannot control the needle; 242)

> Celestina: y dizen los sabios que la *cura* del lastimero *médico* dexa mayor señal, y que nunca peligro sin peligro se vence. (and wise men say that the *cure* of the fainthearted *doctor* leaves a bigger scar, and that danger can only be conquered by danger; 243)

The final reference to medicine during this interview is truly sacrilegious, for it implies that God, being the source (i.e., Creator) of the "wound," which, in this instance, can also mean "burning passion," is also the one who provides the "remedy" that is to be ministered through Calisto. Celestina assures Melibea of her cure with these words: "No desconfíe, señora, tu noble juventud de salud; que cuando el alto *Dios* da la *llaga*, tras ella embía el *remedio*. Mayormente que sé yo al mundo nascida una flor que de todo esto te delibre" (Don't doubt a cure, my noble young lady. Since almighty *God* gives *the wound*, He sends *the remedy* for it afterward. Moreover, I know of a flower born into the world who will deliver you from all of this; 244).[8]

Since Melibea knew perfectly well what she wanted, it does not take her long to discard most of her pretensions. Like the young girl in the Portuguese story, Melibea is also mindful of preserving her honor, however. With the following words, she wonders why the old bawd needs her permission to cure her: "¿De licencia tienes tú necessidad para me dar la salud? . . . Di, di, que siempre la tienes de mí, tal que mi *honrra* no dañes con tus palabras" (You need my permission to give me health? . . . Speak out; speak out, for you will always have my permission, provided that your words do not damage my *honor*; 241). It could be argued that Melibea merely worries about her reputation, a kind of honor different from the exclusively physical connotation given to a girl's "honor" in the folk story. The words used by Melibea when she finally capitulates to Celestina's machinations indicate otherwise, however, for she equates her honor with the wounding of her body and the tearing of her flesh: "Agora toque en mi *honrra*, agora dañe mi *fama*, agora lastime mi *cuerpo*, *aunque sea romper mis carnes* para sacar mi dolorido coraçón, te doy mi fe ser segura, y si siento alivio, bien galardonada" (Now let it [your remedy] touch *my honor*; now let it harm *my reputation*; now let it hurt *my body, even if it means tearing my flesh* in order to extract my aching heart. I assure you of my trust, and, if I feel some relief, you will be handsomely rewarded; 242).

There are too many significant coincidences here for the reader to suppose that Melibea does not understand what she is getting into. Her willingness to have her flesh torn is especially suggestive. As Handy observed, these are indeed piercing cries of surrender (1983, 22).

The folkloric reference to the *novelos* and *linhas* or *fio* also sheds new light on the euphemistic meaning of the *hilado* that plays such a vital role in Celestina's career. Both stories and the conundrum make it clear that the yarn balls designate testicles, and that the thread is a euphemism for semen.

Celestina is a *labrandera*, or "seamstress," an occupation which, as indicated by Pármeno (110), serves to camouflage her real profession. The imagery of sewing is also clearly emphasized in the etiologic joke, and it is in her capacity as seamstress, a euphemism for both whore and procuress, that Celestina, with her needle and thread, weaves the compromising entanglements which are indispensable to her profession. In view of this, the fact that, together with the *hilado*, Celestina also takes needles and pins into the homes of her prospective victims acquires a renewed and comic significance. At one point she tells Sempronio: "Aquí llevo un poco de *hilado* en esta mi faltriquera, con otros aparejos que conmigo siempre traygo para tener causa de entrar donde mucho no só conoscida la primera vez: assí como gorgueras, garvines, franjas, rodeos, tinazuelas, alcohol, alvayalde y solimán, hasta *agujas* y *alfileres*" (I am carrying a little bit of *yarn* in my pouch, together with other trifles that I always bring along as an excuse to enter for the first time into houses where I am not very well-known: ruffs, hair-nets, fringes, edging, tweezers, mascara, blot powder, cleanser, and even *needles* and *pins*; 145).

The euphemistic value of *hilado* also leads to a reinterpretation of the famous words pronounced by Celestina when Sempronio wonders if Calisto and Melibea's is the first commission that she has undertaken. Celestina replies that few maidens in town have "opened up shop" without first availing themselves of the "yarn" that constitutes the mainstay of her business: "¿El primero, hijo? Pocas virgines, a Dios gracias, has tú visto en esta ciudad que hayan abierto tienda a vender, de quien yo no haya sido corredora de su primer hilado" (The first one, son? Few virgins, thank God, have you seen opening up shop in order to sell in this city, without me brokering their first yarn; 141).

There is no doubt that this thread (or yarn), which, significantly, Celestina carries rolled up in *madejas* (skeins; 89) together with a jumble of things including the already mentioned pins and needles as a pretext for entering the homes of maidens like Melibea in order to hunt and trap them (83), euphemistically denotes semen; while the *madejas*, the equivalent to the Luso-Brazilian yarn balls, doubtless designate testicles.

A fairly recent (and, I hasten to add, excellent) translation of this passage reads as follows: "My first? I should say it is not! There are few virgins in this town who have opened up shop without my help in selling their first yarn" (Singleton 1975, 61).

A virgin does not have any "yarn" to sell when she first opens up shop, however. The expression indicates availability for sexual commerce, but, since Celestina finds it necessary to bring these maidens into her fold, what is meant here is that they have reached an age appropriate to engage in sex. The yarn will be brought to them by the partners arranged by Celestina, the procuress (*corredora* still has that meaning). The first Italian and French translations, as well as Cohen's recent English translation, come closer to the original's intent, because they convey a clearer sexual connotation:

> La prima, figliol mio? Poche uergene hai tu uiste in questa cita che habiano aperta botega auendere, dele quale io non habia guadagnate la prima sensalia. (The first one, my son? Few virgins have you seen opening up shop in order to sell in this city, whose fee I have not been the first to earn; Kish 1973, 85)

> Le premier, mon filz? Tu as veu peu de jeunes filles pucelles, graces á Dieu! en cette ville qui ayent ouvert bouticque pour vendre de quoy que je n'aye esté la premiere courtiere. (The first one, my son? Few young virgins have you seen, thank God, opening up shop in order to sell in this city without me being their first broker; Brault 1963, 59)

> The first, my son? You haven't seen many virgins set up shop in this town, praise God! whose goods I haven't been the first to peddle. (Cohen 1966, 63)

James Mabbe's English translation of 1631, however, which preserves the reference to *hilado*, offers a more precise rendition of the levels of meaning in Rojas's phrases: "The first, (my sonne?) Few virgins (I thanke Fortune for it) hast thou seene in this Citty, which have opened up their shops, and traded for themselves, to whom I have not beene a broaker to their first spunne thread, and holpe them vent their wares" (1967, 70). Mabbe's translation of *hilado* as "thread" also brings to mind the colloquial English (and American) expression "to thread the needle," which means "to copulate" (Holder 1995, 372a).[9]

Since Melibea has no difficulty in understanding the old bawd's language, she is far from being the witless, innocent victim of Celestina's cunning that some critics envisioned. She is attracted to Calisto and her lust is aroused by her awareness of the constant, unrelenting "toothache" that he suffers on her account. Until very recently, this aspect of *La Celestina* escaped modern readers because, lacking the crucial cultural background, including an awareness of folk literature and folk beliefs, they failed to understand the nuances of the language used by the author. Fernando de Rojas, however, did not intend to be cryptic. Quite the opposite: he was very conscious that the vast majority of his audience would easily catch the double entendre, since both he and his public shared a common store of linguistic knowledge derived from the oral tradition.

As attested by the Chinese motif indexed by Stith Thompson, and by the colloquial English and American expression "to thread the needle," the utilization of similar euphemisms surviving into modern times constitutes a universal linguistic phenomenon. In the Portuguese oral tradition, as we have seen, those euphemisms are found in a conundrum, an etiologic joke, and a folk story that is also adapted in a Brazilian chapbook. Since the later is better developed, gathering all the terms used by Rojas, including the central, euphemistic reference to a maiden's honor, it is likely that he was inspired by a similar story, and expected his readers to know it as well as he did. Even if they did not, they would no doubt find the euphemisms easy to understand, since, as we shall see, they belonged to an even broader folk tradition. Moreover, Rojas's readers were familiar with courtly poetry, which also makes extensive use of similar linguistic techniques (Whinnom 1981). The latter notwithstanding, the Luso-Brazilian story indicates that Rojas's most probable source was the oral tradition.

The modern oral tradition is not alone in providing a key to some of the euphemisms used in *La Celestina*, however. Other writers frequently use sewing, threading, weaving, and related words in order to refer to the activities of prostitutes throughout the sixteenth and seventeenth centuries. Not surprisingly, such terms are particularly abundant in Francisco Delicado's *La Lozana andaluza* (1528), whose protagonist, Lozana, happens to be a prostitute.

Writing to a group of fellow prostitutes in order to allay their fear of losing revenue after the havoc caused by the sack of Rome by the forces of Charles V in 1527, Lozana concludes: "Por ende, sosegad que, sin duda por munchos años, podéis *hilar* velas largas luengas" (For that reason, do not worry, for no doubt you still have many years to *spin* big, long candles; 1985, 505). At the beginning of the novel, Lozana's aunt informs her that the merchant Diomedes, who is waiting for the girl in front of the house, wants her to weave for him with these words: "Descí, sobrina, que este gentilhombre quiere que le *tejáis un tejillo*, que proveeremos de premideras" (Come down, niece, for this gentleman would like you *to weave for*

him a girdle-band, for which we will supply the treadles [of the
loom]; 181). That there is a double meaning here is confirmed by the
Portuguese conundrum (the baby is made with two yarn balls and a
needle) and by the words used by Lozana to tell Rampín, while she is
making love to him, to indicate that his prowess is beginning to get
the best of her: "Mi vida, ya no más, que basta hasta otro día, que yo
no puedo mantener la *tela*" (My love, no more, let's leave it for another day, for I can no longer hold up the *fabric*; 236).

In addition to *hilar* and *tejer,* in an equally euphemistic fashion,
Delicado also places the words *aguja, alfiler,* and *labrar* (in the sense
of sewing) on the lips of his protagonist and her aunt. When the or-
phaned heroine shows up at the latter's house in Seville, the aunt,
apparently preoccupied with her young niece's future—what she really wants is to get rid of her—informs her that the merchant
Diomedes, who had been there the day before, "me dará *remedio* para
que vos seáis *casada y honrada,* mas querría él que supiésedes
labrar" (will give me the *remedy* [means] for you to be *married and
honorable,* but he would like you to know how *to do needlework*; 179).
The "remedy" that she suggests recalls the remedy or medicine that
is frequently mentioned during the second interview between Celestina and Melibea. "Casada y honrada" is an oblique way of referring to coitus, for marriage implies consummation and, although a
woman can be "honrada" through marriage, the hasty juxtaposition
of that word to "casada" causes it to mean exactly the opposite.[10]
Labrar may mean "to embroider," another sewing activity, but it can
also be taken in the sense of "to plough," which, as evidenced by
Lozana's response, is also related to coitus: "Señora tía, yo aquí traigo
el *alfiletero,* mas ni tengo *aguja* ni *alfiler,* que *dedal* no faltaría para
apretar, y por eso, señora tía, si vos queréis, yo le hablaré antes que
se parta, porque no pierda mi ventura, siendo huérfana" (My lady-
aunt, I've got the *needle cushion* here, but I've neither a *needle* nor a
pin, though I certainly have the *thimble to push* [clutch, tighten]
them with, and for that reason, aunt, I'll speak with him before he
leaves, so as not to lose my good fortune, being an orphan; 179–80).[11]
In other words, Lozana's vagina (*alfiletero,* "needle cushion") is more
than ready, but she is still lacking a phallus, no matter its size (*aguja,
alfiler,* "needle," "pin"), for she certainly has the vulva (*dedal,* "thimble") that it would take to push or clutch (*apretar*) it with. Thus, it is
clear that these terms also had widespread folkloric currency during
the sixteenth and seventeenth centuries. Indeed, thanks to a splendid compilation of erotic Golden Age poetry (Alzieu, Jammes, and Lissorgues 1984), it is possible to document them even further.

Two of the poems that Alzieu and his collaborators anthologized gather numerous sewing and weaving terms in just two strophes. In the first, a lady asks a shoemaker what he is about,[12] to which he replies:

El cuero ablando primero	I first soften the hide
25 que la *costura* se junta,	where the *seam* is placed,
y encero depués la *punta*	and then I wax the *tip*
porque atiña al *agujero*	for it to reach the *hole*,
y pase el *hilo* ligero,	and the *thread* will run smoothly,
blando, suave, amoroso.	soft, smooth, and loving.
30 *Señora, coso, coso.*	*Madam, I'm sewing; I'm sewing.*

(no. 76)

In this context, *costura* connotatively refers to the "seam" left unfinished by the woman in the Portuguese etiologic joke due to the lack of thread. The word also possesses a denotative meaning, however: it means to sew and, as the shoemaker repeats in the refrain, that is precisely what he is doing. There is an implicit reference to a needle, since the cobbler waxes its tip to run the thread smoothly through the *agujero*, or "opening."

In the second poem, a young girl who has just spun some yarn into three *ovillos* (clews; i.e., the Portuguese and Brazilian *novelos* [yarn balls] and Rojas's *madejas* [skeins]), sets out to weave them to see if her "cloth" will gain in size:

Acabó la niña	The little girl finished
de *hilar* su *tela*,	*spinning* her *fabric*;
5 hizo tres *ovillos*,	she made three *clews*
a *tejer* los lleva;	and took them to weave;
quiere hacer prueba	she wants to test
si su *tela* crece.	whether her *fabric* grows.
Quien bien hila y tuerce	For whoever spins and twists well,
10 *bien se le parece.*	it looks good.

(no. 77)

Clearly, the word *tela* is used to designate the body as a whole or, more specifically, perhaps the vagina; if this last interpretation is correct, the young woman's wishes to get it "stretched." In another poem, a lover begs his lady to place herself at his disposal with the following words: "Mandaréis luego tener / a mi servicio la *tela*" (You will at once command the *fabric* to be at my service; no. 3).

Weaving, which produces new *tela* or *trama*, refers to sexual intercourse: "Acá vengo a que me lo hagáis: hacédmelo presto. / *Tejedlo* con lo colorado" (I'm coming here for you to do it to me; do it quickly. *Weave* it with the red part; no. 143.5 [p. 300]). This connotation, which calls to mind the Portuguese conundrum (where the infant's cape is made with one yarn ball and two needles, while the baby is made with two yarn balls and one needle), can also be found in a sonnet where the pleasures of lovemaking are evoked by a young man: "aquel urdir después la dulce *trama*, / luego despacio, luego más aprisa. . . ." (That subsequent warping of the sweet *weft*, at times slowly, at times faster. . . . no. 15).

There are numerous additional examples of these terms having sexual connotations, but the ones presented suffice to demonstrate their widespread currency in the language of the late Middle Ages and the Golden Age. Cervantes was familiar with another, similar tradition of euphemism, as can be seen in the words of the innkeeper's wife in *Don Quijote*, when she demands the return of an oxtail that the barber used in a disguise: "Para mi santiguada, que no se ha aún de aprovechar más de mi *rabo* para su *barba*, y que me ha de volver mi *cola*; que anda *lo de* mi marido por esos suelos, que es *vergüenza*; digo, el *peine*, que solía yo *colgar* de mi *buena cola*" (By my faith, you are no longer to use my *tail* as your *beard*, and you must give the *tail* back to me, for my husband's *thing* is tossed on the floor, which is *shameful* [also: the genitalia]. I mean, his *comb* [*peine* = *pene*, "penis"], which I used to *hang* on my good *tail*; 1978, 1: 392; the double entendres are self-evident and require no further elaboration).

In Cervantes's interlude *El viejo celoso*, Ortigosa, the nosy neighbor, offers the following services to the decrepit Cañizares: "Si vuestra merced hubiere menester algún pegadillo para la *madre*, téngolos milagrosos, y si para *mal de muelas*, sé unas palabras que quitan el dolor *como con la mano*" (If you need some sticking plaster for the *uterus*, I've got miraculous ones, and if for *toothaches*, I know some words that take away the pain, *as if by hand*; 1976, 214). She is, of course, referring to the menstrual pains which, according to Celestina's advice to Areúsa, are best cured with intercourse (203)—ironically, the very thing that Cañizares fears most for his fifteen-year-old wife's discomfort, since he is unable to provide such a remedy for her. As he confesses to a friend a earlier in the play, he had married her solely for the sake of company, since desire, at his age, had long left him: "¡Que no había que abrasar en mí, señor compadre, que con la menor llamarada quedara hecho ceniza!" (There was nothing left to set afire in me, friend; the smallest flame would have turned me to ashes! 209). Moreover, Ortigosa's incantations for toothaches are doubtless a reference to the folk prayer of Saint Appolonia (the same prayer Celestina asks Melibea to provide in order to cure Calisto's dental pain). Saint Appolonia's prayer, it is believed, can cure a toothache as if only by a slight passing of the hand over the affected area. It follows, then, that since a toothache is a euphemism for physical desire, the reference to the hand compounds the joke and embodies an oblique, comical reference to masturbation.

As shown by his reply, Cañizares fails to understand Ortigosa's reference, choosing only to interpret her words in a literal sense: "Abrevie, señora Ortigosa; que doña Lorenza, *ni tiene madre, ni dolor de muelas*; que todas las tiene sanas y enteras, que en su vida se ha sacado muela alguna" (Cut it short, Mrs. Ortigosa. Doña Lorenza has neither a *mother* nor a *toothache*. All of her teeth are healthy and whole, for she hasn't had to pull one all of her life; 214). The connotation is that Lorenza is still a virgin,[13] and that Ortigosa plans to "remedy" this situation by smuggling a young *galán* into the house. She hints at the planned cure when she tells Cañizares that, God willing, Lorenza will eventually pull some teeth, at the same time alluding to his impotence by declaring that old age eventually causes all of one's teeth to fall out: "Ella se las sacará, placiendo al cielo, porque le dará muchos años de vida; y la vejez es la total destruición de la dentadura" (She will eventually pull some, Heaven willing, for she will live yet for many years; old age brings about the complete destruction of one's teeth; ibid.). Enraged, Cañizares catches on and throws Ortigosa out of the house.

Similarly, in *Don Quijote*, Sansón Carrasco advises the protagonist's distraught housekeeper to recite Saint Appolonia's prayer when she suspects that her employer is about to sally forth for a third time. As suggested in her astonished reply, Don Quijote's infirmity was altogether different: "¡Cuitada de mí! ¿La oración de Santa Apolonia dice vuestra merced que rece? Eso fuera si mi amo lo hubiera de las muelas; pero no lo ha sino de los cascos" (Poor me! You want me to say the prayer of Saint Appolonia? That would do if my master suffered from a toothache, but his problem is in the brain; 1978, 2: 86).

While the spell and the allusions just discussed demonstrate that Cervantes was very much aware of the same folk tradition relied upon by Fernando de Rojas, they have little in common with the sewing euphemisms that *La Celestina* shares with the Luso-Brazilian tradition. Cervantes, however, employs some of those very terms in other contexts. When Don Quijote and Sancho encounter Dorotea disguised as a boy in Sierra Morena, for example, she describes the manner in which she lived in her father's house with these words: "Los ratos que del día me quedaban, después de haber dado lo que convenía a los mayorales, a capataces y a otros jornaleros, los entretenía en ejercicios que son a las doncellas tan lícitos como necesarios, como son los que ofrece *la aguja* y la *almohadilla*, y *la rueca* muchas veces" (As for the moments of leisure left me after having paid fairly the head shepherds, overseers, and the other laborers, I spent them in those occupations that are as legitimate as necessary in young girls, such as the ones provided by the *needle* and the *needle cushion*, and often the *distaff*; 1, 348–49). The reference to the *aguja* brings to mind *La Celestina* and the Luso-Brazilian tales, while the word *rueca*, as indicated in the opening *villancico* of a Golden Age poem, becomes capable of an equally salacious interpretation: "*Bras quiere hacer / a Juana una güeca / y ella dábale con la rueca*" (Bras wishes to give Juana a notch with his spindle, and she hit him over and over with her *distaff*; Alzieu, Jammes, and Lissorgues 1984, no. 45). The metaphoric significance of this word is even more striking in a proverb collected by Gonzalo Correas: "Abreme, hilandera de *ruekka*, haréte la güeka" (Open, open, woman who spins with a *distaff*; I will give you a notch with my spindle; qtd. in ibid., no. 45n). The *rueca*, a staff for holding spinning wool, designates the female genitalia;[14] the wool itself is rolled from the *rueca* around the masculine *huso*, the phallic spindle,[15] as it is transformed into yarn.

While it could be argued that my interpretation of the passage cited is farfetched, since it might be unreasonable to attribute to Dorotea the sort of character that the two terms seem to imply, the suggestiveness of both the poem and Correas's proverb remains. While the wordplay in Cervantes could be just that, wordplay, it is important to note that the subject of "los entretenía" is ambiguous; it could refer either to the free moments of the day Dorotea had left, in which case the expression in question would mean "to spend the time"; or it could signal the workers whom she paid, thus causing the expression in question to signify that she "entertained them" with the frequently euphemistic chores of "sewing" (or "embroidering") and the spinning of wool. It is significant that Cervantes takes pains to qualify Dorotea's activities as being legitimate (*lícitos*), thereby suggesting the possibility of an opposite sense. Consequently, it is quite possible that this is a deliberate ambiguity in an author well-known for being ambiguous, and that the passage points to the euphemistic use of the two words in question.

There is similar ambivalence when Sancho, after bringing Don Quijote a false message from Dulcinea, carelessly admits that he had never seen her, and then goes on to correct himself with a reference to *puntos*: "—Digo que no la he visto tan despacio que pueda haber notado particularmente su hermosura y *sus buenas partes punto por punto*; pero así, a bulto, me parece bien" (I mean that I did not see her with enough time to be able to take particular notice of her beauty and her *charms point by point*; but just like that, on the whole, she seems fine to me; 1978, 1, 378–79). At first glance, it appears that Sancho does indeed seem to be saying that he failed to inspect Dulcinea closely, "to take particular notice of her beauty or of her charms point by point" (Jones and Douglas 1981, 234), without further implications. If that were the case, however, why does Sancho refer to what Ormsby's excellent translation renders as "her charms," as "sus buenas partes," while adding that he failed to have the time to examine them "stitch by stitch," "punto por punto"?

Cervantes also knew a variant of a proverb that uses the word *hilar*. Having caught Dorotea kissing Don Fernando at the inn, Sancho tells Don Quijote, when the latter suggests that it is time to leave, that "será mejor que nos estemos quedos, y cada puta *hile*, y comamos" (it will be better for us to stay still; let each slut *spin* her yarn, and let's eat; 1978, 1: 552). In López Pinciano's variant from 1596, "Cuando la puta *hila* con *mal* anda" (When the slut *spins* her yarn, she is sick),[16] the proverb does not mean that when the prostitute spins she fails to exercise her profession on account of illness, as I once proposed (Costa Fontes 1984, 8–9, and n20). Rather, *mal*, or "illness," embodies the idea of *el mal de amores*, "lovesickness," as well as *mal de muelas*. Hence, the proverb really implies that it is precisely when the prostitute suffers most from that illness that she begins to spin. With this, Sancho's statement makes perfect sense: Dorotea is obviously suffering from lovesickness, since she has been kissing Don Fernando. Consequently, rather than leave, Don Quijote should allow her time to do some "spinning." Cervantes's abbreviated use of the proverb indicates that it was so well-known that he expected his readers to understand its use without difficulty. The second sense of the allusions remains lost to contemporary audiences unfamiliar with the oral tradition, however.

In sum, it is abundantly clear that Cervantes uses some of the words and images examined in a fashion betraying his acquaintance with their ribald folk meanings, and, more specifically, with how they are used both in *La Celestina* and in the modern Luso-Brazilian oral tradition.

Two of the euphemisms in question can also be documented in Shakespeare. According to Eric Partridge, in *"Henry V*, II.1.36, the term [needle] bears a literal sense, then there is a reference to the *eye* of the needle, and there is an allusion to *prick"* (1968, 153). And in *The Passionate Pilgrim*, "wound" has a meaning equivalent to that of Melibea's *llaga*:

> See in my thigh, quoth she, here was the sore:
> She showed hers; he saw more *wounds* that one,
> And blushing fled, and left her all alone.
> 　　(Shakespeare 1937, 1275a
> 　　　　[stanza 7])

As noted by Partridge, the pudenda is clearly implied (1968, 222).

The folkloric and literary evidence presented here, besides documenting the interpretations of Rosario Ferré and Otis Handy, suggests that Fernando de Rojas, Francisco Delicado, Cervantes, and Shakespeare, rather than inventing the euphemisms examined in *La Celestina, La Lozana andaluza, Don Quijote, Henry V*, and in *The Passionate Pilgrim*, were inspired by their widespread folkloric currency. The fact that the central motif, for which Stith Thompson lists a Chinese source, has served in Iberia as the basis for a joke, a riddle, and a proverb also testifies to its venerable antiquity (no pun intended) and great popularity at one time. The reduced number of known versions cannot be taken as indicative of its disappearance from the modern oral tradition, for field investigators are obviously reluctant to include material of this sort in their collections. By using such allusions, Rojas was not trying to embody in his text sexual meanings hidden from of his readers. On the contrary, he knew that, like practically anyone who hears the joke and the conundrum today, they would be roaring with laughter, for he was drawing on a well-known folkloric tradition. This may have had something to do with his early decision to call his work a *comedia*.

Although Rojas himself stresses in his prefatory and concluding verses that erotic humor constitutes an integral part of *La Celestina*, being indispensable to a proper understanding of that work, by and large modern criticism has chosen to avoid it (M. E. Lacarra 1996, 421–22). As Lacarra reiterates, however, "el humor afecta a la construcción de los personajes y al significado de la trama, por lo que silenciarlo afecta nuestra percepción de la obra" (since humor contributes to the creation of the characters and to the meaning of the plot, its suppression affects our understanding of the work; 1996, 431; see also Lacarra 1990, 42–50; 1992; 1993; 1995, x–xiv).

The folkloric and literary evidence presented here confirms that, whatever his purposes in writing *La Celestina* may have been (see Castro 1965; Costa Fontes 1988; 1990–91; 1993a), there can be no question that Rojas conceived the story of Calisto and Melibea as a tale of mutual, unadulterated, and undisguised passion, for lust is what attracts them to each other. That is why they never think about marriage. In such a context, the question of their respective lineages is irrelevant.[17] The destructive nature of their self-centered, all-consuming love, provide all the explanation that is needed. This aspect of *La Celestina* constitutes, as Rojas states, an edifying "reprehensión de los locos enamorados" (reprimand of mad lovers; 82). Here the lesson reflects didactic, universal values, and religious or ethnic background has no relevance at all.

5

El idólatra de María:
An Anti-Christian Jewish Ballad?

El idólatra de María (The Idolater of the Virgin; *ó–a*) is a relatively rare ballad that survives only in conservative lateral areas:
Northeastern Portugal, Galicia, Asturias, Catalonia, the Canary Islands, and among the Eastern Sephardim of Salonika, Rhodes, Sarajevo, and Tekirdağ.[1] The ballad was not printed in the collections
published during the sixteenth and seventeenth centuries (See Rodríguez-Moñino 1973), nor in any of the *pliegos sueltos* (broadsides)
that have come down to us (1997). There are three Eastern Sephardic
incipits, one certain (ca. 1836) and two probable (1684, 1753; see
Armistead and Silverman 1981a, nos. 45A–C), but the earliest known
texts remain the two Eastern versions from 1794 and 1860 (Catalán
1970, 271, 273). This lack of earlier versions notwithstanding, the
ballad's present geographic distribution indicates that it was already
sung in the Iberian Peninsula before the expulsion of the Jews in
1492. Since the Sephardic poem is violently anti-Marian and the Virgin behaves in an uncharacteristic manner in some Christian versions, refusing to help the mariner who seeks her protection during a
tempest, the ballad has been regarded as a Jewish composition that
was subsequently adopted by the Christian population (279). The
purpose of this chapter is to suggest the opposite. *El idólatra* is more
probably a Christian ballad that acquired its violently anti-Marian
character as it was transmitted among the Sephardim.

    In the first place, in the Christian versions it is not absolutely
certain that the Virgin refuses to help the mariner. Briefly summarized, the ballad tells the story of a sailor who goes out to sea with
his crew on the day (or on the eve) of the feast devoted to Our Lady

81

and comes upon a storm. He begs the Blessed Mother for her protection. The last time she helped him, he reminds her, he gave her a crown of gold; if she saves him now, he vows, he will dress her in gold as well and will build either a chapel or "casa santa" (holy dwelling) in honor of her Son in Rome.

The versions from the Canaries end at this point:

> Navegaba Saninés   un día, una noche toda,
> 2   sin saber la noche que era,   noche de Nuestra Señora.
> Lloraban los marineros,   lloraba la gente toda,
> 4   sólo Saninés no llora   que es una rica persona.
> Cuando al medio de esas mares   se le aparece una bola:
> 6   —¡Madre santísima 'el Puerto   librarásnos de esta bola!
> de l'otra que me libraste   de oro te di la corona,
> 8   a tu santísimo Hijo   le hice una casa en Roma,
> con escaleras pal cielo,   ventanas para la Gloria.
>
> (Catálan et al. 1969, no. 147)

(Saninés sailed a whole day and night not knowing what night it was, the night of Our Lady. The sailors cried; everyone cried; Saninés alone did not; he was a rich person. In the middle of the seas a big wave appeared to him: "Holy Mother of the Harbor, deliver us from this wave! When you last delivered me I gave you a gold crown, for your Holy Son a house I made in Rome, with stairs leading to Heaven, windows toward glory.")

The lack of a conclusion enables listeners to assume whatever they want but, since in traditional religious poetry the Virgin usually helps those who seek her protection (see Catalán 1970, 279), listeners familiar with the tradition are likely to assume that the same thing will happen here.[2]

The Portuguese tradition does not leave any doubts regarding the mariner's fate, however, for the Virgin stops the storm as soon as he makes his plea. The sailor then goes on to thank the Virgin, saying that she has just performed her greatest miracle. Our Lady rebukes him: whenever he is in danger he addresses her as a noble lady; otherwise, he calls her a mean dog:

> Palavras não eram ditas,   o navio saiu da *ola*.
> 8   —Louvada sejais, ó Virgem,   ó Virgem Nossa Senhora;
> dos milagres que tendes feito,   o maior foi o d'agora.
> 10   —Quando vos vedes em perigo,   chamais-me nobre Senhora;
> quando vos não vedes nele,   chamais-me perra traidora.
>
> (VRP, no. 616)

(As soon as those words were said, the ship came out of the wave. "Blessed art thou, oh Virgin, oh Virgin, Our Lady. Of all your miracles this one is the greatest." "When you find yourself in danger you call me a noble lady; when you are not in danger you call me a mean bitch.")

It is in the Galician and Catalan versions that the Virgin seems to forget her role as the protector of sinners, refusing to help the scared mariner. In Catalonia the sailor concludes his plea impatiently, saying that he is beginning to think that she is deaf. The Virgin replies that he had cursed her while playing at dice, and that now he calls her queen and lady only because he is in trouble. The ballad ends with *El marinero al agua* (The Sailor Who Fell into the Sea; *á–a*; see CMP, U3; RPI, U39), also known as *La tentación del marinero* (The Temptation of the Sailor; Catalán 1970, 276):

6 *—Valeu-nos, Virgen, valeu-nos,   valeu-nos, Virgen senyora!
   que si ara me valéis,   de oro us faré una corona,
8 y al vostre fillet amat   un altar li faré a Roma.
   Valeu-me, Virgen, valeu-me,   que ja m'apar que sou sorda!
10 —Ja te sento, cristiano,   no só sorda en aquesta hora:
   Quan tu jugaves a daus,   maleives ma corona;
12 ara que te veus en treballs,   reclames reina i senyora.—
   Já en respon un mal demoni   de l'altra parte de l'aigua....
                                                              (277)

("Help us; help us; help us, Virgin Lady! If you help me now I will make a gold crown for you, and for your beloved Son an altar I will build in Rome. Help me, Virgin, help me; it's beginning to seem you're deaf!" "I hear you well, Christian, I'm not deaf at this juncture: When you were playing dice, you cursed my crown; now that you are in trouble, you shout Queen and Mother!" A mean devil replied from the other side of the water. . . .)

Although the Catalan poem does not explicitly state that the Virgin rejects the sailor's prayer, the concluding contamination with *El marinero* certainly implies it. In that ballad, the devil tempts a drowning sailor, asking him what he would give in order to be saved. The sailor offers one or more ships laden with gold and silver, but the devil will take only his soul. The sailor usually replies that he would rather drown: the sea can have his body, but his soul belongs to God. In the following rendition, which is appended to a Catalan version of *El idólatra* (the numerous Castilianisms are in italics), the sailor says that he places his soul in God's hands and that his body and heart are for the Virgin Mary, Mother of the Forsaken:

	El dimoni li *responde* de l'atra *parte* de l'aygua:
6	«*¿Que me darás, marinero* que yo te trauré de l'aygua?»
	«Yo te donaré mi un navio *cargado de oro y de plata.*»
8	«*Y no te quiero tu navío ni tu oro ni tu plata,*
	Sino quant te morirás que m'entregues la tev'ánima.»
10	«L'ánima la entrego *a Dios y el cuerpo a la Virgen Santa,*
	Y el corazón a María, Madre de los Desamparados,
12	Que m'en ampari a mí y a *todos los cristianos.*
	Mis pecados son muchos, son muchos y muy graves.»

(Milá 1882, 41–42 [no. 34A1])

(The devil replied to him from the other side of the water: "What will you give me, Sailor, if I take you out of the water?" "I'll give you my ship loaded with gold and silver." "I want neither your ship, nor your gold and silver, only that when you die you give me your soul." "I gave my soul to God, the body to the Holy Virgin, and my heart to Mary, Mother of the Forsaken. May she help me and all Christians. My sins are many, many and very grave.")

Taken as a whole, then, the Catalan ballad ends on a positive note, for the mariner rejects the devil. The Virgin's apparent refusal to save his life is indispensable in the opening verses that correspond to *El idólatra*. Had she saved him, the contamination with *El marinero*, which begins with the shipwrecked sailor already drowning, would not have made any sense whatsoever. In other words, the contamination in question is what caused the Virgin to act out of character in the first ballad. To make her changed role even more plausible, the Catalan poem interpolated the sailor's disrespectful assertion that she seemed to be deaf.

This explains the Virgin's refusal to help the sailor in the Galician versions as well. In that ballad, the Virgin rebukes the sailor for calling her a mean dog while playing cards and, to render the contamination with *El marinero* more plausible, she adds that he is about to die. In the version quoted in the next section, the devil seeks to replace the Virgin, promising to save the mariner. The Galician ballad, which is mostly in Castilian, also ends in a positive manner, for the salvation of the sailor's soul is implicit. Note that the sailor refers to the Blessed Mother in his rejection of the devil's bargain:

10   —Cuando juegas a los naipes,   me llamas perra traidora;
      ahora te ves en peligro,   me llamas noble persona.
12   Ahí morirás, Siselinos,   ahí morirás ahora.—
      Respóndele el enemigo   de la otra banda del mar:
14   —¿*Cuánto me das, Siselinos?   Yo te libraré del mar.*
      —*Yo te daré mis navíos   cargados de oro y plata.*
16   —*No te quiero tus navíos,   ni tu oro, ni tu plata,*
      quiero que cuando te mueras   a mí me dejes tu alma.
18   —*¡Arreda, arreda, demonio,   con esas malas palabras!*
      que mi alma es de Dios   que me la ha dada emprestada,
20   *el corazón de María   al pie de su rostro estaba,*
      miñas carnes pecadoras   ós peixiños do mar vaian.
                              (Valenciano, *Os romances*, no. 89)

("When you're gambling at cards you call me a mean bitch; finding
yourself now in danger, you call me a noble person. There you'll die,
Siselinos; there you'll now die." The enemy replied to him from the
other side of the sea: "How much will you give me, Siselinos, if I deliver you from the sea?" "I'll give you my ships loaded with gold and
silver." "I want neither your ships, nor your gold and silver, only
that when you die you leave me your soul." "Go away, devil; go
away, you and those evil words! My soul belongs to God, He has
loaned it to me; Mary's heart is next to His face. Let my sinning
flesh go to the little fish in the sea.")

There is no question, therefore, that the Virgin's uncharacteristic behavior in the Catalan and Galician versions of *El idólatra* represents a change brought about by its contamination with *El
marinero* in those two traditions. Two versions from the Canaries
also display the same contamination (Catalán et al. 1969, no. 40;
Trapero 1990, no. 60.10) but, since it occurs at the beginning rather
than at the end of the ballad, it does not affect *El idólatra*, which, as
already stated, on those islands leaves the conclusion up to the audience. The Portuguese poem, in which the Blessed Mother saves the
sailor's life as expected, is much closer to the ballad's early form because the contamination in question did not affect it.

These factors suggest that the ballad is originally Christian, but
there is additional evidence to support this claim. The basic concept
that led to the creation of the ballad depends on the fact that, in addition to her role as Mediator between the faithful and her Son, the
Blessed Mother was also regarded as the patroness of mariners. This
came about because of a linguistic pun on her name: "One [of her ti-
tles] was the identification of the Virgin as 'Mary, the star of the sea
[Maria maris stella]', a name that was said to have been given her

from on high" (Pelikan 1978, 162). This title, which has been documented as far back as a ninth-century poem, gained wide currency.
As a result, in the Middle Ages Mary was portrayed as "guiding the
ship of faith" as well as "the lodestar of voyagers through life" (ibid.).
These images appear frequently in medieval Iberian literature. For
example, Alfonso X's *Cantigas de Santa María* include several miracles where the Virgin appears as the patroness of mariners
(1959–72, nos. 33, 36, 112, 172, 313, 339). She has great power over
the sea and the winds ("Gran poder á de mandar / o mar e todo-los
ventos," no. 33) and can stop sea storms everywhere ("poder á d'as
tormentas / toller en todos logares," no. 172); when in trouble, people
should always call upon the Virgin, star of the sea ("Nas coitas deve-
mos chamar / a Virgen, estrela do mar," no. 112). The following quatrain from Gonzalo de Berceo's introductory allegory to his *Milagros
de Nuestra Señora* includes the image of Mary as the star who, besides guiding mariners, also guides the ship of faith on which all
human beings sail in this life:[3]

> 32   La benedicta Virgen   es estrella clamada,
>   estrella de los mares,   guïona deseada,
>   es de los marineros   en las cuitas guardada,
>   ca quando éssa veden,   es la nave guiada.
>
> (1985, 75)

> (The blessed Virgin is called star, star of the sea, sought-after
> guide; sailors seek her in their afflictions, for when they see her the
> ship is saved.)

The ballad may well have contained similar images. The sailor
could be regarded as the sinner who travels through life in the ship
of faith and who, in a moment of affliction, calls on the Blessed
Mother for assistance. Such an interpretation would have been particularly acceptable to a medieval audience more accustomed to
think in allegorical terms.

At another, more literal level, either through forgetfulness (i.e.,
Catalán et al. 1969, nos. 147–51) or, even worse, as a deliberate act
(i.e., no. 410), the sailor fails to observe a holy day, precisely the one
reserved to honor the Virgin. Thus, the storm is a form of divine punishment for having set sail on that day (Canary Islands and Galicia)
or the night before (Portugal; cf. VRP, no. 616). This helps to explain
the Virgin's anger. Nevertheless, she helps the sailor, berating him afterward for calling her a mean dog when he loses at cards or at dice.

In this context, it is interesting to note that, in the *Cantigas de Santa María*, the Virgin punishes a furrier for working on the March day reserved for the feast of the Annunciation (no. 199). A man from Huesca who stopped believing in her after losing everything he owned gambling with dice loses his speech (no. 163). In another miracle, a *jograr* (jongleur) who insulted God and the Virgin in Guimarães because he had lost at dice was possessed by the devil, died, and went straight to hell (no. 238).

The Sephardic versions and those from the Canary Islands indicate that, though no longer sung in central Spain, the ballad was originally composed in Castilian. As a central zone, Castile constituted the most important area of dissemination in Iberia, exporting many of its ballads to the more conservative, less innovative lateral areas. Moreover, the Galician ballad is mostly in Castilian; the Catalan version just quoted includes several Castilian words and even sentences, and two Portuguese versions use the Castilianism *ola* (Port. *onda*; see Alves 1934, 573, vv. 3*b*, 7*b*, and VRP, no. 616.7*b*).

It is true that synthetic versions constitute approximations at best; since ballads exist simultaneously in numerous variants, such versions always betray their multifaceted character to some extent. On the other hand, synthetic versions can be most useful. The new evidence presented in this chapter makes it possible to reconstruct the early prototype of *El idólatra* as follows:

	*Navegaba el capitán un día, una noche toda,
2	sin saber el día que era, día de Nuestra Señora,
	y allá en medio de esas mares se le levanta una ola.
4	Si altas ivan las nubes, más altas ivan las olas.
	Lloraban los marineros, lloraba la gente toda,
6	no lloraba el capitán, que es una noble persona.
	—¡Valedme, Virgen del Puerto, valedme, Reina y Señora!
8	De l'otra que me libraste de oro te di la corona
	y ahora si me favoreces de oro te cuvro toda.
10	A tu Santísimo hijo le haré una ermita en Roma,
	las paredes de marfil, las cadenas de oro todas,
12	las ventanas para el cielo las puertas para la gloria.—
	Esas palabras diciendo la nave salió de la ola.
14	—¡Bendita seas, la Virgen, la Virgen Nuestra Señora!
	—Cuando juegas a los dados me llamas perra traidora,
16	ahora te ves en peligro me llamas Reina y Señora.[4]

(The captain sailed a whole day and night, not knowing it was the feast of Our Lady, and in the middle of those seas there rose a great wave. If the clouds were high, the waves were even higher. The sailors cried, everyone cried, but the captain did not; he was a noble person. "Help me, Virgin of the Harbor, help me, my Queen and Lady. When you last delivered me I gave you a gold crown; if you help me now I will cover you in gold. For your Holy Son I will build a hermitage in Rome with walls of ivory, all locks of gold, windows facing the Heavens, doors facing glory." As he said these words the ship came out of the wave. "Blessed art thou, Virgin, o Virgin, Our Lady!" "When you play dice you call me a mean bitch; finding yourself now in danger, you call me your Queen and Lady.")

Since the captain's name varies from version to version,[5] I chose to call him "el capitán," as in one of the Sephardic versions from Sarajevo (Catalán 1970, 271) and the one from Tekirdağ (Benmayor 1979, no. 9). In Galicia, the fact that the captain begins his voyage on the holy day devoted to Our Lady does not seem to matter to him (i.e., Valenciano, *Os romances*, no. 89). Since the Virgin forgives him, however, the versions from the Canary Islands, where he more often than not sets sail without realizing what day it is, make more sense here. Variants of verse 4 appear at the beginning of several Sephardic versions (Armistead and Silverman 1979, no. A2; Benmayor 1979, no. 9; Catalán 1970, 271), suggesting that the verse might be quite ancient. The captain invokes Our Lady of Guadalupe, del Carmen (Catalán et al. 1969, nos. 149–50), and so on, but I preferred the versions where he invokes La Virgen or Madre del Puerto (nos. 40, 147; Sampedro y Folgar and Figueira Valverde 1942, no. 271) because the latter is a more logical choice under the circumstances, appearing in many of Alfonso X's *Cantigas* as well (nos. 328, 356–59, 364, 366–68, 371–72, 375, 377–79, 381, 385, 389, 391–93). Since the captain had already vowed to dress the Virgin in gold, his promise to erect a chapel or "holy house" (the latter could be a convent) in Christ's honor in Rome may seem superfluous. The wide geographic distribution of this vow—it appears in Galicia, Catalonia, and in the Canary Islands (see Catalán 1970, 275–77)—suggests that the verses in question may go far back in time, however. In the Galician versions, the Virgin accuses the captain of cursing her while playing cards rather than dice, as in Catalonia. I preferred the latter because, as already indicated, the *Cantigas* document similar situations.

The versions that the Sephardim took with them when they left Spain in 1492 were very similar to the synthetic version just presented. The ballad eventually divided into two forms, one independent, the other contaminated with *La tormenta calmada* (The

Quieted Storm, *á–e*; CMP, U1), a poem derived from a late sixteenth-century learned ballad (see Yoná 138–40) that now exists only among the Eastern Sephardim.

In the independent versions, the protagonist invokes "Siñora, la mi Siñora" (Lady, my Lady; Benmayor 1979, no. 9), "Fedyonda" (*hedionda* [one who stinks]; Armistead and Silverman 1979, A2), or "Hadolla" (*imagen religiosa* ["religious image"]; Catalán 1970, 271 and n4). The captain drowns, but the sailors, who, in one version, pray to the "Dio Alto" (High God) instead (Benmayor 1979, no. 9), always escape. The low regard in which the Virgin is held is clear; she is a hideous, graven image, and only God can perform miracles.

In the contaminated versions, the invocation of the Virgin causes the Ruler of the World to make the waves even wilder. The captain ("captains" in the example that follows) blasphemes violently against the Blessed Mother, stating that miracles come only from God, at which point the storm stops:

> —Vate, vate, puta María,   que sos falsa y mintirośa;
> 14   tenemos un Dió muy grande,   que muchas maravillas haće,
> que quita naves de golfo   y la parida cuando pare;
> 16   mo las haga agora y siempre   y deprisa y no detadre.
> Esto oyó el Patrón del mundo,   *abonacheó* las mares. . . .
> (Attias 1961, no. 59; = Catalán 1970, 273)[6]

("Go away, you whorish Mary; you are false and deceitful. We have a very great God who works many wonders, who delivers ships from the gulf and women who give birth. May He do it for me now, quickly, without delay." The Master of the World heard this and calmed the sea.)

The brutal epithet that these contaminated versions apply to the Virgin is well-documented in sixteenth-century Inquisitorial trials (Costa Fontes 1990–91, 33–34). Some of the Jews who remained in Spain and Portugal as *conversos* used it for the same reason as their exiled brethren: to them Our Lady was a bad woman who had a child with a man other than her husband and then made the incredible claim that she was still a Virgin, for the Father was none other than the Holy Spirit (1993b, 201). Most probably, these anti-Marian elements were introduced into the ballad in Spain, when the Jews sang it in the privacy of their own homes, without danger of being heard by Christians. It is very difficult to imagine that they could seriously sing a poem where the Virgin performed a miracle. After their exile, there was even more reason to change the ballad, whose hostility toward the Virgin testifies to the de-Christianization process that Samuel G. Armistead and Joseph H. Silverman so abundantly documented in Sephardic balladry (1982a; see esp. 134).

As Paul Bénichou hypothesized, it is very unlikely that the Jews would have dared to compose and disseminate among Christians a poem that insulted Our Lady. The reason for this is obvious: they could not fail to realize that such an act would have led to prompt retribution. In Bénichou's opinion, the Judaization of the ballad probably depends on an early Christian form where some sacrilegious character blasphemed against the Virgin: "es más probable, quizá, una forma cristiana primitiva, cuyo desenlace ignoramos, y donde tales blasfemias han podido figurar en boca de algún personaje sacrílego—y luego una judaización a base de ese pasaje [?]" (It is more probable, perhaps, that there was an early Christian form, whose conclusion we ignore, where such blasphemies could figure in the mouth of some sacrilegious character—and that this served as a basis for the subsequent Judaization of the poem [?]; 1968a, 289–90 n3). This is precisely what happened. In the early Christian prototype, the Virgin accused the captain of calling her a mean dog when he gambled at dice. The Jews could not agree more with the insult, for it coincided with what they themselves thought, and so they took matters one step further, expanding the ballad in accordance with their own beliefs.

In conclusion, there is no question that *El idólatra de María* originated as a Christian ballad.[7] A sailor goes on a voyage on the day that the Catholic Church reserves to honor the Blessed Mother, probably the feast of the Annunciation, which falls in March, and is punished with a storm for not observing the holy day. Because Catholics looked upon Our Lady as *stella maris*, the "patroness of mariners," the sailor begs her for protection and the tempest stops. At another level, the sailor may be regarded as the sinner who travels through life in the boat of faith guided by Mary. Besides forming the kernel of the ballad, the implicit interdiction and the equally implicit role accorded to the Virgin depend on Christian concepts. In general terms, this is the form of the ballad the Sephardim took with them at the time of expulsion, de-Christianizing it with absolute freedom in their exile, and turning it into an anti-Cristian ballad in the process. Rather than being related to Jewish influence in some way, the Virgin's refusal to help the sailor in Galicia and Catalonia came about because of the ballad's contamination with *El marinero al agua* in those two regions. As we have seen, if the Virgin had granted the captain's petition, the contaminated ballad could not have coalesced into one single, coherent poem, for it would not have made any sense. Consequently, *El idólatra de María* would be better entitled *El marinero y la Virgen María* (The Sailor and the Virgin), at least as far as the early and modern Christian traditions are concerned.

Since the poem was not printed in any of the early collections, the modern versions constitute an excellent example of the manner in which the modern tradition supplements our knowledge of the medieval tradition. The concepts on which the poem is based—Mary as the Star of the Sea, patroness of mariners, and the image of the ship as the Boat of Faith—are unquestionably learned. Thus, this ballad also exemplifies the constant exchange between learned and popular culture, that is, between folklore and literature.

6

Gil Vicente's *Remando Vão Remadores* and *Barca Bela*

Besides supplementing our knowledge of the medieval and Renaissance tradition through its preservation of poems that did not reach print during the sixteenth century, the modern oral tradition can also shed light on the work of early authors. The Portuguese versions of *Puputiriru* are as frank about sex as the fifteenth- and sixteenth-century French versions, which suggests that Juan Timoneda felt compelled to tone down the version he published in 1564. Modern folk metaphors helped to show that, contrary to what scholars used to think, there is no coitus interruptus in Alfonso X's *cantiga d'escarnho* (song of mockery) about a Friday encounter with a *soldadeira* (camp follower, prostitute) and that, since the poem is really a joke—no meat of any kind on Fridays—the poetic voice should not be confused with the king's. Modern folk metaphors have also helped us to understand that the cryptic retraction that Alfonso Martínez de Toledo appended to his misogynistic *Corbacho, o Reprobación del amor mundano* merely purports to apologize to the courtly ladies he had offended, for, in reality, the author reaffirms what he had said about them in his book. A modern Portuguese folk story, an etiologic joke, and a conundrum helped to clarify the meaning of several crucial passages in *La comedia o tragicomedia de Calisto y Melibea*, better known as *La Celestina*, which depend heavily on metaphors nearly impenetrable to readers who no longer possess an intimate knowledge of the oral tradition. So far, these examples have supplemented our knowledge of the early tradition, contributing to a proper understanding of obscure literary passages as well. In the present chapter, I intend to show how a learned

93

writer adapted a popular ballad in order to create a new, highly original poem. The ballad in question is *Barca Bela* (The Beautiful Boat), a religious contrafact of *El conde Arnaldos* (Count Arnaldos), which Gil Vicente rearranged in order to compose *Remando Vão Remadores* (Sailors Row), the beautiful poem with which he opens his *Auto da Barca do Purgatório* (The Boat of Purgatory; 1518).

In its shortest form, *Barca Bela* or *Barca Nova* (The New Boat; RPI, Z2) consists of four verses. It tells about a marvelous boat that has Christ as shipmaster, St. Joseph or some other saint as pilot, angels as oarsmen, the Virgin as the sole passenger, and the flag of Portugal as its ensign:

> Vamos ver a barca nova,   que se deita hoje ao mar;
> 2   Nossa Senhora vai nela   e os anjinhos a remar.
> S. José é o piloto   e Jesus o general;
> 4   que linda bandeira leva,   bandeira de Portugal.
>
> (Can, no. 276)

(Let's go see the new boat being put out to sea today; Our Lady is in it and little angels row. St. Joseph is the pilot; Jesus is the ship-master. What a beautiful flag it carries; it is the flag of Portugal.)

This is the most common form of the ballad, but, today, numerous versions derive from a version popularized by a third-grade reader, *O Livro da 3.ᵃ Classe*, which replaces St. Joseph with St. Vincent as pilot:

> Quem quer ver a barca bela,   que se vai deitar ao mar?
> 2   Nossa Senhora vai nela,   os anjos vão a remar.
> São Vicente é o piloto,   Jesus Cristo o general;
> que linda bandeira levam,   bandeira de Portugal.
>
> (1958, 156)[1]

(Who wants to see the beautiful boat that is being put to sea? Our Lady is in it; the angels row. St. Vincent is the pilot, Jesus Christ the shipmaster. What a beautiful flag they carry; it is the flag of Portugal.)

The poem may indeed be regarded as a children's song, but it had other functions as well. In the Azores, the *foliões* or "jesters" who participated in the annual festivities in honor of the Holy Ghost[2] included it among their songs (Machado Ávila 1948, 291; Braga 1911–13, 2: 82). In Madeira it was also a Christmas song, appearing with *Noite de Natal* (Christmas Night; RPI, U1), a ballad in which St.

Joseph and the Virgin search for a place where Jesus can be born (see vv. 9–12 in the following poem). The example that follows begins with a version of *Barca Bela* derived from *O Livro da 3.ª Classe* (1–4):

Quem que ver a barca bela,   que se vai deitar ao mar?
2   Nossa Senhora vai nela,   os anjos a remar.
S. Vicente é o piloto,   Jesus Cristo é o general;
4   que linda bandeira leva,   bandeira de Portugal.
Vinte quatro remos leva,   outros tantos remadores;
6   como vai acompanhada   Nossa Senhora das Flores!
Nossa Senhora das Flores,   empresta-m'essa maré,
8   p'a eu ir à sua casa,   mais o senhor S. José.
S. José anda de noite   como quem anda de dia,
10   para ajudar a criar   o filho da Virgem Maria.
Quando chegaram a Belém,   já toda a gente dormia;
12   encontraram o Pai Eterno   rezando uma avé-maria.
(Can, no. 273)[3]

(Who wants to see the beautiful boat that is being put to sea? Our Lady is in it; the angels row. St. Vincent is the pilot, Jesus Christ the shipmaster. What a beautiful flag it carries; it is the flag of Portugal. It has twenty-four oars and as many oarsmen; how well Our Lady of the Flowers is accompanied! Our Lady of the Flowers, please send me that tide, so that I can visit your house, together with St. Joseph. St. Joseph walks at night as if it were daytime in order to help raise the Son of the Virgin Mary. When they arrived in Bethlehem everyone was already asleep; they found the Eternal Father praying Hail Mary.)

Barca Bela was also used as a New Year's carol (Gallop 1937, no. 105), and the numerous versions according to which the wondrous boat was built by shepherds ("Aí vem a barca bela, / que a fizeram os pastores" [There comes the beautiful boat that the shepherds made; TM 1240])[4] indicate that, in addition, it was among the carols that people sang as they went from house to house during Epiphany (Pestana 1978, 24); hence the combination of many versions with *Os Três Reis do Oriente* (The Three Wise Men; RPI, U4), in which the three Wise Kings visit Baby Jesus with their gifts:

Ó da casa, nobre gente,   escutai e ouvireis
2   umas cantiguinhas novas   que se cantam pelos Reis.
Santos reis, santos c'roados,   vinde ver quem vos c'roou,
4   e mais quem vos ordenou   no vosso santo caminho.
Mandou Deus dos altos céus,   com tamanho desatino;[5]

6   mandou Deus uma estrela   que lhe ensinasse o caminho.
     A estrela se foi pôr   em cima duma cabana.
8   A cabana era pequena,   não cabiam todos três;
     puseram-se em oração,   cada um por sua vez.
10   Eles todos lh'ofereceram   ouro, incenso e mirra.
     O ouro é como rei,   incenso como martírio,
12   mirra como Deus vivo,   que morreu para nos salvar.
     Vamos ver a barca nova,   que se vai lançar no mar;
14   S. José vai pela proa,   nosso Deus por general;
     arriaram-se as bandeiras,   viva o rei de Portugal.
16   Glória seja a de Deus Padre   e a de Deus Filho também;
     glória seja o 'Sprito Santo   p'ra todo o sempre, amém.
                                           (Pires de Lima 1915, 199)[6]

(Hello there in the house, noble people, listen and you shall hear
some new little songs sung during Epiphany. Holy Kings, crowned
saints, come see who crowned you, and also who commanded you to
undertake your holy journey. From the high Heavens God sent,
with such great folly, God sent a star to show them the way. The
star landed on top of a hut. The hut was small, the three could not
fit inside, and they began to pray, each one in his turn. All three offered him gold, incense, and myrrh: Gold as King, incense as martyrdom, myrrh as living God, who died to save us. Let's go see the
new boat that is being put to sea. St. Joseph goes on the prow; our
God goes as shipmaster. The colors were stricken; long live the king
of Portugal. Glory be to God the Father and God the Son as well;
Glory be to the Holy Ghost for ever and ever, amen.)

Because the short form of *Barca Bela* consists of four verses that
can be easily divided into two quatrains, it has often been regarded
as a popular lyric rather than as a ballad.[7] Manuel Rodrigues Lapa
called attention to the parallelistic character of one version from
Nisa (Alto Alentejo), which he classified as a *vilancico*. Such songs,
of course, are usually lyrical. These parallelistic versions are based
only on the first two verses, discarding the remaining two:

Já lá vem a barca nova,   que fizeram os pelingrinos;
vai Nossa Senhora nela,   toda cheia de cravinhos.

Já lá vem a barca nova,   que fizeram os pastores;
vai Nossa Senhora nela,   toda cheia de flores.

                                           (1929, 275n)

(There comes the new boat that the pilgrims made; on it goes Our
Lady, all covered with little carnations. // There comes the new
boat that the shepherds made; on it goes Our Lady all covered
with flowers.)

Although parallelism could represent an innovation, it usually goes back to the Middle Ages. I found another example of this parallelism, which, as we will see, also exists in the Azores, from the province of Beira Baixa:

> Vamos a vâr a barquinha,   qui fejerem nos pastórse;
> Nossa Sinhöra vai nela,   toda coberta de flórse.
>
> Vamos a ver a barquinha,   qui fejerem nos soldádeso;
> Nossa Sinhora vai nela,   toda coberta de cráveso.
>
> (Monteiro 1943, 168n2)

(Let's go see the little boat that the shepherds made; on it goes Our Lady, all covered with flowers. // Let's go see the little boat that the soldiers made; on it goes Our Lady, all covered with carnations.)

Because of its use during Christmas and Epiphany, *Barca Bela* was combined with *Noite de Natal* and *Os Três Reis do Oriente*, but it became contaminated with other religious poems as well. One frequent contamination is with *O Cordão de Nossa Senhora* (The Blessed Mother's Girdle; RPI, Z3), a children's song in which the protagonist rises early in the morning, sees the Blessed Mother with a golden branch in her hand, and asks for a piece of it (1–11):

	Ergui-me de madrugada, em faixinhas e mantéu,
2	fui correr a via sacra, pelo caminho do céu.
	Encontrei Nossa Senhora com ramo d'ouro na mão.
4	Eu pedi-lhe um bocadinho, ela disse-me que não,
	e tornei-lho a pedir, ela deu-me o seu cordão.
6	Ó meu padre S. Francisco, aqui está este cordão,
	que me deu Nossa Senhora Domingo da Ressurreição:
8	que me desse sete voltas ao redor do coração;
	que me desse outras sete, que chegasse até ao chão.
10	De um lado está S. Pedro, doutro lado S. João;
	no meio está o retrato da Virgem da Conceição.
12	A Virgem da Conceição tem um Menino Jesus
	que foi pela barra fora Domingo de Santa Cruz.
14	Vinde ver a barca nova, que se vai deitar ao mar;
	Nossa Senhora vai dentro, os anjinhos a remar.
16	S. José vai por piloto, Nosso Senhor por general;
	arreiaram-se as bandeiras, viva o rei de Portugal.

(Pimentel 1899, 451)[8]

(I got up in the morning wearing ribbons and diapers, and did the Stations of the Cross, on the road to Heaven. I ran into Our Lady with a golden branch in her hand, asked her for a small piece of it;

she answered no. I asked her again and she gave me her rope belt. Our Father St. Francis, here is this rope belt that Our Lady gave me on Easter Sunday, to give seven turns around my heart and then another seven, so as to reach the ground. St. Peter is on one side, St. John on the other, and in the middle is the picture of the Virgin of the Immaculate Conception. The Virgin of the Immaculate Conception has a Baby Jesus who sailed through the straits on Sunday of the Holy Cross. Come see the new boat that is being put to sea. Our Lady is inside; the angels row. St. Joseph is the pilot, Our Lord is the shipmaster; the colors were stricken; long live the king of Portugal.)

Another contamination is with *As Três Marias* (The Three Marys; RPI, U49), in which the three Marys look for Baby Jesus and find him in Rome next to an altar as he is about to say Mass (5–9):

<blockquote>

Quem quer ver a barca nova,   (ai) que se vai deitar ao mari?

2   Ai, Nossa Sinhora vai dentro,   ai, os anjinhos a remari.

S. José por marinheiro,   S. João por capitão.

4   Já lá vão p'la barra fora,   ai que batalha não farão!

Foram à precura do Sinhori,   ai, nunca o puderam achari;

6   foram dar com ele em Roma,   ai, revestido num altari,

com o seu cal[9] de ouro na mão   ai, a hóstia do consagrari.

8   Missa nova quer dizeri,   ai, missa nova quer cantari.

Não sei que missa há-de seri,   que ela ao céu há-de chigari.

(Dores Galhoz 1987–88, no. 450)[10]

</blockquote>

(Who wants to see the new boat that is being put to sea? Oh, Our Lady is inside; the angels row. St. Joseph goes as sailor, St. John as captain. There they go through the straits; oh, what a battle they shall give! They went looking for the Lord; oh, they could never find Him; then they found Him in Rome, oh, dressed for mass by an altar, with his golden chalice in hand, oh, about to consecrate the host. He wants to say a new mass, a new mass he wants to sing. I do not know which mass it will be, but it will reach Heaven.)

In Brazil, where it enters into a children's game in which girls join hands and sing in a circle (*cantiga de roda*; Santos Neves 1963, 359–60), *Barca Bela* also survives as part of the Epiphany festivities in which people sing as they go from house to house. As in Portugal, some of these versions appear combined with *As Três Marias* (353–55). In addition, the Brazilian ballad is frequently embedded in the popular plays or dramatized folk-dances known as *Auto dos Fandangos* (Fandangos), *Chegança de Marujos* (The sailors), and *Marujada* (Seamen), a type of folk theater that recalls Portugal's old maritime adventures (Câmara Cascudo 1952, 409–36) and the conflict between Moors and Christians or Turks and Christians (Barroso 1949, 31–76). As Luiz Antonio Barreto plausibly argued, the original purpose of this theater was to catechize the Indians and the African slaves, regarded as infidels, by showing them how, being the only true faith, Christianity always prevailed (1996, 33–56).

Like the Portuguese versions discussed so far, the Brazilian renditions usually consist of only four verses. The Blessed Mother sails in a wondrous boat from Heaven with angels as oarsmen; Christ is often the shipmaster, and St. Joseph also appears as the pilot:

> Marujos, vamos à praia,   vamos à praia brincar,
> 2   vamos ver a barca nova,   que do céu caiu no mar.
> Nossa Senhora vai dentro,   com seus anjinhos a remar,
> São José por piloto,   bom Jesus por general.
> (Santos Neves 1963, 357)

(Sailors, let's go to the beach; let's go play on the beach; let's go see the new boat that fell to sea from Heaven. Our Lady is inside, with the little angels rowing. St. Joseph goes as pilot, the good Jesus as shipmaster.)

> Aí vem a barca nova,   que dos céus lançou-se ao mar;
> 2   Nossa Senhora vem dentro   e seus anjinhos a remar.
> Nosso Senhor é o capitão,   São José é o piloto,
> 4   e Maria, Mãe de Graça,   é o nosso seguro porto.
> (Câmara Cascudo 1952, 437)

(There comes the new boat that fell to sea from the Heavens; Our Lady is inside and her little angels row. Our Lord is the captain; St. Joseph is the pilot; and Mary, Mother of Grace, is our safe harbor.)

Note the change of rhyme to *ó–o* in verses 3–4 of the second sample (cf. Alencar Pimentel 1978, 21). Some Brazilian versions change those verses to *ão* ("São Francisco é o piloto, / São José o capitão; // ambos levam a bom porto / a feliz embarcação" [St. Francis is the pilot, St. Joseph the captain; both take the happy ship to safe harbor; Barroso 1949, 76; cf. Santos Neves 1963, 356]). The flag of Portugal is never mentioned in Brazil, perhaps for nationalistic reasons, but this change also characterizes several Portuguese versions, such as the parallelistic ones that we have already seen.

As in the first example that was just cited, which is from Espírito Santo, some Brazilian versions open with an invitation to walk or play on the beach and to see the boat that has fallen from

Heaven, thus making it clear that the ballad also functioned as a children's song. There are similar versions in Bahia:

> Vamos, maninha, vamos   à praia passear,
> 2   vamos ver a barca nova,   que do céu caiu ao mar.
>> (Bahia; Xavier Alcoforado and Suárez Albán 1996, 194)

> (Let's go, little sister; let's go for a stroll on the beach; let's go see the new boat that fell to sea from Heaven.)

This form of the ballad may have been first brought to Brazil by immigrants from Madeira, for, on that island, some versions begin:

> Meninei, se querei,   vamos à praia do má brincare,
> 2   para ver a barca nova,   que se deita hoje ao mare.
>> (Dores Galhoz 1987–88, no. 451)

> (Children, if you want, let's go play on the beach, and see the new boat being put out to sea today.)

> —Menina da saia branca,   que fazeis neste quintal?
> 2   —Estou lavando o meu lencinho   para a noite do Natal.
> —Menina, aviai depressa,   não se ponha a brincar,
> 4   se quere ver a barca bela,   que hoje se bota ao mar.
>> (Pita Ferreira 1956, 104)

> ("Little girl with the white skirt, what are you doing in this back-yard?" "I'm washing my little handkerchief for Christmas Eve." "Hurry up, little girl, don't begin to play, if you want to see the beautiful boat being put out to sea today.")

Barca Bela, then, used to be sung during Christmas, New Year's, the Epiphany, and as a children's song. There were lyrical, parallelistic versions based on the first two verses. Many versions existed in combination with other ballads and, in Brazil, the ballad was also embedded in folk plays.[11]

Since names are changed with great ease in oral transmission, St. Joseph's place as pilot is frequently usurped by some other saint—St. Francis (Barroso 1949, 76; Santos Neves 1963, 356), St. Peter (Santos Neves 1963, 356), St. John (Gomes Pereira 1911, 142), St. Anthony (Can, no. 266), or St. Vincent (*O Livro da 3.ª Classe* and derivatives). Two versions even replace Christ as shipmaster (Alvarenga 1946, 439 [St. Joachim]; Barroso 1949, 76 [St. Joseph]).

Nevertheless, in the earliest form of this ballad, the boat was no doubt sailed by the Holy Family, with angels as oarsmen, thus representing the Ship of Faith. During the Middle Ages, worldly life was regarded as a temporary, short journey to the true, eternal life, and human beings were seen as travelers or sailors who had to avoid the many pitfalls of sin in order to reach their destination. The Ship of Faith was supposed to guide them to a good, safe harbor—that is, to salvation.[12] In Christian symbolism, the ship also represented the Church (Cirlot 1971, 295).

The texts from Continental Portugal end with the four verses examined. Those from the Azores and Madeira at times go on to specify that there are twenty-four oars and as many oarsmen, and the Virgin often assumes the form of Our Lady of Sorrows or Our Lady of Flowers. In one version, however, she is merely called Our Lady, and cries for the sake of sinners:

> Leva vinte e quatro remos,   vinte quatro remadores;
> olha como vai contente   Nossa Senhora das Dores.
> (Can, no. 268)[13]

(It has twenty-four oars, twenty-four oarsmen; see how happily Our Lady of Sorrows goes.)

> Se vinte e quatro remos,   outros tantos remadores;
> como vai acompanhada   Nossa Senhora das Flores.
> (Canuto Soares 1914, 146)[14]

(If it has twenty-four oars, it has as many oarsmen; see how Our Lay of Flowers is accompanied.)

> Leva vinte e quatro remos   e outros tantos remadores;
> Nossa Senhora vai dentro,   chorando pelos pecadores.
> (Can. no. 267)

(It has twenty-four oars and as many oarsmen; Our Lady is inside, crying for the sake of sinners.)

These verses are echoed in the Continental versions which, because of the use of the ballad during Epiphany, recall the visit of the shepherds by introducing the word *pastores*; besides retaining the rhyme in *-ores*, these versions also preserve the reference to oarsmen, which suggests that it must be very old:

> Aí vem a barca bela,   que a fizeram os pastores;
> Nossa Senhora vai nela   e os anjos a remadores.
> (TM, no. 1240)

(There comes the beautiful boat that the shepherds made; in it goes
Our Lady and the angels go as oarsmen.)

So far, *Barca Bela* is relatively short, but five extremely rare
Azorean renditions continue the ballad beyond this point. One version
replaces the beginning with four unique, senseless verses about a divine frigate which, despite its poverty, after a nine-month journey un-
loads in Bethehem a rich cargo destined to be sold in India (vv. 1–4).
The ballad then continues with three verses from *Barca Bela* (5–7),
ending with a contamination from *Os Três Reis do Oriente* (8–11):

1.

Uma fragata divina   nove meses navegou,
2   achou o mar em bonança,   em Belém descarregou.
Ela parece que é pobre,   traz fazendas excelentes,
4   para ir vender à Índia,   a partes do Oriente.
Marinheiros que vão nela,   levam um tão doce cantar:
6   as aves dos altos céus   nos mastros lhe vêm poisar;
os peixinhos do mar fundo   à borda vêm escutar.
8   Os três reis do Oriente,   todos três em romaria,
foram visitar Deus-Homem,   filho da Virgem Maria.
10   Guiados por uma estrela   que a todo o mundo dá luz,
iam ver outra mais bela   que era o Menino Jesus.
(Braga 1869, no. 63)[15]

(A divine frigate sailed for nine months; the sea was calm and it un-
loaded in Bethlehem. It seemed to be poor but it brought rich fabrics
to sell in India and throughout the East. The sailors in it sang such
a sweet song: The birds of the high Heavens perched on its masts;
the little fish of the deep sea came to listen at the sides. The Three
Wise Men, all three made a pilgrimage to visit the Man God, Son of
the Virgin Mary. Guided by a star that gave light to the whole world,
they were going to visit even a brighter star—Baby Jesus.)

Unfortunately, this is the only version from São Jorge. The remaining four are from Flores. Since they are relatively brief and crucial to the synthetic version that follows, I now present them,
beginning with the least complete:

2.

Vamos ver a barca nova,   que do céu caiu ao mar;
2   Nossa Senhora vai nela,   os anjinhos vão a remar.

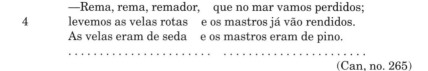

     —Rema, rema, remador,   que no mar vamos perdidos;
4   levemos as velas rotas   e os mastros já vão rendidos.
     As velas eram de seda   e os mastros eram de pino.
. . . .
                                   (Can, no. 265)

(Let's go see the new boat that fell to the sea from Heaven. Our Lady is in it; the angels go as oarsmen. "Row, oarsman, row, for we are lost at sea; the sails are torn, the masts already broken." The sails were of silk; the masts were of pine.)

3.

     Vamos ver a barca nova,   que do céu caiu ao porto.
2   Nossa Senhora vai nela,   S. José vai de piloto.
     Vamos ver a barca nova,   que do céu caiu ao mar;
4   Nossa Senhora vai nela,   os anjos vão a remar.
     —Remai, remai, remadores,   que nós já vamos perdidos,
6   pois as velas já vão rotas   e os mastros já vão rendidos.
     As velas eram de seda,   não quiseram abrandar;
8   os mastros eram de pinho,   não quiseram envergar.
                                  (Fraga 1963, 15)

(Let's go see the new boat that fell to the port from Heaven; Our Lady is in it; St. Joseph goes as pilot. Let's go see the new boat that fell to sea from Heaven; Our Lady is in it; the angels go as oarsmen. "Row, oarsmen, row, for we are lost at sea; the sails are torn; the masts are broken." The sails were of silk and could not be undone; the masts were of pine and refused to bend.)

4.

     Vamos ver a barca nova,   que do céu caiu ao porto;
2   Nossa Senhora vai nela,   S. José vai de piloto.
     Vamos ver a barca nova,   que do céu caiu ao mar;
4   Nossa Senhora vai nela,   e os anjos vão a remar.
     Rema, rema, remador,   que no mar vamos perdidos;
6   levamos as velas rotas   e os mastros já vão rendidos.
     As velas eram de seda   e não puderam abainar;
8   os mastros eram de pino   e não quiseram avergar.
     Os peixes que andam no mar   às bordas vieram escutar;
10   as aves que andam no céu   aos mastros vieram pousar.
                                  (NI, no. 125)

(Let's go see the new boat that fell to the port from Heaven; Our Lady is in it; St. Joseph goes as pilot. Let's go see the new boat that fell to sea from Heaven; Our Lady is in it; the angels go as oarsmen. "Row, oarsman, row, for we are lost at sea; the sails are torn; the masts are broken." The sails were of silk and could not be undone; the masts were of pine and refused to bend. The fish of the sea came to listen at the sides; the birds of Heaven came to perch on the masts.)

5.

Já chigou a barca nova, que do céu descende ao mar;
2 Nossa Senhora vem nela e os anjos a remar.
Já chigou a barca nova, que do céu descende ao porto;
4 Nossa Senhora vem nela e San José de piloto.
Ó que forte maresia, ó que grande temporal!
6 Barca nova corre p'rigo, barca nova a naufragar.
As velas eram de seda, não puderam abrandar;
8 os mastros eram de pinho, não puderam avergar.
San Miguel tomou-l'o leme e se pôs a manobrar.
10 Bom Jasus baixa do céu e à proa se vai sentar.
Logo as áuguas se tornaram de rosas e d'alecrim;
12 barca nova vai salvada, vai varar em Porto Pim.
(Silveira 1961, 483)

(The new boat has arrived that comes to sea from Heaven; Our Lady is in it and the angels row. The new boat has arrived that comes to the port from Heaven; Our Lady is in it and St. Joseph goes as pilot. Oh, how the sea swells; what a great storm! The new boat is in danger; it is about to be lost. The sails are of silk; they cannot be undone; the masts are of pine; they cannot bend. St. Michael takes the helm and begins to maneuver. Good Jesus descends from Heaven and sits at the bow. The water turns at once into roses and rosemary. The new boat is saved; it lands in Porto Pim.)

The contaminated version from São Jorge (no. 1) lacks the beginning of the ballad, but three of the others (nos. 3–5) open with parallelistic verses. Since this parallelism is of medieval origins, and can be documented in Beira Baixa and Alto Alentejo as well, the early prototype probably began in a similar manner.

Although missing here, the verses regarding the presence of the Holy Family, with Christ as shipmaster, St. Joseph as pilot, the Virgin as passenger, and the angels as oarsmen, which characterize the short versions of *Barca Bela* in Portugal and Brazil, go far back in time as well. They transform the marvelous boat from Heaven into the medieval Ship of Faith that leads those who journey through earthly life to salvation. The reference to the Portuguese flag may replace an earlier allusion to some sort of divine ensign. The enumeration of the oarsmen appears in Madeira and in the Azores, being echoed in mainland Portugal as well. This geographic distribution suggests that it must be very old. Since this is the Ship of Faith that leads people through the pitfalls of life to salvation, the version in which the Blessed Mother cries for sinners seems preferable to those that portray her as being very happy. The main role of the Virgin during the Middle Ages was that of mediator between sinners and her Son, Jesus. These findings enable us to reconstruct the beginning of the ballad as follows:

	*Vamos ver a barca nova,	que do céu caiu ao porto;
2	Nossa Senhora vai nela,	S. José vai de piloto.
	Vamos ver a barca nova,	que do céu caiu ao mar;
4	Nossa Senhora vai nela	e os anjos vão a remar.
	S. José é o piloto	e Jesus o general;
6	que linda bandeira leva,	bandeira de Portugal.
	Leva vinte e quatro remos	e outros tantos remadores;
8	Nossa Senhora vai dentro,	chorando pelos pecadores.[16]

(Let's go see the new boat that fell to the port from Heaven; Our Lady is in it; St. Joseph goes as pilot. Let's go see the new boat that fell to sea from Heaven; Our Lady is in it and the angels go as oarsmen. St. Joseph is the pilot; Jesus is the shipmaster; what a beautiful flag it carries; it is the flag of Portugal. It has twenty-four oars and as many oarsmen; Our Lady is inside, crying for the sake of sinners.)

Thanks to the five rare Azorean renditions, it is possible to attempt a reconstruction of the remainder of the ballad. I decided to eliminate verses 9–10 of the last version, from Flores, because they do not appear in the other three versions from that island (nos. 2–4). It does not make any sense to suppose that St. Michael suddenly appears in order to take over St. Joseph's place as pilot, and that Jesus, who is already in the boat, descends from Heaven in order to sit at the bow.[17] The last two verses of this version (11–12) do not appear elsewhere, and Porto Pim is a place on the island of Pico. A late, local addition is involved here. Nevertheless, since those verses echo a passage in the medieval *El conde Arnaldos*, which is related to *Barca Bela*, they must have replaced a similar idea in earlier versions. My reconstitution is as follows:

10
12
14
16
18

*Ó que forte maresia,   ó que grande temporal!
Barca nova corre p'rigo,   barca nova a naufragar.
—Rema, rema, remador,   que no mar vamos perdidos;
levamos as velas rotas   e os mastros vão rendidos.
As velas eram de seda,   não quiseram abrandar;
os mastros eram de pinho,   não quiseram envergar.
Marinheiros que vão nela,   levam um tão doce cantar:
as aves dos altos céus   nos mastros lhe vêm poisar;
os peixinhos do mar fundo   à borda vêm escutar.
Logo as áuguas se tornaram   de rosas e d'alecrim;
barca nova vai salvada,   vai varar em Porto Pim.[18]

(Oh, how the sea swells; what a great storm! The new boat is in danger; it is about to be lost. "Row, oarsman, row, for we are lost at sea; the sails are torn and the masts are broken." The sails are of silk; they cannot be undone; the masts are of pine; they refuse to bend. The sailors in it sing such a sweet song. The birds of the high Heavens perch on its masts; the little fish of the deep sea come to listen at the sides. The water turns at once into roses and rosemary. The new boat is saved; it lands in Porto Pim.)

Synthetic versions betray the oral tradition, constituting approximations at best. We will never know for certain what the early *Barca Bela* was like. Nevertheless, synthetic versions can be very useful, and the one just presented enables us to envision what *Barca Bela* must have been like before it began to disintegrate and become contaminated and modified through oral transmission: (1) There comes from Heaven a marvelous sailboat with Christ as shipmaster, St. Joseph as pilot, angels as oarsmen, and the Virgin as the only passenger; (2) it flies the flag of Portugal (3) and has a total of twenty-four oarsmen; the Virgin cries (i.e., prays) for sinners; (4) there begins a terrible tempest; the boat almost capsizes, but the sails and masts are strong; (5) the sailors begin to sing a wondrous song that causes the birds to perch upon the masts and the fish to listen at the sides; (6) and the becalmed waters turn into roses and rosemary.

Although the ballad rhymes mostly in *á* (11 out of 19 vv., with 8 having consonance in *-ar* rather than assonance), the existence of verses in *ó–o* (1–2), *-ores* (7–8), *-idos* (11–12), and *-im* (18–19) suggests a polyassonanted prototype. The verses in *ó–o*, we recall, are due to the parallelistic beginning of the ballad in the Azores, Beira Baixa, and Alto Alentejo. Note that some Brazilian versions also include couplets with the words "porto" and "piloto" in rhyme position: "Nosso Senhor é o capitão, / São José é o piloto, // e Maria, Mãe de Graça, / é o nosso seguro porto" (Our Lord is the captain, St. Joseph is the pilot, and Mary, Mother of Grace, is our safe harbor; Câmara Cascudo 1952, 437; cf. Alencar Pimentel 1978, 21). The reiteration of the two verses in -*ores* in widely separated lateral areas of archaicity, such as the Azores, Madeira, and Trás-os-Montes, would seem to endow them with considerable antiquity. The verses in -*idos* appear in three of the five Azorean continuations (2–4), and their absence in the one from São Jorge (1) is probably due to the fact that it is a contaminated fragment. The verses in -*im*, which convey the results of the wondrous song, correspond to a similar passage in *El conde Arnaldos*. In sum, the verses that do not rhyme in *á* fit well within the context of the ballad. The hypothesis that they might constitute interpolations grafted on through oral transmission does not hold. I am unaware of any other ballad from which they could have descended, and the fact that they fall short of standing as complete units in themselves bars their classification as intrusive popular quatrains.

Teófilo Braga (1869, 458–59) called attention to a similar ballad in Hernando del Castillo's *Cancionero general* (1511), in which a great tempest arises when Christ travels by sea with his disciples. They awaken him, and he puts an end to the storm:

	Durmiendo yua el Señor en vna naue en la mar,
2	sus discípulos con él, que no le osan recordar.
	El agua con la tormenta començóse a leuantar;
4	las olas cubren la naue, que la quieren anegar.
	Los discípulos, con miedo, començaron de llamar,
6	diziendo: —Señor, Señor, quieras nos presto saluar.
	Y despiertó el buen Jesu, començóles de hablar:
8	—O hombres de poca fe, ¿qué teméis? Quered pensar
	quan gran ofensa es a Dios de su gran poder dubdar.
10	Y levántose, mandando a los vientos y a la mar.
	Gran espanto puso entr'ellos y muy más marauillar,
12	diziendo: —¿Quién es aqueste que el tiempo hace mudar?

(1967, xiv[r.])

(The Lord was asleep on a ship, at sea, and his disciples did not dare to awaken him. With the storm the water began to swell; the waves covered the ship; they were about to flood it. Fearful, the disciples began to call, saying: "Lord, Lord, please save us quickly." Good Jesus awoke and began to speak to them: "Oh men of little faith, what do you fear? Remember how great an offense it is to God to doubt His power." And He got up, commanding the winds and the sea. He caused them great fright and even greater wonder, and they said: "What man is this, who can change the weather?")

Although the similarity between the two ballads is purely coincidental, it shows that such poems existed at the beginning of the sixteenth century. Moreover, *Barca Bela* is obviously related to the controversial *El conde Arnaldos*, first written down (1430–40) in a version contaminated with *El Conde Niño* (Count Niño) by Juan Rodríguez del Padrón, "el más antiguo colector de romances conocido" (the oldest known ballad collector; R. Menéndez Pidal 1953, 2: 208), and preserved in its secular form in the oral tradition of the Sephardim (CMP, H15; see also RPI, H6).[19]

Conde Arnaldos can be summarized as follows: While hunting with his falcon in the morning of St. John's Day, Count Arnaldos sees a galley with silken sails and rigging of sendal. The sailor in charge sings a song that becalms the sea, abates the wind, and causes the fish to surface and the birds to perch on the mast. Arnaldos asks the sailor to repeat his song, but he will teach it only to those who sail with him. As the correlation that follows indicates, *Barca Bela* reworks *Arnaldos* "a lo divino" transforming it into a religious contrafact that preserves the description of the marvelous boat and the effects of the sailor's wondrous song with hardly any change:

Arnaldos		*Barca Bela*	
	¡Quién hubiese tal ventura	3	Vamos ver a barca nova,
	sobre las aguas de mar		que do céu caiu ao mar.
2	como hubo el conde Arnaldos		
	la mañana de San Juan!		
	Con un falcón en la mano		
	la caza iba cazar,		
4	vio venir una galera		
	que a tierra quiere llegar.		
	Las velas traía de seda,	13	As velas eram de seda,
	la ejercia de un cendal,		*não quiseram abrandar.*
6	marinero que la manda	15	Marinheiros que vão nela,
	diciendo viene un cantar		levam um tão doce cantar.
	que la mar facia en calma,	18	Logo as áuguas se tornaram
	los vientos hace amainar,		de rosas e d'alecrim.
8	los peces que andan nel hondo	17	os peixinhos do mar fundo
	arriba los hace andar,		à borda vêm escutar.
	las aves que andan volando	16	as aves dos altos céus
	en el mástil las face posar.		nos mastros lhe vêm poisar.
10	Allí fabló el conde Arnaldos,		
	bien oiréis lo que dirá:		
	por Dios te ruego, marinero,		
	dígasme ora ese cantar.		

12 Respondióle el marinero,
tal respuesta le fue a dar:
—Yo no digo esta canción
sino a quien conmigo va.
(*Primavera*, no. 153)

Translation:

Would it that
one could be so fortunate
on the water of the sea
2 as was Count Arnaldos
on St. John's morn!
Falcon in hand,
he was going hunting
4 and saw a galley coming
as it approached the shore.
Its sails were of silk,
the rigging of gauze,
6 and the sailor who commanded it
sang a song
that calmed the sea,
slackened the winds,
8 and made the fish from the bottom
come above,
and makes the flying birds
perch on the mast.
10 There spoke Count Arnaldos,
you shall hear what he said:
"By God I pray thee, oh sailor,
to teach me that song now."
12 The sailor answered;
this was his reply:
"I only tell this song
to those who sail with me."

3 Let's go see the new boat
that fell to sea from Heaven.

13 The sails are of silk;
they cannot be undone.
15 The sailors in it
sing such a sweet song.
18 The water turns at once
into roses and rosemary.
17 The little fish of the deep sea
come to listen at the sides.
16 The birds of the high Heavens
perch on its masts.

The correlation of the opening verses of *Barca Bela* with the beginning of *Arnaldos* is rather tenuous; those lines could easily correspond to verse 4 of the Spanish ballad. Despite the different rhymes, verse 18 of *Barca Bela* was correlated with verse 7 of *Arnaldos* because the image conveyed—calmness of the sea—seems to be essentially the same.

Arnaldos exerted some influence on the composition of Andrés Ortiz's *Floriseo y la reina de Bohemia* (Floriseo and the Queen of Bohemia), a lengthy secular ballad whose plot is taken from *Floriseo*

que por otro nombre es llamado el Caballero del Desierto, el qual por
su gran esfuerzo y mucho saber alcanzó a ser rey de Bohemia, a romance by Fernando Bernal (Valencia, 1516) (Hauf and Aguirre 1969,
107). Ortiz's ballad opens with a description of the joy that Floriseo
feels when the beautiful Queen of Bohemia sends for him:

      Quien hubiese tal ventura   en haberse de casar,
2   como la hubo Floriseo   cuando se fue a desposar,
      que con su grande alegría   no podía reposar,
4   y la causa fuese aquesta: como l'envió a llamar
      esa noble, linda reina   de Bohemia natural.
6   El no era perezozo,   allá la fuera a hablar.

                                      (Durán 1945, no. 287)

(Would that one could be so fortunate upon marrying as was
Floriseo when he took a spouse. His joy was such that he could not
sleep, and the reason was this: That he had been sent for by that
noble, beautiful queen, lady of Bohemia. Being far from lazy, he
went to speak to her.)

The first two verses are from *Arnaldos*, but those that follow are inspired by *Conde Claros insomne* (Sleepless Count Claros; CMP, B11;
RPI, B3), which tells how Count Claros is unable to sleep because of
his love for Claraniña:

      Media noche era por filo,   los gallos querían cantar,
2   conde Claros con amores   no podía reposar:
      dando muy grandes sospiros   que el amor le hacía dar,
4   porque[20] amor de Claraniña   no le deja sosegar.

                                    (*Primavera*, no. 190)

(It was midnight on the dot, the cocks were about to sing, and the
lovesick Count Claros was unable to sleep: He gave great sighs
caused by love; his love for Claraniña did not permit him to stay
still.)

Later on, when Floriseo rests from battle on an enchanted isle,
a maiden arrives by boat with a message from her mistress, who
seeks his assistance in redressing an injury. The maiden's song is inspired by *Arnaldos*:

54   Lo qu'en el barco venía   era cosa de mirar,
      que venía entretejido   con guirnaldas de arrayán,
56   y de aquel barco salía   una música de amar.

58
60

El estándolo mirando   del barco vieron saltar
una doncella hermosa   que cantando iba un cantar.
Las aves que iban volando   al suelo hacía bajar,
los peces qu'están nadando   todos juntos hace estar,
las naves que van remando   no podían navegar.

(What came in a boat was a wonder to see, for it was interwoven with garlands of myrtle, and from that boat came a music to make love by. While he looked at it, from the boat was seen landing a handsome maiden who was singing a song that caused the flying birds to descend to the ground, the swimming fish to gather together, and the ships being rowed could no longer move.)

Floriseo refuses the maiden's request, explaining that he has to go to Constantinople in order to report to the emperor. The maiden plays a lute and sings a song that puts everyone to sleep, kidnaps Floriseo, and takes him to her mistress:

90
92
94

La canción qu'ella decía   era gloria d'escuchar:
a todos los que la oían   adormecido les ha.
Ansí hizo a Floriseo,   qu'en el suelo vido estar.
Desque lo vido dormido   en el barco lanzado lo ha,
y su música tañendo   a un castillo llegado ha.

(The song she sang was glorious to hear: All who listened to it fell asleep. And so it happened to Floriseo, whom she saw on the ground. As soon as she saw him sleeping, she threw him in the boat, and playing her music she arrived at a castle.)

Some early versions of *Arnaldos* end when the sailor tells the count that he will teach his song only to those who sail with him; other versions include the text of the song (R. Menéndez Pidal 1958c, 60–64). The modern Sephardic ballad supplements this. Arnaldos goes aboard the galley and falls asleep right away because of the sound of the water (see Armistead's summary in CMP, 1: 294–95), but, in one version, it is the singing that puts him to sleep: "Al son de los dulces cantos / el conde dormido se ha" (At the sound of the sweet songs the count fell asleep; Bénichou 1968a, 207). This parallels the effects of the maiden's song on Floriseo, and indicates that, even though the full version of the early *Arnaldos* did not reach print, Andrés Ortiz was familiar with it.

Arnaldos also influenced three traditional religious ballads. Some Spanish and Chilean versions of *La Magdalena* (*Maria Madalena Busca Jesus* [Mary Magdalene in Search of Jesus]; RPI, U48), which report how Mary Madgalene searched for Christ when he was on his way to Calvary, begin with verses adapted from *Arnaldos*:

> ¡Quién tuviera tal fortuna,   tal fortuna y tal bondad,
> 2   como Magdalena tuvo   cuando a Cristo fue a buscar!
> Le buscaba de huerto en huerto,   en rosalito en rosal.
>   (R. Menéndez Pidal 1958b, 30; from Segovia, Spain)[21]

(Would that one could have such fortune, such fortune and goodness as the Magdalene found when she went looking for Christ! She searched from garden to garden, in rosebushes and rose trees.)

> ¡Quién tuviera tal ventura   sobre las aguas del mar
> 2   como tuvo Magdalena   cuando a Cristo fue a buscar!
> Lo buscó de villa en villa   y de villar en villar.
>   (Vicuña Cifuentes 1912, no. 85; from Chile)[22]

(Would that one could have such fortune on the waters of the sea as the Magdalene found when she went looking for Christ! She searched from town to town; from town to town she searched.)

In Asturias, *La Pasión* (The Passion) also begins with an adaptation of verses from *Arnaldos*. The Virgin sails in a boat made of crystal and with golden oars, and faints when the oarsman sings that Christ can be found by following the trail of blood that he has left behind:

> Navegando va la Virgen,   navegando por la mar;
> 2   los remos trae de oro,   la barquilla de cristal:
> el remador que remaba   va diciendo este cantar.
> 4   —Por aquella cuesta arriba,   por aquel camino real,
> por el rastro de la sangre   a Cristo hemos de encontrar.
> 6   La Virgen que aquello oyó   desmayadita se cae. . . .
>   (J. Menéndez Pidal 1986, no. 92)[23]

(The Virgin is sailing, she sails on the sea, the oars are of gold, the little boat of crystal, and the oarsman who rows sings this song: "Up that hill, on that highway, by the trail of blood Christ we shall find." The Virgin, hearing that, fell senseless to the ground.)

In Galicia, during Christmas groups of children used to sing going from door to door *Hoy es día de alegría* (Today is a Day of Joy), which also adapts the beginning of *Arnaldos*, as an *aguinaldo* or "song" in which they asked for some sort of gratification:

Hoy es día de alegría,   olvidar todo el pesar,
2   que anda el Redentor del mundo   navegando por la mar.
Navega en una galera   que en mi vida he visto tal:
4   las bandas eran de lienzo,   los remos de virginal.
El piloto que la guía   traía este cantar:
6   —Si nos han de dar aguinaldo   no nos hagan esperar,
que somos niños chiquillos,   traemos muito que andar.
(González 1994, no. 9.1)[24]

(Today is a day of joy; let's forget all sorrow, for the Redeemer of the World is sailing on the sea. He sails on a galley as I have never seen: The sails are of cloth, the oars of virginity. The pilot who guides it sings this song: "If you are going to reward us, do not make us wait, for we are small children and have a long ways to go.")

The first two of these religious ballads open with verses adapted from the beginning of *Arnaldos*, but then continue with different subjects. Except for the beginning and concluding verses, the *aguinaldo* consists only of verses adapted from *Arnaldos*, but what we have in these three instances is a partial adaptation. *Barca Bela*, on the other hand, adapts the secular *Arnaldos* much more extensively, constituting, therefore, a "religious contrafact" or *a lo divino* adaptation of that ballad. This adaptation is exclusively Luso-Brazilian.[25] An Argentinian and Colombian traditional poem recalls *Barca Bela*, but there is no genetic relationship between the two. The poem in question, *Entre San Pedro y San Juan* ([Between] St. Peter and St. John; *é–o*), tells how St. Peter and St. John make a new, golden boat with oars of steel. St. Peter serves as pilot, St. John as sailor, and Jesus as shipmaster. It exists in contamination with *El marinero al agua* (The Sailor Who Fell into the Sea; *á–a*; CMP, U3; RPI, U39), in which a drowning sailor rejects the devil's offer to save his life in exchange for his soul when he dies. In the Argentinian version, *Entre San Pedro y San Juan* introduces *El marinero*:

Entre San Pedro y San Juan   hicieron un barco nuevo;
2   el barco era de oro,   los remos eran de acero.
San Pedro era piloto,   San Juan era marinero,
4   y capitán general   era Jesús Nazareno.
En una noche oscurita   cayó un marinero al agua. . . .
(Carrizo 1939, 28)[26]

(St. Peter and St. John made a new boat. The boat was of gold; the oars were of steel. St. Peter was the pilot, St. John was a sailor, and the shipmaster was Jesus of Nazareth. On a dark night a sailor fell into the water. . . .)

One version of *El marinero al agua* from Santander, Colombia, begins and concludes with verses from this poem:

> Entre San Juan y San Pedro   hicieron un arca nueva;
> 2   el arca era de oro,   su arquilla era de acero.
> Una noche muy oscura   cayó un marinero al agua. . . .
> > (Dougherty 1977, 248–49)

(St. John and St. Peter made a new ark: The ark was of gold; the little ark was of steel. On a very dark night a sailor fell into the water. . . .)

The conclusion is unclear. Having rejected the devil's offer, the sailor commends his soul to God, his wife and children to the Virgin. Then he seems to seek help from St. John, St. Peter, and Jesus:

12	De San Juan iba a San Pedro,	From St. John he would go to St. Peter,
	de San Pedro iba a San Juan.	from St. Peter he would go to St. John.
	De capital general	From shipmaster
	iba a Jesús Nazareno.	he would go to Jesus of Nazareth.
14	De capital general,	From shipmaster
	iba a Jesús Nazareno.	he would go to Jesus of Nazareth.

Having Christ as shipmaster and a saint as pilot, this poem recalls the beginning of *Barca Bela* but, since it rhymes in *é–o* and not in *á*, the similarity is purely concidental. This is also true of a lyrical quatrain from Asturias about a love-boat with twenty-five oars and as many oarsmen, rhyming in *ó–e*, just like the corresponding passage of *Barca Bela*, where there are twenty-four oars:

—A la mar abajo va	Down the seas goes
la lancha de mis amores;	the launch of my beloved;
veinticinco remos lleva	it has twenty-five oars
y otros tantos remadores.	and as many oarsmen.
	(Cabal 1931, 208)

The image of the love-boat is well-known in literature.[27] Although that does not seem to be the case here, the boat, which moves to and fro with the action of the waves, often represents the woman, and the sailor stands for her lover. The first verse of the Asturian quatrain corresponds to an openly erotic sixteenth-century *seguidilla* (type of stanza) in which a girl named Catalina undertakes a "sea-voyage" with a monk:

Por la mar abajo	Down the seas
va Catalina,	goes Catalina,
las piernas de fuera,	with bare legs
un fraile encima.	and a monk on top.

(Alzieu, Jammes, and Lissorgues 1984, no. 135)

Given the erotic, albeit more subdued character of the first Asturian quatrain, its resemblance to a passage of *Barca Bela* is no doubt coincidental as well.[28]

Barca Bela, then, is the most extensive adaptation of *Arnaldos* "a lo divino," and there is nothing like it in the other pan-Iberian subtraditions. Unfortunately, *Barca Bela* was not included in any of the early collections (see Rodríguez-Moñino 1973); to my knowledge, it did not appear in any *pliego suelto* (see Rodríguez-Moñino 1997; Di Stefano 1972), and Carolina Michaëlis de Vasconcelos (1934) does not mention it as one of the ballads cited or alluded to by Portuguese medieval and Renaissance writers. Nevertheless, its relationship to *Remando Vão Remadores*, the moving ballad Vicente composed to usher in his *Auto da Barca do Purgatório*, indicates its currency in the late fifteenth century, for it takes a few years for a ballad to become traditional:

	Barca Bela		*Remando Vão Remadores*
	Vamos ver a barca nova,	1	Remando vam remadores
	que do céu caiu ao mar;	2	barca de grande alegria.
4	Nossa Senhora vai nela	5	Anjos eram os remeyros,
	e os anjos vão a remar.	6	que remavão a profia.
	S. José é o piloto	3	O patrão que a guiava,
	e Jesus o general;	4	filho de Deus se dezia.
6	que linda bandeira leva,	7	Estandarte d'esperança,
	bandeira de Portugal.	8	ho quam bem que parecia!
	. . . .		
	As velas eram de seda,	11	A vella, com fé cosida,
	não quiseram abrandar;	12	todo mundo esclarecia.
14	os mastros eram de pinho,	9	O masto de fortaleza
	não quiseram envergar.	10	como cristal relozia.
	. . . .	13	A ribeyra muy serena,
		14	que nenhum vento bolia.

(1979, 78)[29]

Translation:

Let's go see the new boat	1 Oarsmen rowed
that fell to sea from Heaven;	2 a boat of great joy.
4 Our Lady is in it	5 The oarsmen were angels;
and the angels go as oarsmen.	6 they competed with each other.
St. Joseph is the pilot;	3 The shipmaster who guided the boat
Jesus is the shipmaster;	4 called himself the Son of God.
6 what a beautiful flag it carries;	7 The standard was of hope;
it is the flag of Portugal.	oh how great it looked!
. . . .	
The sails are of silk;	11 The sail, sewed with faith,
they cannot be undone.	12 brightened the whole world.
14 The masts are of pine;	9 The mast, made of fortitude,
they refuse to bend.	10 shone like crystal.
. . . .	13 The shore was so serene
	14 that no wind stirred.

Vicente's (1) "barca de grande alegria" (boat of great joy) corresponds to the boat "que do céu caiu ao mar" (that fell to sea from Heaven) in *Barca Bela*; (2) both ballads have angels as oarsmen and (3) Christ as shipmaster; (4) also, Vicente's "estandarte d'esperança" (standard of hope) parallels the flag of Portugal in the modern versions of *Barca Bela*. Since Vicente was interested in evoking an image of serenity, the tempest and the wondrous song in *Barca Bela* were eliminated, yet both ballads go on to refer to (5) the sails and to (6) the masts of the marvelous boat.

Coincidences are always possible, especially when dealing with the same image—Vicente's ballad also depicts the Ship of Faith—, but there are too many elements in common here for this to be a matter of pure coincidence. *Barca Bela* cannot derive from *Remando*, for a ballad in *-ía* could not have been altered to such an extent through oral transmission. Consequently, it is *Remando* that must derive from *Barca Bela*. The different sequence in which the elements they share are arranged hardly complicates the correlation here posited. Vicente probably took what he needed from *Barca Bela*, rearranging it in the order most convenient for his purposes. His choice of the rhyme *-ía* versus the predominant rhyme in *á* of *Barca Bela* fits well the climate of peace that he intended to create, for *-ía* seems much softer than the tempestuous *á*.

Remando Vão Remadores, then, should not figure among Vicente's original compositions in ballad form, as asserted by Carolina Michaëlis de Vasconcelos (1934, 235, 271–72n6) and Ramón Menéndez Pidal (1953, 2: 104). Obviously, this does not detract in any way from the originality of what Vicente did with something that already existed in the oral tradition.

Despite its marked beauty, *Remando* was not included in *pliegos sueltos* nor in any of the Spanish collections printed during the sixteenth and seventeenth centuries. This exclusion was probably because it was written in Portuguese,[30] although, as Dámaso Alonso has demonstrated, it is possible to translate it into Castilian without loss of its pristine beauty (1958, 153–54). The only subsequent echo of it that I have managed to discover is in one of Juan Timoneda's ballads, where it appears transformed, as the title indicates, into a *romance de amores* (love ballad):

Remando		*Romance de amores*
Remando vam remadores		Nauegando va la Naue
barca de grande alegria;		por el mar de el alegria,
		en popa voy assentado
		y puesto a mi fantasia:
	5	fletada va de plazeres,
		porque Descanso la guia:
o patrão que a guiava,		el Patron es el Contento,
filho de Deus se dezia.		el Sossiego el que regia,
5 Anjos eram os remeyros,		y los marineros son
que remavão a profia;	10	Regozijo, y Melodia,
estandarte d'esperança,		Espacio, Fauor, y Gusto
ho quam bem que parecia!		que siruen sin rebeldia:
O masto de fortaleza		
10 como cristal relozia;		
a vella, com fé cosida,		las velas mis pensamientos
todo mundo esclarecia;		que gozo las estendia,
a ribeyra muy serena,	15	deleyte, y prosperidad
que nenhum vento bolia.		quien de viento las enchia. . . .
		(1963, xiiii–xv)

Translation:

1 Oarsmen rowed	The ship goes sailing
a boat of great joy.	on the sea of joy,
	I am sitting at the stern,
	giving reins to my imagination:
	5 The boat is packed with pleasure
	because Repose guides it:
The shipmaster who guided the boat	The shipmaster is Happiness,
called himself the Son of God.	Peace the one who governs it,
5 The oarsmen were angels;	and the sailors are
they competed with each other.	10 Joy and Melody,

The standard was of hope;
oh how great it looked!
The mast, made of fortitude,
10 shone like crystal.
The sail, sewed with faith,
brightened the whole world.
The shore was so serene
that no wind stirred.

Space, Favor, and Liking;
they serve without protest:

The sails are my thoughts
and pleasure stretches them out;
15 delight and prosperity
fill them with wind.

Timoneda's skill in turning a religious poem into a love ballad brings to mind the controversy surrounding *Conde Arnaldos* ever since John Gibson Lockhart suspected in 1823 that "more is meant [by *Arnaldos*] than meets the ear" and that "some religious allegory is intended to be shadowed forth" (259), a suggestion Thomas R. Hart took up in 1957. Others have seen *Arnaldos* as a ballad of magic "whose theme is the conflict of man with the supernatural forces of nature" (Spitzer 1955, 183; 1956),[31] or as an erotic poem (Hauf and Aguirre 1969). There has been no dearth of other studies and interpretations.[32] Although *Barca Bela* lends validity to the religious one, we must recognize the fact that the "multivocidad natural del símbolo" (the multiplicity of meaning inherent in symbols; Suárez Pallasá 1975, 136) makes it difficult to decide between any two interpretations, and that one interpretation does not necessarily exclude the viability of all the rest.

In sum, *Barca Bela* lives on in the Portuguese and Brazilian oral traditions in three forms that complement each other. The shortest, which tells about the marvelous boat from Heaven sailed by the Holy Family with angels as oarsmen, is found throughout Portugal and Brazil. The second variant, specifying that there are twenty-four oars and as many oarsmen, and allowing the Virgin, who prays for sinners, to assume the form of "Nossa Senhora das Dores" (Our Lady of Sorrows) or "Nossa Senhora das Flores" (Our Lady of Flowers) is remembered only in two archaic lateral areas, the Azores and Madeira. The third, which enables one to establish a clear connection between *Barca Bela* and *Arnaldos*, survives in the Azores and among Azorean New World immigrants because, in the islands, the ballad in question has been incorporated into the ancient festivities in honor of the Holy Ghost.[33] Although *Barca Bela* was not printed at an early date, its relationship with Vicente's *Remando Vão Remadores*, which it inspired, proves that *Barca Bela* was already traditional in the late fifteenth century. Thus, once again, modern oral tradition sheds light upon the past, disclosing facts that might otherwise have remained shielded from knowledge.

7

The Oral Transmission of *Flérida*

Gil Vicente (ca. 1465–ca. 1536) was perhaps the greatest European playwright of his time (Alborg 1970–96, 1: 699–700), and folk literature played a crucial role in his plays. His indebtedness to the oral tradition, especially the ballad, the popular lyric, and the folktale are well-known,[1] but the oral tradition is also greatly indebted to him.

During the Middle Ages, Castilians regarded Galician-Portuguese as more appropriate than Spanish for lyric poetry, writing many of their poems in that language. In the sixteenth century, Portuguese authors penned some of their works in Castilian, and *Flérida*, the beautiful ballad that Vicente composed to end one of his Spanish plays, the *Tragicomedia de don Duardos* (ca. 1525), became extremely popular.

Don Duardos was inspired by *Primaleón* (1512), a romance of chivalry by Floriano de Silva.[2] In that play, Don Duardos, an English prince, falls in love with Flérida, daughter of Palmeirín, emperor of Constantinople. On the advice of Princess Olimba, Don Duardos disguises himself as a peasant and enters into the service of Julián, Flérida's gardener, who pretends that the prince is a son of his, also named Julián. Flérida falls in love with the new gardener but suspects from his manners and speech that he is not what he seems to be. Don Duardos eventually promises to reveal his identity to Flérida and to one of her ladies-in-waiting, Artada, at night in the garden. He shows up dressed as a prince but still refuses to say who he is, even though he expects Flérida to elope with him in an awaiting fleet. Flérida agrees to go. The play concludes with a ballad that is divided among three characters, Artada, Flérida, and Don Duardos, who also sing it together afterward. This ballad, which Vicente entitled *Romance para final del Auto*, soon became known as *Flérida*. It has been collected in Spanish, Judeo-Spanish, and Portuguese, and is probably still being sung in those three languages.[3]

Unfortunately, we do not have a satisfactory edition of *Don Duardos*. The early editions exhibit many important variants,[4] and this is also true of *Flérida*, the ballad with which Vicente concluded his play.

Don Duardos has 2,054 verses, and the first known edition is a fragment of 61 verses (958–1017) used to complete a *pliego suelto* published in Seville by Bartolomé Pérez on 28 January 1530 (Infantes 1982, 687–89). This fragment probably survived by accident, because it was customary to fill in the blank space on the last page of broadsides with poems which, as a result, often appear truncated. As Víctor Infantes plausibly argued, this is the reason for the inclusion of the said fragment in Pérez's *pliego*. Since it would not make any sense for the printer to typeset a fragment from the middle of a play as a fill-in, Pérez probably used a page from an edition that he was preparing (Infantes 1982, 672, 679–80). Although that edition has not survived, it helps to set the date of the first printed version of *Flérida*.

That version is a gloss by António Lopes, a Portuguese student from Trancoso at the University of Salamanca. It exists in a single, undated *pliego suelto* (Rodríguez-Moñino 1997, no. 273; ed. in *Pliegos . . . góticos* 1957–61, 1: 221–26) published before 1539, because it was of one the items in the library of Fernando Colón (b. 1488), who died in that year. This gloss is entitled "Romance sacado de la farsa de don duardos que comiença enel mes era de abril nueuamente glosado por Antonio Lopez" (Ballad that begins "It was in the month of April," taken from the farce of Dom Duardos and newly glossed by Antonio Lopez), thus indicating that its source was the *Tragicomedia* itself, in an edition that classified it as a *farsa*. Since Spanish printers applied the word *farsa* indiscriminately to a variety of works, Lopes is almost surely referring to a Spanish edition, which could well be the one that Bartolomé Pérez was typesetting in 1530 (Infantes 1982, 682 and n107; 700). As Arthur L.-F. Askins suggests, this edition is probably either the same or a very close relative of one acquired by Colón in Alcalá de Henares in January or February 1534 (1991, 304n5B). Thus, the version that António Lopes glossed before 1539 could date from 1530, that is, only five years after the composition of the play, while Vicente was still living.

The second version of *Flérida* appeared in Martín's Nucio's *Cancionero de romances impreso en Amberes sin año* (ca. 1548) and five subsequent editions of that work (1550–81), as well as in the *Silva de romances (Zaragoza 1550–1551)* and three additional *Silvas* (1550–61) (Rodríguez-Moñino 1973, 2: 469).

The third version, published twenty-six years after the poet's death, is in the *Copilaçam de todalas obras de Gil Vicente* prepared by his son, Luís Vicente (1562). A fourth version, in a *pliego suelto* published in Valladolid in 1572 (Rodríguez-Moñino 1997, no. 1608; *Pliegos . . . Catalunya* 1976, 2: 302–3), is carelessly printed and incomplete. It does not help to restore Vicente's original, but it enables us to document that the ballad was being orally transmitted in the 1570s, even though it probably became traditional much earlier. (I will study this version at the end of the section in this chapter dedicated to the modern Spanish versions of *Flérida*.) The fifth version is in a second *Copilaçam* of Vicente's works published in Lisbon in 1586.[5]

These five versions are in the original Spanish, but there was yet another sixteenth-century version, in Portuguese, in a manuscript copied by Francisco Xavier de Oliveira (1702–83), better known as the Cavaleiro de Oliveira. Although João Baptista de Almeida Garrett claimed that he saw it in London, including it in his *Romanceiro* (1843–51; see Almeida Garrett 1963, 3: 137–39), its existence was in doubt. As Carolina Michaëlis de Vasconcelos observed, it is an excellent translation of the version found in the *Copilaçam* of 1562 (1934, 117n1). Nevertheless, there are indications that this early Portuguese version did exist, even though it is no longer available. The Cavaleiro de Oliveira had glued pieces of paper with notes between the pages of one of his books, but the person who subsequently rebound the book in question did not hesitate to pull out and destroy those pages (see Lindley Cintra 1967, 108–10). Since Garrett's so-called copy follows the *Copilaçam* of 1562 in almost every detail, the chances are that he decided to "correct" it. As a good Romantic, he did not hesitate to "reconstruct" the poems that he discovered, believing that, in so doing, he was merely restoring them to their pristine beauty.

In the nineteenth century, Agustín Durán included Nucio's version of *Flérida* in his *Romancero general o Colección de romances Castellanos anteriores al siglo XVIII*, first published in five volumes between 1828 and 1832 (1945, no. 288). Strangely, Fernando J. Wolf and Conrado Hofmann omitted it from their *Primavera* (1856), which perhaps explains its absence from the five major anthologies dedicated to Spanish ballads during the last thirty years.[6]

In any case, *Flérida* has been frequently reprinted through the centuries. Since there are considerable differences among the versions published by António Lopes (1530s), Nucio (ca. 1548), the *Copi-*

laçam of 1562, and the *Copilaçam* of 1586,[7] they must be taken into account when studying the modern renditions. A first reconstruction of the original, attempted by Michaëlis de Vasconcelos (1934, 132), was subsequently refined by Israel S. Révah (1952). Révah's reconstruction is excellent, but I disagree with it in one detail and would like to propose an emendation.

The worst of the four early versions just listed is the one in the *Copilaçam* of 1562 (1968, 225–27) which omits verses 6–8, 15b–16a, and 21b–22a (see the next section). The *Copilaçam* of 1586 omits verses 15b–16a and 21 (Reckert 1977c, 446–61). Nucio's version (1945, 253v.–254v.) omits only verses 15b–16a. These three versions also exhibit important variants. At the end of two consecutive strophes, António Lopes's glossed version adds two octosyllables (15b–16a; emphasis mine), but the last verse of the second strophe breaks the rhyme in *-ía*:

a)   alli hablo don duardos   there spoke Don Duardos,
     bien oyreys lo que dezia   you will hear what he said:
b)   pues vuestro mal me quebranta   since your grief pains me,
     no lloreys señora infanta.   do not cry, my lady and princess.
              (*Pliegos . . . góticos* 1957–61, 1: 223)

As Révah demonstrated (1952, 111), unlike the remainder of the gloss, the strophe in question (b) consists of nine instead of ten verses, a mishap obviously due to a printer's error. Fortunately, the missing verse, "no lloreys mi alegria" (do not cry, my joy), can easily be restored through a comparison with the other three versions. Therefore, Lopes's version should read at this point:

alli hablo don duardos   *bien oyreys lo que dezia*
no lloreys señora infanta   no lloreys mi alegria.

(there spoke Don Duardos, *you will hear what he said*: *Do not cry, my lady and princess*; do not cry, my joy.)

Révah eliminated from his reconstruction the two italicized verses on the grounds that, lacking in the other three versions, they could not possibly belong to Vicente. I believe otherwise. António Lopes's version of *Flérida* is the oldest. He took it from a printed edition of the play, and a cursory reading suffices to show that it does not yet bear any signs of oral transmission. If the two octosyllables in question were new, chances are that there would be significant changes elsewhere, but there aren't any. From an artistic point of view, these two octosyllables are excellent, fitting well within the ballad tradition that Vicente knew so well. The formulaic "bien oyreis lo que dezia" (you will hear what he said) is an introduction to dialogue that appears in many other ballads (Webber 1951, 183–85), and the parallelism that "no lloreys señora infanta" (do not cry, my lady and princess) adds to the following octosyllable, "no lloreys mi alegria" (do not cry, my joy) belongs to the traditional pattern in which "the second line is an exact reproduction of the preceding line except the last element" (224). In fact, these two octosyllables improve the text, softening the directness of Don Duardos's reply to Flérida. For these reasons, I believe that they belong to Vicente, and decided to add them (see the next selection) to Révah's otherwise impeccably reconstructed version (1952, 136–37):[8]

	*En el mes era de abril, de mayo antes un día,
2	quando los lirios y rosas muestran más su alegría,
	en la noche má serena que el cielo hazer podía,
4	quando la hermosa infanta Flérida ya se partía,
	en la huerta de su padre a los árboles dezía:
6	—Jamás, en quanto biviere, os veré tan sólo un día,
	ni cantar los ruiseñores en los ramos melodía.
8	Quédate a Dios, agua clara, quédate a Dios, agua fría,
	quedaos con Dios, mis flores, mi gloria que ser solía.
10	Voyme a tierras estrañas, pues ventura allá me guía.
	Si mi padre me buscare que grande bien me quería,
12	digan que el amor me lleva, que no fue la culpa mía:
	tal tema tomó comigo que me venció su porfía.
14	¡Triste, no sé donde voy, ni nadie me lo dezía!—
	Allí habló don Duardos, bien oiréis lo que decía:
16	—No lloréis, señora infanta, no lloréis, mi alegría,
	que en los reinos de Inglaterra más claras aguas avía
18	y más hermosos jardines, y vuestros, señora mía.
	Ternéis trezientas donzellas de alta genelosía;
20	de plata son los palacios para vuestra señoría,
	de esmeraldas y jacintos toda la tapecería,
22	las cámaras ladrilladas de oro fino de Turquía,
	con letreros esmaltados que cuentan la vida mía:
24	cuentan los bivos dolores que me distes aquel día,
	quando con Primaleón fuertemente combatía.
26	¡Señora, vos me matastes, que yo a él no lo temía!
	Sus lágrimas consolava Flérida, que esto oía.
28	Fuéronse a las galeras que don Duardos tenía:
	cincuenta eran por cuenta; todas van en compañía.
30	Al son de sus dulces remos la infanta se adormecía

en braços de don Duardos   que bien le pertenecía.
32   Sepan quantos son nacidos   aquesta sentencia mía:
que contra la muerte y amor   nadie no tiene valía.

(It was in the month of April, one day before May, when irises and
roses show more of their beauty, on the most peaceful night that the
Heavens could display, when the beautiful princess Flérida was departing. In her father's garden she was saying to the trees: "Never,
for as long as I live, shall I see you even one day, nor hear in your
branches the melody of the nightingales. Stay with God, clear
water; stay with God, cold water; stay with God, my flowers, which
used to be my pride. I am going to strange lands, for fate guides me
there. If my father looks for me, whose love for me is so great, tell
him that love takes me, that the fault is not mine: It was so stubborn with me that its persistence vanquished. Woe is me, I know
not where I go, nor does anyone tell me!" There spoke Don Duardos,
you will hear what he said: "Do not cry, my lady and princess; do
not cry, my joy, for in the Kingdom of England the waters are even
clearer, the gardens more beautiful, and they are yours, my lady.
You will have three hundred maidens of great rank. The palaces for
your ladyship are of silver; all the tapestry is of emeralds and hyacinths; the rooms have walls of fine Turkish gold and enameled
signs that relate my life story: They relate the great suffering you
caused me that day when with Primaleón I fiercely fought. My lady,
you were killing me, for him I did not fear!" His tears consoled
Flérida, upon hearing this. They went toward the galleys that Don
Duardos had: They were fifty in all; all of them departed together.
At the sweet sound of the oars the princess fell asleep, in the arms
of Don Duardos; she belonged to him well. Let those who have been
born know this maxim of mine: In the face of death and love no one
has any recourse.)

There are some lines right after this ballad, but, being spoken by
the shipmaster, they are set apart from the ballad itself because of
their change in rhyme, and have left no vestiges in the oral tradition:

Lo mismo iremos cantando   The same we shall go on singing
por essa mar adelante,   as we travel through the seas,
a las serenas rogando   asking the sirens for help
y vuestra alteza mandando   if your highness commands
que en la mar siempre se cante.   us to always sing in the ocean.
                                  (Vicente 1968, 227)[9]

As we have already mentioned, this ballad has been collected in
the Portuguese, Spanish, and Sephardic traditions. The study that

follows begins with the Sephardic versions because they have remained most faithful to the original.

a. The Sephardic Ballad

The Sephardic tradition can be divided into two main branches. The Western tradition refers to North Africa and especially to Morocco, where most of the fieldwork has been conducted; the Eastern tradition refers to the Eastern Mediterranean—what used to be Yugoslavia, Greece, Turkey, Israel, Bulgaria, and Romania. Besides *Flérida*, the Sephardim preserve *El falso hortelano* (The False Gardener), which also derives from *Don Duardos* (ca. 1525). Thus, both of these ballads constitute good examples of the continued contact between the Sephardim and their Iberian homeland after the expulsion of 1492. Interestingly, *Flérida* seems to be exclusively Moroccan; *El falso hortelano* has been discovered only in the East.

The synthetic version that follows is based on eleven splendid renditions collected in Tangier, Tetuan, Larache, and Alcazarquivir between 1904 and 1916.[10] They were sent to me from the Menéndez Pidal Archive, in Madrid, which houses the largest corpus of ballads in the world, including rich collections from the Iberian Peninsula, Latin America, and the Eastern and Western Sephardic traditions.[11]

Other Sephardic versions of *Flérida* have been published by Oro Anahory-Librowicz (1988, no. 19), Armistead and Silverman (1977, no. 49), Arcadio de Larrea Palacín (1952, no. 157), and Juan Martínez Ruiz (1963, nos. 37c, 66).[12] I will refer to them in my discussion, but chose to base the synthetic version on the eleven versions from the Menéndez Pidal Archive because they include all of the ballad's main features. Since I received permission to edit them here (appendix B), thus enabling readers to see them directly, I did not feel that a lengthy, complex list of variants to each verse was necessary. I have indicated my sources in parenthesis:

> *Entrar quiere el mes de mayo   y el de abril antes de un día,
> 2   cuando las rosas y flores   amuestran sus alegrías,
> cuando la señora infanta   Flérida ya se partía.
> 4   De los sus ojos lloraba,   de la su boca decía:
> —Adiós, adiós, aguas claras,   adiós, adiós, aguas frías;   (2.1, vv. 1–5)
> 6   adiós, mis ricos vergeles,   donde yo me divertía;   (2.1, v. 7)
> adiós, mis ricas donzellas,   las que conmigo dormían;   (2.2, v. 8)
> 8   adiós, mi padre y mi madre,   los que a mí mucho querían.   (2.1, v. 8)
> Si mi padre os preguntare,   el que a mí mucho quería,

10 decidle que el amor me lleva,   que la culpa no es mía,   (2.3, vv. 9–10)
   que al amor y a la muerte   naide los pone a porfía.
12 Tanto porfió el amor   que a mí venció su aporfía.—
   Con ciento de sus donzellas   a la mar se bajaría;   (2.2, vv. 11–13)
14 en treinta y cinco navíos   Flérida se embarcaría.
   Al son de los dulces remos   el sueño la vencería;
16 con el ruido del agua   Flérida dispertaría.
   De los sus ojos lloraba,   de la su boca decía: (2.1, vv. 13–16)
18 —¡Ay, válgame Dios del cielo,   qué grande desdicha mía!,   (2.2, v. 18)
   que no sé donde me llevan,   ni menos donde yo iría,
20 si me llevan para Francia,   o para la Andalucía,
   si me llevan a Inglaterra,   donde yo pertenecía.   (2.1, vv. 19–21)
22 Oído lo había don Luguardo,   que junto a ella estaría: (2.2, v. 22)
   —No lloredes vos, mi alma,   no lloredes vos, mi vida;   (2.1, v. 22)
24 para Francia, mi señora,   a Francia la bien querida.   (2.2, v. 24)
   Si ricos vergeles dejasteis,   mejores los hallarías;   (2.4, v. 25)
26 si ricas doncellas dejas,   mejores las hallaríais;   (2.1, v. 25)
   si ricas casas dexates,   ricas casas hallarías,
28 los techos aleonados,   pintados a la Turquía;   (2.2, vv. 25–26)
   las paredes son de oro,   los suelos de plata fina,   (2.6, v. 21)
30 los cerrojos de la puerta   de aljófar y piedras finas.
   Si padre y madre dexates,   suegro y suegra hallarías;   (2.2, vv. 27–28)
32 si hermanos y hermanas dejas,   ricos cuñados tendríais.—
   Ellos en estas palabras,   los dolores la darían;   (2.1, v. 28)
34 en la halda de don Duardos   un niño parido había.   (2.5, v. 18)
   —Volve, volve, la mi madre,   vólvela donde venía.   (2.3, v. 21)
36 Y en un barquito de cañas   la niña se volvería.   (2.4, v. 29)

(The month of May wanted to enter, and it was April, one day before, when roses and flowers displayed their joy, when the lady and
Princess Flérida was about to depart. She cried from her eyes; from
her mouth she said: "Farewell; farewell, clear waters; farewell;
farewell, cold waters; farewell, my beloved gardens, where I used to
enjoy myself; farewell, beloved maidens, who used to sleep with me;
farewell, Father and Mother, you loved me a great deal: If my father asks you, he loves me so much; tell him that love takes me,
that the fault is not mine, for love and death no one can defy. Love
was so stubborn that its persistence vanquished me." With two
hundred of her maidens she went down to the sea; in thirty-five
ships Flérida would embark. At the sound of the sweet oars sleep
vanquished her; with the sound of the water Flérida woke up. She
cried from her eyes, from her mouth she said: "Oh, may God in
Heaven help me; what a great misfortunate is mine; I do not know
where I am being taken, even less where I will end up, if I am being
taken to France, or to Andaluzia, if I am being taken to England,
where I really belong." Luguardo had heard this; he was right next

to her: "Do not cry, my soul; do not cry, my life; you are being taken to France, to France, the well-beloved. If you have left rich gardens, better ones you shall find; if you are leaving dear maidens, better ones you shall find; if you are leaving rich houses, rich houses you shall find, with reddish-gold roofs painted in the Turkish style; their walls are of gold, the floors of fine silver, the locks of the door of seed pearls and precious stones. If you have left Father and Mother, Father and Mother you shall find; if you are leaving brothers and sisters, loving brothers and sisters-in-law you shall have." They were speaking these words when she got birth pains; on the lap of Don Duardos she gave birth to a boy. "Send her back; send her back, Mother; send her back whence she came." In a little reed boat back went the little girl.)

Although the Sephardic poem is remarkably faithful to the Vicentine original, it also changes it significantly. Only one version preserves Flérida's name (S2.1). Some merely refer to her as "la señora infanta" (the lady and princess; cf. 2.2), "la querida infanta" (beloved princess; 2.10–11), or "la niña" (the little girl; Martínez Ruiz 1963, no. 66), and others change "Flérida," which is an unusual name, to the adjective "ferida" (wound, wounded), thus implicitly stating that she has been wounded by love: "cuando la señora infanta / ferida ya se sentía" (when the lady and princess already felt wounded; 2.6); "cuando la señora infanta / de herida ya se partía" (when the lady and princess left because she was wounded; 2.3). One version takes matters even further, making the princess suffer from lovesickness: "cuando la señora infanta / enferma de amor se sentía" (when the lady and princess felt sick with love; 2.2). A version that begins by replacing her name with "querida infanta" (beloved princess) later refers to her as "reina Elena" (Queen Helen; 2.10). This is a substitution triggered by a ballad about Helen of Troy, *El robo de Elena* (The Abduction of Helen), which is popular among both the Eastern and the Western Sephardim. In the Moroccan versions, "París" lures "reina Elena" to a ship and sails off with her (CMP, F5). Although Flérida is not abducted, she also sails together with her lover.

Don Duardos's name is preserved more frequently (2.4–5, 2.8), but it is also changed to Don Alguardos (2.6), Don Luardo (2.7), and even to Don Fernando (2.1). One version begins by calling him Eduardo, but later refers to him as Don Duardos (2.5). In Larrea's rendition, the unnamed hero is one of two suitors, one of whom is a Moor: "cuando morito y el infante / de amores la requería" (when the little Moor and the prince sought her love; 1952, no. 157). This version then fails to specify with which of them the princess elopes. The oral tradition does at times take some surprising turns.

Verse 13, according to which Flérida goes to the seashore accompanied by one hundred maidens, appears only in another version (2.4). I included it because it echoes one verse of the Vicentine original: "Fuéronse a las galeras / que don Duardos tenía" (They went to the galleys that Don Duardos had; 28).

The number of ships is usually thirty-five (14), but one version changes it to twenty-five (2.8), and two versions reduce these numbers to just one ship (2.2; Larrea 1952, no. 157). The sound of rowing causes the princess to fall asleep, and the noise of the water later awakens her (15–16). In two versions, it is the singing of Frenchmen that either puts her to sleep (2.10; Martínez Ruiz 1963, no. 66) or awakens her (2.9; Martínez Ruiz 1963, no. 66), and there is one version in which singing monks disturb the girl's sleep (2.11). The presence of the Frenchmen was no doubt triggered by Flérida's subsequent mention of France as one of her unknown destinations (20). Three versions add that she wakes up very frightened: "Recordó despavorida / con un pavor ya tan grande" (She woke up in a fright, with such a great fright; 2.4; cf. 2.6, 2.11).

The princess then complains that she does not know if she is being taken to France, Andaluzia, or England, where she belongs (18–21). The reference to England, of course, reflects the hero's nationality, and the fact that he was supposed to be taking Flérida home with him. Some versions precede this complaint with Flérida's request for a scribe or scribes, so that her misfortune can be put into writing, presumably as a warning to others, even though the text does not say so explicitly. These versions make her realize right away that her elopement was a terrible mistake:

8   Venid aquí mis escribanos,   lo que aquí se escribanía.
       Escribid y yo notalda   la grande desdicha mía.   (2.8)

(Come here, my scribes, for what is to be written here. You write, and I will dictate my great misfortune.)

16   —Vení acá, mis escribanos,   daca aquí esa escribanía.
       Escribiré yo y notaré   esta desdicha la mía.   (2.7)

("Come here, my scribes, bring that writing here. I shall write and put down this misfortune of mine.")

This interpolated request was probably triggered by Flérida's sadness about not knowing where she was being taken in the Vicentine original: "¡Triste, no sé donde voy, / ni nadie me lo dezía!" (Woe is me; I know not where I go, nor does anyone tell me; 14). Here the word "triste" (woe is me; sad) can be interpreted to mean "misfortunate," paralleling the "desdicha" (misfortune) in the modern versions, but the reference to the scribes is also related to similar reactions on the part of characters who meet with disaster in popular balladry.[13]

Flérida invariably lists England, which also appears as Ingalaterra (S2.2), Ingalatierra (2.4), Inglaletierra (2.7), and "la india tierra" (the Indian land; 2.3), as one of her possible destinations. When the hero bothers to reveal where he is taking her, he mentions either France (2.2) or "Artalucía" (corrupted form for "Andaluzia"; 2.3).

The reddish-gold roofs painted in the Turkish manner (28) that Flérida is supposed to find in her new home correspond to Vicente's rooms with walls of fine Turkish gold (22). The only other echo of this gold is displaced to Flérida's farewell, in the version in which she says good-bye to black servants dressed in the Turkish style: "y adiós, mis ricos negritos, / vestidos a la turquía" (and farewell, my dear little blacks, dressed in the Turkish style; Martínez Ruiz 1963, no. 37c).

As Don Duardos finishes his reassurances, Flérida feels labor pains and deposits a baby boy on his lap (33–34). Some versions merely state that she goes back where she came from, implying that the hero loses interest in her right away (2.2, 2.4–6, 2.8–9, 2.11), but in others he is very explicit, asking his mother (2.3) and his knights (2.1, 2.7; Anahory-Librowicz 1988, no. 19) to send her back for him. In Anahory-Librowicz's version, he tells the princess that now she looks like a black woman to him: "Entre mis ojos luceros, / una negra paresía" (Before my shining eyes, a black woman you seem).

The boat in which the princess returns is usually made of reeds (2.1, 2.4–6, 2.8, 2.11; Martínez Ruiz 1963, no. 37c), but she also travels in a boat constructed with boards (2.7), shells (2.9), bedspreads (2.3), and even in a broken boat (2.2). For good measure, two versions add a proverb that compares wandering women to lost chicken: "la mujer y la gallina / por andar se perdería" (women and chicken get lost for wandering off; 2.11; Martínez Ruiz 1963, 37c).

A direct comparison between the synthetic version and its source will better display the differences already discussed and several others. The Roman numerals correspond to the narrative stages into which I divide Vicente's text afterward:

Gil Vicente's Text	Sephardic Versions
I. En el mes era de abril, de mayo antes un día,	Entrar quiere el mes de mayo y el de abril antes de un día,

2 quando los lirios y rosas
 muestran más su alegría,
 en la noche má serena
 que el cielo hazer podía,
4 quando la hermosa infanta
 Flérida ya se partía,
 en la huerta de su padre
 a los árboles dezía:
6 II. —Jamás, en quanto biviere,
 os veré tan sólo un día,
 ni cantar los ruiseñores
 en los ramos melodía.
8 Quédate a Dios, agua clara,
 quédate a Dios, agua fría,
 quedaos con Dios, mis flores,
 mi gloria que ser solía.

10 Voyme a tierras estrañas,
 pues ventura allá me guía.
 III. Si mi padre me buscare
 que grande bien me quería,
12 digan que el amor me lleva,
 que no fue la culpa mía:
 tal tema tomó comigo
 que me venció su porfía.

14 ¡Triste, no sé donde voy,
 ni nadie me lo dezía!—

IV. Allí habló don Duardos,
 bien oiréis lo que decía:
16 —No lloréis, señora infanta,
 no lloréis, mi alegría,
 que en los reinos de Inglaterra

 más claras aguas avía
18 y más hermosos jardines,

---

2 cuando las rosas y flores
 amuestran sus alegrías,

 cuando la señora infanta
 Flérida ya se partía.
4 De los sus ojos lloraba,
 de la su boca decía:

 —Adiós, adiós, aguas claras,
 adiós, adiós, aguas frías;
6 adiós, mis ricos vergeles,
 donde yo me me divertía;
 adiós, mis ricas donzellas,
 las que conmigo dormían;
8 adiós, mi padre y mi madre,
 los que a mí mucho querían.

 Si mi padre os preguntare,
 el que a mí mucho quería,
10 decidle que el amor me lleva,
 que la culpa no es mía,
12 Tanto porfió el amor
 que a mí venció su aporfía.—
17 De los sus ojos lloraba,
 de la su boca decía:
18 —¡Ay, válgame Dios del cielo,
 qué grande desdicha mía!,
 que no sé donde me llevan,
 ni menos donde yo iría,
20 si me llevan para Francia,
 o para la Andalucía,
 si me llevan a Inglaterra,
 donde yo pertenecía.
22 Oído lo había don Luguardo,
 que junto a ella estaría:
 —No lloredes vos, mi alma,
 no lloredes vos, mi vida;
24 para Francia, mi señora,
 a Francia la bien querida.

 Si ricos vergeles dejasteis,

y vuestros, señora mía.
Ternéis trezientas donzellas
de alta genelosía;
20 de plata son los palacios
para vuestra señoría,
de esmeraldas y jacintos
toda la tapecería,
22 las cámaras ladrilladas
de oro fino de Turquía.

26 mejores los hallarías;
si ricas doncellas dejas,
mejores las hallaríais;
si ricas casas dexates,
ricas casas hallarías,

28 los techos aleonados,
pintados a la Turquía;
las paredes son de oro,
los suelos de plata fina,
30 los cerrojos de la puerta
de aljófar y piedras finas.
Si padre y madre dexates,
suegro y suegra hallarías;
32 si hermanos y hermanas dejas,
ricos cuñados tendríais.—

. . . .

28 V. Fuéronse a las galeras
que don Duardos tenía:
cincuenta eran por cuenta;
todas van en compañía.
30 Al son de sus dulces remos
la infanta se adormecía

13 Con ciento de sus donzellas
a la mar se bajaría;
14 en treinta y cinco navíos
Flérida se embarcaría.
Al son de los dulces remos
el sueño la vencería;
16 con el ruido del agua
Flérida dispertaría.
33 Ellos en estas palabras,
los dolores la darían;
34 en la halda de don Duardos
un niño parido había.

en braços de don Duardos
que bien le pertenecía.
32 VI. Sepan quantos son nacidos
aquesta sentencia mía:
que contra la muerte y amor
nadie no tiene valía.

11 que al amor y a la muerte
naide los pone a porfía.
35 —Volve, volve, la mi madre,
vólvela donde venía.
36 Y en un barquito de cañas
la niña se volvería.

Translation:

I. It was in the month of
April,
one day before May,
2 when irises and roses
show more their beauty,

*The month of May wanted to
enter,
and it was April, one day before,
2 when roses and flowers
displayed their joy,

on the most peaceful night
that the Heavens could display,
4 when the beautiful princess
Flérida was departing.
In her father's garden
she was saying to the trees:
6 II. "Never, for as long as I live,
shall I see you even one day,
or hear in your branches
the melody of the nightingales.
8 Stay with God, clear water;
stay with God, cold water;
stay with God, my flowers,
which used to be my pride.

10 I am going to strange lands,
for fate guides me there.
III. If my father looks for me,
whose love for me is so great,
12 tell him that love takes me,
that the fault is not mine:
It was so stubborn with me
that its persistence vanquished.

14 Woe is me, I know not where
      I go,
nor does anyone tell me!"

IV. There spoke Don Duardos;
you will hear what he said:
16 "Do not cry, my lady and
      princess;
do not cry, my joy,
for in the Kingdom of England

the waters are even clearer,

when the lady and Princess
Flérida was about to depart.
4 She cried from her eyes,
from her mouth she said:

"Farewell, farewell, clear waters;
farewell, farewell, cold waters;
6 farewell, my beloved gardens,
where I used to enjoy myself;
farewell, beloved maidens,
who used to sleep with me;
8 farewell, Father and Mother;
you loved me a great deal:

If my father asks you,
he loves me so much,
10 tell him that love takes me,
that the fault is not mine,
12 Love was so stubborn
that its persistence vanquished
      me."
17 She cried from her eyes,
from her mouth she said:
18 "Oh, may God in Heaven help me;
what a great misfortunate is mine;
I do not know where I am being
      taken,
even less where I will end up;
20 if I am being taken to France,
or to Andaluzia,
if I am being taken to England,
where I really belong."
22 Luguardo had heard this;
he was right next to her:
"Do not cry, my soul;

do not cry, my life;
24 you are being taken to France,
to France, the well-beloved.

18 the gardens more beautiful,
and they are yours, my lady.
You will have three hundred
    maidens
of great rank.
20 The palaces for your ladyship
are of silver;
all the tapestry is
of emeralds and hyacinths;
22 the rooms have walls
of fine Turkish gold."

If you have left rich gardens,
better ones you shall find;
26 if you are leaving dear maidens,

better ones you shall find;
if you are leaving rich houses,
rich houses you shall find;

28 with reddish-gold roofs
painted in the Turkish style;
their walls are of gold,
the floors of fine silver,
30 the locks of the door
of seed pearls and precious stones.
If you have left Father and
    Mother,
Father and Mother you shall find;
32 if you are leaving brothers and
    sisters,
loving brothers and sisters-in-law
    you shall have."

. . . .
28 V. They went toward the
    galleys
that Don Duardos had:
They were fifty in all;
all of them departed together.
30 At the sweet sound of the oars
the princess fell asleep,

13 With two hundred of her maidens

she went down to the sea;
14 in thirty-five ships
Flérida would embark.
At the sound of the sweet oars
sleep vanquished her;
16 with the sound of the water
Flérida woke up.
33 They were speaking these words
when she got birth pains;
34 on the lap of Don Duardos
she gave birth to a boy.

in the arms of Don Duardos;
she belonged to him well.
32 VI. Let all those who have
    been born
know this maxim of mine:
In the face of death and love
no one has any recourse.

11 for love and death
no one can defy.
35 "Send her back; send her back,
Mother; send her back whence she
    came."
36 In a little reed boat
back went the little girl.

The division of the Vicentine original into six narrative stages helps us to understand its survival in the oral tradition. Verses 23–27, regarding a duel of Don Duardos with Primaleón and the suffering that Flérida had caused him at the time have been completely eliminated by the oral tradition, and understandably so, because the episode has nothing to do with the elopement that constitutes the central theme of the ballad.[14] For this reason, I decided to omit those verses from the six narrative stages into which I have divided the poem:

1. The season in which the action takes place   (1–5);
2. Flérida's farewell to her garden   (6–10);
3. The excuse for her father regarding the power of love and her misgivings   (11–14);
4. Don Duardos's reassurance, describing the water, gardens, maidens, and palaces that await her   (15–22);
5. Their departure in Don Duardos's galleys. Flérida falls asleep in his arms   (28–31);
6. Human beings' helplessness before death and love (32–33).

The Sephardic ballad preserves stage 1, but discards as superfluous the verse about the serenity of the night on which the action takes place (3). The verse that precedes the beginning of Flérida's farewell (5) is changed to "de los sus ojos lloraba" (she cried from her eyes) a weeping formula that is frequent in medieval epicry and balladry (Webber 1951, 198). In stage 2, Flérida's allusion to the nightingales (7) is eliminated, but her farewell is expanded, perhaps more reasonably, with allusions to her maidens and to the parents she is leaving behind. Stage 3 is left practically intact but, perhaps as a warning to young singers, Flérida's misgivings are expanded as well. Whereas in the original she merely complains that she does not know her destination, now she does not know whether she will end up in France, Andaluzia, or England. The reference to England is displaced for, in Vicente's text, it appears within Don Duardos's reply. In stage 4, rich homes replace the silver palaces that Flérida will find, and door locks encrusted with seed pearls and other precious stones replace the tapestries embroidered with emeralds and hyacinths (20). The Sephardic poem also expands the hero's reassurances: in her new home, Flérida's in-laws will be like parents to her, and her brothers-in-law will take the place of her brothers and sisters. Thus, once again, there is an emphasis on the importance of the family. Stage 5, which describes the departure, is at first retained, but then the modern ballad takes an unexpected turn. In the original, Flérida falls asleep in her lover's arms. Now she suddenly gives birth to a baby boy and deposits him on his lap. What begins as a transformation of a detail (arms > lap) becomes a rather surprising interpolation, and the hero loses all interest in his beloved from one moment to the next, sending her back home, and in a very fragile boat at that. Although the sixth and final stage regarding man's helplessness before death and love is preserved, the Sephardic ballad displaces it, putting it right after stage 3, where Flérida also mentions love, referring to its power in the excuse that she leaves for her father.

The oral transmission of this ballad, then, is characterized by phenomena that we may as well label as the vicissitudes of oral transmission, for they apply to other ballads as well. (1) Substitution is often observed with proper names, which can be exchanged for others with great ease, but at times some passages are replaced with verses and formulas which, although different, exercise essentially the same function. Substitution is also at work when (2) corruption takes place, as when Flérida's unusual name becomes "herida" (wound, wounded), or "Inglaterra" (England) is somehow transformed into "india tierra" (Indian land). (3) Condensation occurs when, although retained, a narrative unit or stage is either shortened or compressed by discarding some verses. (4) Elimination, on the other hand, discards stages that are regarded as superfluous but, of course in many instances it comes about because of forgetfulness. (5) Expansion occurs when an idea already present in the original is increased with additional, related data. It differs from (6) interpolation, which consists of completely new, interjected material. As observed especially with stage 6, (7) displacement, in which a passage is moved elsewhere within the ballad, is very frequent. Another common vicissitude of oral transmission is (8) the contamination with other text-types, but this phenomenon, which is usually triggered by thematic similarity, has barely affected the Sephardic *Flérida*; it was observed only in one version, which designates the heroine as *reina Elena* (Queen Helen), a change no doubt caused by the similarity of her situation to that of Helen of Troy in *El robo de Elena*.

Besides testifying to the conservatism of the Sephardic tradition, the Sephardic versions of *Flérida* also bear witness to the creative character of the oral tradition, which, no matter how conservative, does not restrict itself to the passive transmission of what it has inherited from the past, often introducing innovations in the process.[15] The displacement of stage 6, which brought the original to an end with a statement regarding the helplessness of men and women in the face of love, as if it were the same as death, was no doubt also motivated by the fact that Sephardic singers did not have much use for such an excuse, anyway. Clearly, they did not want their daughters singing a poem that seemed to justify and even glorify elopements. Hence the expansions that emphasize the importance of the family, and Flérida's return, alone, helpless, and dishonored at the end of the ballad. As Samuel G. Armistead and Joseph H. Silverman vehemently protest, this unexpected conclusion does irreparable damage to the poem, annihilating its beautiful, lyrical portrayal of idealized love: "De una espléndida evocación lírica del amor idealizado, según los textos antiguos, el romance ha pasado a ser portavoz de una didáctica barata, pesada y machacona" (From a splendid lyrical evocation of idealized love, as found in the early texts, the ballad has become the spokesperson for a cheap, heavy, and tiresome didacticism; 1977, 156). This is very true, but the conservative Sephardim were not about to encourage in their daughters notions of idealized love, much less elopements, which challenged parental authority, and changed the poem accordingly.

b. The Spanish Ballad

In Spain, *Flérida* seems to be exclusively Asturian, and is usually followed by contaminations with *El moro cautivo* (The Captive Moor; *Canta, Mouro* [Sing, oh Moor]; RPI, H4; CMP, H7) and *La Devota de la Virgen en el yermo* (*í–a*; The Girl Devoted to the Virgin in the Uninhabited Land; *A Devota do Rosário* [The Girl Devoted to the Rosary]; RPI, U45). I know of only four versions. The earliest, previously unedited rendition is located in the Menéndez Pidal Archive and was collected in 1860 by José Amador de los Ríos from the eighteen-year-old Micaela Díaz del Valle in Roza de Parres:

1.

	Tan alta iba la luna como el sol del mediodía,
2	cuando la querida infanta partir de Francia quería.
	De las huertas de su padre de esta manera decía:
4	—Adiós, adiós, agua clara, adiós, adiós, agua fría;
	adiós, damas y doncellas, con quien yo me divertía.
6	Si mis padres por mi lloran, de lo bien que me querían,
	digo que el amor me lleva y que la culpa no es mía,
8	que otras muchas de mi tiempo marido e hijos tenían.—
	Doce remos iban de oro, las lanchas de plata fina,
10	y al son de los doce remos la niña se va dormida.
	En el medio de la mar dispertó despavorida. . . .

(The moon was as high as the sun at noon, when the beloved princess wanted to leave France. In her father's gardens she spoke thus: "Farewell; farewell, clear water; farewell; farewell, cold water; farewell, ladies and maidens with whom I amused myself. If my parents cry because of their love for me, I say that love takes me and that the fault is not mine, for many others of my age already have a husband and children." Twelve oars were of gold, the launches of fine silver, and at the sound of the sweet oars the little girl fell asleep. In the middle of the sea she awoke in a fright.)

The second version, collected in Proaza, was first published by L. Giner Arivau in 1886, and subsequently reprinted by Marcelino Menéndez Pelayo. Unlike the other versions, it opens with *El moro cautivo* (1–3), but then it continues with *Flérida* and with the usual contaminations (*Moro, Devota*):

2.

4   De las damas y doncellas   la niña se despedía:
     —Adiós, damas y doncellas,   que andáis en mi compañía.
5   Y si os pregunta mi padre,   de lo bien que me quería,
     que él se ha tenido la culpa   que yo marche pa Turquía.—
8   A eso de la media noche,   cuando amanecer quería,
     marchan los enamorados   para el reino de Turquía.
10   En los brazos de Leonardo   la niña se adormecía. . . .
                    (Menéndez Pelayo 1945, 9: 266)

(To the ladies and maidens the little girl said farewell: "Farewell, ladies and maidens who keep me company. If my father asks you because of his love for me, he is the one to blame for my departure to Turkey." Around midnight, when dawn was about to break, the two lovers eloped to the Kingdom of Turkey. In the arms of Leonardo the little girl fell asleep.)

The third version, from Naveces (Castillón, Avilés), was collected in 1914; it opens with a refrain often used to conclude religious ballads:

3.

    ¡Nuestra Señora me valga,   *válgame Santa María!*
    Cuando la querida infanta   de Francia partir quería,
2   de las huertas de su padre   se anda dispidiendo un día:
     —Adiós, las fuentes del oro,   donde yo beber solía;
4   adiós, rosas y claveles,   las que el mi jardín tenía;
     adiós, damas y doncellas,   las de la mi compañía.

6   Si el rey mi padre pregunta   por el bien que me quería,
        diréis que el amor me lleva   y que la culpa no es mía,
8   que la culpa suya era,   que soltera me tenía.—
        Veinticinco embarcaciones   vinieron buscar la niña;
10   los navíos son de oro,   los remos de plata fina.
        Al son de los remecillos   la niña se adormecía;
12   en el medio de la mar   dispertó despavorida. . . .

                                              (Cid 1993, no. 15)

(*May Our Lady help me; may Holy Mary help me!* When the beloved princess wanted to leave France, she said farewell to her father's gardens one day: "Farewell, golden fountains where I used to drink; farewell, roses and carnations, those that were in my garden; farewell, ladies and maidens, those who kept me company. If the king my father asks because of his love for me, say that love takes me away and that the fault is not mine, that the fault is his, for having kept me single." Twenty-five vessels came to pick up the little girl; the ships were of gold, the oars of fine silver. At the sound of the little oars the little girl fell asleep; in the middle of the sea she woke up in a fright. . . .)

The fourth, previously unedited version, from Avilés, was collected by A. Gamoneda in 1914, and is also located at the Menéndez Pidal Archive:

4.

        Tan alta iba la luna   como el sol al mediodía,
2   cuando la señora en Francia   de Francia salir quería.
        De las huertas de su padre   se fue despidiendo un día:
4   —Adiós, rosas y claveles,   los que mi jardín tenía;
        adiós, damas y doncellas,   las de la mi compañía;
6   adiós, fuentes, las del oro,   donde yo beber solía.
        Si el mi padre por mí entroga,   por lo bien que me quería,
8   dile que el amor me lleva,   la culpa que no era mía.
        La culpa que era d'él,   que soltera me tenía.—
10   Veinticinco embarcaciones   vienen a buscar la niña;
        las cadenas son de oro,   los remos de plata fina.
12   Al son de los cuatro remos,   la niña se adormecía. . . .

(The moon was as high as the sun at noon when in France the lady from France wanted to leave. She said farewell to her father's gardens one day: "Farewell, roses and carnations, those that my garden has; farewell, ladies and maidens, those who kept me company; farewell, fountains, those of gold, where I used to drink. If my father asks my whereabouts because of his love for me, say that love takes me away; the fault is not mine. The fault is his, for having kept me single." Twenty-five vessels came to pick up the girl; their chains were of gold, their oars of fine silver. At the sound of the four oars the little girl fell asleep. . . .)

Since the contaminations that follow constitute an integral part of the poem, I will comment on them before resuming discussion of the part that corresponds to *Flérida*. The ballad continues with *El moro cautivo*, where a princess asks a captive Moor why he will not sing, and he replies that he cannot, because he is in irons. She frees him and they elope together. As they are about to arrive in his land, the princess wonders whether he is taking her as wife or as mistress. In Amador de los Ríos's previously unedited version (no. 1, *supra*), he reveals that he is taking her as a slave for his beautiful wife, adding that she will live in the stable and will be fed like his greyhound. The contamination with *Flérida*, of course, was triggered by the elopement motif:

12   —Por Dios te pido, Abelardo,   por Dios y Santa María,
        que me digas la verdad,   no me niegues la mentira:
14   si me llevas por esposa,   o me llevas por querida.—
        —Ni te digo la verdad,   ni te niego la mentira,
16   ni te llevo por esposa,   ni te llevo por querida,
        que te llevo por esclava   de una linda mujer mía,
18   para ponerte en la cuadra   donde el caballo comía,
        para darte de comer   de lo que el galgo comía.—

("By God I beg you, Abelardo, by God and the Holy Mary, that you tell me the truth, and don't deny the lie: If you are taking me as wife, or taking me as mistress." "I'm not telling you the truth, or denying the lie to you: I'm not taking you as wife; I'm not taking you as mistress; I'm taking you as slave for my beautiful wife, and to put you in the stable where my horse eats, and to give you as food the same I give to my greyhound.")

In the version from 1886 (no. 2), where the protagonists elope to Turkey, the princess wonders about the shining towers that she sees in the distance before asking whether she is being taken as a wife or as a girlfriend:

        —¿De quién son aquellas torres   que relucen en Turquía?
14   —Una era la del rey,   otra de doña María,
        otra es la de mi esposa,   de mi esposa Lazandría.
                                   (Menéndez Pelayo 1945, 9: 266)

("Whose are those towers that shine in Turkey?" "One belongs to the king, another to Doña María, another to my wife, my wife, Lazandría.")

These verses, which often appear in contamination with *El moro cautivo*, derive from the historical *Abenámar* (CMP, C5; RPI, C2):

> ¿Qué castillos son aquellos?   ¡Altos son y relucían!
> —El Alhambra era, señor,   y la otra la mezquita;
> los otros los Alixares,   labrados a maravilla.
> (Primavera, no. 78a)

("What castles are those? They are so tall and shiny!" "One is the Alhambra, sir, and the other is the mosque; the other ones, the Alixares, which are wondrously carved.")

Independent versions of *El moro cautivo* conclude when the princess prays to the Blessed Mother. She is miraculously returned home, and the treacherous Moor goes back to his cell (for two Spanish examples, see Pedrosa 1994–95, 69–70). The protagonists usually travel by land, however, which suggests that the action takes place in the Peninsula, during the Moorish occupation. Contrary to the version contaminated with *Flérida* that was just quoted, there is no mention of Turkey.

The other three Asturian versions of *Flérida* continue with verses that seem to belong to another ballad. Upon discovering what the Moor plans to do with her, the girl begins to pray and begs God and the Virgin for the boat to be lost at sea. A tempest begins and the sailors ask for her to be thrown into the water, but her abductor suggests that she be left on a rock instead:

> La niña, que aquesto oyó,   en oración se ponía. (Amador, v. 20)
> —Permita Dios de los cielos,   la Virgen Santa María,
> 20   que la mar se entorpeciese   y el barco pierda la guía.—
> Entre estas razones y otras   ya la mar se entorpecía.
> 22   Todos dicen a una voz: —¡Tiren al mar esa niña!—
> Arrespondiera Belardo,   que era el que menos valía:
> 24   —Arrimémosla a una peña,   que algún dios la valería.
> (Cid 1993, no. 15)

(Hearing this, the little girl began to pray. "May God in Heaven permit, and the Holy Virgin Mary, the sea to swell and the boat to lose its way." For these reasons and others the sea began to swell. All say with one voice: "Throw that girl into the sea!" Belardo answered, the least worthy of them all: "Let's leave her on a rock; some god may come to help her.")

These verses bring to mind the medieval story of the empress of Rome whose brother-in-law attempts to seduce her during her husband's absence on a pilgrimage to Jerusalem. When the emperor returns, his brother accuses the empress of attempting to commit adultery with him. In the version included by Alfonso X in the *Cantigas de Santa María* (Songs of Holy Mary; no. 5), the empress is handed over to a sailor in order to be drowned at sea:

> O maryeiro, poi-la ena barca meteu, ben come fol   110
> disse-lle que fezesse seu talan, e seria sa prol;
> mas ela diss'enton: "Santa Maria, de mi non te dol,
> neno teu Fillo de mi non se nenbra, como fazer sol?"
> Enton vẽo voz de ceo, que lle disse: "Tol
> tas mãos dela, se non, farey-te perecer."   115
> *Quenas coitas deste mundo ben quiser soffrer. . . .*
>
> Os maryeiros disseron enton: "Pois est'a Deus non praz,
> leixemo-la sobr'aquesta pena, u pod'aver assaz
> de coita e d'affan e pois morte, u outra ren non jaz,
> ca, se o non fezermos, en mal ponto vimos seu solaz."   120
> (Alfonso X 1959–72, 1: no. 5)

(Having put her in the boat, the sailor, like a fool, told her to do what he wanted, and that it would be to her advantage, but then she said: "Holy Mary, if you do not feel sorry for me, or your Son fails to remember me, what can I do, being alone?" Then there came a voice from Heaven, which said to him: "Take your hands away from her; if not, I will make you perish." *Whoever the afflictions of this world wishes to endure well. . . .* The sailors said: "Since it does not please God, let us leave her on this rock, where she can undergo plenty of suffering, anxiety, and then die; there is nothing else there, and, if we do not do this, we will pay dearly for taking pleasure from her.")

In a note to a second, handwritten copy of the version sent to him by Amador de los Ríos, Ramón Menéndez Pidal refers to A. Wallensköld's study of this story (1907), and adds: "Al episodio fundamental de la mujer forzada por el capitán y salvado su honor por una tormenta, se une en algunas versiones el detalle de depositarla en una roca donde la socorre la Virgen. . . . En el *Patrañuelo* y en *La peregrina doctora* (versiones españolas del cuento de la emperatriz) falta el episodio del marinero" (To the fundamental episode of the

woman being forced by the captain, and whose honor is saved by a
storm, some versions add the detail of placing her on a rock where
the Virgin comes to her assistance. . . . The *Patrañuelo* and *La peregrina doctora* [Span. versions of the story of the empress] lack the
episode of the sailor).[16] This story became very popular in Portugal
and Brazil, where it is known as *A Imperatriz Porcina* (The Emper-
ess Porcina).[17] If the coincidences with the medieval story are not
fortuitous, what we have here is a fragment of a Spanish ballad
which, as far as I know, has not been identified elsewhere.

The poem then concludes with *La devota de la Virgen en el
yermo*, in which the Virgin takes the king's daughter (or a shep-
herdess), who is very devoted to her, to live in some uninhabited
mountains. A dove brings her food and water. Seven years later the
Virgin appears to the girl and asks her if she wants to be married or
to become a nun. The girl chooses the latter:

	Allí estuviera siete años	en sin ver alma nacida;
26	al cabo de los siete años	bajó la Virgen María,
	y si no, una palombita,	que de comer la traía;
28	en el pico lleva el agua	y en las alas la comida.
	Entre estas razones y otras	bajó la Virgen María:
30	—¿Niña, tú quieres ser monja,	tú quieres ser monja, niña?
	Si te quieres poner monja,	convento te buscaría,
32	y si te quieres casar	yo marido te daría.
	—Monja, monja, la señora,	monja de Santa María.

(Cid 1993, no. 15)

(She stayed there for seven years without seeing one born soul; at
the end of seven years the Virgin came down and, if not, a little
dove brought her food to eat. She carried the water on her beak and
the food on her wings. For these reasons and for others down came
the Virgin Mary: "Girl, do you want to be a nun? Do you want to be
a nun, girl? If you want to become a nun, I will find you a convent,
and if you wish to marry, I will give you a husband." "A nun, my
Lady, a nun, a nun of Holy Mary.")

The contamination of *Flérida* with *El moro cautivo*, then, was
triggered by thematic similarity, since both ballads deal with elopements. In one version, *El moro cautivo* retains the contamination
with *Abenámar*, which is frequent in independent versions of that
ballad. The verses in which the princess prays to God and the Virgin
for the boat to be lost at sea may perpetuate a medieval legend; they
were added to the poem because, in *El moro cautivo*, the princess

also prays to the Blessed Mother for help. In its turn, this triggered the contamination with *La devota*, in which the Virgin takes a princess who is devoted to her to some uninhabited mountains. Contaminations such as this, of course, are first brought about by poor memory but, in time, they become traditional, creating what amounts to a new poem (see Silverman 1979).

A synthetic version combining the narrative elements that appear in the portion of this poem that corresponds to *Flérida* will enable us better to understand how that ballad has survived in the Spanish tradition. I indicate, in parenthesis, which of the four versions just presented I have used as sources:

	*Tan alta iba la luna como el sol del mediodía, (1.1)
2	Cuando la querida infanta de Francia partir quería. (3.1)
	De las huertas de su padre de esta manera decía:
4	—Adiós, adiós, agua clara, adiós, adiós, agua fría; (1.3–4)
	adiós, fuentes, las del oro, donde yo beber solía; (4.6)
6	adiós, rosas y claveles, las que el mi jardín tenía;
	adiós, damas y doncellas, las de la mi compañía.
8	Si el rey mi padre pregunta por el bien que me quería,
	diréis que el amor me lleva y que la culpa no es mía,
10	que la culpa suya era, que soltera me tenía, (3.4–8)
	que otras muchas de mi tiempo marido e hijos tenían.— (1.8)
12	Veinticinco embarcaciones vienen a buscar la niña;
	las cadenas son de oro, los remos de plata fina. (4.10–11)
14	Al son de los remecillos la niña se adormecía;
	en el medio de la mar dispertó despavorida. (3.11–12)

(The moon was as high as the sun at noon, when the beloved princess wanted to leave France. In her father's gardens she spoke thus: "Farewell; farewell, clear water; farewell; farewell, cold water; farewell, fountains, those of gold, where I used to drink; farewell, roses and carnations, those that were in my garden; farewell, ladies and maidens, those who kept me company. If the king my father asks because of his love for me, say that love takes me away and that the fault is not mine, that the fault is his, for having kept me single, for many others of my age already have a husband and children." Twenty-five vessels came to pick up the little girl; their chains were of gold, their oars of fine silver. At the sound of the little oars the little girl fell asleep; in the middle of the sea she woke up in a fright.)

It is readily apparent that, with its 15 verses, the Spanish ballad preserves much less of Vicente's poem than its Sephardic coun-

terpart (36 verses). A comparison between the Spanish *Flérida* and
its source will show much more clearly what has happened:

Gil Vicente's Version		*Spanish Version*	
	I. En el mes era de abril,		*Tan alta iba la luna
	de mayo antes un día,		como el sol del mediodía,
2	quando los lirios y rosas		
	muestran más su alegría,		
	en la noche má serena		
	que el cielo hazer podía,		
4	quando la hermosa infanta	2	Cuando la querida infanta
	Flérida ya se partía,		de Francia partir quería.
	en la huerta de su padre		De las huertas de su padre
	a los árboles dezía:		de esta manera decía:
6	II. —Jamás, en quanto biviere,		
	os veré tan sólo un día,		
	ni cantar los ruiseñores		
	en los ramos melodía.		
8	Quédate a Dios, agua clara,	4	—Adiós, adiós, agua clara,
	quédate a Dios, agua fría,		adiós, adiós, agua fría;
			adiós, fuentes, las del oro,
			donde yo beber solía;
	quedaos con Dios, mis flores,	6	adiós, rosas y claveles,
	mi gloria que ser solía.		las que el mi jardín tenía;
			adiós, damas y doncellas,
			las de la mi compañía.
10	Voyme a tierras estrañas,		
	pues ventura allá me guía.		
	III. Si mi padre me buscare	8	Si el rey mi padre pregunta
	que grande bien me quería,		por el bien que me quería,
12	digan que el amor me lleva,		diréis que el amor me lleva
	que no fue la culpa mía:		y que la culpa no es mía,
		10	que la culpa suya era,
			que soltera me tenía,
			que otras muchas de mi tiempo
			marido e hijos tenían.—
	tal tema tomó comigo		
	que me venció su porfía.		
14	¡Triste, no sé donde voy,		
	ni nadie me lo dezía!—		
	IV. Allí habló don Duardos,		
	bien oiréis lo que decía:		
16	—No lloréis, señora infanta,		
	no lloréis, mi alegría,		

que en los reinos de Inglaterra
más claras aguas avía
18 y más hermosos jardines,
y vuestros, señora mía.
Ternéis trezientas donzellas
de alta genelosía;
20 de plata son los palacios
para vuestra señoría,
de esmeraldas y jacintos
toda la tapecería,
22 las cámaras ladrilladas
de oro fino de Turquía.
. . . .
28 V. Fuéronse a las galeras
que don Duardos tenía:
cincuenta eran por cuenta;   12 Veinticinco embarcaciones
todas van en compañía.   vienen a buscar la niña;
                                              las cadenas son de oro,
                                              los remos de plata fina.
30 Al son de sus dulces remos   14 Al son de los remecillos
la infanta se adormecía   la niña se adormecía;
                                              en el medio de la mar
                                              dispertó despavorida.
en braços de don Duardos
que bien le pertenecía.
32 VI. Sepan quantos son nacidos
aquesta sentencia mía:
que contra la muerte y amor
nadie no tiene valía.

Translation:

I. It was in the month of April,   The moon was as high
one day before May,   as the sun at noon,
2 when irises and roses
show more their beauty,
in the most peaceful night
that the Heavens could display,
4 when the beautiful princess   2 when the beloved princess
Flérida was departing.   wanted to leave France.
In her father's garden   In her father's gardens
she was saying to the trees: she said thus:
6 II. "Never, for as long as I live,
shall I see you even one day,
nor hear in your branches

the melody of the nightingales.
8 Stay with God, clear water;
stay with God, cold water;

stay with God, my flowers,
which used to be my pride.

10 I am going to strange lands,
for fate guides me there.
III. If my father looks for me,
whose love for me is so great,
12 tell him that love takes me,
that the fault is not mine:

4 "Farewell; farewell, clear water;
farewell; farewell, cold water;
farewell, fountains, those of gold,
where I used to drink;
6 farewell, roses and carnations,
those that were in my garden;
farewell, ladies and maidens,
those who kept me company.

8 If the king my father asks
because of his love for me,
say that love takes me away
and that the fault is not mine,
10 that the fault is his,
for having kept me single,
for many others of my age
already have a husband and
children."

It was so stubborn with me
that its persistence vanquished.
14 Woe is me, I know not where I go;
nor does anyone tell me!"
IV. There spoke Don Duardos,
you will hear what he said:
16 "Do not cry, my lady and princess;
do not cry, my joy,
for in the Kingdom of England
the waters are even clearer,
18 the gardens more beautiful,
and they are yours, my lady.
You will have three hundred maidens
of great rank.
20 The palaces for your ladyship
are of silver;
all the tapestry is
of emeralds and hyacinths;
22 the rooms have walls
of fine Turkish gold."
. . . .
28 V. They went toward the galleys
that Don Duardos had:
They were fifty in all;
all of them departed together.

12 Twenty-five vessels came
to pick up the little girl;
their chains were of gold,

their oars of fine silver.

30 At the sweet sound of the oars   14 At the sound of the little oars
the princess fell asleep,   the little girl fell asleep;
                                             in the middle of the sea
                                             she woke up in a fright.
in the arms of Don Duardos,
she belonged to him well.
32 VI. Let all those who have been born
know this maxim of mine:
Before death and love
no one has any recourse.

Vicente's beautiful opening lines about the season in which the action takes place (stage 1) have been compressed to a mere formula designed to indicate the time of day: the moon is as high in the sky as the sun is at noon (1). This verse is used to begin the early *Romance de Valdouinos* (Ballad of Valdevinos; Nucio 1945, 194v.) and *El conde Alemán y la reina* (Count Alemán and the Queen; *Conde da Alemanha* [The German Count]; Nucio 1967, 256), some modern Spanish and Portuguese versions of *La pobreza de la Virgen recién parida* (The Poverty of the Virgin After Having Just Given Birth; *Noite de Natal* [Christmas Night], *í–a* [RPI, U1]; see González 1994, nos. 7.1, 57.8; TM, nos. 943–76), as well as modern Spanish versions of *Belardo y Valdovinos* (Petersen et al. 1982, nos. 10.1–5). It would be possible to find additional examples, but this suffices to show that the formula is common in the oral tradition.

The farewell (stage 2) is expanded with a reference to the golden fountains where Flérida used to drink (5). The roses and carnations mentioned (6) match the princess's farewell to her flowers in the original, but they may also reflect the irises and roses in stage 1, thus constituting a case of displacement. The farewell to the maidens, which is absent from Vicente's poem, parallels the Sephardic ballad. The heroine now leaves from France, probably because, being unusual, her name, Flérida, became "Francia" through oral transmission.

Stage 3, Flérida's excuse to her father regarding the power of love, is expanded. Now she also blames him for keeping her single, when others of her age already have husbands and children (10–11). This situation brings to mind *El conde Alarcos* (Count Alarcos; CMP, L1; RPI, L1), whose protagonist complains to her father, the king, in a similar manner: "todas do meu tempo se casam, / só eu fico solteirinha" (all of my age get married; I alone remain single; TM, no. 339); "Mosas qu'eran de quince años, / marido e hijos tenían" (Fifteen-year-old girls already have husbands and children; Armistead and Silverman 1981b, no. 27). Since I was unable to find textual Spanish parallels—the examples just given are Portuguese and Sephardic—it is impossible to claim that a contamination with *Alarcos* is definitely involved, but the idea is the same. Note that, in the Spanish poem, the princess does not express any misgivings at this point. The Sephardic ballad, on the other hand, emphasizes her fears considerably, expanding them in relation to the original.

Since Flérida no longer seems to have any misgivings, it stands to reason that stage 4, in which Don Duardos reassures her, should also be omitted. As we recall, the Sephardic poem preserves this stage fairly well, expanding it with references to the new family that Flérida will find at her destination.

Stage 5, the departure in Don Duardos's galleys, is well preserved, with a reference to their number, which it cuts in half, and to the rowing sound that puts Flérida to sleep. As we saw, the Sephardic ballad displaces this stage, placing it right after Flérida's excuse for her father (stage 3) and the statement regarding helplessness before death and love (stage 6), which the Sephardic poem also displaces. This last stage is absent from the Spanish ballad, but the concluding verse, in which the princess awakens terrified, parallels the Sephardic versions in which Flérida "recordó despavorida, / con un pavor ya tan grande" (woke up in a fright, with such a great fright; S2.4; cf. 2.6, 2.11).

Whereas the Sephardic ballad preserves all six stages of *Flérida*, albeit in a different sequence (1, 2, 3, 6, 5, 4), the Spanish poem compresses the opening verses of stage 1 to a one-verse formula, eliminating stages 4 and 6. Nevertheless, the two ballads coincide on two important points absent from their source: the farewell to the maidens and Flérida's terror upon awakening after falling asleep at sea. This suggests that these two details must go far back in time.

The Sephardic ballad concludes with the addition regarding the birth of a baby during the voyage, Don Duardos's sudden loss of interest in Flérida, and her immediate return. The Spanish poem continues with a contamination from *El moro cautivo* in which the princess, upon discovering the fate that awaits her, prays to the Virgin for deliverance, and ends with a contamination from *La devota de la Virgen* that places her under the Virgin's protection. This, of course, amounts to a new, completely different poem.

As we saw, the Sephardic ballad undermines Vicente's portrayal of idealized love by emphasizing the role of the family and by changing the conclusion, in which a dishonored Flérida is abandoned and forced to return home alone right after giving birth to a boy. This reflects the views of a very conservative community, with no toleration for unsanctioned amorous entanglements, and even less for the elopements to which they could lead. The Spanish ballad is quite different in this respect. In its only expansion regarding the family the princess displays an attitude of rebellion, blaming her father for not having married her off sooner. In other words, she justifies the serious step that she is about to take. Her elopement is punished when she discovers the fate that awaits her, but this is achieved through a contamination and not with an addition specifically created for the part that corresponds to *Flérida*, as in the Sephardic poem. After eloping and being subsequently abandoned while still single in a conservative Iberian society, a young lady would be automatically disgraced and ineligible for marriage but, whereas the Sephardic Flérida returns home dishonored without any hope in the future, her Spanish counterpart is rescued by the Virgin. She meets with forgiveness and salvation. Consequently, the Spanish ballad ends in a positive note, reflecting a Christian society which, although conservative, would seem to be more liberal, understanding, and tolerant in such matters.

The two details absent from Vicente's text that the Sephardic and the Spanish ballads have in common—the farewell to the maidens and Flérida's terror upon awakening at sea—, I repeat, must go far back in time. Luis Vélez de Guevara (1579–1644) used in one of his plays, *El príncipe viñador*, a version that includes ample evidence of oral transmission, proving that *Flérida* was traditional during the seventeenth century:

	Por el mes hera de Abril primero de Mayo un día,
2	quando la hermosa infanta Flérida ya se partía;
	de las güertas de su padre a los árboles deçía:
4	—Adiós, adiós, aguas claras, adiós, adiós, aguas frías,
	adiós, flores, adiós, plantas, mi plaçer que ser solía;
6	adiós, dueñas y doncellas, las cosas que más quería,
	adiós, palaçios y rexas, adiós, salas de oro ricas,
8	que ya mientras yo viviere no os pienso ver sólo un día.
	Si mi padre os preguntare por hija dél tan querida,
10	deçid quel amor me lleva, que la culpa no fue mía.—
	—Calléis, infanta, calléis, calléis, vida de mi vida,
12	que en el reino de Navarra ricos palaçios avía;
	las salas encamaradas, labradas a maravilla;
14	las paredes heran de oro, los techos de plata fina;
	condesas ay y marquesas para donçellas que os sirvan;

<pre>
16   de oro son mesas y camas,   de esmeraldas las vagillas;
      muchas insines ciudades,   muchos castillos y villas,
18   y este coraçón que es vuestro,   que es mayor riqueça en cifra.
      Vamos, que el luçero viene   denunçiando el alva fría,
20   porque quando nasca el sol,   tenga a los vuestros enbidia.
                              (R. Menéndez Pidal 1933, 497–98)
</pre>

(It was in the month of April, the first of May in one day, when the beautiful princess Flérida was departing; in her father's gardens she was saying to the trees: "Farewell; farewell, clear waters; farewell; farewell, cold waters; farewell, flowers; farewell, plants, which used to be my pleasure; farewell, ladies and maidens, things that I loved most; farewell, palaces and railings; farewell, rich golden salons, for as long as I live I do not think I shall see you even one day. If my father asks you for his beloved daughter, tell him that love takes me, that the fault was not mine." "Be silent, princess; be silent; be silent, oh life of mine, for in the Kingdom of Navarre there are rich palaces; their salons are full of grain and fruit, with wondrous work; their walls are of gold, the roofs of fine silver. There you will find countesses and marquises to serve you as maidens; tables and beds are of gold, the dishes of emeralds. There you will find many famous cities, many castles and towns, and this heart that belongs to you, and is worth even more. Let us go, for Venus appears, announcing the cold dawn, so that, upon being born, the sun will envy the brightness of your eyes.")

A detailed comparison between Vicente and Guevara's texts will reveal several signs of oral transmission:

Gil Vicente Version	*Vélez de Guevara's Version*
I. En el mes era de abril,	Por el mes hera de Abril
de mayo antes un día,	primero de Mayo un día,
2 quando los lirios y rosas	
muestran más su alegría,	
en la noche má serena	
que el cielo hazer podía,	
4 quando la hermosa infanta	2 quando la hermosa infanta
Flérida ya se partía,	Flérida ya se partía;
en la huerta de su padre	de las güertas de su padre
a los árboles dezía:	a los árboles deçía:
6 II. —Jamás, en quanto biviere,	8 que ya mientras yo viviere
os veré tan sólo un día,	no os pienso ver sólo un día.
ni cantar los ruiseñores	
en los ramos melodía.	

8   Quédate a Dios, agua clara,
     quédate a Dios, agua fría,
     quedaos con Dios, mis flores,
     mi gloria que ser solía.

4   —Adiós, adiós, aguas claras,
     adiós, adiós, aguas frías,
     adiós, flores, adiós, plantas,
     mi plaçer que ser solía;
6   adiós, dueñas y doncellas,
     las cosas que más quería,
     adiós, palaçios y rexas,
     adiós, salas de oro ricas,

10   Voyme a tierras estrañas,
     pues ventura allá me guía.
     III. Si mi padre me buscare
     que grande bien me quería,
12   digan que el amor me lleva,
     que no fue la culpa mía:
     tal tema tomó comigo
     que me venció su porfía.
14   ¡Triste, no sé donde voy,
     ni nadie me lo dezía!—
     IV. Allí habló don Duardos,
     bien oiréis lo que decía:
16   —No lloréis, señora infanta,
     no lloréis, mi alegría,
     que en los reinos de Inglaterra
     más claras aguas avía
18   y más hermosos jardines,
     y vuestros, señora mía.
     Ternéis trezientas donzellas
     de alta genelosía;
20   de plata son los palacios
     para vuestra señoría,
     de esmeraldas y jacintos
     toda la tapecería,
22   las cámaras ladrilladas
     de oro fino de Turquía.

     Si mi padre os preguntare
     por hija dél tan querida,
10   deçid quel amor me lleva,
     que la culpa no fue mía.

     —Calléis, infanta, calléis,
     calléis, vida de mi vida,
12   que en el reino de Navarra

15   condesas ay y marquesas
     para donçellas que os sirvan;
12b ricos palaçios avía;

13   las salas encamaradas,
     labradas a maravilla;
14   las paredes heran de oro,
     los techos de plata fina;
16   de oro son mesas y camas,
     de esmeraldas las vagillas;
     muchas insines ciudades,
     muchos castillos y villas,
18   y este coraçón que es vuestro,
     que es mayor riqueça en cifra.
     Vamos, que el luçero viene
     denunçiando el alva fría,
20   porque quando nasca el sol,
     tenga a los vuestros enbidia.

....
28   V. Fuéronse a las galeras
      que don Duardos tenía:
      cincuenta eran por cuenta;
      todas van en compañía.
30   Al son de sus dulces remos
      la infanta se adormecía
      en braços de don Duardos
      que bien le pertenecía.
32   VI. Sepan quantos son nacidos
      aquesta sentencia mía:
      que contra la muerte y amor
      nadie no tiene valía.

Translation:

I. It was in the month of April,   It was in the month of April,
    one day before May,   the first of May in one day,
2 when irises and roses
    show more their beauty,
    on the most peaceful night
    that the Heavens could display,
4 when the beautiful princess   2 when the beautiful princess
    Flérida was departing.   Flérida was departing;
    In her father's garden   in her father's gardens
    she was saying to the trees: she was saying to the trees:
6 II. "Never, for as long as I live,   8 for as long as I live
    shall I see you even one day,   I do not think I shall see you
                                               even one day.

    nor hear in your branches
    the melody of the nightingales.
8 Stay with God, clear water;   4 "Farewell, farewell, clear waters;
    stay with God, cold water;   farewell, farewell, cold waters;
    stay with God, my flowers,   farewell, flowers, farewell, plants,
    which used to be my pride.   which used to be my pleasure;
                                         6 farewell, ladies and maidens,
                                             things that I loved most;
                                             farewell, palaces and railings;
                                             farewell, rich golden salons,

10 I am going to strange lands,
    for fate guides me there.
    III. If my father looks for me,   If my father asks you
    whose love for me is so great,   for his beloved daughter,
12 tell him that love takes me,   10 tell him that love takes me,
    that the fault is not mine: that the fault was not mine."

It was so stubborn with me
that its persistence vanquished.

14 Woe is me; I know not where I go;
nor does anyone tell me!"

IV. There spoke Don Duardos;
you will hear what he said:

16 "Do not cry, my lady and princess;
do not cry, my joy,
for in the Kingdom of England
the waters are even clearer,

18 the gardens more beautiful,
and they are yours, my lady.
You will have three hundred
   maidens
of great rank.

20 The palaces for your ladyship
are of silver;
all the tapestry is
of emeralds and hyacinths;

22 the rooms have walls

of fine Turkish gold."

"Be silent, princess; be silent;
be silent, oh life of mine,

12 for in the Kingdom of Navarre

15 there you will find countesses
and marquises
to serve you as maidens;

12*b*   there are rich palaces;

13 their salons are full of grain and
   fruit,
with wondrous work;

14 their walls are of gold,
the roofs of fine silver.

16 Tables and beds are of gold,
the dishes of emeralds.
There you will find many famous
   cities,
many castles and towns,

18 and this heart that belongs to you,
and is worth even more.
Let us go, for Venus appears,
announcing the cold dawn,

20 so that, upon being born,
the sun will envy the brightness
   of your eyes."

. . . .

28 V. They went toward the galleys
that Don Duardos had:
They were fifty in all;
all of them departed together.

30 At the sweet sound of the oars
the princess fell asleep,
in the arms of Don Duardos;
she belonged to him well.

32 VI. Let all those who have been born
    know this maxim of mine:
    In the face of death and love
    no one has any recourse.

   The action takes place on the last day of April, just before the
beginning of May, but, like the modern Sephardic versions, Guevara's opening verse does not make much sense, and there are
compressions, eliminations, expansions, displacements, and substitutions that could arise only through prolonged transmission.
   Having set the time for the action in that brief first verse, the
ballad goes right to the one that mentions Flérida's departure (4).
Verses 2–3, 7, 10, 13–15, 17b–18, 20b–21, and 28–33 are eliminated.
Displacement is seen in verses 8, 12b, and 15, which have been
moved elsewhere. In verses 12a and 15, the references to Navarre
and countesses and marquises replace England and highborn ladies
in the original. Don Duardos's reassurances are greatly expanded.
Even though unique to this version, the numerous cities, castles,
and towns that Flérida will find in her exile could have been traditional; they fit well within the riches that the ballad enumerates at
this point. That is not the case with the verses that follow (18–20),
however. Don Duardos's reference to his own heart and his gallant
comparison of Flérida's eyes to the morning star when it is at its
brightest, just before dawn, are clearly learned. Vélez de Guevara
eliminates Flérida's embarkation and the remainder of the ballad
because he does not need it for his purposes, but there is little doubt
that he knew them.
   In addition to the signs of oral transmission just listed, Vélez de
Guevara's version coincides with the modern tradition in important
details. (a) The action takes place on the last day of April, just before
the beginning of May, but, like the modern Sephardic versions, Guevara's opening verse does not make much sense. (b) The elimination
of verses 2–3 coincides with the ballad's modern Asturian counterparts. (c) As Ramón Menéndez Pidal pointed out (1933, 498), the interpolated verse where Flérida says good-bye to her maidens (6)
parallels the modern Sephardic and Asturian renditions. (d) This
also applies to the replacement of the original's "buscare" (to look for;
11) with "preguntar" (to ask for). (e) The replacement of "no lloréis"
(do not cry; 16) with the more direct "calléis" (be silent) also occurs in
one Azorean version (R. Menéndez Pidal 1933, 498–99; see Braga
1869, no. 56). (f) Don Duardos's enumeration of the rich rooms and
roofs (or ceilings; the Span. word means both, and the context is not

very clear) of the palaces that Flérida will find overseas (13–14) coincides with the Moroccan ballad (R. Menéndez Pidal 1933, 498).

In sum, Vélez de Guevara's rendition proves that *Flérida* was traditional in the seventeenth century, matching several of the features found in its modern counterparts. The ballad probably begun to be sung soon after the performance of the play in 1525, however. There is no way to prove this conclusively, but an earlier, defective, incomplete version published in a 1572 *pliego suelto* documents that it was traditional during the sixteenth century:

	En el mes era de Abril, de mayo antes vn día,
2	quando los lirios y rosas muestran más su alegría,
	en la noche más serena que el cielo poder hazía,
4	quando la hermosa infanta Flérida ya se partía,
	en el huerto de su padre a los árboles dezía:
6	—Quedaos a dios, aguas frías, mi gloria que ser solía,
	jamás en quanto biuiere os veré tan sólo vn día:
8	voyme a tierras estrañas, pues ventura allá me guía.
	Si mi padre preguntare, que grande bien me quería,
10	digan quel amor me lleua y no fue la culpa mía.
	¡Triste, no sé donde voy, ni nadie no me lo diga!
12	Allí hablara don Duardos: —No lloréys, mi alegría,
	quen los reynos de Inglaterra más claras aguas auía,
14	y más hermosos jardines que vuestros, Señora mía.
	De plata son los palacios para vuestra Señoría,
16	de Esmeraldas y Jacintos toda la tapicería,
	las cámaras ladrilladas de oro fino de Turquía,
18	con letreros esmaltados que tienen la vida mía
	[. . . . .] que distes en aquel día
20	quando con Primaleón fuertemente combatía.
	¡Señora, vos lo matastes, que y[o] a él no lo temía!

(Pliegos . . . Catalunya 1976, 2: 302–3)

(It was in the month of April, one day before May, when irises and roses show more their beauty, on the most peaceful night that the Heavens could display, when the beautiful princess Flérida was departing. In her father's garden she was saying to the trees: "Stay with God, cold waters, which used to be my pride; never, for as long as I live, shall I see you even one day. I am going to strange lands, for fortune guides me there. If my father asks for me, whose love for me is so great, tell him that love takes me, that the fault was not mine. Woe is me; I know not where I go, and let not anyone tell me." There spoke Don Duardos: "Do not cry, my joy, for in the Kingdom of England the waters are even clearer, and the gardens more beautiful than yours, my lady. The palaces for your ladyship are of silver, all the tapestry is of emeralds and hyacinths, the rooms have walls of fine Turkish gold, and enameled signs that contain my life, [. . .] which you gave that day, when, with Primaleón I fiercely fought. My lady, you killed him, for him I did not fear!")

I must once again place this version next to the original in order to show clearly what happened. I have put the most significant lexical variants in italics:

Gil Vicente's Version		*Pliego suelto*	
	I. En el mes era de abril,		En el mes era de Abril,
	de mayo antes un día,		de mayo antes vn día,
2	quando los lirios y rosas	2	quando los lirios y rosas
	muestran más su alegría,		muestran más su alegría,
	en la noche má serena		en la noche más serena
	que el cielo hazer podía,		que el cielo *poder hazía*,
4	quando la hermosa infanta	4	quando la hermosa infanta
	Flérida ya se partía,		Flérida ya se partía,
	en la huerta de su padre		en *el huerto* de su padre
	a los árboles dezía:		a los árboles dezía:
6	II. —Jamás, en quanto biviere,	7	jamás en quanto biuiere
	os veré tan sólo un día,		os veré tan sólo vn día:
	ni cantar los ruiseñores		
	en los ramos melodía.		
8	Quédate a Dios, agua clara,		
	quédate a Dios, agua fría,	6	—*Quedaos* a dios, *aguas frías*,
	quedaos con Dios, mis flores,		
	mi gloria que ser solía.	6*b*	mi gloria que ser solía,
10	Voyme a tierras estrañas,	8	voyme a tierras estrañas,
	pues ventura allá me guía.		pues ventura allá me guía.
	III. Si mi padre me buscare		Si mi padre *preguntare*,
	que grande bien me quería,		que grande bien me quería,
12	digan que el amor me lleva,	10	digan quel amor me lleua
	que no fue la culpa mía:		y no fue la culpa mía.
	tal tema tomó comigo		
	que me venció su porfía.		
14	¡Triste, no sé donde voy,		¡Triste, no sé donde voy,
	ni nadie me lo dezía!—		ni nadie *no me lo diga*!
	IV. Allí habló don Duardos,	12	Allí *hablara* don Duardos:
	bien oiréis lo que decía:		
16	—No lloréis, señora infanta,		
	no lloréis, mi alegría,		—No lloréys, mi alegría,
	que en los reinos de Inglaterra		quen los reynos de Inglaterra
	más claras aguas avía		más claras aguas auía,

18 y más hermosos jardines,
y vuestros, señora mía.
Ternéis trezientas donzellas
de alta genelosía;
20 de plata son los palacios
para vuestra señoría,
de esmeraldas y jacintos
toda la tapecería,
22 las cámaras ladrilladas
de oro fino de Turquía,
con letreros esmaltados
que cuentan la vida mía:
24 cuentan los bivos dolores
que me distes aquel día,
quando con Primaleón
fuertemente combatía.
26 ¡Señora, vos me matastes,
que yo a él no lo temía!
Sus lágrimas consolava
Flérida, que esto oía.
28 V. Fuéronse a las galeras
que don Duardos tenía:
cincuenta eran por cuenta;
todas van en compañía.
30 Al son de sus dulces remos
la infanta se adormecía
en braços de don Duardos
que bien le pertenecía.
32 VI. Sepan quantos son nacidos
aquesta sentencia mía:
que contra la muerte y amor
nadie no tiene valía.

14 y más hermosos jardines
que vuestros, Señora mía.

De plata son los palacios
para vuestra Señoría,
16 de Esmeraldas y Jacintos
toda la tapicería,
las cámaras ladrilladas
de oro fino de Turquía,
18 con letreros esmaltados
que *tienen* la vida mía
[. . . . .]
que distes en aquel día
20 quando con Primaleón
fuertemente combatía.
¡Señora, vos *lo* matastes,
que y[o] a él no lo temía!

Translation:

I. It was in the month of April,
one day before May,
2 when irises and roses
show more their beauty,
on the most peaceful night
that the Heavens could display
[*hazer podía*],
4 when the beautiful princess
Flérida was departing.
In her father's garden [*huerta*]
she was saying to the trees:

It was in the month of April,
one day before May,
2 when irises and roses
show more their beauty,
on the most peaceful night
that the Heavens *could display*
[*podía hazer*],
4 when the beautiful princess
Flérida was departing.
In her father's *garden* [*huerto*]
she was saying to the trees:

6 II. "Never, for as long as I live,
shall I see you even one day,
nor hear in your branches
the melody of the nightingales.
8 Stay with God, clear water;
stay with God, cold water;
stay with God, my flowers,
which used to be my pride.
10 I am going to strange lands,
for fate guides me there.
III. If my father looks for me,
whose love for me is so great,
12 tell him that love takes me,
that the fault is not mine:
It was so stubborn with me
that its persistence vanquished.
14 Woe is me; I know not where I go;
nor does anyone tell me!"
IV. There spoke [*habló*] Don
   Duardos
you will hear what he said:
16 "Do not cry, my lady and princess;
do not cry, my joy,
for in the Kingdom of England
the waters are even clearer,
18 the gardens more beautiful,
and they are yours, my lady.
You will have three hundred
      maidens
of great rank.
20 The palaces for your ladyship
are of silver;
all the tapestry is
of emeralds and hyacinths;
22 the rooms have walls
of fine Turkish gold,
and enameled signs
that relate my life story:
24 They relate the great suffering
you caused me that day
when with Primaleón
I fiercely fought.
26 My lady, you were killing me;
for him I did not fear!"
His tears consoled Flérida,
upon hearing this.

7 never, for as long as I live,
shall I see you even one day.

6 "Stay with God, *cold waters*,

6b which used to be my pride;
8 I am going to strange lands,
for fortune guides me there.
If my father *asks for me*,
whose love for me is so great,
10 tell him that love takes me,
that the fault was not mine.

Woe is me, I know not where I go,
and let not anyone tell me."

12 There *spoke* [*hablara*] Don
   Duardos:

"Do not cry, my joy,
for in the Kingdom of England
the waters are even clearer,
14 and the gardens more beautiful
than yours, my lady.

The palaces for your ladyship
are of silver;
16 all the tapestry is
of emeralds and hyacinths;
the rooms have walls
of fine Turkish gold,
18 and enameled signs
that *contain* my life,
[. . . . .]
which you gave that day,
20 when, with Primaleón
I fiercely fought.
My lady, *you killed him*,
for him I did not fear!"

28　V. They went toward the galleys
　　　that Don Duardos had:
　　　They were fifty in all;
　　　all of them departed together.
30　　At the sweet sound of the oars
　　　the princess fell asleep,
　　　in the arms of Don Duardos;
　　　she belonged to him well.
32　VI. Let all who have been born
　　　know this maxim of mine:
　　　In the face of death and love
　　　no one has any recourse.

The *pliego* version eliminates many verses (7, 8a, 9a, 13, 15b–16a, 19, 24a, 27–33) and there is one important displacement (7). Some of the lexical variants could be justified as carelessness on the part of the printer (3b, 5a, 12a, 19b), but that is unlikely with those that corrupt the original in a vulgar, plebeian manner. Vicente's Flérida complains that no one tells her where she is being taken (14); now she does not even wish to be told, and with a redundant, grammatically incorrect negative at that. Of course the printer could have misread "que" for "no," but there are other examples of the sort. In the original, Don Duardos informs Flérida that the gardens are even more beautiful in England and that they will belong to her (18); now he says that the English gardens are more beautiful than hers, which is rather impolite. The Primaleón episode, which this version still retains, is poorly modified as well. In Vicente's text, Don Duardos states that the signs tell the story of his life, including the grief that Flérida had caused him to suffer on the day of his fight with Primaleón (24–25); now he says that those signs "contain" ("tienen") the life that she had given him on that day. The statement that it was Flérida who killed Primaleón is ridiculous. Eliminations, displacements, substitutions, and corruptions such as these are characteristic of oral transmission. It is possible to hypothesize that the informant who provided this version did not know the end of the ballad, but its omission could also mean that, since the poem was fairly popular at the time, there was no point in including it. Last but not least, whereas in the original Flérida states "si mi padre me buscare" (11a), now she is made to say "si mi padre preguntare," which coincides with Vélez de Guevara's rendition as well as with the modern Sephardic and Spanish versions. Notwithstanding the carelessness of the printer, what we have here is an oral rendition from the sixteenth century.

c. The Portuguese Ballad

The Portuguese versions of *Flérida* can be divided into two main groups. The second group, from mainland Portugal, may bear some relationship to the Asturian ballad. The first group, represented by one single version from the island of São Jorge, Azores, published in 1869, is remarkably faithful to Vicente's text:

Era pelo mês d'Abril,   de Maio antes um dia,
2   quando a bela infanta   já da frota se espedia.
Fora ao jardim de seu pai,   ela chorava e dizia:
4   —Fica-te embora, mil flores,   meus jardins d'água fria,
qu'eu te não torno a ver   senão hoje, neste dia.
6   Se meu pai te perguntar,   pelo bem que me queria,
diz-lhe que o amor me leva,   que me venceu uma porfia.
8   Não sei p'ra onde me leva   nem que ventura é a minha.
Respondeu D. Duardos,   que escutava o que dizia:
10   —Calai-vos, bela infanta,   calai-vos, pérola minha!
Em portos de Inglaterra   mais claras águas havia,
12   mais jardins e arvoredos   para vossa senhoria.
Também isto quero, donzela,   para vossa companhia.
14   Chegados são às galeras   que D. Duardos trazia;
a mar lhe catava honra   e as ondas cortesia.
16   Ao doce remar dos remos   a menina adormecia
no colo do seu amor,   pois assim lhe convencia.
(Braga 1869, no. 56)[18]

(It was in the month of April, one day before May, when the beautiful princess said farewell to the fleet. She went to her father's garden, where she cried and said: "Farewell, one thousand flowers, my gardens of cold water, for I will not see you again, only today, on this day. If my father asks you, because of his love for me, tell him that love takes me, that obstinacy vanquished me. I know not where it is taking me, nor what fate awaits me." Replied Don Duardos who listened to what she said: "Be silent, beautiful princess; be silent, oh pearl of mine! In the ports of England there are even clearer waters, more gardens and groves for your ladyship. I also wish this, maiden, to keep you company." They arrived at the galleys that Don Duardos brought; the sea paid her honor and the waves courtesy. At the sweet rowing of the oars the girl fell asleep on the lap of her beloved, for he convinced her so.)

Once again, it is necessary to place this version next to the original, line by line, so as to show precisely how the Azorean ballad relates to it:

Gil Vicente's Version		*São Jorge*	
	I. En el mes era de abril,		Era pelo mês d'Abril,
	de mayo antes un día,		de Maio antes um dia,
2	quando los lirios y rosas		
	muestran más su alegría,		
	en la noche má serena		
	que el cielo hazer podía,		
4	quando la hermosa infanta	2	quando a bela infanta
	Flérida ya se partía,		já da frota se espedia.
	en la huerta de su padre		Fora ao jardim de seu pai,
	a los árboles dezía:		ela chorava e dizia:
6	II. —Jamás, en quanto biviere,	5	qu'eu te não torno a ver
	os veré tan sólo un día,		senão hoje, neste dia.
	ni cantar los ruiseñores		
	en los ramos melodía.		
8	Quédate a Dios, agua clara,		
	quédate a Dios, agua fría,	4b	meus jardins d'água fria,
	quedaos con Dios, mis flores,	4a	—Fica-te embora, mil flores,
	mi gloria que ser solía.		
10	Voyme a tierras estrañas,		
	pues ventura allá me guía.	8b	nem que ventura é a minha.
	III. Si mi padre me buscare	6	Se meu pai te perguntar,
	que grande bien me quería,		pelo bem que me queria,
12	digan que el amor me lleva,		diz-lhe que o amor me leva,
	que no fue la culpa mía:		
	tal tema tomó comigo		
	que me venció su porfía.		que me venceu uma porfia.
14	¡Triste, no sé donde voy,	8a	Não sei p'ra onde me leva
	ni nadie me lo dezía!—		
	IV. Allí habló don Duardos,	9	Respondeu D. Duardos,
	bien oiréis lo que decía:		que escutava o que dizia:
16	—No lloréis, señora infanta,	10	—Calai-vos, bela infanta,
	no lloréis, mi alegría,		calai-vos, pérola minha!
	que en los reinos de Inglaterra		Em portos de Inglaterra
	más claras aguas avía		mais claras águas havia,
18	y más hermosos jardines,	12	mais jardins e arvoredos
	y vuestros, señora mía.		para vossa senhoria.
	Ternéis trezientas donzellas		Também isto quero, donzela,
	de alta genelosía;		para vossa companhia.
20	de plata son los palacios		
	para vuestra señoría,		
	de esmeraldas y jacintos		
	toda la tapecería,		
22	las cámaras ladrilladas		
	de oro fino de Turquía.		

. . . .

28   V. Fuéronse a las galeras
que don Duardos tenía:

cincuenta eran por cuenta;
todas van en compañía.

30   Al son de sus dulces remos
la infanta se adormecía
en braços de don Duardos
que bien le pertenecía.

32   VI. Sepan quantos son nacidos
aquesta sentencia mía:
que contra la muerte y amor
nadie no tiene valía.

14   Chegados são às galeras
que D. Duardos trazia;
a mar lhe catava honra
e as ondas cortesia.

16   Ao doce remar dos remos
a menina adormecia
no colo do seu amor,
pois assim lhe convencia.

Translation:

I. It was in the month of April,
one day before May,

2   when irises and roses
show more their beauty,
on the most peaceful night
that the Heavens could display,

4   when the beautiful princess
Flérida was departing.
In her father's garden
she was saying to the trees:

6   II. "Never, for as long as I live,
shall I see you even one day,
nor hear in your branches
the melody of the nightingales.

8   Stay with God, clear water;
stay with God, cold water;
stay with God, my flowers,
which used to be my pride.

10   I am going to strange lands,
for fate guides me there.
III. If my father looks for me,
whose love for me is so great,

12   tell him that love takes me,
that the fault is not mine:
It was so stubborn with me
that its persistence vanquished.

14   Woe is me; I know not where I go;
nor does anyone tell me!"

It was in the month of April,
one day before May,

2   when the beautiful princess
said farewell to the fleet.
She went to her father's garden,
where she cried and said:

5   for I will not see you again,
only today, on this day;

4*b*   my gardens of cold water,
4*a*   "Farewell, one thousand flowers,

8*b*   nor what fate awaits me."
6   If my father asks you,
because of his love for me,
tell him that love takes me,

that obstinacy vanquished me.
8*a*   I know not where it is taking me,

IV. There spoke Don Duardos,
you will hear what he said:

16 "Do not cry, my lady and lady
princess;
do not cry, my joy,
for in the kingdom of England
the waters are even clearer,

18 the gardens more beautiful,
and they are yours, my lady.
You will have three hundred
maidens
of great rank.

20 The palaces for your ladyship
are of silver;
all the tapestry is
of emeralds and hyacinths;

22 the rooms have walls
of fine Turkish gold."
. . . .

28 V. They went toward the galleys
that Don Duardos had:

They were fifty in all;
all of them departed together.

30 At the sweet sound of the oars
the princess fell asleep,
in the arms of Don Duardos;
she well belonged to him.

32 VI. Let all those who have been born
know this maxim of mine:
In the face of death and love
no one has any recourse.

9 Replied Don Duardos
who listened to what she said:

10 "Be silent, beautiful princess;

be silent, oh pearl of mine!
In the ports of England
there are even clearer waters,

12 more gardens and groves
for your ladyship.
I also wish this, maiden,

to keep you company."

14 They arrived at the galleys
that Don Duardos brought;
the sea paid her honor
and the waves courtesy.

16 At the sweet rowing of the oars
the girl fell asleep
on the lap of her beloved,
for he convinced her so.

It is readily apparent that this unique version from São Jorge compresses the original through the elimination of several verses, changing the sequence of others as well, but, nevertheless, it retains the initial verse and the first five of the six stages into which I have divided Vicente's text. It also keeps the consonance in *-ía* except for two verses (8*b*, 10*b*) that show assonance instead. The rhyme is impaired when one translates Sp. *mía* (my, mine) into Portuguese, where it becomes *minha*. Though the given lines do not appear as a direct translation of *mía*, this still applies. Note that the hero's name (9*a*, 14*b*) and the reference to England (11*a*) are preserved. This version of *Flérida* is therefore remarkably faithful to the Vicentine original, so much so that its traditional character could seem somewhat suspicious, especially in view of the fact that versions of this type have not been subsequently discovered.[19] There are additional factors that testify to its traditional character, however. One verse (15) constitutes a contamination with the exclusively Azorean *A Filha Desterrada (D. Maria)* (The Banished Daughter; RPI J7). Dona Maria was set adrift in the sea by her father, the king, as punishment for falling in love with a captain of whom he disapproved. When the ship returned against his expectations, her father asked her how the voyage had been, whereupon she answered: "Os mares me cataram honra / e os ventos cortesia" (The seas paid me honor and the winds courtesy; Braga 1869, no. 43). This verse does not alter the original narrative in any major way, but, together with the eliminations and the displacements just observed, it lends additional credence to the ballad's traditional character. Furthermore, like the sixteenth-century *pliego*, Vélez de Guevara's rendition, and the modern Sephardic and Spanish versions, this version changes the original's "si mi padre me buscare" (if my father looks for me; 11*a*) to "se meu pai te perguntar" (if my father asks you). As R. Menéndez Pidal observed (1933, 498–99), the substitution of the repeated "no lloréis" (do not cry) in Don Duardos's reassurance of Flérida (16) by the more direct "calai-vos" (be silent; 10) parallels the rendition preserved thanks to Vélez de Guevara (11).

As in the Sephardic ballad, the princess falls asleep in the hero's lap (17), rather than in his arms. Contrary to the Sephardic ballad, however, the heroine fails to surprise him with a baby, and her elopement does not end in disgrace. Besides remaining remarkably faithful to Vicente's text, then, this Azorean version also preserves its depiction of idealized love.

The Portuguese versions belonging to the second group are exclusive to the northeastern province of Trás-os-Montes. I have constructed a synthetic version, listing my sources and all the important variants afterward:

	*Meio-dia era em ponto,	quando o sol revolvia,
2	quando a bela infanta	do seu palácio saía,
	indo-se ela a despedir	dum jardim que seu pai tinha.
4	—Adeus, cravos, adeus, rosas,	adeus, fontes de água fria;
	adeus, jardim das flores,	onde eu me divertia;
6	adeus também, hortelão,	Deus te deia boa vida.
	Se por aqui vier meu pai,	aquele que tanto me queria,
8	dizei-lhe que o amor me leva,	e a culpa não era minha.
	Eu vou-me com um jornaleiro,	ao jornal ganhar a vida.

10   Eu não sei se vou ganhada,   eu não sei se vou perdida.
      —Ganhada ides, senhora,   ganhada, que não perdida.
12   Nos campos da Inglaterra   mais lindos jardins havia,
      também há cravos e rosas   para vossa regalia,
14   também há ricas donzelas   para vossa companhia.
      Achareis muito do ouro,   muito mais da prata fina,
16   achareis casas telhadas   ao uso da mouraria,
      achareis salas douradas   para passear de dia.
18   Entre as mourinhas todas   vós sereis a mais querida.

(It was exactly midday; the sun turned around and around, as the beautiful princess was leaving her palace to bid farewell to a garden her father owned. "Farewell, carnations; farewell, roses; farewell, fountains of cold water; farewell, garden of flowers where I used to enjoy myself; farewell to you, gardener; may God give you a good life. If my father comes here, he who loved me so much, tell him that love takes me away, and that the fault was not mine. I am leaving with a journeyman to earn a living as a day worker. I know not whether I have been won, or whether I have been lost." "You have been won, my lady, won, and not lost. In the meadows of England there are more beautiful gardens, also carnations and roses that will give you pleasure, and you will also find rich maidens to keep you company. You will find much gold, much more fine silver; you will find houses tiled in the manner of the Moors; you will find golden salons to stroll in during the day. Among all the Moorish women you will be the most beloved.")

Sources

Alves	= Alves 1934, 563
AF	= Armistead and Costa Fontes 1998, no. 31A
AP	= Aragão Pinto 1990, 6–7
DGalhoz	= Dores Galhoz 1987–88, no. 374
DM	= Dias Marques 1984–87, no. 31
DS	= Dias Marques and Reis da Silva 1984–87, no. 51
Tav.	= Tavares 1903–6, no. 20
TM	= TM (see the bibliography), nos. 719–25
VRP	= VRP (see the bibliography), nos. 276–80[20]

Variants:

1: Meio-dia era em ponto / quando o sol revolvia (VRP 276; cf. AF; Alves; AP; DM; DS; TM 721–25; VRP 277); Chegadinha era la hora / ao pino do meio-dia (VRP 278; cf. DGalhoz; TM 720; VRP 279–80); Alta vai a lua, alta, / mais que o sol ao meio-dia (Tav.).

2: quando a bela infanta / do seu palácio saía (VRP 276; cf. AP; DM; DS; TM 719–23; VRP 277–78); quando a bela infanta / meter-se freira queria (VRP 279); quando a bela infanta / de freirinha se metia (VRP 280); quando aquela donzela / do seu palácio saía (TM 724); quando aquela senhora / meter de freira se queria (TM 725); quando a bela infanta / de casa de seu pai saía (Alves); quando aquela donzela / vesti de freira se qu'ria (AF); quando aquela donzela / meter freira se ela qu'ria: Tav.

3: indo-s'ela a despedir / do jardim que seu pai tinha (VRP 276; cf. AP; DGalhoz; Tav.; TM 720); fora a casa de seu pai, / fora a dar a despedida (VRP 277); fora-se p'r'à sua horta / e dela se despedira (VRP 279); ao jardim d'el-rei, seu pai, foi fazer a despedida (VRP 280); Ela s'ia a despedir / dum jardim que seu pai tinha (TM 719; cf. TM 722); Ela ia visitare / um palácio que o pai tinha (TM 721); Ela se bai despedir / do jardim que seu pai tinha (DS).

4: —Adeus, cravos, e adeus, rosas, / adeus, fontes d'águas frias (VRP 276; cf. Alves; AP; DS; Tav.; TM 719, 721–23); Adeus, casa de meu pai, / adeus, fontes de água fria (VRP 277; cf. TM 724); Adeus, cravos, adeus, rosas, / adeus, tanques de água fria (VRP 278; cf. DGalhoz; DM; TM 720; VRP 280); Adeus, casa de meu pai, / adeus, adeus, horta minha (VRP 279); Adeus, cravos, adeus, rosas, / com quem m'eu adevertia (TM 724; cf. VRP 277).

5: adeus, jardins das flores, onde eu me divertia (Tav.); adeus, belo jardineiro, / com quem eu me divertia (VRP 280); adeus, jardim de meus pais, / fonte da i-água fria (TM 725).

6: adeus também, hortelã, / qu'era a erva qu'eu mais qu'ria (VRP 276; cf. TM 719); adeus também, jardineiro, / Deus te deia boa vida (VRP 277; cf. DGalhoz; DM; TM 720, 724); adeus também, jardineiros, / a quem tanto meu pai queria (VRP 278); adeus também, hortelã, logra-te da boa vida (TM 722; cf. DS); adeus também, hortelão, / leva-te mui boa vida (Alves).

6+: adeus tam'ém, janelas / do palácio que o meu pai tinha (TM 723); aideus, tan altus palácius, / donde m'eu vi alguns dias (AP).

7: Se por qui vier meu pai, / aquel' que tanto me qu'ria (VRP 276); Se por qui vier meu pai, / em busca da sua filha (VRP 277; cf. Alves; AP; TM 719, 724); Se aqui vier meu pai / homem que tanto me queria (VRP 280); Se vires por aí o meu pai / perguntar por sua filha (TM 721); Se vier por qui meu pai, / perguntar por sua filha (TM 722; cf. DS); Se vier por qui meu pai, / procurar a sua filha (TM 723); Se virais por aqui meu pai, / aquele que tanto me queria (DM); Se por aqui passar meu pai, / meu pai que tanto me queria (Tav.).

8: dizei-le que o amor me leva, / mas a culpa não é minha (VRP 276; cf. Alves; TM 724); diga que amores me levam, / mas a culpa não é minha (VRP 277); diga-le que o amor me leva / e a culpa não era minha (TM 722; cf. DS).

9: Eu me vou c'um jornaleiro, / ao jornal ganhar a vida (VRP 276; cf. Alves; DGalhoz; DM; TM 720; VRP 278, 280); Eu vou com um jornaleiro, / ganhar jornal cada dia (VRP 277; cf. TM 724–25); qu'eu vou-me c'um jornaleiro / a ganhá-la minha bida (VRP 279); Dizei que fui com um jornaleiro, / ao jornal ganhar a vida (TM 719; cf. AP; Tav; TM 723).

10: Eu não sei se vou ganhada, / eu não sei se vou perdida (VRP 276; cf. Alves; DGalhoz; DM; DS; Tav.; TM 719–20, 722, 725; VRP 277–80); Dizem que eu vou roubada, / ou dizem que eu vou perdida (TM 721).

11: —Ganhada vai a senhora, / ganhada, que não perdida (VRP 276; cf. Alves; DS; AP; Tav.; TM 719–20, 722, 724–25; VRP 277); Ganhada ides, senhora, / ganhada e não perdida (VRP 278; cf. DM; VRP 280); Ganhada vai, minha senhora, / ganhada bai, não perdida (VRP 279); Ganhada vai, ó menina, / ganhada e não perdida (DGalhoz).

12: Nos campos d'Inglaterra / lindas cadeiras havia (VRP 280).

13: também há cravos e rosas / para vossa regalia (VRP 280).

14: também há lindas donzelas / para vossa companhia (VRP 280); achareis ricas donzelas / para vossa companhia (Tav.); achará moço e moça / para sua serventia (VRP 279).

14+: também há lindas varandas / para se passeiar, menina (VRP 280); também há pentinhos d'ouro / para se pentear, menina (VRP 280).

15: Achareis muito do ouro, / muito mais de prata fina (VRP 276; cf. Alves; AP; Tav.; TM 719); Na mourama achará ouro, / muitas sedas, prata fina (VRP 277); qu'achará casas douradas, / defronte da mouraria (VRP 279); Se tem muito ouro, / muito mais tem prata fina (TM 724); Achará muito dinheiro, / muito mais da louça fina (VRP 279).

16: achareis casas telhadas / ao uso da mouraria (VRP 276; cf. AP; TM 719); e as casas lajeadas / ao uso da mouraria (VRP 277); ao chegar àquelas terreiras / ao uso da mouraria (TM 720); tem a casa coberta / ao ouro da mouraria (TM 724); ò chegar às casas terreiras, / ò uso da mouraria (DGalhoz).

17: achareis sala dourada / para passear de dia (Tav.).

18: Entre as mourinhas todas / vós sereis a mais querida (VRP 276; cf. Alves; DGalhoz; AP; TM 720; VRP 277); lá entre os mouros e as mouras / há-de ser a mais querida (TM 722; cf. DS); entre as criadas mouras / serás tu a mais querida (DM); entre mouros e mouramas / vós sereis a mais querida (VRP 278).

The opening verse of this ballad, "Meio-dia era em ponto / quando o sol revolvia" (It was exactly midday; the sun turned around and around), constitutes a formula to indicate the time of day. The most common alternative, "Chegadinha era la hora, / ao pino do meio-dia" (The hour had arrived, at the apex of midday), means essentially the same. Referring both to the sun and the hour of noon, "Alta vai a lua, alta, / mais que o sol ao meio-dia" (High goes the moon, high, more than the sun at midday) is a related *incipit*, but it appears only in one version. The first two formulas, however, seem to be exclusive to the Portuguese *Flérida*; the third one, which is characteristic of its Spanish counterpart, is used to open several other ballads, both early and modern.

Ironically, rather than stating that the protagonist, whose name is never mentioned, is leaving her father's house (2), some versions maintain that she wanted to become a nun, even though soon after they reveal that she is eloping with a journeyman (Tav.; TM 725; VRP 280). The word used to designate the garden to which Flérida says good-bye is almost always *jardim*, which means "flower garden" (3). The *huerta* in Vicente's original (5) could not be accurately translated with the corresponding *horta*, which, in Portuguese, means "vegetable garden."

In her farewell, Flérida says good-bye to a *jardineiro* or *jardineiros* (gardener, gardeners), but, in some versions, she refers to this gardener with the masculine *hortelão* (6), as well as with the feminine *hortelã*. Don Duardos, we recall, had disguised himself as an *hortelano* in order to earn her love. Since she was eloping with the disguised prince, it would not make any sense for her to take leave of him. Therefore, this *hortelão* must refer to the older gardener, also named Julián, who had taken Don Duardos into his service. The feminine *hortelã*, of course, could refer to Julián's wife, Costanza, but it is more likely to be a corruption. In some versions, the word is used with a second meaning, "mint," and the princess says good-bye to it, specifying that it is the herb that she most likes. In any case, since neither Julián nor his wife is in the garden when Flérida is about to elope, and Vicente's ballad does not mention an *hortelano*, what we have here is an interpolation derived from the play itself.

As she expresses her misgivings about the step she is about to take, Flérida says that she is eloping with a journeyman (9). Once again, the modern ballad interpolates information derived from the play itself. Although Don Duardos pretends to be a gardener, at one point, when Flérida probes his identity, the former professions that he lists transform him precisely into a journeyman:

De moço guardé ganado	As a young man I was a shepherd
y arava:	and used to plough:
esto sé yo bien hacer.	I know how to do this well.
Después dexé el arado	Then I left the plough
y trasquilava.	and used to shear.
Después estuve a soldada	Then I worked by the day
y acarreava harina	and carried the flour
de un molino.	of a mill.

(Vicente 1968, 216)[21]

The unnamed hero's reference to England (12) appears only in one striking version, which states that, in her new home, the princess will also find carnations and roses, verandas on which to walk, golden combs, and beautiful maidens to keep her company:

Nos campos d'Inglaterra   lindas cadeiras havia;
também há cravos e rosas   para vossa regalia;
também há lindas varandas   para se passeiar, menina;
também há pentinhos d'ouro   para se pentear, menina;
também há lindas donzelas   para vossa companhia.
(VRP, no. 280)

(In the fields of England there are beautiful chairs; there also are carnations and roses that will give you pleasure; there also are pretty verandas for you to stroll in, girl; there also are little golden combs for you to comb your hair with, girl; there also are pretty maidens to keep you company.)

According to the first verse that was just quoted, however, what Flérida will find in the fields of England are beautiful chairs, which does not make any sense. I retained the first hemistich, but changed the second one to "mais lindos jardins havia" (there are more beautiful gardens; 12), because gardens constitute a more logical alternative, fitting better with the carnations and roses in the following verse, which I also retained (13). Although these two verses are not documented in any of the other versions of this type, they are unquestionably traditional. The reference to the maidens (14), on the other hand, appears in three versions.

The riches that Flérida will find in her new home—gold, fine silver, and houses with roofs in the Moorish style (15–16)—are listed in numerous versions. The houses in the Moorish style, of course, give a new twist to the ballad, for, rather than going to England, the princess is now being taken to Moorish territory. Somehow, Don Duardos is turned into a Moor. Further confirming this, he informs the princess that, among all the Moorish women, she will be the most beloved (18).

A line by line comparison of this reconstructed version with the Vicentine original will better reveal the structural changes that have occurred as the modern Portuguese ballad was orally transmitted across the centuries:

Gil Vicente's Version		*Portuguese Version*	
	I. En el mes era de abril,		*Meio-dia era em ponto,
	de mayo antes un día,		quando o sol revolvia,
2	quando los lirios y rosas		
	muestran más su alegría,		
	en la noche má serena		
	que el cielo hazer podía,		
4	quando la hermosa infanta	2	quando a bela infanta
	Flérida ya se partía,		do seu palácio saía,
	en la huerta de su padre		indo-se ela a despedir
	a los árboles dezía:		dum jardim que seu pai tinha.
6	II. —Jamás, en quanto biviere,	4	—Adeus, cravos, adeus, rosas,
	os veré tan sólo un día,		
	ni cantar los ruiseñores		
	en los ramos melodía.		
8	Quédate a Dios, agua clara,		
	quédate a Dios, agua fría,		adeus, fontes de água fria;
	y quedaos con Dios, mis flores,		adeus, jardim das flores,
	mi gloria que ser solía.		onde eu me divertia;
		6	adeus também, hortelão,
			Deus te deia boa vida.
10	Voyme a tierras estrañas,		
	pues ventura allá me guía.		
	III. Si mi padre me buscare		Se por aqui vier meu pai,
	que grande bien me quería,		aquele que tanto me queria,
12	digan que el amor me lleva,	8	dizei-lhe que o amor me leva,
	que no fue la culpa mía:		e a culpa não era minha.
	tal tema tomó comigo		

que me venció su porfía.

Eu vou-me com um jornaleiro,
ao jornal ganhar a vida.

14 ¡Triste, no sé donde voy,
ni nadie me lo dezía!—
IV. Allí habló don Duardos,
bien oiréis lo que decía:

10 Eu não sei se vou ganhada,
eu não sei se vou perdida.

16 —No lloréis, señora infanta,
no lloréis, mi alegría,
que en los reinos de Inglaterra
más claras aguas avía

18 y más hermosos jardines,

—Ganhada ides, senhora,
ganhada, que não perdida.

12 Nos campos da Inglaterra

y vuestros, señora mía.
Ternéis trezientas donzellas
de alta genelosía;

20 de plata son los palacios
para vuestra señoría,
de esmeraldas y jacintos
toda la tapecería,

22 las cámaras ladrilladas
de oro fino de Turquía.

bem lindos jardins havia,
também há cravos e rosas
para vossa regalia,

14 também há ricas donzelas
para vossa companhia.
Achareis muito do ouro,
muito mais da prata fina,

16 achareis casas telhadas
ao uso da mouraria,
achareis salas douradas
para passear de dia.

18 Entre as mourinhas todas
vós sereis a mais querida.

. . . .

28 V. Fuéronse a las galeras
que don Duardos tenía:
cincuenta eran por cuenta;
todas van en compañía.

30 Al son de sus dulces remos
la infanta se adormecía
en braços de don Duardos
que bien le pertenecía.

32 VI. Sepan quantos son nacidos
aquesta sentencia mía:
que contra la muerte y amor
nadie no tiene valía.

Translation:

I. It was in the month of April,
one day before May,

2 when irises and roses

It was exactly midday,
the sun turned around and
around,

show more their beauty,
on the most peaceful night
that the Heavens could display,
4 when the beautiful princess
Flérida was departing.
In her father's garden
she was saying to the trees:
6 II. "Never, for as long as I live,

shall I see you even one day,
nor hear in your branches
the melody of the nightingales.
8 Stay with God, clear water;
stay with God, cold water;
stay with God, my flowers,
which used to be my pride.

10 I am going to strange lands,
for fate guides me there.
III. If my father looks for me,
whose love for me is so great,
12 tell him that love takes me,
that the fault is not mine:
It was so stubborn with me
that its persistence vanquished.

14 Woe is me, I know not where I go;

nor does anyone tell me!"
IV. There spoke Don Duardos,
you will hear what he said:
16 "Do not cry, my lady and princess;
do not cry, my joy,
for in the Kingdom of England
the waters are even clearer,
18 the gardens more beautiful,

and they are yours, my lady.
You will have three hundred
   maidens
of great rank.
20 The palaces for your ladyship
are of silver;
all the tapestry is

2 as the beautiful princess
was leaving her palace
to bid farewell
to a garden her father owned.
4 "Farewell, carnations; farewell,
   roses;

farewell, fountains of cold water;
farewell, garden of flowers
where I used to enjoy myself;
6 farewell to you, gardener,
may God give you a good life.

If my father comes here,
he who loved me so much,
8 tell him that love takes me away,
and that the fault was not mine.

I am leaving with a journeyman
to earn a living as a day worker.
10 I know not whether I have been
   won,
or whether I have been lost."

"You have been won, my lady,
won, and not lost.
12 In the meadows of England

there are more beautiful gardens,
also carnations and roses
that will make you pleasure,
14 and you will also find rich maidens

to keep you company.
You will find much gold,
much more fine silver,

of emeralds and hyacinths;
22 the rooms have walls
   of fine Turkish gold."

16 You will find houses tiled
   in the manner of the Moors;
   you will find golden salons
   to stroll in during the day.
18 Among all the Moorish women
   you will be the most beloved."

. . . .
28 V. They went toward the galleys
   that Don Duardos had:
   They were fifty in all;
   all of them departed together.
30 At the sweet sound of the oars
   the princess fell asleep,
   in the arms of Don Duardos;
   she belonged to him well.
32 VI. Let all those who have been born
   know this maxim of mine:
   In the face of death and love
   no one has any recourse.

The eliminations that caused the original to be compressed considerably are readily apparent. Several passages were replaced by verses which, although different enough, convey essentially similar meanings (5, 14, 16, 20). One striking change occurs when, rather than complaining that she ignores where she is being taken (14), the heroine wonders whether she has been won or lost. In his reply, the hero no longer tells her not to cry (16), maintaining instead that she has been won. The ideas expressed here are more or less the same: the princess is uncertain about her fate, and the hero attempts to reassure her.

In the modern ballad, Flérida's farewell begins with the carnations and roses in her garden (4), thus bringing to mind the "rosas y claveles" (roses and carnations) also enclosed within the Asturian ballad's farewell (6). This, we recall, may represent a case of displacement, echoing the "lirios y rosas" (irises and roses) found at the beginning of Vicente's poem (2).

As we have seen, the interpolations regarding a gardener (6) and a journeyman (9) derive from the play itself. This suggests that those who first began to sing the ballad were also familiar with the play, and that the Portuguese ballad became traditional at a very early period, soon after the performance.

The third and last important interpolation (16–18) may have begun as a substitution. The original's rooms with walls of fine Turkish gold (22) probably became houses roofed in the Moorish style because, being Moslims, the Turks were also viewed as Moors. This led to the replacement of England with Moorish territory, and to the transformation of the prince into a Muslim. Since, during the first part of the sixteenth century, the days of the Moorish occupation were still well remembered, there was no longer any need for a sea voyage, and the remainder of Vicente's ballad (28–33) was eliminated.

The correlation just presented also enables us to see more clearly the narrative stages that have been preserved despite the eliminations, compression, substitutions, and interpolations just discussed, and better to compare this Portuguese form of *Flérida* with its Spanish counterpart. The Portuguese ballad preserves stages 1 (season), 2 (farewell), 3 (excuse for the father), and 4 (prince's reassurances), eliminating stages 5 (embarkation) and 6 (helplessness before death and love). The Spanish ballad also retains the first three stages, but it eliminates the prince's reassurances (4). It preserves the crucial departure in his galleys (5), however.

These are important differences, but, nevertheless, the two ballads still have much in common. Both reduce the beginning of stage 1 to a formula which, rather than describing the season, merely sets the time of the day. These formulas do not seem to depend on each other, however.[22] Being quite different, they do not reveal a direct relationship.

The interpolations also differ considerably. In the Spanish ballad, the princess blames her elopement on her father, who failed to marry her off sooner, with words that may derive from *El conde Alarcos*. With its references to a gardener and to a journeyman, the Portuguese ballad interpolates material that reveals knowledge of the play itself. The Portuguese ballad concludes with the prince's false reassurances—he is really a Moor and is taking the girl to Moorish territory. They travel by land. The Spanish ballad eliminates those reassurances, and the protagonists elope by sea.

The Spanish ballad, however, always continues with *El moro cautivo*, which leads to a similar result—the hero turns out to be a Moor as well. In the Portuguese ballad, this transformation is triggered by the reference to Turkish gold in Vicente's text and, therefore, occurs within *Flérida*. In the Spanish ballad, the transformation results from a contamination with a separate text-type, *El moro cautivo*. Because the heroine of that ballad is rescued by the Virgin, this leads to a contamination with yet another poem, *La devota de la Virgen en el yermo*.

I know of two Portuguese examples, both from Trás-os-Montes, in which *Flérida* also appears in contamination with *El moro cautivo*, known as *Canta, Mouro* in Portugal. The first example is brief, consisting of only three (9–11) verses:

<pre>
        —Ganhada ides, senhora,   ganhada e não perdida.
8   O pão vo-lo darei por onças   e a água por medida.
        —Volta atrás, ó meu cavalo,   que ainda remédio havia.
10   Abra-me a porta, meu pai,   que aqui tem a sua filha,
        que venho de S. Tiago,   de cumprir a romaria.
</pre>

(VRP, no. 278)

("You have been won, my lady, won and not lost. I will feed you bread by the ounce and very little water." "Turn back, my horse, it is not yet too late. Open the door, my father; here you have your daughter; I'm returning from Santiago; I've completed the pilgrimage.")

Right after the hero reassures her that she has been won, not lost, the girl reacts in a manner indicating that the verses in which he reveals that he is taking her to live among the Moors are missing. She commands her horse to return at once and then lies to her father, claiming that she has been on a pilgrimage to Santiago, so as to avoid even more trouble. Note that the miraculous intervention of the Blessed Mother is also omitted here.

My wife and I recorded in Vinhais, in 1980, the second version of *Flérida* in contamination with *Canta, Mouro*:

<pre>
        —Canta, mouro, canta, mouro,   canta pela tua vida.
2   —Como cantarei eu, senhora,   se eu com prisões não podia?
        —Canta, mouro, canta, mouro,   da prisão te livraria.
4   Prepara-te, ó mourinho,   p'r'amanhã ao meio-dia;
        eu me vou fazer a despedida   ao jardim que meu pai tinha.
6   —Adeus, cravos, adeus, rosas,   adeus, tanques d'água fria;
        adeus, jardim de flores,   ond'eu passava o meu dia;
8   adeus, casa de meus pais,   e o espelho donde m'eu via.
        Lá no meio do caminho   altas torres relumbriam.
10   —De quem são aquelas torres   que tanto relumbriam?
        —Ũa é da minha mãe,   outra é da minha tia,
12   e aquela que mais relumbria   da minha esposa linda.
        —Diz-me aqui, ó mourinho,   diz-me pela tua vida,
14   se me levas por escrava,   ou me levas por amiga?
        —Nem te levo por esposa,   nem tão-pouco por amiga;
16   levo-te por escrava   da sala e da cozinha.
</pre>

—Valha-me Nossa Senhora,   valha-m'a Virgem Maria!
18   Tornai-me o perro mouro   para a prisão dond'eu ia.
S'a prisão era grande,   eu ainda (?) lha dobraria.

(TM, no. 113)

("Sing, oh Moor; sing, oh Moor; sing for your life." "How can I sing,
Madam? With these chains, I cannot." "Sing, oh Moor; sing, oh Moor;
I will deliver you from prison. Get ready, dear Moor, for tomorrow at
noon. I'm going to say farewell to a garden my father owns."
"Farewell, carnations; farewell, roses; farewell, tanks of cold water;
farewell, garden of flowers where I used to spend the day; farewell,
house of my parents, and mirror where I used to see myself." Further down the road high towers shone. "Whose towers are those,
which shine so much?" "One belongs to my mother, another belongs
to my aunt, and that one, which shines most, belongs to my beautiful wife." "Tell me here, dear Moor, tell me by your life if you take me
as a slave, or if you take me as mistress?" "I don't take you as a wife,
or as a mistress either; I'm taking you as a slave for the living room
and the kitchen." "Help me here, Our Lady; help me here, Virgin
Mary! Please return the Moorish dog to the prison I used to visit. Although the prison is harsh, I will make it twice as bad.")

This version opens with *Canta, Mouro* (1–4),[23] continues with
Flérida (5–8), and then ends with *Canta, Mouro* (10–19), including
two verses from *Abenámar* (10–12), which is often contaminated
with that ballad.[24] The infatuated princess promises to free the captive Moor in exchange for a song. The day after she says farewell to
her garden and to her father's house, and elopes with him. Seeing
some towers in the distance, she wonders who owns them. The
Moor reveals that one belongs to his mother, another to his aunt,
and that the one that shines most belongs to his beautiful wife. The
princess then asks whether she is being taken as a slave or as a
mistress. Discovering that he plans to make her a slave, she prays
to the Blessed Mother to return the Moorish dog[25] to the prison
where he was.

This contamination could have originated in Castile, which,
being a centrally located center of dissemination, has exported many
ballads to its neighbors, but it could also have arisen independently
in Portugal, as a result of thematic similarity, since both *Flérida* and
Canta, Mouro deal with elopements. The discovery of more variants
would perhaps enable us to reach a firmer conclusion in this respect,
but, for now, I favor the second hypothesis. Although this Portuguese
form of *Flérida* shares some features with the Spanish ballad, it developed separately, becoming popular in Portugal at a very early pe-

riod. The two examples with *Canta, Mouro* are contaminated with the Portuguese, rather than with the Spanish form of *Flérida*, and they fail to include the additional contamination with *La devota de la Virgen* that characterizes the Spanish ballad. Moreover, in the Portuguese tradition, the two contaminations with *Canta, Mouro* constitute an exception, not the rule.

From a sociological perspective, the Portuguese poem is quite different from the Asturian ballad as well. The princess elopes with a journeyman, who turns out to be a Moor. Although he promises her all sorts of riches, and that, among all the Moorish women, she will be his dearest, this is a very bad fate for any Christian girl. Unlike the Azorean rendition, which, somehow, retained Vicente's portrayal of idealized love, this Portuguese form of the ballad implicitly condemns such elopements, probably embodying a condemnation of unions between different social classes as well. The Spanish ballad, we recall, ends on a positive note, for the Virgin rescues and then takes the girl under her protection.

Although the Portuguese forms of *Flérida* are now restricted to the Azores (group 1) and Trás-os-Montes (group 2), the contamination of the part of the poem that corresponds to Flérida's farewell with several other ballads documents that it was sung throughout the whole country at one time. In Castelo Branco (Beira Baixa), Elvas (Alto Alentejo), and the district of Beja (Baixo Alentejo), it appears at the end of the combinations of *A Aposta Ganha* (*La apuesta ganada* [The Wager Won]; RPI, T2) + *Conde Claros Vestido de Frade* (*Conde Claros fraile* [Count Claros Disguised as a Friar]; RPI, B4; CMP, B12)[26] and *Aliarda* (*Aliarda y el alabancioso* [Aliarda and the Boastful Lover]; RPI, R1; CMP, R1) + *Conde Claros Vestido de Frade*.[27] In the Carolingian *Claros Frade*, upon discovering that his daughter is pregnant, the emperor decides to have her burned at the stake. Her lover, Count Claros, disguises himself as a monk, pretends to confess her, and rescues her at the very last moment. As they escape, the princess says farewell with words taken from *Flérida*. In the example that follows, she refers to the nightingales which, although present in Vicente's text (7), no longer appear in the Sephardic, Spanish, and Portuguese forms of that ballad:

> —Adeus, casa do meu pai,   adeus, tanque da água fria,
> 50   já não torno a ouvir cantar   rouxinol ao meio-dia.
> (Ferré et al. 1987, no. 6)

("Farewell, house of my father; farewell, tank of cold water; I will no longer hear the singing of the nightingale at midday.")

Except for the unique version from São Jorge, the modern Portuguese *Flérida* eliminates the sea-voyage, and the princess elopes by land. Two versions from Elvas append to *Claros Frade* a farewell which, besides mentioning the nightingale, also refers to an awaiting ship. In the first example, their destination is no longer England but Hungary, because, being in rhyme position, the word needs to rhyme in *í–a*. Somehow, the second example divides the farewell between the princess and the hero:

—Adeus, casa de meu pai,   rouxinol canta ao meio-dia;
44   eu também tenho um navio   pronto a partir para Hungria.

(Tomás Pires 1986, no. 13)

("Farewell, house of my father, nightingale that sings at midday; I also have a ship ready to leave to Hungary.")

50   —Adeus, casa de meu pai,   onde o galo canta ao meio-dia.
   —Venha-se embora, menina,   não fale com fantasia,
52   que eu tenho um navio no mar   [. . . . .]
   onde canta o rouxinol   quer de noite, quer de dia.[28]

(no. 12)

("Farewell, house of my father, where the cock sings at midday." "Let's leave now, girl; try to be more realistic, for I have a ship at sea [. . .] where the nightingale sings all day and night long.")

Flérida's farewell also appears in contamination with *O Cego* (The Blind Man; *El raptor pordiosero* [The Abductor in Beggar's Guise]; RPI, O3; CMP, O3), in which a man who pretends to be blind asks a girl to show him the way and then kidnaps her. Realizing what has happened, and that her mother conspired with the abductor, the girl says good-bye to her (31–32), adding two verses taken from *Flérida* (33–34):

—Adeus, minha casa,   adeus, minha terra,
32   adeus, minha mãe,   que bem falsa me era.
   Adeus, moços e moças   com quem m'eu deverti,
34   adeus, fontes, águas claras,   ond'eu água bobi.

(Armistead and Costa Fontes 1997, no. 23F)

("Farewell, my home; farewell, my land; farewell, my mother; you were false to me. Farewell, boys and girls with whom I had a good time; farewell, fountains, clear waters, where I used to drink.")

This example is from Trás-os-Montes. In another example, from the district of Évora (Alto Alentejo), the girl replaces the nightingale with a lark, and the feigned beggar reassures her with words that correspond to Don Duardos's reassurance of Flérida, including a reference to the maidens who will keep her company in her new home:

12   (E) adeus, ó meu mõnti,   (e) adeus, tanque de água fria,
        já não oiço a calhandra   na hora do meio-dia.
14   —Também lá tens a calhandra,   que é astro do dia,
        também doze donzelas   p'ra vossa companhia.
                                    (Dores Galhoz 1987–88, no. 301)

("Farewell, my mountain; farewell, tank of cold water, I no longer hear the lark at the hour of noon." "Yonder you will also have the lark, which is the star of the day, and also twelve maidens in order to keep you company.")

The most frequent contamination with *Flérida*, however, is enclosed within *O Conde Alarcos* (RPI, L1; CMP, L1). The king commands Count Alarcos to kill his wife so that he can marry his daughter. The countess's farewell often includes words from *Flérida*. The examples that follow are from Santarém (Ribatejo), Madeira, and Brazil:

        —Deixa-me ir dar um passeio   da sala para a cozinha.
36   Adeus, criados e criadas,   adeus também, ó vizinha.
        Deixa-me ir dar um passeio   da sala para o jardim.
38   Adeus, cravos, adeus, rosas,   tudo para mim tem fim.
                                    (Dores Galhoz 1987–88, no. 176)

("Let me take a stroll from the living room to the kitchen. Farewell, servants and maids; farewell to you too, neighbor. Let me take a stroll from the living room to the garden. Farewell, carnations; farewell, roses; everything is ending for me.")

36   —Deixa-me dar um passeio   da sala para o jardim.
        Adeus, cravos, adeus, rosas,   adeus, flores d'alecrim.
38   Deixa-me dar um passeio   da sala par'à cozinha.
        Adeus, cravos, adeus, rosas,   adeus, criadas minhas.
                                    (Ferré et al. 1982, no. 123)

("Let me take a stroll from the living room to the garden. Farewell, carnations; farewell, roses; farewell, flowers of rosemary. Let me take a stroll from the living room to the kitchen. Farewell, carnations; farewell, roses; farewell, maids of mine.")

—Adeus, adeus, minhas aias,   com quem eu me advertia;
adeus, espelho real,   onde me mirava e vestia;
adeus, casa tão querida,   que de mim fica vazia;
adeus, minha gente toda,   que é chegado o meu dia.

(Lopes 1967, 130)

("Farewell, my ladies-in-waiting, with whom I had a good time; farewell, oh royal mirror where I saw myself and dressed; farewell, beloved house, you no longer have me; farewell, all of my people, for now my day has come.")

Although the modern Portuguese versions of *Flérida* are now restricted to the province of Trás-Montes, these contaminations, I repeat, show that the ballad was very popular throughout the country at one time. Since the references to a gardener and to a journeyman derive from the *Tragicomedia*, the poem became popular soon after the performance, when people still remembered the play. Nevertheless, the Portuguese versions condense Vicente's original tremendously, transforming the hero into a Moor, and the protagonists no longer elope by sea. The Spanish ballad, which is now apparently restricted to Asturias, preserves the crucial embarkation, but it condenses Vicente's original considerably as well, and the additions from *El moro cautivo* and *La devota de la Virgen* transform it into a different poem. Since the ballad dates from ca. 1525, the Sephardim received it already in exile, but, as in many other instances, the Judeo-Spanish versions are much more faithful to the original than their Portuguese and Spanish counterparts, thus testifying, once again, to the great wealth and conservatism of the Sephardic tradition.

8

Three New Ballads Derived from *Don Duardos*

Flérida became extremely popular, and, since it concentrated on the elopement of the princess with the English prince, people felt a need to know something about what caused her to take such a drastic step, and created two new ballads in order to fill the gap. This happened at a later stage, when Gil Vicente's play was no longer well remembered. Both ballads take background material from *Don Duardos* and are exclusively Portuguese. *O Hortelão das Flores* (The Flower Gardener; RPI, S3; provinces of Beira Alta and Beira Baixa) places emphasis on Don Duardos's ruse to conquer Flérida's love, disguising himself as a gardener. *Lizarda* (RPI, S2; Madeira, Azores, Brazil), on the other hand, emphasizes the role of the go-between, Artada. Since Flérida sees the prince hunting and falls in love with him at once, this eliminates the need for the disguise. These two ballads conclude with the elopement, that is, with verses taken from *Flérida*. A third new ballad, *El falso hortelano* (The False Gardener; CMP, R8), is exclusively Sephardic and goes beyond *Don Duardos*, for it purports to explain what happened to Flérida after her departure. With no less than four popular ballads derived from his play, Vicente is one of those few learned authors whose work has received the honor of being accepted and transmitted anonymously by the folk as if it were something of their own creation.

1. *O Hortelão das Flores*

O Hortelão exists only in two versions, one from Covilhã (Beira Baixa; Braga 1906–9, 1: 426–28; = A),[1] the other from Mangualde

181

(Beira Alta; VRP, no. 275; = B).[2] This ballad fails to follow the characteristic *romance* form, which consists of two heptasyllabic verses (7 + 7; octosyllabic by Spanish count) divided by a "pause" or caesura, with a single assonance in the second hemistich. *O Hortelão* consists of strophic quatrains. Interestingly, whereas *A* is mostly hexasyllabic, in *B* it is the heptasyllable that prevails.[3] Since the two versions differ so much from each other, it is impossible to construct a satisfactory synthetic text. For this reason, I will use both versions in the analysis that follows, referring to them as *A* (Covilhã) and *B* (Mangualde). For the sake of those readers who would like to read them easily as wholes, without being broken up by analysis, I have edited them in appendix C.

A follows the *Tragicomedia* in numerous details. It begins with a conversation between Don Duardos and an old woman, to whom he says, very rudely, that the purpose of his visit is not to see or honor her. Rather, he seeks her advice because he has been conquered by love and he wishes to see the princess, who is like the sun to him:

	—Não venho por te ver,	nem por te dar valor,
2	venho por erguer olhos	e a vista no sol pôr.
	Falar quero à princesa,	o amor me traz rendido;
4	a ti peço conselho,	velha do tempo antigo.

("I don't come to see you, or to honor you; I come for something better, and see the sun itself. I want to speak with the princess; love has made me surrender; and so I ask your advice, old woman of the olden days.")

B eliminates the first two verses, transposes verses 3–4, and the hero behaves in a more direct, less romantic manner. Rather than saying that love has conquered him, he states immediately that he wishes to marry the princess:

	—Venho pedir-te conselho,	velha dos tempos antigos:
2	quero falar à princesa,	quero que case comigo.

("I'm coming for your advice, old woman of the olden days. I want to speak with the princess; I want her to marry me.")

Both texts parallel a comparable episode in the play where Don Duardos, after telling the Infanta Olimba how much he loves Flérida, asks her:

Dezidme, señora ifanta: Pray tell me, my lady and princess:
Flérida, ¿cómo la haveré? (174) How can I have Flérida?

In *A*, the old woman advises him:

    —Vista traje mudado,   cante em seu bandolim,
6   boquinha de cristal,   faces de serafim.

(Put on different clothes; sing and play your mandolin, you little
mouth of crystal with the face of an angel.)

The advice offered in *B* is more specific:

    —Conselho, conselho,   que conselho lhe hei-de dar?
4   Vista-se em trajo de pastor,   vá à porta do pomar.

("Advice, advice, what advice shall I give you? Dress yourself as a
shepherd; go to the entrance of the orchard.")[4]

The play is different—Olimba tells Don Duardos here:

Iros hes a su hortelano,	You shall go to her gardener
vestido de paños viles,	dressed in vile clothes
con paciencia,	and be patient,
de príncipe hecho villano,	changed from prince into peasant,
porque las mañas sotiles	for subtle cunning
son prudencia,	is prudence,
y assentaros hes con él,	and his employee you'll become
después que le prometiéredes	after promising him
provecho,	profit,
y avisaros hes de él,	and you shall watch out for him,
que no sinta en lo que hizierdes	so that from your actions he won't
vuesso hecho. (175–76)	suspect your affair.

Olimba then continues:

Llevad estas pieças de oro	Take these golden coins
y esta copa de las hadas	and this vase of the wonderful
preciosas;	fairies;
ternéis las noches de moro	you will work all night, like a Moor,[5]
y ternéis las madrugadas	and you will have very tearful
muy llorosas.	mornings.
Hazed que beva por ella	Make Flérida drink from it,
Flérida, porque el amor	and the love that you feel
que le tenéis	for her

a ella, os terná ella,   she will feel for you,
y perdida de dolor   and when she surrenders to the pain
la cobraréis.   (176)   you will win her.

Thus, the old woman corresponds to Olimba, who has been transformed into a "velha dos tempos antigos" (old woman of the olden days), that is, a witch, because of the magic vase that she gives to Don Duardos. This vase and the gold coins are missing in the ballad, however, and the reaction of Don Duardos, who thanks Olimba profusely in the *Tragicomedia*, is entirely different. In *B*, he fears: "Se nesse trajo me virem, / não farão caso de mim" (If they see me in those clothes, they will ignore me; 5). In *A*, however, he says:

      —Um bom conselho, velha,   me deste para mim!
8   Não farão de mim caso   se me virem assim.
      Com Deus te fica, velha,   mais a tua porfia;
10   mas se eu a render, velha,   tens tença cada dia.

(What good advice, old woman, you have given me! They will just ignore me if they see me dressed thus. Stay with God, old woman, you and your persistence; but if I conquer her, old woman, you will have a pension for life.)

The attitude of the prince toward Flérida is clearly vulgar. Then he adds, also in a rude manner, that he is going to hunt with a falcon in the woods,[6] as if the princess were a bird to be preyed upon, and threatens the old woman if her advice turns out to be of no avail:

      Eu vou bater o mato,   caçar altenaria,
12   mas, se ela me escapar,   em ti me vingaria.

(I'm going to the woods to hunt with a falcon, but if she escapes from me I shall take revenge upon you.)

These verses recall *Lizarda* (see the next section of this chapter), where the episode in which the hero disguises himself as the gardener's son disappears, and he meets the princess while hunting. Contrary to the play, where the gardener is unaware of Don Duardos's identity, in the ballad the hero states that he has disguised himself in order to speak with his beloved:

      —Abri lá essas portas,   ó hortelão das flores!
14   Venha [sic] em traje mudado   falar aos meus amores. (*A*)

("Open there those doors, oh gardener of the beautiful flowers, for I come in changed clothes, in order to speak with my beloved.")

8   —Abre-me a porta, jardim,   hortelão das belas flores,
        que eu venho em trajo mudado   p'ra falar aos meus amores. *(B)*

("Open the door for me, garden, oh gardener of the beautiful flowers, for I come in changed clothes, in order to speak with my beloved.")

A adds two verses that make it clear that the gardener recognizes Don Duardos:

        —Senhor, podeis entrar,   que tendes sempre acerto;
16   senhor, sois D. Duarte,   que bem vos reconheço.

("Sir, you may enter, for you are always right; sir, you are Don Duarte, I recognize you well.")

In the *Tragicomedia*, Julián at first refuses to allow the disguised Don Duardos, who tells him that he is from England, to enter into the garden. Julián agrees to do so only when the prince asks to be his apprentice and bribes him by pretending that he is the only one who knows where a gold treasure is buried. This treasure, of course, consists of the gold coins that Olimba had advised Don Duardos to use as a pretext to convince Julián to hire him:

Querría ser hortelano   I would like to become a gardener
si vos me lo enseñáis;   if you would teach me the job;
y quiero dezirlo llano: and I want to say this clearly:
en esta huerta, señor,   In this garden, Sir,
está terrible tesoro   there is a great treasure
que infinitas peças d'oro,   of countless coins of gold,
y sólo yo soy sabidor. (179)   and I alone know this.

In a passage missing in *B*, in *A* Don Duarte then wonders if the princess ever walks in the verandas that he sees and instructs the gardener that, should she inquire about him, he ought to say that he is a son of his who has just returned from abroad:

        —Oh que varandas altas   com cem palmos de alteza!
18   Diz, velho de bom tempo,   se ali vem a princesa.
        —Para as varandas altas,   para tomar a fresca,
20   costuma vir sozinha   quasi sempre a princesa.

—Se ela te perguntar   quem é o estrangeiro,
22   dize que é um teu filho   vindo lá doutro reino.
         Que varandas tão altas,   que jardim bem plantado!
24   Soubera o que hoje sei,   que o tinha passeado.

("Oh, what tall verandas, a hundred handbreadths in height! Pray tell me, old man of the good days, if the princess goes there." "To those tall verandas, in order to take the breeze, the princess is almost always wont to come alone." "Should she ask you who the stranger happens to be, tell her he is a son of yours who has come from another kingdom. What tall verandas; what a well-planted garden! Had I known what I know now, I would already have strolled on it.")

In the *Tragicomedia*, it is the gardener's wife who suggests to her husband that Don Duardos could pass himself off as their son:

JULIÁN   A la infanta ¿qué diremos   What shall we tell the princess
           se os viere aquí andar?   if she sees you around here?
COSTANZA   Por hijo puede passar;   He can pass himself off as our son;
           Julián le llamaremos.   (179)   we will call him Julián.

When Flérida comes into the garden, she wonders where Julián is, and Costanza tells her that he has taken the day off because their son has returned. Costanza then summons him to meet Flérida:

¡Julián, mi hijo, mi diamán!,   Julián, my son, my diamond!
llámaos la Princesa   Princess Flérida
Flérida. (181)   is calling you.

This situation is paralleled in *A*, where an unidentified speaker asks the new gardener to speak with the princess:

—Ó regador dos cravos,   venha para mais perto,
26   conversar a princesa   com prazer discreto.
         Ó regador dos cravos,   venha para o mirante,
28   olhar para a princesa   com olhos de diamante.

("Oh man who waters the carnations, please come closer, to talk to the princess with discrete pleasure. Oh man who waters the carnations, please come to the belvedere, to look at the princess with eyes of diamond.")

In *B*, the heroine invites her mother to see the new gardener, whose eyes she tastelessly compares to ivory. The mother then tells her to ask him to come nearer:

10   —Venha ver, ó minha mãe,   este nosso hortelão,
        que ele tem olhos de marfim,   mas ele prega-os no chão.
12   —Chama-mo cá, minha filha,   chama-mo cá p'ra mais perto,
        [. . . . .]   que ele me parece ser discreto.

("Mother, come see this gardener of ours; he has eyes of ivory, but
he looks at the ground." "Pray call him, daughter, call him nearer,
[. . .] for he seems to be discrete.")

The diamond eyes in *A* (28*b*), which become eyes of ivory in *B*,
probably echo Costanza's description of her putative son as a diamond when she informs him that Flérida would like to meet him.
Flérida's mother replaces Costanza because the latter is also a
mother. Note that in his reply the prince also mentions his own eyes,
stating that they are not worthy of seeing the most divine eyes that
the gods have created:

Y vos, mis ojos indignos,   And you, my unworthy eyes,
¿quáles hados os mandaron   what fate commanded you,
    siendo humanos,   being human,
ir a ver los más divinos   to see the most divine ones
que los dioses matizaron   that the gods fashioned
    con sus manos? (182)   with their hands?

As the play continues, after eating some fruit that Costanza had
given her, a thirsty Flérida asks Amandria to bring her a glass of
water:

Amandria, hazedme presta   Amandria, bring me quickly
    agua fría. (193)   some cold water.

Costanza replies that she will fetch it herself, and offers the
water in the magic vase that Olimba had given to Don Duardos, who
is present (193). In the ballad, it is the prince who gives the water to
Flérida. In *A*, he can hardly believe his luck when told to present
himself before the princess. She asks him for a cup of water and, as
he offers it to her, he adds that no one will sate the unquenchable
thirst that he himself feels:

        —Mandaram-me cá vir?   Não sei se é verdade.
30   —Tão verdade não fora,   espelho belo e claro.
        —Tendes-me aqui, senhora,   mandai como a vassalo;
32   já estive em noite escura,   agora é dia claro.
        —Dai-me, que tenho sede,   um pucarinho de água.

34 —Aqui vos mato a sede, espelho belo e claro.
    A mim não há quem mate a sede continuada.

("Have you sent for me? I cannot believe it!" "Of course it is true,
you handsome, clear mirror." "Here I am, Madam, command; I am
your vassal; before I was in darkness; now the day is bright." "Pray
give me, for I'm thirsty, a small cup of water." "Here I quench your
thirst, you beautiful, clear mirror, but no one cares to quench the
relentless thirst I feel.")

In *B*, having implicitly called for the hero, as her mother told
her, the girl states that she is dying of thirst as she asks him for the
water. Comparing her to an Easter lily as he tenders it to her, the
prince also refers to his own, unquenchable thirst:

14 —Dai-me uma pinguinha d'água, que estou morrendo à sede.
    —Aí te apago a sede, açucena bela e clara.
16 Minha sede não se apaga, pois ela é tão continuada!

("Give me a drop of water, for I'm dying of thirst." "There I quench
your thirst, you beautiful, clear Easter lily. My own thirst cannot be
quenched, for it is so relentless.")

Although *O Hortelão* never refers to the magic vase which, according to Olimba, would make Flérida fall in love with Don Duardos
as soon as she drank from it, the princess's sudden, unexpected reaction suggests that something magical must be at work. Apparently
aware that she herself is the only remedy for the hero's great thirst,
the princess immediately decides to elope with him the morning after,
and asks him to take her away secretly, on a female donkey:

36 —Vem cá falar comigo amanhã de madrugada.
    Aluga uma burrinha, que o não saiba ninguém,
38 que eu quero para sempre ir daqui para além. (*A*)

("Come to speak with me tomorrow morning, at dawn. Rent a little
donkey and let no one know it, for I want, for ever, to leave here, to
go far away.")

    —Amanhã de manhã, cedo, amanhã, de madrugada,
18 traga-me uma burrinha, muito bem aparelhada.
    [. . . . .] Que o não saiba ninguém:
20 que eu quero ir consigo, estrangeirinha, p'r'i além. (*B*)

("Tomorrow morning, early, tomorrow, at dawn, bring me a little donkey, very well harnessed. [. . .] Let no one know it, for I want to go with you abroad, far away.")

The only explanation for the princess's sudden decision to take such a serious step, right after drinking the water, is that at one point *O Hortelão* must have included some sort of reference to the magical properties of the vessel from which she drinks.

Here the ballad differs considerably from the *Tragicomedia* where, having already drunk from the vase, Flérida wavers considerably before deciding to elope, saying to Don Duardos that she is worried about her parents and her reputation:

Queréis que pierda el amor	You want me to forget my love
a mi padre y a mi señora	for my father and mother
y al sossiego,	and tranquillity itself,
y a mi fama y a mi loor	to forget my reputation and praise
y a mi bondad, que se desdora	and even my kindness, which is being tarnished
en este fuego. (223)	because of this fire.

Unlike in the *Tragicomedia*, where it is Don Duardos who tries to convince the princess to elope with him, in the ballad the prince attempts to make her reconsider, stating that his real father is a lowly butcher. The princess refuses to change her mind, however. In *A*, she replies that she could not care less; in *B*, she repeats her request for him to come early in the morning with the donkey:

```
     —Como a levarei, senhora,   com quem ireis daqui?
40   Filho de um corta-carne,   que apregoa aqui!
     —Não se me dá que o sejas   ou que apregoe aqui. (A)
```

("How can I take you, Madam? Do you realize with whom you will be leaving? I'm the son of a butcher and hawk goods here!" "I care not what you are, or whether you hawk here.")

```
     —Sendo vós filha d'el-rei,   que nunca pagou à justiça,
22   eu filho do corta-carnes,   como pode ser assim?
     —Amanhã de manhã, cedo,   amanhã, de madrugada,
24   traga-me uma burrinha   muito bem aparelhada.
     [. . . . . . . . . . . . . . . . . . . . . . .]   Que o não saiba ninguém:
26   que eu quero ir consigo,   estrangeirinha, p'r'i além. (B)
```

("Since you are the king's daughter, who never paid anything to jus-
tice, and I the butcher's son, how can that possibly be?" "Tomorrow
morning, early, tomorrow, at dawn, bring me a little donkey, very
well harnessed. [. . .] Let no one know it, for I want to go with you
abroad, far away.")

The hero's insistence on his low social status reflects the play's
emphasis on love for the sake of love. Although Don Duardos relies
on the magic vase to make Flérida fall in love with him, he also
wants her to love him as a person, not just because he happens to be
a prince. When Flérida wonders if he does not wish he were at least
a squire, he replies:

Oh, señora, ansí me quiero:	Madam, I want myself as I am:
hombre de baxas maneras;	A man of low manners.
que el estado	It is not in rank
no es bienaventurado,	that good fortune lies.
que el precio está en la persona. (194)	Goodness is in the person.

While reflecting the play's insistence on love for the sake of love,
however, the hero's attempt to make the princess reconsider by
maintaining that he is the son of a butcher is rather plebeian, to say
the least. Being a butcher was regarded as a demeaning profession.
The reason for this transformation, it would seem, was a desire to
astonish by exaggerating the power of the magic vase. Here the popular muse seems to have forgotten that, by attempting to make the
princess reconsider her decision to elope, the hero contradicts his
stated intention at the beginning of the ballad to hunt down and to
make Flérida surrender to him, as if she were a bird to be caught.
Clearly, *O Hortelão* is far removed from the world of pure, idealized
love portrayed in the *Tragicomedia*.

Although the protagonists elope on a donkey rather than in the
galleys that play such a prominent role in the concluding ballad, *O
Hortelão* goes on to adapt some passages from *Flérida*. *B* retains stages
3 (Flérida's excuse for her father) and 4 (Don Duardos's reassurances),
interpolating some new material as well. The princess's name is now
Aboladoura (from *abalar*, "to leave in a hurry," "to flee") and, although
the protagonist had just told her that his real father was a butcher,
now she declares that she is eloping with a herder of cattle:

> —Se meu pai perguntar   pela D. Aboladoura,
> 28   dizei-lhe que amores me levam,   a culpa não é só minha,
> que irei com um pastor de gado   para maior perdição minha.

30   —Abala, abala, Aboladoura,   deixa teus bens à profia,
        que entre Inglaterra   águas claras havia;
32   também há salas douradas,   d'ouro fino ou cutia (?);
        também há belas senhoras   para a vossa companhia.

("If my father asks for Doña Aboladoura, tell him that love takes me
away; the fault is not mine alone, that I shall go with a herder of
cattle as an even greater disgrace." "Take off; take off, Aboladoura;
persist in leaving your possessions, for in [between] England there
are clear waters; there also are golden salons of fine gold or *cutia* (?);
there are also beautiful ladies to keep you company.")

As we have already seen, the hero's transmutation from a gardener's son into a herder is due not to the popular muse alone. In the
Tragicomedia, when Flérida probes the identity of Don Duardos he
answers that he used to guard cattle and to plow: "De moço guardé
ganado / y arava" (216).

In *A*, the adaptation of *Flérida* begins when the princess says
farewell to her garden, including a reference to the singing nightingales (stage 2). This stage is missing in *B*. The princess then leaves
an excuse for her father (stage 3) and the prince reassures her (stage
4). As he begins to calm Flérida, Don Duardos asks her not to cry
with the word *cala-te* (lit., shut up), thus matching Vélez de Guevara's seventeenth-century version as well as the version from São
Jorge. The hero then refers to the princess as "Madalena" and mentions her tears, a development no doubt brought about by the copious tears shed by the repentant Mary Magdalene as she washed the
feet of Jesus:

        —Adeus, ó fontes claras   e poços de água fria;
44   eu já não ouço aqui   rouxinóis ao meio-dia.
        Se meu pai perguntar   quem é que me queria,
46   dizei que a desgraça   não é a que me guia.
        —Cala-te, Madalena,   lágrimas de peregrina!
48   Nos reinos estrangeiros   melhor água haveria.
        Também há claras fontes,   poços de água fria,
50   e canta o rouxinol   à hora do meio-dia.

("Farewell, clear fountains and pools of cold water; here I no longer
hear nightingales at midday. If my father asks who is it that loves
me, tell him that misfortune is not what guides me." "Be silent,
Magdalene, with your pilgrim's tears! In foreign kingdoms there is
even better water. There are also clear fountains, pools of cold
water, and the nightingale also sings at the hour of noon.")

The hero's reassurance would have been a satisfactory conclusion, but *A* then continues with material absent from *B*. Flérida recognizes "D. Duarte" and, instead of leaving (stage 5), she decides to return to the palace to report to her mother what has happened, ready to be punished for her aborted elopement. In the *Tragicomedia* Flérida's father is the emperor of Constantinople. *A* nationalizes the story, placing it in a more familiar Iberian context—Flérida's father is now "lord of all Spain." The final reference to the power of love, of course, corresponds to stage 6, but the assertion that love is very blind embodies a reference to Cupid as well:

	—Pareces D. Duarte! Oh que fortuna a minha!
52	Tornemos ao palácio, a dizê-lo à rainha.
	Rainha e mãe, senhora, humildo-me ao castigo;
54	aqui está D. Duarte, que vem por meu marido.
	Rainha e mãe, senhora, que pena me acompanha
56	de não achar meu pai, senhor de toda a Espanha.
	Rainha e mãe, senhora, humildo-me com dor;
58	não tem a quem pôr culpa, é mui cego o amor.

("You look like Don Duarte! What good fortune is mine! Let's go back to the palace and let the queen know about it. Queen and Mother, my lady, I submit willingly to punishment; here is Don Duarte; he comes as my husband. Queen and Mother, my lady, what sorrow assails me for not finding here my father, lord of all of Spain. Queen and Mother, my lady, I submit myself with grief; you cannot blame anyone else, for love is very blind.")

As we have seen, this second metamorphosis of *Don Duardos* takes a generous slice of background from the *Tragicomedia* itself, thus explaining the circumstances leading to the elopement in the concluding ballad. People wanted to know more. They liked *Flérida* because of its portrayal of idealized love. The union between a princess and a commoner, with the commoner turning out to be a prince, was fascinating to them. It was the stuff of fairy tales.

To conclude, *O Hortelão* draws especially on the episode in which Don Duardos disguises himself as the gardener's son in order to conquer Flérida's love. Although the portion that corresponds to *Flérida* eliminates the season in which the action takes place (stage 1) and the sea-voyage (stage 5), overall it is more faithful to the Vicentine original than group 2 of *Flérida*. Except for this part of the ballad, which rhymes in *í–a*, the rest of the poem is strophic. This suggests that it derives from a "chapbook," a *folheto de cordel* that adapted a portion of the play in quatrains. Since *O Hortelão* is exclusively Portuguese, the *folheto* in question was probably composed in Portugal, and probably failed to make its way into neighboring Spain.

Except for the Azorean rendition of *Flérida* (group 1), which retains the spirit of idealized love found in the original, the other modern versions of the ballad find it necessary to condemn the elopement that it portrays, either in an explicit or in an implied, implicit manner. The elopement always leads to disaster, even though, in the Spanish versions, the princess eventually meets with redemption thanks to the intervention of the Virgin Mary. In *O Hortelão*, however, the heroine does not pay dearly for the step she has taken. *B* concludes with the elopement and fails to reveal what happened afterward. In *A* the princess discovers that her lover is Don Duardos and returns home in order to tell her mother what happened. In both versions, however, the hero had told her that he was the son of a butcher, a startling revelation which, nevertheless, did not cause her to change her plans to elope. She could not have cared less. This suggests that disparate unions were condoned, pointing to a period that encouraged social climbing. Given the paucity of the evidence, it is impossible to determine when such a poem was composed, but it is very unlikely to be earlier than the beginning of the eighteenth century.

2. Lizarda

Like *O Hortelão das Flores*, *Lizarda* also concludes with *Flérida*, drawing background material from the *Tragicomedia* in order to explain the princess's elopement. The background material is equally strophic, thus pointing to another late adaptation of Vicente's play.

In *Lizarda*, while in her garden, Flérida sees the prince hunting and falls in love with him at once. She seizes the initiative by sending her lady-in-waiting to Don Duardos to learn if he reciprocates her feeling. This move eliminates the need for the ruse employed by the prince in *Hortelão das Flores* and in the play itself. On the other hand, the role played by the intermediary receives heavier emphasis here.

In Portugal, *Lizarda* is found only on the islands, and there are three Brazilian versions as well. The first Azorean version, from the island of São Jorge, dates from 1869 (Braga 1869, no. 36; = Braga 1906–9, 1: 439–42). In 1971 and 1972, I recorded two highly condensed versions from immigrants from São Jorge in Manteca and Modesto, California (Cal, nos. 104–5;[7] see also Costa Fontes 1978–79), and in 1977, while in São Jorge, I found a fragment in the village of

Rosais (SJ, no. 154). The other Azorean versions are from Flores (Silveira 1986, no. 2;[8] Cortes-Rodrigues 1987, 318–19) and São Miguel (Can, no. 198). The last one is a fragment recorded in 1978 by an immigrant in Toronto. There are two excellent versions from Madeira (Rodrigues de Azevedo 1880, 191–201; = Braga 1906–9, 1: 432–39). In Brazil, *Lizarda* has been collected in Pernambuco (Pereira da Costa 1908, 302–9; 2 versions) and Sergipe (Silva Lima 1977, no. 24).[9]

Unlike with *O Hortelão*, these twelve versions of *Lizarda* do not differ so much from each other as to render impossible the construction of a synthetic text:

	*No jardim do seu recreio passeava uma donzela
2	tão linda como engraçada, como as mesmas flores bela.
	Seus cuidados e disvelos era no jardim das flores,
4	por não saber até ali que haviam outros amores.
	Seu nome era Lizarda, única filha, herdeira,
6	filha do rei d'Aragão, por ser na casa a primeira.
	Saindo à tarde à caça a um monte que ali 'stava,
8	a um monte sobranceiro, o príncipe à caça andava.
	Lizarda botou seus olhos ao príncipe, como inocente,
10	e já com setas d'amor seu peito ferido sente.
	—Lo amor não tem alteza, eu vou arriscar quem sou;
12	vou arriscar minha fama, d'amor já lhe falar vou.
	—Assossegue voss'alteza, repare que nã lhe convém
14	arrical'a sua fama por amor desse qu'rer bem.
	É necessário primeiro do príncipe o intento ver
16	para então poder seguir e declarar seu bem querer.
	—Dizes bem, querida dama; disfarçarei entre as flores;
18	e do príncipe vai saber si por mim morre de amores.
	—Tomo isto a minha conta, e detenha-se vossa alteza;
20	a passos cheios andando irei com toda a presteza.
	—Daquele monte sobranceiro, mirando este jardim,
22	eu vi estar ũa flor que parecia um jasmim.
	—Esse jasmim, meu senhor, que procura vossa alteza,
24	é deste jardim senhora e deste reino princesa.
	Louquinha de amor me disse, si algum bem vós lhe quereis,
26	na porta do seu jardim de noite falar-lhe ireis.
	—Esta jóia, bela dama, de alvíçaras te ofereço,
28	si eu chegar a lograr uma flor que não mereço.
	—Diga, senhor, não me engane, seus passos, sua tenção?
30	—As vias que eu venho no meu coração estão.
	—Adeus, senhor Dom João, haja segredo e cautela,
32	que lhe dou minha palavra de ser sua essa flor bela.
	—Adeus, minha rica dama, dizei ao meu serafim
34	que à noite sem falta estou na porta do seu jardim.

—Agora, minha senhora,   pode ficar bem segura
36   que lo nobre forasteiro   por seu amor s'aventura.
Que el'é de nobre sangue   bem podeis ficar segura;
38   no amor dele, senhora,   nã vos faltará ventura.
'Stá por vós louco d'amor   e, se bem algum lhe qu'reis,
40   esta noit'àquela porta   dar-lh'uma fala podeis.
—Cala-te, querida dama,   não mo digas, porqu'estou
42   tão perdida pelo príncipe,   que quasi morrendo estou.
Esta tard', ó aia minha,   minhas jóias ajuntar,
44   que eu à noite pertendo   com meu amor m'ausentar.
Ó sol, que a quarenta raios   luzes ao mundo vás dando,
46   apressa mais os teus passos,   que por amores 'stou penando.
—Chega, chega, noit'escura,   dos amantes desejada,
48   p'ra que feliz eu alcance   prenda de mim tão amada.
—À porta do meu jardim   ouço passos; quem será?
50   é a flor por quem eu morro,   que em meu peito está?
—Vós 'stais 'í, qu'rida minha,   minha princes'adorada?
52   —Eu estou cá, luz dos meus olhos,   minha rica prenda amada.
—Dá-me cá esses teus braços   e juntamente o querer;
54   quero apagar o fogo   que no peito sinto arder.
—Toma lá estes meus braços,   também o meu coração;
56   também podeis aceitar   por esposa a minha mão.
Vamos imbora daqui,   antes qu'eu seja sentida,
58   que logo toda pessoa   saberá minha fugida.
—Montai-vos aqui, senhora,   às ancas neste cavalo,
60   que bem segura vós is,   sem sofrer nenhum abalo.
—Adeus, meu jardim das flores,   minha fonte d'água fria,
62   que em quanto eu mais viver,   te verei tão só lo dia;
adeus, adeus, rouxinol,   que cantais ao meio-dia;
64   adeus, palácio, adeus, jardim,   onde eu me divertia;
adeus, aia da minh'alma,   com quem eu tanto me qu'ria.
66   Mal la fortuna me leva,   mal la fortuna me guia;
não sei se me furta um rei,   s'homem de baixa valia.
68   Adeus, ó pai de minh'alma,   adeus, mãe de minha vida,
que para sempre se aparta   tua prenda mais querida.
70   Se meu pai te perguntar,   pois que muito me queria,
dize-lhe que o amor me leva,   a culpa que não é minha.
72   E s'alguém quer saber mais   parte da minha fugida,
pergunt'ò deus dos amores,   que dele me vou bem f'rida.
74   —Calai-vos, senhora rainha,   nã choreis, minh'alegria,
qu'eu sou lo filho dum rei,   príncipe d'alta valia:
76   que também na Inglaterra   tem águas la fonte fria;
los jardins têm passarinhos   que cantam todo lo dia;
78   tem la corte muitas damas   que vos farão companhia;
lá tenho paços reais   de oiro e pedraria,
80   tudo isto e muito mais   pera vossa senhoria.

(In her garden of recreation there strolled a maiden, both pretty and spirited, as beautiful as the very flowers. Her concern and devotion were about the flower garden, because she did not know that other love existed. Her name was Lizarda, only daughter and heir, daughter of the king of Aragon; she was his firstborn. Having left in the afternoon for a nearby mountain, a towering mountain, the prince was hunting. Lizarda set her eyes innocently on the prince and at once, with love arrows, she feels her bosom wounded. "Love has no rank; I am going to take a risk; I shall risk my reputation and speak to him of love now." "Pray calm down, your highness; note that it is not becoming to risk your reputation for the sake of that love. First it is necessary to see the intentions of the prince, to be able to continue and then declare your love." "You speak well, dear lady; I will dissimulate among the flowers while you go and find out if he is dying of love for me." "I will take care of the affair. Please hold back, your highness. I will walk with big strides and go as quickly as possible." "While on that towering mountain I looked at this garden, and saw a beautiful flower; it looked like a jasmine." "That jasmine, my lord, for which you are looking, is the owner of this garden and a princess in this kingdom. Madly in love, she told me that if you feel anything for her, by the door of this garden you will speak with her tonight." "This jewel, beautiful lady, I offer you as reward if I am able to obtain that flower, which I don't deserve." "Pray tell me, Sir, do not deceive me, your motives and intentions?" "The paths that I follow are imprinted in my heart." "Farewell, Lord Don João; let there be secrecy and caution, and I give you my word, that beautiful flower will be yours." "Farewell, my dear lady; let my angel know that tonight, without fail, I will be by the door of her garden." "My lady, now you can be absolutely certain that the noble stranger is interested in your love. He is of noble blood, of that you can be certain; in his love, my lady, you will not lack happiness. He loves you madly and, if you care for him at all, tonight, by that door, you can speak with him." "Be silent, dear lady, do not even say that to me; I'm so much in love with the prince, I am almost ready to die. This afternoon, my lady-in-waiting, put my jewelry together, for tonight I intend to elope with my love. Oh sun, which with forty rays gives light to the world, quicken more your steps, for I suffer much with love." "Hurry, hurry, dark night, which lovers so much desire, so that I can happily attain the gift that I love so." "By the door of my garden I hear steps; who could it be? Is it the flower for whom I'm dying and that is in my bosom?" "Are you there, my beloved, my adored princess?" "I am here, light of my eyes, my dear, beloved gift." "Give me your arms, together with your love; I want to put out the fire that I feel burning in my bosom." "Take these arms of mine and the heart as well; you can also accept my hand as wife. Let's leave here at once, before my ab-

sence is noticed; soon everyone will know that I have run away."
"Pray mount here, my lady, on the back of this horse, for you will be
very safe, and will not feel any discomfort." "Farewell, my garden of
flowers, my fountain of cold water; no matter how long I live, this is
the last day I see you; farewell; farewell, nightingale, who sings at
midday; farewell, palace; farewell, garden, where I used to enjoy
myself; farewell, lady-in-waiting of my soul, whom I so much loved.
Fortune is carrying me away me badly; badly fortune guides me; I
know not if I elope with a king, or a man of low rank. Farewell, father of my soul; farewell, mother of my life; it is forever that your
dearest daughter is leaving. If my father asks for me, for he loved
me very much, tell him that love takes me, that the fault is not
mine. Should anyone wish to know more details of my elopement,
let him ask the god of love, for he has wounded me deeply." "Be
silent, my lady and queen, do not cry, my joy, for I'm the son of a
king, a high-ranking prince: For also in England the cold fountain
has water; the gardens have little birds that sing all day long; the
court has many ladies who shall keep you company; there I own
royal palaces of gold and precious stones. All of this and much more
awaits your ladyship.")

Sources

Az. 1	= Rodrigues de Azevedo 1880, 191–96 (Madeira)
Az. 2	= Rodrigues de Azevedo 1880, 196–201 (Madeira)
Cantos	= Braga 1869, no. 36 (São Jorge)
SJ	= SJ, no. 154 (São Jorge)
Cal 104	= Cal, no. 104 (São Jorge)
Cal 105	= Cal, no. 105 (São Jorge)
Can	= Can, no. 198 (São Miguel)
Silv.	= Silveira 1986, no. 2 (Flores)
CR	= Cortes-Rodrigues 1987, 318–19 (Flores)
PC 1	= Pereira da Costa 1908, 302–5 (Pernambuco)
PC 2	= Pereira da Costa 1908, 305–9 (Pernambuco)
SL	= Silva Lima 1977, no. 24 (Sergipe)

Variants

1–2: Cantos; cf. Az. 2; SJ; Can; Silv.; CR; PC 1–2.

3–4: Cantos; cf. Az. 1–2; SJ; Cal 104–5; Silv.; CR; PC 2. 4*b*: que coisa fos-
sem amores (Az. 1–2); "qu'havia o rei dos amores" (SJ; cf. Cal 104–5);
"que havia deus dos amores" (Silv.; CR; PC 2).

5–6: Cantos; cf. Silv.; CR; PC 1–2. 5*a*: rei de Abraão (SJ); rei Adragão
(Cal 104); 6*b*: e da c'roa la herdeira (Az. 2); 6*b* + : Retirou-se p'ra outras

quintas, / suas aias divertia; // com correntes de cristal / alegre passava o dia (Silv.; cf. PC 2).

7–8: Cantos; cf. Az. 1–2; Um dia lá estava ela, / cantando à fidalguia, // nisto passa um cavaleiro, / dela se namoraria (Cal 104; cf. Cal 105).

9–10: Cantos; cf. Az. 1; Silv.; CR; PC 1–2; Ele le põe los olhos, / ela que fica manente; // cada olhar, cada ferro / cravado no peito sente (Az. 2); 10*b* + Quando o príncipe a viu / foi tal a inquietação // que aos olhos lhe arrebentaram / lágrimas do coração (Cantos).

11–12: Az. 1; —Nã sei p'ra onde me vá, / nem me conheço quem sou; // 'stou louca d'amor por ele, / ao monte falar-lhe vou (Az. 2); Vem cá tu, minha rica ama, / discreta entre as mais flores; // vai-me saber daquele homem / se ele morre dos meus amores (Silv.); —Até agora, aia minha, / [. . .] // viveu quieto meu peito, / e nele o deus dos amores (CR); —Até agora, minhas damas, / vivia quieto o meu peito, // pois o cego deus do amor / seus tiros não tinha feito. // Sem atender quem eu sou, / ponho em risco a minha fama, // e sem nela reparar / ao príncipe falar me vou (PC 1; cf. PC 2).

13–14: Az. 1; cf. Az. 2; Cantos; —Senhora ama e princesa, / isso à minha conta fica, // mas recolha-se vossa alteza; recolha-se, que nã convém // arriscar a sua vida / por amor dum querer bem (Silv.); Nisto logo lhe acudiu / sua mais querida dama: // —Detenha-se vossa alteza, / advirto-lhe, não convém // que semelhante passo dê / em troca de querer bem (PC 1; cf. PC 2).

15–16: PC 1; cf. PC 2.

17–18: PC 2; cf. Az. 1–2; Cantos; PC 1; —Ô criada, ô criada, / vai fazer os meus mandados, / se algum bem me quisesse / uma palavra me desse / de noite no meu jardim (SL).

19–20: PC 2; —Isso fic'à minha conta, / recolha-se voss'alteza, // que los passos p'ra nós guia / ele já com gran lesteza (Az. 1; cf. Az. 2; Cantos).

21–22: Silv.; cf. Az. 1–2; Cantos; PC 1–2; 17*b* da brancura do jasmim (Az. 1); also note the following Brazilian variant:

> —Vinde, vinde, bela dama,   que vos quero perguntar
> 28   que caminho é este aqui,   qu'eu não sei onde vai dar.
> Eu não sei por onde irei,   nem mesmo por onde vim,
> 30   por causa de uma bela flor   que vi naquele jardim.
> Essa flor, si não me engano,   que vi naquele jardim,

32 essa flor, si não me engano, pareceu-me ser jasmim.
   Desde que tal jasmim vi, tão perdido me deixou,
34 que não sei de onde vim e nem sei para onde vou.
   Dizei-me, dama galharda, onde essa flor se encerra,
36 porque com setas de amor todo meu peito é guerra.

                 (PC 2; cf. PC 1)

23–24: PC 1; cf. Az. 1–2; Cantos; Silv.; PC 2.

25–26: PC 2; cf. Az. 1–2; Cantos.

27–28: PC 2; cf. Az. 1, 2 (anel); Cantos (anel); Cal 105 (anel); PC 1; —Se eu pensasse de lograr / um jardim que eu não mereço. . . . (SL).

29–30: PC 2. *Missing in all others.*

31–32: PC 2; cf. Az. 1 (rico senhor), 2 (generoso forasteiro); Cantos; PC 1.

33–34: PC 2; cf. Az. 1, PC 1.

35–36: Az. 1; cf. Az. 2, PC 1–2.

37–40: Az. 2. *Missing in all others.*

41–42: PC 2. *Missing in all others.*

43–44: Az. 1; cf. Az. 2; Cantos; PC 1–2.

45–46: Cantos; cf. Az. 2, PC 1–2; SL. *The speaker is not always clear.*

47–48: Az. 1; cf. Az. 2; Cantos; Noite de mim desejada, / com tuas sombras escuras, // permiti que venturosa / goze das minhas venturas (PC 2). *The speaker is not always clear.*

49–50: PC 2; cf. PC1; La noit'escura chegou, / passos mansinhos vêm lá; // serão ambos ou um só? / Algum deles faltará? (Az. 2).

51: Az. 1; cf. Az. 2; Cantos; Silv.; PC 1–2.

52: Silv.; cf. Az. 1–2; Cantos; PC 1–2.

53–54: Cantos; cf. Az. 1; Silv.; PC 2; SL.

55–56: Silv.; cf. Cantos; PC 2; —Aqui tendel'os meus braços, / junto vai lo coração. // —Vinde ser minha mulher, / aqui tendes minha mão (Az. 1); —

Vinde comigo, princesa, / dona do meu coração. // —Mas haveis d'arrece-
ber-me / por mulher, na vossa mão. // —Agora vinde comigo, / ao mais nã
digo que não (Az. 2).

57–58: Az. 1. *Missing in all others.*

59–60: Az. 1; cf. PC 1–2; Amonta-se nesse cavalo / a senhora sem mais
abalo (SL).

61–62: Cantos; adeus, janelas tão altas, / janelas de ond'eu via // correrem
las águas claras, / las águas da fonte fria (Az. 1); —Ficai, meu jardim das
flores, / ficai, fontes d'água fria (Az. 2); —Adeus, casa de meus pais, /
adeus, mimoso jardim; // hoje se aparta uma flor / para séculos sem fim
(Cal 104; cf. Cal 105); Adeus, aias e criadas, / adeus, jardim, adeus, flores,
// que eu pretendo esta noite / ir com o deus dos amores (Silv.); —Adeus,
palácio real, / adeus, jardim, adeus, flores (PC 2).

63: PC1; onde cantam passarinhos / todal'as horas do dia (Az. 2).

64: PC1; Adeus, palácios reais, / palácios ond'eu vivia (Az. 1); Ficai-vos,
paços reais / de oiro e pedraria (Az. 2).

65: Az. 1; Ficai vós, dama fiel, / que mais fiel nã n'havia (Az. 2); Fica-te
embora, Menónia, / minha leal companhia (Cantos).

66–67: Az. 1; ficai-vos vós, pai e mãe, / pai e mãe qu'eu tanto qu'ria. //
Furta-me nã sei s'um rei, / s'homem de baixa valia (Az. 2).

68–69: PC 1; cf. PC 2; —Or'adeus, pai da minh'alma, / qu'eu me vou p'ra
terr'alheia; // la vossa casa vazia / fôra p'ra mim sempre cheia. // Or'adeus,
mãe da minh'alma, / adeus, mãe da minha vida; // hoje s'ausenta de vós /
la vossa filha tão qu'rida (Az. 1); Adeus, casa, adeus, espelhos, / adeus, pai
da minha vida, // que hoje de ti se aparta / uma prenda tão querida (Cantos); Adeus, pai da minha alma, / adeus, mãe da minha vida, // que tão má
paga vos deu / vossa prenda mais querida (Silv.); 69*b* + : Bem sei que o
nome de ingrata / requer minha crueldade, // de deixar quem me criou / em
uma tão pouca idade (PC 1; cf. PC 2).

70–71: Cantos; Se meu pai cá perguntar / por uma filha que tinha, //
digam que me lev'amor, // muito por vontade minha (Az. 2; cf. PC 1); que
por ser amante firme / me leva o deus dos amores (PC 2).

72–73: Az. 1; —S'alguém procurar quiser / parte da minha fugida, // no
reino d'amor procure, / que p'ra lá vou de corrida (Az. 2); Quem melhor
quiser saber / partes da minha fugida, // pergunte a quem tem amores, /
pois que eu deles vou perdida (PC 2).

74: Az. 1; —Nã vos vades tão soidosa, / não choreis, minh'alegria (Az. 2); —Não chore, rica princesa, / que não tem porque chorar (SL).

75: Az 2.

76: Az. 1; Também lá na minha terra / tem águas la fonte fria (Az. 2).

77: Az. 2.

78: Az. 2; Tenho vinte-quatro damas, / que são nobre companhia (Az. 1); Eu tenho duzentas criadas / todas vestidas e trajadas / só p'ra vossa senhoria (SL).

79: Az. 2; Lá tenho paços, janelas, / e coisas de mais valia (Az. 1).

80: Az. 1; lá tenho pais que serão / pais de vossa senhoria (Az. 2).

In some versions, the princess lavishes all her attention on her garden because, rather than failing to know what love was (4a), she is unaware that there was a "king" or "god" of love (4a). In two instances she does not see the hunting prince from her garden (7–8), but from a country house she was visiting with her ladies-in-waiting. The versions from Pernambuco expand considerably the prince's reaction to the beautiful girl he had seen (21–22). Utterly dazzled, he has forgotten whence he came and does not even know his destination, for love arrows have pierced his heart. Although the princess takes the initiative, proposing marriage just before eloping (55–56), in one instance the prince is the one who asks her to marry him.

The portion of the ballad that corresponds to *Flérida* (61–80) was especially difficult to reconstruct because it varies considerably from version to version, ranging from 2 (Cal 104–5) to 19 verses (Az. 1). The versions that condense *Flérida* to 2 verses also change the original's rhyme from *í–a* to *í*:

> —Adeus, casa de meus pais,   adeus, mimoso jardim;
> 16   hoje se aparta uma flor   para séculos sem fim.
>
> (Cal 104)

("Farewell, house of my parents; farewell, delicate garden; today is departing a flower for centuries without end.")

The earliest version from São Jorge preserves Flérida's farewell to her garden (41–42; stage 2) and the excuse for her father regarding the power of love (44–45; stage 3), but then it goes back to the farewell to the garden (46–47; stage 2). Note that in this version the lady-in-waiting, to whom the princess also says good-bye (43), is named Menónia:

> Adeus, casa, adeus, espelhos,　adeus, pai da minha vida,
> 42　que hoje de ti se aparta　uma prenda tão querida.
> Fica-te embora, Menónia,　minha leal companhia.
> 44　Se meu pai te perguntar,　pois que muito me queria,
> dize-lhe que o amor me leva,　a culpa que não é minha.
> 46　Adeus, meu jardim das flores,　minha fonte d'água fria,
> que em quanto eu mais viver,　te verei tão só lo dia.
>
> (Cantos)

("Farewell, house; farewell, mirrors; farewell, father of my life, for today is departing from you such a beloved gift. Farewell to you, Menónia, my loyal companion. If my father asks for me, for he loved me very much, tell him that love takes me, that the fault is not mine. Farewell, my garden of flowers, my fountain of cold water; no matter how long I live, this is the last day I see you.")

In one of the versions from Madeira, the part that corresponds to *Flérida* begins when the prince invites the princess to mount on his horse (43–44):

> —Montai-vos aqui, senhora,　às ancas neste cavalo,
> 44　que bem segura vós is,　sem sofrer nenhum abalo.
> —Mal la fortuna me leva,　mal la fortuna me guia;
> 46　não sei se me furta um rei,　s'homem de baixa valia.
> Adeus, palácios reais,　palácios ond'eu vivia;
> 48　adeus, janelas tão altas,　janelas de ond'eu via
> correrem las águas claras,　las águas da fonte fria;
> 50　adeus, aia da minh'alma,　com quem eu tanto me qu'ria.
> —Calai-vos, senhora rainha,　nã choreis, minh'alegria,
> 52　que também na Inglaterra　tem águas la fonte fria.
> Lá tenho paços, janelas,　e coisas de mais valia.
> 54　Tenho vinte-quatro damas,　que são nobre companhia,
> tudo isto e muito mais　pera vossa senhoria.
> 56　—Or'adeus, pai da minh'alma,　qu'eu me vou p'ra terr'alheia;
> la vossa casa vazia　fôra p'ra mim sempre cheia.
> 58　Or'adeus, mãe da minh'alma,　adeus, mãe da minha vida;
> hoje s'ausenta de vós　la vossa filha tão qu'rida.
> 60　E s'alguém quer saber mais　parte da minha fugida,
> pergunt'ò deus dos amores,　que dele me vou bem f'rida.
>
> (Az. 1)

("Pray mount here, my lady, on the back of this horse, for you will be very safe, and will not feel any discomfort." "Fortune is taking me badly; badly fortune guides me; I know not if I am eloping with a king or a man of low rank. Farewell, royal palaces, palaces where I used to live; farewell, tall windows, windows where I used to watch the clear water run, the water of the cold fountain; farewell, lady-in-waiting of my soul, whom I so much loved." "Be silent, my lady and queen, do not cry, my joy, for also in England the cold fountain has water. There I own palaces, windows, and things of greater worth. I have twenty-five ladies; they are noble company. All of this and much more awaits your ladyship." "Farewell, father of my soul, I'm leaving to a strange land; your house is now empty, but it was always full for me. Farewell, mother of my soul; farewell, mother of my life; today withdraws from you your beloved daughter. Should anyone wish to know more details of my elopement, let him ask the god of love, for he has wounded me deeply.")

Although in a different rhyme (*á–o*), the first two verses correspond to the departure in Don Duardos's galleys (stage 5). The princess then expresses misgivings by referring to her fortune (45–46). This could correspond either to stage 3 or to the part of stage 2 in which she uses *ventura*, a variant of the word *fortuna*: "Voyme a tierras estrañas, / pues ventura allá me guía" (I am going to strange lands, for fate guides me there; 10). The ballad continues with the princess's farewell (47–50; stage 2), the prince's reassurances (51–55; stage 4), and then returns to the farewell with two interpolated quatrains (56–59), the first of which rhymes in *-eia*. The concluding reference to the god of love (60–61) could either be an expansion of the excuse that Flérida leaves for her father, in which she mentions the power of love (stage 3), or correspond to the original's statement regarding the powerlessness of human beings before death and love (stage 6). The latter is in the third person, however. Since here these words are spoken by Flérida, in the reconstructed version I treated them as part of stage 3, because it was it was impossible to fit them properly at the very end.

Some versions include contaminations. The most common one, which I have retained in the synthetic version, is in verse 1, "No jardim do seu recreio / passeava uma donzela" (In her garden of recreation there strolled a maiden), which appears, with minor variants, in no less than 8 of the 12 versions (Az. 2; Cantos; SJ; Can; Silv.; CR; PC 1–2). It recalls the early *incipit* of the epic *As Ameias de Toro* (*Las almenas de Toro* [The Battlements of Toro]; RPI, A9; CMP, A6), "Por las almenas de Toro / se pasea una doncella" (On the battlements of Toro there strolls a maiden; Menéndez Pelayo 1945, 9: 86–87), a ballad about King Sancho II's siege of his sister Elvira in order to dispossess her of the city of Toro, which she had inherited from her father, Fernando I (see Armistead and Silverman 1986, 161–86). This contamination was first noticed by Samuel G. Armistead and Joseph H. Silverman, who in their introduction to my *Romanceiro Português dos Estados Unidos*, 1: *Nova Inglaterra*, pointed out that, "as elsewhere in modern tradition, the toponymic reference to Toro (in v. 1) has been replaced by some more general *lectio facilior*" (NI, x). Rather than walking on the battlements of Toro, the maiden now strolls in her garden.[10]

The second version from Flores is a fragment. Having seen the prince, Lizarda informs her lady-in-waiting that she has fallen in love, and the word "love" triggers a contamination with the part of *Não me Enterrem em Sagrado* (Bury Me Not in Holy Ground; *El testamento del enamorado* [The Lover's Testament]; RPI, K5; CMP, K12) in which the dying protagonist states that lovesickness does not have a cure, and that whoever perishes from it ought not to be buried in holy ground:

> —Mal de amores não tem cura,   que é um mal apaixonado.
> 14   Quem morre de mal de amores   não se enterra em sagrado,
>   enterra-se em campos verdes   onde se apastora o gado,
> 16   [. . . . .]   com um letreiro letrado,
>   para quem passar ver e ter: "Morreu de mal de amores, coitado".
>   (CR)

(Lovesickness has no cure; it is a difficult illness. Whoever dies of lovesickness cannot be buried in holy ground, only in the green meadows where the cattle is herded, [. . .] and with an enameled sign for passersby to see and behold: "He died of lovesickness, poor man.")

Since this version ends at this point, what we have here is a case of poor memory; it does not really affect the structure of the ballad.[11] Much more interesting are the contaminations in the two highly condensed versions from São Jorge collected in California, which begin:

> Era uma triste donzela,   filha dum rei Adragão;
> 2   seu pai apartou-a de si   por causa da sua feição.
>   Ele tinha sete filhas,   ela era a escolhida:
> 4   mandou-a fechar numa torre   p'ra ela não ser pretendida.
>   (Cal 104)

(There was a sad maiden, daughter of a king of Aragon ["Adragon"]; her father pushed her away because of her looks. He had seven daughters; she was the chosen one; he had her locked up in a tower so that no one would court her.)

The heroine loses her name and no longer spends her time happily among the flowers in the garden, becoming a "triste donzela" (sad maiden) instead. Although she still remains daughter of the king of Aragon, these versions add that she is one of seven daughters, and this, together with the name "Aragon," brings to mind *Donzela Guerreira* (*La doncella guerrera* [The Warrior-Girl]; RPI, X5; CMP, X4), a ballad in which an old warrior complains that he himself has to go to the wars being fought between France and Aragon because his wife failed to give him a male son to take his place:

> —Grandes guerras 'stão armadas   entre França e Aragão!
> 2   Mal o hajas tu, mulher,   mais a tua criação;
> sete filhas que tiveste   sem nenhuma ser varão!
> (Braga 1906–9, 1: 95)

("Great wars are taking place between France and Aragon! Cursed be thee, woman, together with everything you bred; you had seven daughters and not even one son.")

The heroine is presented as her father's favorite daughter (3). This resulted from the compression of the passage that designates Lizarda as successor to the throne (vv. 5–6 of the synthetic version). Being her father's favorite, however, constituted no boon for the girl: He had her imprisoned in a tower to prevent anyone from courting her (4). Such a fate is explainable through contamination with *Delgadinha* (RPI, P2; CMP, P2), a ballad whose heroine—indeed her father's "favorite"—is locked up in a tower for rejecting his incestuous advances:[12]

> Seu pai, quando isto ouviu,   não mandou fazer mais nada;
> mandou fazer uma torre   para Deolinda ser fechada.
> (VRP, no. 500)

(Her father, hearing this, had nothing but this done: he had a tower built to lock up Deolinda.)

Clearly, the two highly condensed versions of *Lizarda* collected in California change the ballad to such an extent that they practically amount to a different text-type. The ballad continues as follows:

mandou fazer um jardim   p'rà menina passear;
6   era de manhã e à noite,   nele s'ia recreiar.
  Um dia lá estava ela,   cantando à fidalguia,
8   nisto passa um cavaleiro,   dela se namoraria.
  —Que fazes aí, menina,   nessa estreita morada?
10   Hoje se sobe um príncipe   para seres resgatada.
  —Meu cuidado e desvelo   é neste jardim de flores;
12   nunca pensei que no mundo   houvesse o rei dos amores.
  —Deixe-me subir a este muro,   quero-lhe dar minha mão;
14   se não a levo comigo   estala meu coração.
  —Adeus, casa de meus pais,   adeus, mimoso jardim;
16   hoje se aparta uma flor   para séculos sem fim.

                        (Cal, no. 104)

(he had a garden made for the girl to go strolling; both morning and night she enjoyed herself there. One day there she was, singing in the noble manner, when a knight went by and fell in love with her. "What are you doing, girl, in such a narrow dwelling? Today a prince shall climb it in order to rescue you." "My concern and devotion is about this garden of flowers; I never thought that in the world there was a King of Love." "Let me climb this wall; I want to marry you; if I fail to take you with me my heart will break." "Farewell, house of my parents; farewell, delicate garden; today is departing a flower for centuries without end.")

Having locked up his daughter in a tower in order to fend off all suitors, the king nevertheless has a garden made for her and she is there from morning until evening (5–6). A prince goes by, falls in love, and decides to rescue her (7–10). This is quite different from the other versions, where the princess falls in love first and then takes the initiative. Rather than eloping, here she is rescued from her father's prison. The part that corresponds to *Flérida* is reduced to a two-verse farewell (15–16).

Even in the more complete versions of *Lizarda*, the background material leading to the elopement is not as clearly related to the *Tragicomedia* as *O Hortelão das Flores*, and there are important differences between the ballad and the play. Whereas Flérida visits her garden frequently, Lizarda spends all of her time in the garden, centering her attention on its beautiful flowers because she does not know any other type of love (1–4). Thus this garden, which is the topical *locus amoenus* that serves as stage for lovers' trysts, receives even more emphasis than in the *Tragicomedia*.

The instant manner in which Lizarda falls in love with the prince when she sees him hunting nearby (7–10) is also quite different from the play, where Don Duardos disguises himself as the gardener's son in order to earn Flérida's love. The prince's hunt, of course, brings to mind the hunt of love mentioned in *O Hortelão* but, unlike the *Tragicomedia* and *O Hortelão*, here the princess is the one who takes the initiative. She informs her lady-in-waiting that she must speak to the prince at once, even though she is risking her reputation (11–12). This passage has its counterpart in the *Tragicomedia*, when Flérida confesses to Artada her love for the gardener's son:

¡Oh, Artada, mi amiga,	Oh Artada, my friend,
llave de mi coraçón!:	key of my heart!
tal me hallo,	I feel such
que no sé cómo os diga	that I neither know how to tell you
ni calle tanta passión	nor how to keep to myself as much passion
como callo. (197)	as I do.

Shocked, Artada wonders:

¡Jesús!, y vuessa grandeza,	Jesus! What about your greatness,
vuesso imperio y merecer,	your power and worth?
¿qué le dirán? (198)	What will people say?

In the ballad, right after Lizarda's confession the lady-in-waiting warns her not to risk her reputation (13–16). This confirms the relationship with the play at this point, for the sequence is the same.

Accepting the lady-in-waiting's advice to inquire about the prince's feelings, Lizarda decides to allow her to address the prince, while she herself remains among the flowers (17–18). In the play, unable to forget the new gardener after a self-imposed three-day absence, the love-stricken Flérida also "manda primero a Artada" (sends Artada first; 208).

When the lady-in-waiting arrives, the prince compares Lizarda, whom he had seen, to a jasmine. The lady reveals that Lizarda is in love with him and that, if the feeling is mutual, Lizarda would like to meet him by the door of the garden in the evening (21–26). Flérida is much less forward in the *Tragicomedia*. She sends Artada to ascertain who the hero really is, because his manners and speech do not seem to be those of a gardener's son. Wondering why Flérida has not appeared for three days in the garden, Don Duardos asks her, "No verná, por vuessa fe?" (Won't he come, as far as you know? 210), to which Artada replies: "No, hasta ser sabidora, / quien sois vos" (No, not until she knows who you are; 210). Although he would like very much to see Flérida, Don Duardos still refuses to reveal his identity. Obsessed with the idea of love for the sake of love, he wants the princess to love him regardless of his social standing:

Quien tiene amor verdadero	The one who loves truly
no pergunta	does not ask
ni por alto ni por baxo	about high or low rank,
ni igual ni mediano.	or even equal or median rank.
Sepa, pues,	Know, then,
que el amor que aquí me traxo,	that even if I were a low peasant
aunque yo fuesse villano,	the love that brought me here
él no lo es. (210)	is not low.

Convinced that he is of noble blood, Artada advises Flérida to approach him herself (213). When she does, Don Duardos is the one who arranges a meeting in the evening, promising to disclose his identity to her at that time:

Será a horas y en lugar	It will be at a time and place
que estén solas las estrellas	when the stars alone
de presente,	will be present,
los árboles sin lunar	the trees bereft of the moon,
y Artada allí con ellas	Artada among them,
sin más gente.	and no one else.
Allí os descobriré	There I shall reveal to you
quién soy, y seréis servida	who I am, and your will shall be done,
pues queréis	for you refuse
no crer quién yo soy, por fe,	to believe who I am through faith alone,
que por vos tomé esta vida	and that for your sake I chose
que me veis. (218)	this profession you see.

In the ballad, where the encounter has been arranged by the lady-in-waiting at Lizarda's request, the prince displays his gratitude by offering her a jewel, upon which she recommends secrecy and care, promising that Lizarda will be his. When the lady then informs the princess that the meeting has been arranged, she adds that the hero is of noble blood (27–40). In the *Tragicomedia*, Artada also informs Flérida, right after her meeting, that Don Duardos must be a great nobleman: "Señora, no es villano, / mas gran cosa" (Madam, he is not a peasant, but a great lord; 213). It is only after this episode that Artada, who until then opposed Flérida's love for Don Duardos, advises her mistress to speak to him: "Mas, señora, vaya allá / sola vuessa señoría" (But Madam, your ladyship should go there alone; 213).

In the ballad, the love-stricken Lizarda decides to elope before the meeting and bids her lady-in-waiting to gather her jewelry (41–44). The ballad goes on to describe how eagerly both lovers wait for the appointed hour (45–48). In the *Tragicomedia*, Flérida decides to elope only after she herself has spoken to Don Duardos, stating that she is placing herself in the hands of Fortune (224). She does, however, express some anxiety just before the meeting, saying to Artada:

> Ardo en fuego de contino   I burn continuously with fire,
> con ansias que no han nombre   with longings that do not have a name
> ni medida. (219)   and cannot be restrained.

Nevertheless, it is impossible to establish a direct textual parallel between the ballad and the play at this point. Like the ballad (45–46), the play also refers to the sun, but it is Artada who mentions it in order to remind Flérida that it is time for her tryst with Don Duardos: "Acuérdeseos, señora, que el Sol es partido" (Pray remember, Madam, that the sun is down; 220).

The ballad goes on to describe the meeting of the two lovers in the garden. Lizarda hears the prince's footsteps as he arrives and ends up asking him to marry her and to take her away at once, before her absence is noticed (49–58). In the play, Don Duardos shows up dressed as a prince but still fails to tell Flérida his name, and the princess worries about her parents and her reputation before boarding the waiting galleys (222–24).

The background material in *O Hortelão das Flores*, then, is more clearly related to the *Tragicomedia* than that in *Lizarda*. In *O Hortelão*, the old woman from whom the hero seeks advice in order to conquer the princess corresponds to Olimba, and the advice she gives him is essentially the same: to disguise himself in humble attire in order to enter the garden. The gardener who lets the prince in parallels Julián, and the princess falls in love right after drinking water, which recalls the magical vase that Olimba had given to Don Duardos. The prince's insistence just before eloping that he is the son of a lowly butcher brings to mind Don Duardos's insistence on love for the sake of love. The ballad then concludes with *Flérida* but, rather than undertaking a sea voyage, the protagonists elope on a donkey.

Because of its elimination of the hero's disguise, *Lizarda* is not as clearly related to the play. The garden is still there, acquiring an even more prominent role, but Lizarda sees the prince hunting on a nearby hill, falls in love with him instantly, and then seizes the initiative, sending her lady-in-waiting to speak with him. Although the hunting episode recalls *O Hortelão*, where the hero informs the old woman that he intends to hunt and trap the princess as if she were a bird to be caught, the situation here is quite different from the *Tragicomedia*. Nevertheless, the lady-in-waiting corresponds to Artada, the courtly go-between who plays such a prominent role in Flérida's affair with Don Duardos. After Flérida confesses her love for Don Duardos, Artada warns her about her reputation. The lady-in-waiting does exactly the same in *Lizarda*. Flérida "manda primero a Artada" (sends Artada first), and Lizarda also agrees to send her lady-in-waiting to speak with the prince first. Upon her return, Artada tells Flérida that the gardener's son must be of noble lineage, and the lady-in-waiting also stresses the hero's noble blood to Lizarda. Contrary to the *Tragicomedia*, where Flérida agrees to meet Don Duardos in the garden in the evening in order to find out his true identity, here the lady-in-waiting is the one who arranges the tryst, but this tryst also takes place in the garden, in the evening, and Lizarda's eagerness for the appointed hour to arrive corresponds to Flérida's anxiety in the play. Lizarda's decision to elope and her forwardness in suggesting this to the hero are quite different from the Vicentine original, but the ballad then concludes with *Flérida*, just like the play. Notwithstanding important differences, then, there is no question that the background material in *Lizarda* is also taken from the *Tragicomedia*.

In order to better understand and appreciate the manner in which *Lizarda* adapts *Flérida*, it is necessary to correlate it with Gil Vicente's original:

Gil Vicente's Version		*Lizarda*
I. En el mes era de abril,		
de mayo antes un día,		
2 quando los lirios y rosas		
muestran más su alegría,		
en la noche má serena		
que el cielo hazer podía,		
4 quando la hermosa infanta		
Flérida ya se partía,		
en la huerta de su padre		
a los árboles dezía:		
6 II. —Jamás, en quanto biviere,	62	que em quanto eu mais viver,
os veré tan sólo un día,		te verei tão só lo dia;
ni cantar los ruiseñores	63	adeus, adeus, rouxinol,

en los ramos melodía.
8 Quédate a Dios, agua clara,
  quédate a Dios, agua fría,
  quedaos con Dios, mis flores,
  mi gloria que ser solía.

10 Voyme a tierras estrañas,
   pues ventura allá me guía.

III. Si mi padre me buscare
   que grande bien me quería,
12 digan que el amor me lleva,
   que no fue la culpa mía:

   tal tema tomó comigo
   que me venció su porfía.
14 ¡Triste, no sé donde voy,
   ni nadie me lo dezía!—
   IV. Allí habló don Duardos,
   bien oiréis lo que decía:
16 —No lloréis, señora infanta,
   no lloréis, mi alegría,

   que en los reinos de Inglaterra
   más claras aguas avía
18 y más hermosos jardines,
   y vuestros, señora mía.
   Ternéis trezientas donzellas
   de alta genelosía;
20 de plata son los palacios
   para vuestra señoría,
   de esmeraldas y jacintos
   toda la tapecería,
22 las cámaras ladrilladas
   de oro fino de Turquía.

. . . .

   que cantais ao meio-dia;
61 —Adeus, meu jardim das flores,
   minha fonte d'água fria,
64 adeus, palácio, adeus, jardim,
   onde eu me divertia;
65 adeus, aia da minh'alma,
   com quem eu tanto me qu'ria.
66 Mal la fortuna me leva,
   mal la fortuna me guia;
   não sei se me furta um rei,
   s'homem de baixa valia.
68 Adeus, ó pai de minh'alma,
   adeus, mãe de minha vida,
   que para sempre se aparta
   tua prenda mais querida.
70 Se meu pai te perguntar,
   pois que muito me queria,
   dize-lhe que o amor me leva,
   a culpa que não é minha.
72 E s'alguém quer saber mais
   parte da minha fugida,
   pergunt'ò deus dos amores,
   que dele me vou bem f'rida.

74 —Calai-vos, senhora rainha,
   nã choreis, minh'alegria,
   qu'eu sou lo filho dum rei,
   príncipe d'alta valia:
76 que também na Inglaterra
   tem águas la fonte fria;
   los jardins têm passarinhos
   que cantam todo lo dia;
78 tem la corte muitas damas
   que vos farão companhia;
   lá tenho paços reais

   de oiro e pedraria,
80 tudo isto e muito mais
   pera vossa senhoria.

28 V. Fuéronse a las galeras
    que don Duardos tenía:

    cincuenta eran por cuenta;
    todas van en compañía.
30 Al son de sus dulces remos
    la infanta se adormecía
    en braços de don Duardos
    que bien le pertenecía.
32 VI. Sepan quantos son nacidos
    aquesta sentencia mía:
    que contra la muerte y amor
    nadie no tiene valía.

59 —Montai-vos aqui, senhora,
    às ancas neste cavalo,
60 que bem segura vós is,
    sem sofrer nenhum abalo.

Translation:

I. It was in the month of April,
   one day before May,
2 when irises and roses
   show more their beauty,
   on the most peaceful night
   that the Heavens could
       display,
4 when the beautiful princess
   Flérida was departing.
   In her father's garden
   she was saying to the trees:
6 II. "Never, for as long as I live,
   shall I see you even one day,
   nor hear in your branches
   the melody of the nightingales.
8 Stay with God, clear water;
   stay with God, cold water;
   stay with God, my flowers,

   which used to be my pride.

10 I am going to strange lands,

   for fate guides me there.

62 no matter how long I live,
    this is the last day I see you;
63 farewell; farewell, nightingale,
    who sings at midday;
61 "Farewell, my garden of flowers,
    my fountain of cold water;
64 farewell, palace, farewell,
        garden,
    where I used to enjoy myself;
65 farewell, lady-in-waiting of my
        soul,
    whom I so much loved.
66 Fortune is carrying me away
        badly,
    badly fortune guides me;
    I know not if I elope with a
        king,
    or a man of low rank.

68 Farewell, father of my soul;
    farewell, mother of my life;
    it is forever
    that your dearest daughter is
        departing.

III. If my father looks for me,
    whose love for me is so great,
12 tell him that love takes me,
    that the fault is not mine:

70 If my father asks for me,
    for he loved me very much,
    tell him that love takes me,
    that the fault is not mine.

It was so stubborn with me
    that its persistence vanquished.
14 Woe is me; I know not where
        I go,
    nor does anyone tell me!"
    IV. There spoke Don Duardos,
    you will hear what he said:
16 "Do not cry, my lady and
        princess;
    do not cry, my joy,

72 Should anyone wish to know
    more details of my elopement,
    let him ask the god of love,
    for he has wounded me deeply."

74 "Be silent, my lady and queen;

    do not cry, my joy,
    for I'm the son of a king,
    a high-ranking prince:

for in the Kingdom of England
    the waters are even clearer,
18 the gardens more beautiful,
    and they are yours, my lady.
    You will have three hundred
        maidens
    of great rank.
20 The palaces for your ladyship
    are of silver;
    all the tapestry is
    of emeralds and hyacinths;
22 the rooms have walls
    of fine Turkish gold."

76 For also in England
    the cold fountain has water;
    the gardens have little birds
    that sing all day long;
78 the court has many ladies

who shall keep you company;
there I own royal palaces

of gold and precious stones.
80 All of this and much more
    awaits your ladyship."

. . . .
28 V. They went toward the
        galleys
    that Don Duardos had:

59 "Pray mount here, my lady,

on the back of this horse,
60 for you will be very safe,
    and will not feel any
        discomfort."

They were fifty in all,

all of them departed together.
30 At the sweet sound of the oars
   the princess fell asleep,
   in the arms of Don Duardos;
   she well belonged to him.
32 VI. Let all those who have been born
   know this maxim of mine:
   In the face of death and love
   no one has any recourse.

In *Lizarda*, *Flérida* begins with the elopement of the protagonists on horseback (59–60), which corresponds to their departure in
Don Duardos's galleys. Thus stage 5 is displaced to the beginning of
the ballad. This manner of transportation is also related to *O Hortelão das Flores*, where the protagonists elope on a donkey, and to
the independent Portuguese versions where they travel by land. The
ballad then continues with the princess's farewell to her garden
(61–64; stage 2), changing the verse sequence considerably and interpolating a good-bye to the lady-in-waiting (65), whom Vicente had
omitted from his ballad, probably because Artada is one of the three
characters who sing it. This farewell matches the farewell to the
ladies and maidens in Vélez de Guevara's seventeenth-century version and in the modern Spanish versions, paralleling Flérida's
farewell to her maidens in the Sephardic versions as well. Although
the princess's apprehensions (66–67) could correspond to the misgivings voiced right after the excuse for her father in Vicente's original
(14; stage 3), the synonymity between the words *fortuna* and *ventura*
(fate) and the coincidental use of the word *guia* (guide) in rhyme position (66*b*) show that this verse is part of the farewell. The verse in
which Lizarda wonders whether she is being taken away by a prince
or a low-born man (67) is, of course, an interpolation derived from
the play itself, also matching the independent Portuguese versions
in which the princess wonders whether she has been won or lost.
Lizarda's excuse for her father and others (68–72) corresponds to
stage 3, in which the princess also blames her elopement on love, but
this passage is expanded with a reference to her mother, and the
power of love is increased even more, for love is now personified in
the god of love who has wounded the princess so deeply (73). The
prince's concluding reassurances (74–80) clearly correspond to stage
5, but now the prince also reveals that his father is a king (75),
which amounts to an interpolation, and Don Duardos's description of
the palaces that await Flérida in England is condensed to two
verses: the palaces are of gold and precious stones (78–79) and the
heroine will find even more riches where she is going (80).

In *O Hortelão*, the princess falls in love as soon as she drinks the water that recalls Olimba's magic vase. *Lizarda* replaces this love-inducing vase with none other than Cupid himself. In some versions, she centers all her attention on her flowers because she does not yet realize "qu'havia o rei dos amores" (that the king of love existed; SJ; cf. Cal 104–5), or "que havia deus dos amores" (that the god of love existed; Silv.; CR 2; PC 2). As we saw, when she leaves the excuse for her father, Lizarda says that anyone who wants to know why she is eloping should ask the god of love (72–73).

These references derive from the play itself. When Julián and Costanza attempt to convince their putative son to marry Grimanesa, a peasant-girl whom Julián describes as "una moça valiente" (a strong girl), "baxa, doblada" (short, hunchbacked), "pretallona" (dark), "tan salada / que no la mira persona / que no quede enamorada" (so saucy that no one who looks at her fails to like her; 204–5), Don Duardos blames Cupid for having brought him to such an exasperating situation:

¡Oh, mi dios, señor Copido,   Oh my god, Lord Cupid,
loado seas por esto,   may you be praised for this,
que a tal punto me has traído! (206)   for having brought me to
                                             such desperate straits!

Later, complaining that Flérida has not appeared in her garden for three whole days, Don Duardos appeals to the love god once again:

Dios de amor, ¿no te contentas,   God of love, doesn't it satisfy you
que te quiero dar la vida   that I wish to give you my life
    'n este día,   this day,
la misma que tú atromentas?   that very same life you are torturing?
¡Sácame la dolorida   Take from me this pained
    alma mía!   (207)   soul of mine!

Also, just before eloping, Flérida tells Don Duardos that love is the lord of this world, thus transforming love into a "king," which brings to mind the ballad's alternate reference to Cupid as *rei dos amores*:

Ya me di a la ventura,   I have already surrendered to fate;
    mi señora.   fate is my mistress.
Y pues sabe este pumar   And since this orchard
y la huerta mi dolor   and garden are aware
    tan profundo,   of my great suffering,
quiero que sepa la mar   I also wish the seas to know
que el amor es el señor   that love is the master
    de este mundo.   (225)   of this world.

As in the case of *O Hortelão*, the background material selected from the play, together with the strophic form that it is given, point to a *folheto de cordel*, a broadside composed by a semilearned popular poet, either during the eighteenth or the first half of the nineteenth century. (The earliest version of *Lizarda*, we recall, was published in 1869.) In the part that corresponds to *Flérida*, the elopement is by land rather than by sea, and the princess expresses anxiety regarding the social status of her lover. Since these two elements appear in the Continental versions of *Flérida*, *Lizarda* was probably composed in mainland Portugal, even though it became traditional only on the islands and in Brazil. Although many people from the Azores immigrated to Brazil, the Madeiran versions are more closely related to those from Brazil, with which they share several verses not found in the Azorean ones (33–36, 59–60, 63–64, 72–74, 78). The most striking examples are the elopement on horseback (59–60) and the prince's reassurances of Flérida (stage 4), which are exclusive to the two Madeiran renditions and to the version from Sergipe collected by Jackson da Silva Lima (SL).

With its emphasis on the garden and its transformation of love into an overpowering love god, albeit in a popular, tasteless manner, such as transferring the initiative to the princess, whom it portrays as a rash, volatile character, *Lizarda* still retains much of Vicente's spirit of idealized love. The princess falls in love instantly and elopes from one day to the next, without any apparent ill consequences. Some versions interpolate verses in which she herself confesses that she is being cruel to her parents (see the critical apparatus to vv. 68–69) but, nevertheless, her elopement seems to be condoned. This is quite different from the Sephardic *El falso hortelano*, the fourth metamorphosis of *Don Duardos* in oral tradition.

3. El falso hortelano

El falso hortelano (The False Gardener) is a continuation of *Flérida* and, therefore, goes beyond the *Tragicomedia*. In the Sephardic tradition, we recall, Flérida's elopement leads to disaster. Already pregnant, the princess deposits a baby on the lap of Don Duardos during the voyage and he loses interest, forcing her to return home in a boat made of reeds. Whoever first wrote *El falso hortelano* also wanted to drive home a strong warning against such elopements but, rather than making the princess return right away, invents a new conclusion, showing how misfortunate she was in exile.

El falso hortelano is exclusively eastern. It was collected in Greece, Turkey, and from immigrants from those two countries in the United States. The published Greek versions are from Salonika (Yoná, nos. 21*a–b*;[13] Attias 1961, no. 10; Díaz-Plaja 1934, no. 13;[14] Molho 1960, 72)[15] and from Rhodes (Benmayor 1979, no. 36*d*; collected in Los Angeles),[16] and there is one unedited version from Sérrai (Yoná 277). Thanks to the kind permission of Diego Catalán, director of the Menéndez Pidal Archive, I have edited four versions from Salonika (CMP, R8.2–5) and one from Larisa (CMP, R8.6) in appendix D.[17] The Turkish versions are from Edirne (Danon 1896, 115)[18] and from Istanbul (Levy 1959, no. 4, vv. 1–12; collected in New York); Rina Benmayor collected in Seattle two versions from unspecified towns along the Sea of Marmara (1979, nos. 36*a-b*), recording also an *incipit* from Izmir in Los Angeles (1979, no. 36*c*).[19]

As can be seen from the following synthetic version, *El falso hortelano* is placed in the mouth of an unnamed Flérida, who complains about her fate as follows:

   *—Andando por estas mares, naveguí con la fortuna,
2   caí en tierras ajenas, ande no me conocían:
    ande no cantava gallo, ni menos perro maúlia,
4   ande bramean leones y la leona respondía,
    ande crece la naranja y el limón y la cidra,
6   ande krese yerva sidrera 'i konǧás 'i grave'ínas,
    ande crece ruda menuda, guadria de criaturas,
8   onde cae la nieve a copos y el sol la derretía.
    ¡Ah, Julián, falso y traidor, causante de los mis males!
10   Entrates en mi vergel y me engañates.
    Entrates en mi vergel, un día d'enverano,
12   acogitex la flor de mí, la acogitex a grano a grano.
    Con tu hablar delicado me engañatex.
14   ¿Qué dirán damas de mí, las que a mí me conocían,
    las que con mí se conhortaban, muchas donćellas?
16   Siendo hija de quien so, me casaron con un villano;
    'ižo 'era de 'un gu'ertelano de la mi gu'erta.
18   ¡Ah, Julián, vamos de aquí, de este huerto sin provecho!
    Luvyya kayyga de los syelos 'i mos amože.
20   Los grandes truenos de los cielos vos estropajen.

("Sailing upon the seas at the mercy of fortune, I landed in a strange land where no one knew me: Where no rooster crowed, nor did even less a dog bark, where lions roar and the lioness answers back, where the orange, the lemon, and the citron grow, where lemon-balm and roses and pink carnations grows, where small rue grows, which keeps small children from illness, where the snow falls in flakes and is melted by the sun. Oh Julian, false and treacherous, you are the cause of my woes! You entered my garden and deceived me. You entered my garden on a summer day, you plucked the flower from me; you plucked it little by little. With your fine talk you deceived me. What will the ladies say about me, those who knew me, those who took pleasure in my company, and many maidens as well? Being the daughter of who I am, I was married off to a peasant; he was the son of a gardener of my own garden. Oh Julian, let us leave this place, this garden without any use! May the great thunder from Heaven destroy you.")

Sources

Attias   = Attias 1961, no. 10
Ben   = Benmayor 1979, nos. 36*a–b*
CMP   = Fundación Menéndez Pidal, as classified in CMP (R8.2–6)
Danon   = Danon 1896, 115
DPlaja   = Díaz Plaja 1934, no. 13
Levy   = Levy 1959, no. 4.1–12
Molho   = Molho 1960, 72
Yoná   = Yoná, nos. 21*a–b*

Variants

1: Attias; cf. CMP, R8.2, R8.4, R8.5; Danon; Yéndomi por mares onda[s] / naveguí a la fortuna (Ben 36*a–b*); encontré con la fortuna (CMP, R8.3); A. p. altas mares, / navegando (CMP, R8.6); ¡Aj! índome por estos / navegué (DPlaja); En prinsipios de los mis maliz (Levy); ¡Ah! índome (Molho; Yoná 21*a–b*).

2: Molho; cf. Ben 36*a–b*; CMP, R8.5; DPlaja; Yoná 21*a–b*; onde no(n) me conocía(n) (Attias; CMP, R8.3–4, R8.6); me echaron (CMP, R8.2); donde (Danon); sevdades / ondi (Levy).

3: Molho; cf. Yoná 21*a–b*; onde (Attias); ande gallo(s) no cantava / ni menos amanecía (Ben 36*a–b*); onde (ande, donde) no cantaba(n) gallo(s), / ni menos canta(n) gallina(s) (CMP, R8.3–6; Danon); ni menos gallina (CMP, R8.2); ni menos amanecía (DPlaja); donde no kantó gayo, / ni menos la gayina (Levy).

4: CMP, R8.2; cf. CMP, R8.5; DPlaja; Molho; Yoná 21*a–b*; onde (Attias; CMP, R8.3–4); no b. / y ni l. (CMP, R8.6).

5: CMP, R8.2; cf. DPlaja; Molho; Yoná 21*a–b*; onde (CMP, R8.3–4); donde (Danon); d. krese partukal, / el limón i la naranǧa (Levy).

6: Yoná 21*a*; cf. DPlaja; Molho; Yoná 21*b*; onde crecen rośas y flores, / alhabaca y gravellina (Attias); ande crecen lirios y rosas / y alhabaca y violetas (CMP, R8.5).

7: CMP, R8.5; cf. DPlaja; Molho; Yoná 21*a–b*; onde / guardia (Attias); onde hay rudas menudas, / guadrián (CMP, R8.3); que es guardia de las paridas (CMP, R8.4); donde hay sacsis de ruda / guardian de creatura (Danon).

8: CMP, R8.6; a colmo (CMP, R8.4).

9: CMP, R8.3; cf. CMP, R8.2, R8.5–6; Danon; Julio / cabśador (causante) (Attias; DPlaja; Molho; Yoná 21*a–b*); ¡Ah! maldičo ke me traisionates, / i kavzates los mis males (Levy).

10: CMP, R8.2; chadir (CMP, R8.5; DPlaja); ğadir (Yoná 21*b*); chaddir / mañanica de Sanjiguale (Attias); Me truxites en estas tierras (CMP, R8.3); entratex en el jadire / en la horicas de tadre (CMP, R8.6); te entrates en mis jardines (Danon).

11: Molho; vergil / y ouna tadre (CMP, R8.4); chadir (DPlaja); ğadir (Yoná 21*a–b*); Mañanica d. (CMP, R8.6).

12: CMP, R8.6; cf. Attias; CMP, R8.2; Danon; DPlaja; Molho; Yoná 21*a–b*; arrancates / la acoupites (CMP, R8.4).

13: CMP, R8.6; cf. Attias; CMP, R8.2, R8.4; Danon; DPlaja; Yoná 21*b*; con tus havlas delicadas (Molho; Yoná 21*a*).

14: CMP, R8.2; cf. Attias; CMP, R8.4–5; las que a mí me conhortaban (CMP, R8.6); Damas qué dirán de mí (DPlaja; Molho; Yoná 21*a–b*).

15: Attias; cf. CMP, R8.4, R8.6; m. amigas (CMP, R8.2); m. mujeres (DPlaja); muchachicas (Molho); muğağikas (Yoná 21*a*); muğağikitas (Yoná 21*b*); Con mí se aconsejaban / grandes y chicas (CMP, R8.5).

16: CMP, R8.5; cf. Attias (vilano); Molho (vilano); con un diano (CMP, R8.2); con oun milano (CMP, R8.4); con un llano (CMP, R8.6); con Juliano (Danon); me casates con un vilano (DPlaja; Yoná 21*a-b*); ke siendo iža de bien, / kon ti, maldičo, me kazaron (Levy).

17: Yoná 21*b*; cf. DPlaja; Molho; Yoná 21*a*; hijo es (CMP, R8.4–5); hijo es / del mi huerto (CMP, R8.6); Hijo de un h. (Danon); hortelano de mi huerta (Attias); Me dieron a un marido, / huertelá de las mis huertas (Ben 36*a*); mozo ni es de un güertelano / de la mi güerta (CMP, R8.2).

18: CMP, R8.3; cf. CMP, R8.2, R8.5; Juliano (Attias); de este vergel (CMP, R8.6); de este mundo (Danon); Julio / deste árbole (árvol) sin flores (DPlaja; Molho; Yoná 21*a*–*b*); Juliana / sin provecho louvia cayia (CMP, R8.4).

19: Yoná 21*a*; CMP, R8.6; Danon; DPlaja; Yoná 21*b*; luvi(a) caiga(n) / amoje(n) (Attias; CMP, R8.2); y vos amoje (CMP, R8.3); y que te amoxe (CMP, R8.5); Luvia haze(n) de los cielos / lágrimas de los mis ojos (Ben 36*b*; *the verse is repeated*); y lágrimas de mis ojos (Molho); de los cielos i non la amoja; / yo non la puedo más yevar (CMP, R8.4).

20: CMP, R8.3; *missing in all others*.

In verse 1, some versions intensify the danger of the protagonist's voyage, specifying that she traveled in deep (*mares ondas*) or high seas (*mares altas*) and, in one version, she emphasizes that this voyage was the beginning of her woes: "En prinsipios de los mis maliz, / navigí kon la fortuna" (At the beginning of my woes, I sailed at the mercy of fate; Levy).

Also to stress the desolate character of the land where the girl arrives, in verse 3*b* several versions replace the lack of howling dogs with the lack of clucking chickens, and since the missing crowing of roosters mentioned in the first hemistich normally announces dawn, other versions state that even dawn fails to rise in such a land.

This is indeed a forbidding place, haunted by the roaring of lions (4), but, nevertheless, it is a fertile land, with oranges, lemon, citron, lemon-balm, rue, roses, and carnations (5–7), and some versions add that there are also irises and sweet basil (6).

The name that Don Duardos takes when he disguises himself as the gardener's son, Julián, is often preserved (9, 18), but the hero also appears as "Julio," "Juliano," and, in one version, he is somehow transformed into "Juliana" (9); in another, rather than calling out his name, the girl merely refers to him as *maldičo*, "wretched" or "accursed person."

When the unnamed Flérida accuses Julián of deceiving her in her garden, she uses the word *vergel* (10–11), which also appears as *jardines*, but many versions prefer *chaddir* or *ǧadir*, which, although phonetically close to the Spanish *jardín*, derives from the Turkish *çadir*, meaning "tent" (Yoná 632). Flérida then adds that Julián plucked her flower a little at a time, *a grano a grano* (12), "grain by grain," an expression that corresponds to the Portuguese *grão a grão*, as in the proverb *grão a grão enche a galinha o papo* (lit., "the chicken fills its craw little by little," which corresponds to the Eng.

"little strokes fell great oaks"; "many a pickle makes a nickle"). In one version, she practically accuses Julián of rape, stating that he had ripped off her flower: "arrancates la flor de mí, / la acoupites a grano a grano" (you ripped the flower from me; you plucked it little by little; CMP, R8.4).

Instead of complaining that she had been married to a lowly peasant despite her social rank (16), in one version Flérida berates Julián even more, saying that she had been married to a devil (*diano*, from the Sp. *diaño*) and to a bird of prey (*milano*, [glede, "kite"]). She wishes to leave that useless, barren garden (18), which she also designates as a tree without any flowers or as a sterile world ("mundo sin provecho"; Danon). For good measure, the princess hopes that rain from the Heavens will drench them both (19), but, in two versions, she states instead: "May rain fall from the heavens, and tears from my eyes." The last verse, in which Flérida also wishes for thunder to destroy her companion, appears only in the version indicated; I retained it because the thunder goes along with the rain in the previous verse.

By replacing the Spanish *jardín* (garden) with the Turkish *chaddir* or *ğadir* (tent) (10–11) in several Salonikan versions, the ballad reflects the Ottoman milieu in which the Sephardim existed, a phenomenon that can be easily observed among immigrant communities in the United States and elsewhere, for people gradually adapt into their native tongue terms from the languages of the countries in which they live.[20] Other examples of this are the words *konğás* (6; T. roses) and *sacsis* (T. vase of flowers; Danon). The difference between the Sephardic and the mentioned immigrant communities, of course, is that, in the countries where they have been living since the end of the fifteenth and the sixteenth centuries, the Sephardim are no longer immigrants. In the case of the exiled Spanish Jews, the language of their beloved Hispania became an integral part of their identity.

Three additional terms require further explanation. The *yerva cidrera* (6) that the princess finds corresponds to the Portuguese *erva cidreira*, "lemon-balm," designated in Spanish as *melisa* or *toronjil*, which is well-known for its medicinal properties. In Latin it is *melissa officinalis*, a favorite with bees (Covarrubias 1994, s.v. *toronjil*) whose leaves serve as "anti-espasmódico para os cardíacos e calmante nas irritações gástricas" (an antispasmodic for people who suffer from heart problems and as a sedative for gastric irritations; Pereira 1989–90, 1: 360). According to my mother, who is from the Azores, lemon-bald is good to calm one's nerves; herbalists recommend it for stress, anxiety, cold sores, and even for genital herpes (Gottlieb et al. 1995, 60, 179, 247, 323).

The "ruda menuda" or "small rue" that the ballad recommends for children (7)—according to one version, it is also "guardia de las paridas" (CMP, R8.4), good for women who have given birth recently—has medicinal properties as well. Because of its strong odor, Celestina recommends it to Areúsa for her menstrual cramps, even though, in her opinion, sex is a much more effective remedy.[21] According to Covarrubias, rue helps people to wake up; it is effective against the plague and poisons; painters used to eat it very often because it sharpened their eyesight.[22] Herbalists today recommend it for sprains and sore bones (Gottlieb et al. 1995, 71), but my mother-in-law agrees with Celestina; when rue is placed in a piggin (*selha*; "small wooded pail," but without the handle) with hot water, it gives out a steam that is good for feminine problems. An aunt from Madeira residing in California, on the other hand, recommends a tea made with rue for pregnant women. Among other benefits, it helps to prevent miscarriages.

The term *yerva cidrera* and the expression *a grano a grano* correspond to the Portuguese *erva cidreira* and *grão a grão*, bringing to mind the Portuguese substratum that I often notice in Judeo-Spanish ballads. Many Portuguese Jews joined their Spanish coreligionists already in exile, and, therefore, it is only logical that their language should have had an influence on Judeo-Spanish. On the other hand, besides Catalan and Basque, there is in Spain a rich diversity of dialects, including Galician, which is closely related to Portuguese, and Leonese and Asturian, which also share some features with Portuguese. As a result, it is often extremely difficult to determine with certainty whether apparently Portuguese words represent Castilian archaisms or regionalisms, or derive from Galician, Leonese, or Asturian. Unfortunately, to my knowledge no one has yet attempted a comprehensive study of the Portuguese substratum in Judeo-Spanish.

As Samuel G. Armistead and Joseph H. Silverman pointed out, the beginning of the ballad's prologue—(1) the sea-voyage, (2) the arrival in foreign lands, (3) the absence of roosters and chickens (dogs), and (4) the roaring lions (vv. 1–4)—appears, in varying degrees, in at least seven other Eastern Sephardic ballads: *La choza del desesperado* (The Hopeless Lover's Hermitage; CMP, K3); *El encuentro del padre* (The Encounter of the Father) or *La busca del padre* (The Father-Quest; CMP, G4); *La muerte del duque de Gandía* (The Death of the Duke of Gandía; CMP, C12); *La tormenta calmada* (The Quieted Storm; CMP, U1), *El enamorado y la muerte* (Death and the Lover;

CMP, V2), *El triste amador* (The Sad Lover; Yoná, no. 19), and *La fuerza de la sangre* (The Strength of Noble Blood; *Quem Quiser Viver Alegre* [Whoever Wants to Be Happy]; CMP, G3; RPI, G1) (Yoná 283–88).[23] As Armistead and Silverman conclude, this migrant formulaic complex or Wanderstrophen constitutes a suspense-creating introduction which, in its present form, "is probably largely the work of Eastern ballad singers, for several of its components, especially those referring to plants, have to our knowledge no parallels in other branches of the tradition" (Yoná 288).

The related cluster that appears in some Peninsular poems is quite different. In a dirge printed in 1562, which survives in the Sephardic tradition of Morocco as a funeral dirge, the ill-fated protagonist complains that he was born at an hour when dogs failed to bark and roosters to crow, and inquisitorial trials from the sixteenth century preserve rhymed incantations that consign evil and illnesses to the ocean, where roosters and chicken do not crow and cackle. Similar incantations survive in the modern Portuguese, Galician, and Catalan traditions (290–92). This dirge and incantations, however, refer only to dogs, roosters, and chickens, omitting the roaring lions, fruit trees, herbs, and flowers present in the Sephardic prologue.

The related cluster in some modern Peninsular and Canarian versions of *La infantina* (The Enchanted Princess; CMP, X1; RPI, X2) + *El caballero burlado* (*O Cavaleiro Enganado* [The Baffled Knight]; CMP, T6; RPI, T1), *La penitencia del rey Rodrigo* (King Roderick's Penance; RPI, A2), and *La devota del rosario* (The Girl Devoted to the Rosary; RPI, U45) is equally partial (Yoná 289–90). A singing snake and another snake that sings back recall the roaring lion and the answering lioness, but the action takes place in a dark forest without the rich botanic elements enclosed within the Sephardic cluster, as in the following Asturian example of *La infantina* + *El caballero burlado*. The snowflakes, however, match those in the Sephardic prologue:

> Allá arriba en aquel monte, allá en aquella montiña,
> do cae la nieve a copos y el agua muy menudina,
> donde canta la culebra, responde la serpentina,
> al pie del verdoso roble se veye la blanca niña.
>
> (J. Menéndez Pidal 1986, 156)

(Up there in that forest, in that forest where the snow falls in flakes and the water in a fine mist, where the snake sings and the little serpent answers back, next to the greenish oak tree the fair little girl can be seen.)

Another Asturian version includes the snowflakes, and a lion answers a snake:

> donde cae la nieve a copos,   el agua menuda y fría,
> donde canta una culebra,   un león le respondía.
> (Petersen et al. 1982, no. 46.1)

(where the snow falls in flakes and the water in a mist and cold, where a snake sings and a lion answers back.)

In the Canary Islands, many versions mention the missing roosters and chickens, and there is one version in which a lion also answers a snake:

> donde no cantaban gallos,   menos cantaban gallinas,
> sólo canta una culebra   y un león le respondía.
> (Trapero 1991, no. 2.4)

(where cocks did not sing and even less chicken sang, and only a snake sings and a lion answers back.)

On those islands, one version mentions dogs, and I found two renditions in which a lion answers a "singing" lioness:

> donde no cacareaban   perros, gallos ni gallinas,
> sólo cantan tres culebras,   todas tres cantan al día.
> (Catalán et al. 1969, no. 347)

(where dogs, cocks, or chicken did not cackle, and only three snakes sing; all three sing during the day.)

> donde no canta el gallo   ni le canta la gallina,
> sólo canta la leona,   el león le respondía.
> (Trapero 1987, no. 47)

(where the cock does not sing and even less the chicken, where the lioness sings and the lion answers back.)

> onde no cantaba el gallo,   menos canta la gallina,
> onde canta la leona,   el león le respondía,
> onde canta la culebra   dos horas antes del día.
> (Catalán et al. 1969, no. 442)

(where the cock did not sing and even less the chicken, where the lioness sings and the lion answers back, where the snake sings two hours before daylight.)

Except for the sea-voyage and the foreign lands, then, the roosters, chickens, dogs, lions, and lionesses in the Sephardic cluster of motifs are of Peninsular origin, but that is not the case with the flora that follows, and these differences, as Armistead and Silverman indicated, render the Sephardic prologue unique.

In *Flérida*, the heroine knows perfectly well that she is eloping with Don Duardos, and that he is taking her to England. In *El falso hortelano*, the nameless Flérida complains that she is married to a lowly peasant, son of her gardener. Thus Don Duardos loses his true identity as a prince, remaining the Julián whom he had pretended to be in order to conquer Flérida's love. Although *El falso hortelano* does not state it, this suggests that the hero was really Julián, and that he had pretended to be a prince in order to trick Flérida into marrying him. Rather than sailing to England, as in the play, he takes her to a foreign land inhabited by wild lions. The fruit trees, herbs, and flowers that Flérida finds echo her former garden, and the ladies and maidens about whose opinion she worries are none other than the ladies-in-waiting and maidens that accompany her in the play.

There are 8 verses in *í–a* (2–6, 8, 14), and the remaining 12 exhibit other rhymes (9–10: *á–e*; 11–12: *á–o*), as well as none (1, 7, 13, 15–20). This suggests that the ballad was originally strophic, and the shorter, pentasyllabic verses often found in the second hemistich (10, 13, 15, 17, 20–21) may reflect the *Tragicomedia*'s irregular *coplas de pie quebrado* with two octosyllabic verses followed by a four-syllable verse. Thus, whoever wrote the alternate conclusion that *El falso hortelano* represents probably decided to use the same type of verse as found in the play (Yoná 282). These strophic *pies quebrados*, which were also lengthened in order to conform to the octosyllabic pattern that prevails in balladry, explain the lack of rhyme in so many verses. Since the only sequence in *í–a* is restricted to the prologue (2–6), a good portion of which, as we know, is a formulaic cluster found in several other ballads, the chances are that at least the two verses that enumerate different animals (3–4) and the verse about the melting snow (8) represent a subsequent interpolation. Taking these observations into account, it is possible to attempt a reconstruction which, although highly unsatisfactory, is no doubt closer to the ballad's prototype:

—Andando por estas mares,	Sailing upon the seas,
naveguí con la fortuna,	at the mercy of fortune,
caí en tierras ajenas,	I landed in a strange land
ande no me conocían,	where no one knew me,
5 ande crece la naranja	where the orange

y el limón y la cidra,
ande krese yerva sidrera
'i konǧás 'i grave'ínas,
ande crece ruda menuda,
10 guadria de criaturas.

and the lemon and the citron grow,
where lemon-balm
and roses and pink carnations grow,
where small rue grows,
which keeps small children from illness.

¡Ah, Julián, falso y traidor,
causante de los mis males!
Entrates en mi vergel
y me engañates.

Oh Julian, false and treacherous,
you are the cause of my woes!
You entered my garden
and deceived me.

15 Entrates en mi vergel,
un día d'enverano,
acogitex la flor de mí,
la acogitex a grano a grano.
Con tu hablar delicado
20 me engañatex.

You entered my garden
on a sunny summer day;
you plucked the flower from me;
you plucked it little by little.
With your fine talk
you deceived me.

¿Qué dirán damas de mí,
las que a mí me conocían,
las que con mí se conhortaban,
muchas donćellas?

What will the ladies say about me,
those who knew me,
those who took pleasure in my
company, and many maidens
as well?

25 Siendo hija de quien so,
me casaron con un villano;
'ižo 'era de 'un gu'ertelano
de la mi gu'erta.

Being the daughter of who I am,
I was married off to a peasant;
he was the son of a gardener
of my own garden.

¡Ah, Julián, vamos de aquí,
30 de este huerto sin provecho!
Luvyya kayyga de los syelos
'i mos amože.
Los grandes truenos de los
cielos vos estropajen.

Oh Julian, let us leave this place,
this garden without any use!
May rain fall from the Heavens
and drench us.
May a great thunder from Heaven
destroy you.

Besides using a verse form similar to the *Tragicomedia*, *El falso hortelano* may also have included at least one passage derived directly from the play. Angry with Don Duardos because he had refused to reveal his identity, Flérida turns to Artada and tells her that they should leave, cursing the garden by wishing to see it burned with a bolt of lightning:

Vámonos d'aquí, Artada,
de esta huerta sin consuelo
para nos,
¡de fuego seas quemada,
y sea rayo del cielo,
plega a Dios! (217)

Let's go from here, Artada,
from this garden without any comfort
for us.
May it be burned with fire,
and let it be a lightning bolt from Heaven,
so please God!

These verses are very similar to the ending of the ballad. As Armistead and Silverman observe, although verses 29–30 replace Artada with Julián, they parallel Flérida's first two verses, the word "syelos" in verse 31 corresponds to Flérida's "rayo del cielo" and, although it replaces rain with fire, the ballad's rhyme in ó–e in verses 30–32 is the same as in the play (Yoná 280–81). In the last two verses (33–34), the thunder from Heaven with which the princess curses Julián echoes the bolts of lightning with which Flérida curses her garden, for the play's "rayo del cielo" (lightning bolt from Heaven) corresponds to the ballad's "los grandes truenos de los cielos" (great thunder from Heaven).

The sea-voyage at the beginning of the ballad, of course, brings to mind the boat of love and the image of sailing as a metaphor for lovemaking, often found in early poetry and prose, but this turns out to be a misfortunate voyage.[24] The princess takes a chance, sailing "con la fortuna" (at the mercy of fortune; 1b), and, rather than finding the happiness that she expected, she ends up in foreign lands where no one knows her (2). The horrifying character of this land, where no domestic animals can be heard because of the lions that live there (3–4), clashes with the beautiful, vibrant natural scenery described afterward (5–8). This further strengthens the hypothesis regarding the intrusive character of the animal part of the prologue. Having left her garden with Julián, Flérida ends up in another beautiful garden, but it is not the love-garden that she expected. Unhappy with Julián, she accuses him of deceiving her. (Perhaps by pretending to be what he was not.) He had managed to enter into her garden, and, with his fine talk, he had plucked her flower little by little, petal by petal, that is, he had taken her virginity (9–13). Now the princess worries about what her former ladies-in-waiting and the maidens that used to keep her company will say about her marriage to a lowly peasant, son of her former gardener (14–17). It goes without saying, however, that her reputation is already damaged far beyond repair. The beautiful garden in which she now finds herself with Julián may as well be barren (18), for there no longer exists any love between them, and she sees him for what he really is.

This Flérida, then, is quite different from the girl who elopes with Don Duardos at the end of Vicente's play, falling happily asleep in his arms with great hope for their future. The present Flérida would like to leave the garden to which her lover has taken her because she is very unhappy. There is no future in their relationship, and she knows perfectly well that she cannot return to her former life. That is why she wishes for rain from the Heavens to drench them both, and for a bolt of lightning to destroy Julián, freeing her from him (19–20).

Obviously, the disagreement with Vicente's solution could not be more emphatic. As far as the Sephardic community was concerned, love for the sake of love, albeit a beautiful concept, was extremely dangerous. Besides disturbing the social order, undermining parental authority, the elopements to which such love can lead often cause great misfortune.

↢

With its four popular metamorphoses, *Don Duardos* is a splendid example of the manner in which the folk at times accept as their own the work of a learned author, transmitting it orally from generation to generation, across the centuries. People liked *Flérida* so much that, as the modern Portuguese versions that enclose details derived from the *Tragicomedia* itself suggest, they began to sing it soon after the performance, while it was still fresh on their mind. This ballad, which also exists in Spain (Asturias), is best preserved by the rich oral tradition of the Sephardim. Since the play dates from 1525, the Judeo-Spanish versions testify to the continued contact of the Sephardim with their Iberian homeland after their expulsion from Spain in 1492.

As the analysis of *Flérida* in the Portuguese, Spanish, and Sephardic traditions demonstrated, this ballad also constitutes an excellent vehicle for the study of the factors that affect and transform a poem as it is orally transmitted. These include condensation, the elimination of some passages and the expansion of others, interpolations, substitutions, frequent displacements, corruptions, and contaminations triggered by thematic similarity with other poems. The results are often amazing. In the Sephardic ballad, rather than falling asleep in the arms of the hero during the sea-voyage, Flérida suddenly deposits a baby-boy on his lap instead. In one Sephardic version, she becomes *reina Elena*, a substitution no doubt triggered by *El robo de Elena*, where "París" abducts Helen of Troy. In Asturias, the hero becomes a Moor due to a contamination with *El moro cautivo*, where a princess frees and elopes with a Moor whom her father held captive. She is then rescued by the Blessed Mother thanks to a contamination with *La devota de la Virgen en el yermo*, in which the Virgin takes a girl who is devoted to her to live in the mountains under her protection. In Portugal, the hero's disguise as a gardener in the play causes the princess to elope with a journeyman who turns out to be a Moor and travels by land rather than by sea, and the rooms with walls of fine Turkish gold that Don Duardos promises to Flérida are changed into houses roofed in the Moorish style. As it was orally transmitted in Portugal, Spain, and among the Sephardim, *Flérida* also incorporated the views of those societies about idealized love and elopement. Idealized love may have been fascinating to them—hence the acceptance of *Flérida* by the oral tradition—, but the elopement of their daughters was not. By stressing the importance of the family and by making the princess give birth to a boy at the end of her sea-voyage, only to be promptly dismissed and returned home alone and dishonored, the Sephardic versions reflect the most conservative attitude, being uncompromisingly emphatic in their disapproval. In the Spanish ballad, a rebellious princess blames her elopement on her father for not having married her off sooner. She prays to the Virgin for help when she discovers that her lover plans to give her as a slave to his wife, and he leaves her on a deserted rock in the middle of the ocean. A pigeon brings her food for seven years before the Virgin appears to her, asking her whether she wants to be married or to become a nun, and she chooses the latter. Although she is severely punished, the girl meets with rescue and salvation. Thus, the ballad reflects a Christian society that seems to be somewhat more understanding and tolerant in such matters. The Portuguese ballad exists in two forms that reflect different attitudes. The Azorean form, which is extremely faithful to the sixteenth-century text, preserves its positive description of idealized love. During the voyage Flérida falls asleep on the lap of Don Duardos, with great hope for the future. In the second form of the ballad, which exists in mainland Portugal, the princess is deceived, eloping with a journeyman who turns out to be a Moor. Although he promises her all sorts of riches and to treat her well, this is still a very bad fate for a Christian girl. Thus, the ballad implicitly condemns elopement, reflecting disapproval of the union between different social classes as well.

People liked *Flérida* so much because, in addition to its portrayal of idealized love, the union of a princess with a lowly peasant was the stuff of fairy tales, even if the peasant happened to be a prince in disguise. Since the ballad focused on the elopement, they wanted to know about the circumstances that led to it. In Portugal, this caused the creation of *O Hortelão das Flores* and *Lizarda*, which take generous slices of background action from the *Tragicomedia*, preserving *Flérida* as an ending. Based on Olimba's advice to Don Duardos to disguise himself as a gardener and to make Flérida fall in love with him by making her drink from a magic vase, *O Hortelão* nevertheless retains the original's insistence on love for the sake of love, for the hero tells the princess that he is the son a lowly butcher before eloping with her on a donkey. *Lizarda*, which also exists in Brazil, stresses the power of love, which it personifies as *o rei dos amores* (the king of love), and focuses on the role of Artada, the lady-in-waiting who serves as the intermediary between the protagonists. Here Flérida is the one who takes the initiative. Besides falling in love instantly with the prince when she sees him hunting near her garden, she sends her lady-in-waiting to speak with him and asks him to take her away during their first meeting. They elope on horseback.

Rather than basing itself on the play, we recall, *El falso hortelano*, which exists among the Sephardim of Greece and Turkey, continues the *Tragicomedia*, for it purports to tell what happened to Flérida after she and Don Duardos arrive at their destination. The hero turns out to be the son of her gardener, a lowly peasant rather than a prince, and she is extremely unhappy with him.

These four metamorphoses of Vicente's play, then, vividly illustrate the relationship between folklore and literature, and how, besides using folklore, some early writers assimilated the popular style and spirit so well that the folk accepted works of theirs as their own, transmitting them anonymously to the present. Vicente, who often used the popular ballad, lyric, proverb, and folktale as sources, was greatly indebted to the oral tradition, but there is no question that he also knew how to repay his debt.

Appendix A

1. *Puputiriru*

Version recorded by the septuagenarian Guilherme Alexandre da Silveira, from Cedros, island of Flores, Azores, in Taunton, Massachusetts, on 14 January 1978 (tape 11A251). Mr. Silveira, who never learned to read and write, worked as a farmer and fisherman in the Azores. A talented storyteller, he recorded over seventy folktales, many of which took half hour or more to tell. A comparison between his version and the one that follows will give a good idea of his narrative style.

Era um padre que queria tê ũa entrevista. Nunca tinha visto ũa mulhé. Queria tê ũa entrevista, mas custava-le, já se sabe. Custava-l'a falar. E ele um dia vai pa um hotel e 'tava comendo no hotel, e quando sai do hotel 'tava ũa senhora, a cara mais linda que podia ser haver. E a sua vida era aquela. Tinha-se mudado pr'ali. E vê o padre e começa a namorar o padre. E o padre doido, e ela dá à mão pra ele antrar.

Quando ele entra, ela disse:

—Ah, senhô padre, o senhô padre o que é que deseja?

—Ó seora, ê queria ter ũa entrevista co'a senhora.

—Sim, senhor. Sim, senhor. O senhor vai ter. Olhe, 'tá a nossa barra ali, mas ist'é debaixo d'aposta. Ê vou dizer três palavras. S'o senhor padre mas soiber respondere, olha, 'tá a nossa barra acolá. Tem entrevista e tem tanto dinheiro. E se nã soiber responder a estas três palavras qu'ê disser. . . . Com'é padre, vai saber, mas, se nã soiber, perde tanto dinheiro.

—Sim, senhora. Vamos lá a elas.

231

—Não, senhô, senhô padre. Isto só pode ser às oito horas da noite em ponto.

E ele disse:

—Ó mulher, podia ser agora.

—Não, senhô, senhô padre. Só às oito horas da noite. Olhe, o senhor acerte o seu relógio pelo meu. É só às oito horas da noite em ponto.

Bom, ele ficou doido. Caminhou. Parecia-le que nunca chegava às oito horas. Pois ele nunca tinha visto mulher. Andava p'ũa banda, prà outra. Doido.

Mas quando de tarde um capitão da armada d'ia passando. Ela dá-le d'olho.

Ele vê.

—Olá!

Torna a vir.

—Oh, ê queria ũa entrevista!

E ela disse:

—Sim, senhô, senhô capitão. Olha, está a barra acolá prà gente. 'Tá tudo. Agora o senhor. . . . É debaixo d'aposta. Eu vou-le fazer três preguntas. Se soibé dizê as três preguntas, 'tá certo, e, se nã soibé, perde tanto dinheiro.

—Vamos lá! Vamos lá!

—Não, senhor, senão quando passá dez das oito.

—Ó mulhé, põe-te. . . .

—Nã quero. Já le disse.

Ela disse:

—Bote o sê relógio direito por aquele.

Botou. Caminhou o capitão, tamém sem sabê nada do padre. A passeá p'ũa banda, a passeá pra outra.

Quando daí a pèdaço chega um soldado. Viu aquela cara, e ela sempre a olhar. Mas ela viu ele puxar ũa carteira, e tinha-a recheada. E ela começa a olhá pra ele. Mas quando ele viu aquilo, o soldado vai-le bater à porta.

—O que é que queres, soldadinho?

—Ó senhora, ê queria tê ũa entrevista co'a senhora.

—Tu pensas qu'isto aqui qu'é de cães e gatos? Qu'é de toda a gente?

Ele disse:

—Ó senhora, olhe que dinheiro nã falta.

E amostra a carteira c'o dinheiro que tinha.

E ela:

—Ó *raite*, agora já 'tou vendo que sim. Tens dinheiro bastante. Pois olha, eu vou-te fazê três preguntas. Sei que tu, coma soldado, qu'as vais saberes. E tu vens é a passar um quarto das oito. Vens ter aqui, bates à porta, e abro-t'a porta. Um quarto pàs oito. Se soiberes as doze palavras,[1] olha, 'tá a barra acolá. E ganhas tanto dinheiro. E se nã soiberes, perdes tanto dinheiro.

Ela, coma viu qu'o rapaz que tinha muito dinheiro. . . . Nã foi coma o padre nem o capitão. Foi muito mais.

E ele 'tava doido pa. . . .

—Não, só às oito e meia direitinhas.

Ora, quando chegou às oito horas, o padre batendo à porta.

—Entre, senhô padre!

Agora, a porta fechada. Só ela é que a podia abri co'a chave, por dentro.

—Entre, senhô padre!

—Ó mulhé, cheguei à hora ou nã cheguei?

—Chegou, sim, senhor. Olha, sente-se naquele sofar. Ê tenho ũas coisa a arranjare aqui par dentro, na cozinha.

Ora, o padre ali com'um pateta. Quando daí a pouco [*som de bater à porta*], batendo à porta.

Diz ela:

—Já vai.

Diz o padre:

—Ó senhora! Ó senhora, ond'é que me vou escondê? Ó senhora, ond'é que me vou esconder?

—Cale-se, senhô padre!

Mas ela já abrindo a porta.

—Cale-se, senhô padre! É gente séria. O senhô é um home como os outros são.

Quando o capitão:

—Ê cheguei à hora ò nã cheguei?

—Chegou, sim, senhor. Olha, faz o favor de se santar ao pé do senhor padre.

O capitão:

—Olá! O senhô padre aqui tamém?

O senhô padre, que queria falá e nã podia, todo envèlhècado, todo vermelho.

Vai o capitão:

—Home, o senhor é um senhô com'à gente semos. É a mesma coisa. O senhor é capelão é só na igreja. Agora, cá fora, é igual com'à gente semos.

Até qu'o padre já d'ia tomando mais. . . . [*Falta algo que não consegui entender.*]

Pois ela 'tava lá dentro. Pois era pa quando chegasse às oito e meia. Mas o capitão sempre disse:

—Ó mulhé, tu vens ò nã vens? Diabo, tanto lavar aí par dentro!

—Nã tarda. Cala-te, que 'tá quase.

Ó repaz, quando chega às oito e meia [*som de bater à porta*].

Diz o capitão:

—Que diabo, ist'é pra toda a noite a antrá gente.

E ela:

—Já vai! Já vai!

Abr'a porta e ele entra par dentro. O soldado. Ela fecha a porta.

E ele disse:

—Senhora, o mê navio . . .

O padre e o capitão.

E o soldado disse:

—Senhora, cheguei às oito e meia ò nã cheguei?

—Chegaste. Olha, agora é que vai começar. O senhor assente-se acolá a pé do senhô padre e do senhô capitão.

—Olha, o mê capitão! Ó meu capitão! Perdoe-me. A senhora abra-m'a porta, que quero-me ir embora. Oh, o mê capitão!

E o capitão ali. Pois todo. . . . Parecia o diabo. Nã abriu a boca. E raivoso d'o ver antrar ali.

—Ó meu capitão!

E ela disse:

—Aqui não há capitão, não há ninguém. Quem dentro, dentro, e fora, fora. Assenta-t'acolá a pé dele. E o capitão calado.

Quando ela vem c'um fato. Home, era quase nua. Via-se tudo. O corpo todo. Quase nua.

E quando:

—Bem! Venha cá o senhô padre. Qual é a coisa mais bela?

Vai o padre:

—A coisa mais bela é esta batina qu'ê tenho aqui vestida.

Ela começou a rir:

—Qual é a coisa mais formosa?

—A coisa mais formosa sou eu, que sou um homem simpático, um homem bom, um homem que leva as almas ao céu. 'Tou trabalhando pa levar as almas ao céu.

Ela puxa ũa gaitada.

—E qual é o puputiru?

E vai ele:

—Senhora, puputiru é quando ê mando o mê tisoureiro, o mê sacristão, tocá o sino. Ele 'tá: «Pum! Tirirum! Pum! Tirirum!»

—Vaia-se sentá pr'acolá, que perdeu. É já o capitão.

E puxou ũa gaitada.

—Venha cá o capitão.

O capitão:

—Olha qu'ê nã sou com'ò padre. Nã te faças comigo, qu'ê nã sou com'ò padre.

—Venha cá o capitão.

O capitão chega adiante.

Diz ela:

—Antão, se não és como o padre, qual é a coisa mais bela?

Ele disse:

—A coisa mais bela é eu, que sou um capitão da armada. Olha pò qu'ê tenho aqui. Pa essas divisas.

Ela puxa ũa gaitada.

—Ah! Ah! Tu pensas que me metes medo? Qual é a coisa mais formosa?

Diz:

—A coisa mais formosa é quando eu preparo a minha tropa toda. Tudo armado pa d'i p'ũa guerra, pa matá as que são coma ti.

E ela:

—Ah, ah! Pensas que me metes medo? Antão vais-me dizeres qual é o puputiriru.

Ele disse:

—Digo. Ê nã te sou o padre. O puputiriru é quando ê mando os meus soldados todos virá-se, coma vou mandá: «Virem-se todos contra aquela mulhé!» Mas ê digo ũa, duas, três, mas já nã vai tudo dũa vez. Vai um: «Pupuriru, pupuriru!» E as balas. É tudo.

E ela disse:

—Vai-t'assantá pr'acolá, que perdeste. Perdeste tudo. Ê já sabia.

E tal.

—Venha cá o soldado.

—Ó mê capitão! Mê capitão!

Diz o capitão:

—Eh, tu és um home com'à gente semos. Se tu soiberes, s'é que ganhares, tu amanhã tens um fato de cabo, e daqui a um ano tu tens um fato igual a este se tu ganhares. E tu és um home com'à gente. Faz o que tu. . . .

O rapaz vai.

A mulhé disse:

—Ei, vamos a sabê qual é a coisa mais bela! Olhe pra mim! Olhe pra mim!

Ele disse:

—A coisa mais bela. . . . [*Confusão na fita, porque o informante tem vergonha de falar explicitamente, mas refere-se aos "altares"*].

—E qual é a coisa mais formosa?

—Ora, é a tua linda . . . [*cona*]. [*Gesto*].

Ela ficou!

—E qual é o puputiru?

—Senhora, é este [*pénis*]. [*Gesto*].

Já o levou pra cima da cama. E fez tudo e ganhou aquele dinheiro todo.

E o capitão, foi ũa alegria!

Ele disse:

—Isto nã se diz nada. Qu'a gente e o padre perdemos. Que vinhemos aqui. Mas tu já amanhã vais buscá o tê fato de cabo, e durante um ano tu é que ficas sendo o homem qu'ê sou hoje. Capitão da armada.

E lá está ele. E o rapaz é que ganhou tudo.

Ela mudou-se. Ali era conhecida, qu'ela era muito linda.

2. *A Princesa*

Version told by Rita de Jesus Madeira, eighty-seven years old, in Carvalhal, county (*concelho*) of Bombarral, District of Leiria, in September 1993. Recorded by Michel Giacommetti, who transcribed it with the help of Celeste Amorim. Published in Soromenho and Soromenho 1984–86, 1: 296 (no. 191).

Havia uma princesa que se queria casar, mas era muito rica— uma milionária—e queria-se casar, mas havia de ser com um rapaz que lhe dissese ou que falasse só consoante o desejo dela.

Bem, ora, era milionária muitas vezes, podre de rica. Ora, vejam lá, quando um padre vai ter com ela, vejam lá! Vai um padre ter com ela:

—Ó menina, ó menina, prá minha fortaleza as minhas igrejas; e pra luxo os meus castiçais e para reque-treque os meus sinos!

—Não, senhor, vá-se embora, que você não me serve!

Mandou-o embora.

Veio um capitão tropa:

—Ó menina, ó menina, prà minha fortaleza as minhas tropas; e pra luxo a minha espada e reque-treque os meus tambores!

—Não, senhor, vá-se embora, que não me serve!

Mandou-o embora, também.

Veio um soldado raso. Veio um soldado:

—Ó menina, pra luxo os meus botões; prà minha fortaleza o meu caralho e reque-treque os meus colhões!

—És tu que és meu! És tu que és meu!

Appendix B

Flérida (Sephardic Versions)

Judeo-Spanish versions from Morocco collected by José Benoliel and
Manuel Manrique de Lara in Tangier, Tetuan, Larache, and Alcazarquivir
(1904–15). Held at the Menéndez Pidal Archive, in Madrid, these versions
are edited here for the first time thanks to the kind permission of its director, Diego Catalán. CMP (see the bibliography) refers to Samuel G. Armistead's classification of the Judeo-Spanish materials in the archive.

CMP, S2.1. Tánger. Benoliel. 1904–6.

	Entrar quiere el mes de mayo y el de abril antes de un día,
2	cuando las rosas y flores amuestran sus alegrías,
	cuando la señora infanta Flérida ya se partía.
4	De los sus ojos lloraba, de la su boca decía:
	—Adiós, adiós, aguas claras, adiós, adiós, aguas frías;
6	adiós, mis ricas doncellas, las que conmigo yacían;
	adiós, mis ricos vergeles, donde yo me me divertía;
8	adiós, mi padre y mi madre, los que a mí mucho querían.
	Si mis padres preguntaren, los que a mí tanto querían,
10	decildos que amor me lleva, que la culpa non es mía,
	porque al amor y a la muerte nadie los pone a porfía.
12	Tanto porfió el amor que a mí vencerme podía.—
	En treinta y cinco navíos Flérida se embarcaría.
14	Al son de los dulces remos el sueño la vencería;
	con el ruido del agua Flérida dispertaría.
16	De los sus ojos lloraba, de la su boca decía:
	—Venid cá, mis escribanos, deisme aquí esa escribanía;
18	escribiré y notaré esta gran desdicha mía,

239

que no sé donde me llevan,   ni menos donde yo iría,
20   si me llevan para Francia,   o para la Andalucía,
si me llevan a Inglaterra,   donde yo pertenecía.
22   —No lloredes vos, mi alma,   no lloredes vos, mi vida.
Si ricas casas dejasteis,   mejores las hallaríais,
24   los techos aleonados,   labrados a maravilla.
Si ricas doncellas dejas,   mejores las hallaríais,
26   si padre y madre dejabais,   padre y madre hallaríais,
si hermanos y hermanas dejas,   ricos cuñados tendríais.—
28   Ellos en estas palabras,   los dolores la darían;
en haldas de don Fernando,   un niño parido había.
30   —Volvedla, mis caballeros,   mujeres muchas yo había.—
En un barquito de caña Flérida se volvería.

Variantes: 29a don Lorenzo. —31a de vela.

CMP, S2.2. Tánger. Manrique de Lara. 1915.

Entrar quiere el mes de mayo,   el de abril antes de un día,
2   cuando las rosas y flores   amostran sus alegrías,
cuando la señora infanta   enferma de amor se sentía.
4   De los sus ojos lloraba,   de la su boca dezía:
—Adiós, adiós, aguas claras,   adiós, adiós, aguas frías;
6   adiós, mis ricos vergeles,   donde yo me divertía;
adiós, mi padre y mi madre,   los que a mí mucho querían;
8   adiós, mis ricas donzellas,   las que conmigo dormían.
Si mi padre os preguntare,   el que a mí mucho quería,
10   dizelde que el amor me lleva,   que la culpa no es mía,
que al amor y a la muerte   naide los pone a porfía.
12   Tanto porfió el amor   que a mí venció su aporfía.—
Con ciento de sus donzellas   a la mar se bajaría;
14   alzó velas el navío,   la niña se embarcaría.
Con el ruido del agua   la niña se vencería;
16   al son de los dulces remos   la niña recordaría.
De los sus ojos lloraba,   de la su boca dezía:
18   —¡Ay, válgame Dios del cielo,   qué grande desdicha mía!,
que no sé donde me llevan,   ni menos donde yo iría.
20   Si me llevan para Francia,   o para la Andalucía,
o para Ingalaterra,   donde yo pertenecía.
22   Oído lo había don Luguardo,   que junto a ella estaría:
—No llores tú, mi alma,   no llores tú, mi vida.
24   Para Francia, mi señora,   a Francia la bien querida.
Si ricas casas dexates,   ricas casas hallarías,
26   los techos aleonados,   pintados a la Turquía,
los cerrojos de la puerta   de aljófar y piedras finas.

28   Si padre y madre dexates,   suegro y suegra hallarías.—
      En halda de don Luardo   un hijo parido había.
30   En un barquito quebrado   a la niña volvería.

CMP, S2.3. Tánger. Manrique de Lara. 1915.

      Entrar quiere el mes de mayo,   el de abril después de un día,
2   cuando las rosas y flores   amostran sus maravillas,
      cuando la señora infanta   de herida ya se partía.
4   De los sus ojos lloraba,   de la su boca decía:
      —Adiós, adiós, aguas claras,   adiós, adiós, aguas frías;
6   adiós, mis ricos vergeles,   donde yo me rivertía;
      adiós mi padre y mi madre,   los que a mí mucho querían;
8   adiós mis ricas donzellas,   las que conmigo dormían.
      Si mi padre os preguntare,   el que a mí mucho quería,
10   decidle que el amor me lleva,   que la culpa no es mía.
      Tanto porfió el amor, el amor,   que a mí rendida traía.—
12   En trinta y cinco navíos   la niña se embarcaría.
      Con el ruido del agua   la niña se marearía.
14   —Yo no sé donde me llevan   y no sé donde me traen,
      si me llevan para Francia   o para la india tierra.
16   —Para Artalucía, señora,   donde tú irte querías.
      Si ricas casas dejates,   mejores las hallarías;
18   si padre y madre dejates,   suegro y suegra encontrarías;
      si ricas donzellas dejates,   negros y negras encontrarías.—
20   Ellos en estas palabras,   los dolores la venían.
      —Volve, volve, la mi madre,   vólvela donde venía.
22   En un barquito de colchas   la niña se embarcaría.

CMP, S2.4. Tánger. Manrique de Lara. 1915.

      Entrar quiere el mes de mayo   y el de abril antes de un día,
2   cuando las rosas y flores   amostran sus alegrías,
      cuando la señora infanta   de herida ya se partía.
4   De los sus ojos lloraba,   por la su boca decía:
      —Adiós, adiós, aguas claras,   adiós, adiós, aguas frías;
6   adiós, mis ricos vergeles,   donde yo me divertía;
      adiós, mi padre y mi madre,   los que a mí mucho querían;
8   adiós, mis ricas donzellas,   las que conmigo dormían.
      Si mi padre os preguntare   y el que a mí mucho quería,
10   dizelde que el amor me lleva,   que la culpa no es mía,
      porque al amor y a la muerte   nadie los pone a porfía.
12   Tanto porfió el amor   que a mí rendida traería.—
      Con ciento de sus donzellas   la niña se embarcaría
14   en treinta y cinco navíos.   [....................]

Con el ruido del agua   la niña se vencería;
16   con el ruido del remo   la niña despertaría.
Recordó despavorida,   con un pavor ya tan grande;
18   de los sus ojos lloraba,   por la su boca dezía:
—Yo no sé donde me llevan,   ni menos donde me iría,
20   si me llevan para Francia,   o para la Andalucía,
o para la Ingalatierra,   donde padre y madre tenía.
22   —No llores tú, rosa blanca,   no llores, rosa florida.
Si padre y madre dexasteis,   suegro y suegra hallarías;
24   si ricas casas dejasteis,   mejores las hallarías;
si ricos vergeles dejasteis,   mejores los hallarías;
26   si ricas donzellas dejasteis,   mejores las hallarías.—
Y ellos en estas palabras   y un infante nacería.
28   En haldas de don Duardos   un infante nacería,
y en un barquito de cañas   la niña se volvería.

Variantes: 3b enferma de amor se sentía. —17b u. amor.

CMP, S2.5. Tetuán. Manrique de Lara. 1915.

Entrar quiere el mes de mayo   y el de abril antes de un día,
2   cuando las rosas y flores   amostran sus alegrías,
cuando la señora infanta   ferida ya se partía.
4   De los sus ojos lloraba,   de la su boca decía:
—Adiós, adiós, aguas claras,   adiós, adiós, aguas frías.—
6   En treinta y cinco navíos   la niña se embarcaría.
—Vení aquí, mis escribanos,   los (?) pra (?) aquí se escribanía,
8   escribid y yo notar   la grande disdicha mía.
Adiós, mis ricos vergeles,   donde yo me divertía;
10   adiós, mis ricas doncellas,   las que conmigo dormían;
adiós, mi padre y mi madre,   los que a mí mucho querían.—
12   Oídolo había Eduardo,   que estaba tras de la oliva:
—No lloréis vos, mi alma,   no lloréis vos, mi vida,
14   que si rica casa dijestes,   mejores las hallarías.
Las paredes eran de oro,   labradas en plata fina,
16   los techos salenjornados,   labrados a maravilla,
los ferrojos de la puerta   de aljófar y piedras finas.—
18   En la halda de don Duardos   un niño parido había,
y en un barquito de caña   la niña se volvería.

CMP, S2.6. Tetuán. Manrique de Lara. 1915.

Entrar quiere el mes de mayo   y el abril antes de un día,
2   cuando las rosas y flores   amostran sus alegrías,
cuando la señora infanta   ferida ya se sentía.

4   De los sus ojos lloraba,   de la su boca decía:
–Adiós, adiós, aguas claras,   adiós, adiós, aguas frías;
6   adiós, mi padre y mi madre,   los que a mí mucho querían.
Si mi padre os preguntare,   el que a mí mucho quería,
8   dixilde que el amor me lleva,   que la culpa non es mía,
que al amor y a la muerte   nadie los pone a porfía.
10   Tanto porfió el amor   que a mí propia me vencía.—
En treinta y cinco navíos   la niña se embarcaría.
12   Abrió velas el navío,   la niña se embarcaría.
Con el ruido del agua   la niña se vencería;
14   recordó despavorida,   la niña llora y decía:
—Adiós mis ricas doncellas,   las que conmigo jazían;
16   adiós mis ricos vergeles   donde yo me divertía.—
Oído lo había don Alguardos,   que estaba tras de la oliva.
18   —No lloredeis vos, mi alma,   no lloredeis vos, mi vida.
Si ricas casas dijateis,   mejores las hallarías,
20   los techos aleonados,   labrados a maravilla,
las paredes son de oro,   los suelos de plata fina.
22   Si padre y madre dejasteis,   suegro y suegra hallaríais.—
Con el ruido del agua   la niña se vencería.
24   Recordó despavorida,   muy triste y muy afligida.
En haldas de don Alguardos   un hijo le nacería.
26   Como eso oyera la niña,   en un desmayo se caería.
En un barquito de cañas   la niña se volvería.

CMP, S2.7. Tetuán. Manrique de Lara. 1915–16.

Entrar quiere el mes de mayo   y el de abril antes de un día,
2   cuando las rosas y flores   amostran sus alegrías,
cuando la señora infanta   ferida ya se partía.
4   De los sus ojos lloraba,   de la su boca decía:
—Adiós, adiós, aguas claras,   adiós, adiós, aguas frías;
6   adiós, mis ricos vergeles,   donde yo me divertía;
adiós, mi padre y mi madre,   los que a mí mucho querían.
8   Si mi padre os preguntare,   el que a mí mucho quería,
dizelde que el amor me lleva,   que la culpa non es mía,
10   que al amor y a la muerte   naide los pone a porfía.
Tanto aporfía el amor   que a mí propia vencería.—
12   En treinticinco navíos   la niña se embarcaría.
Con el ruido del agua   la niña se vencería;
14   al son de los dulces remos   la niña recordaría.
De los sus ojos lloraba,   de la su boca dezía:
16   —Vení acá, mis escribanos,   daca aquí esa escribanía.
Escribiré yo y notaré   esta desdicha la mía,
18   que ni sé de ande me llevan   ni menos donde yo iría,

si me llevan para Francia   o para el Andalucía,
20   para la Inglaletierra,   donde yo siempre estaría.
        —Si ricas casas dexateis,   mejores las hallaríais,
22   los techos aleonados,   labrados a maravilla,
        los umbrales de la puerta   de aljófar y piedras finas.
24   Si padre y madre dexateis,   suegro y suegra hallaríais.—
        Y en haldas de don Luardo   un hijo parido había.
26   —Volvedla, mis caballeros,   volvelda de ande venía.
        En un barquito de tablas   la niña se volvería.

CMP, S2.8. Tetuán. Manrique de Lara. 1916.

Entrar quiere el mes de mayo   y el de abril antes de un día,
2   cuando las rosas y flores   amostran sus alegrías,
       cuando la señora infanta   ferida ya se partía.
4   En veinticinco navíos   la niña se embarcaría.
       —Adiós, adiós, aguas claras,   adiós, adiós, aguas frías;
6   adiós, mis ricos vergeles,   donde yo me divertía;
       adiós, mi padre y mi madre,   quien (?) a mí mucho querían.
8   Venid aquí, mis escribanos,   lo que aquí se escribanía.
       Escribid y yo notalda   la grande desdicha mía,
10   que si alguno os preguntare   decidle que la culpa no es mía.—
       Oído la había Eduardo,   que estaba tras de la oliva:
12   —No lloréis vos, mi madre,   no lloréis vos, mi vida,
       que si rica casa dejaste   mejores las hallarías.
14   Las paredes son de oro,   labradas en plata fina,
       los techos salenjornados,   labrados a maravilla,
16   los ferrojos de la puerta   de aljófar y piedras finas.—
       Ellos en estas palabras,   los dolores le vencían;
18   en haldas de don Duardos   un niño parido habría.
       En un barquito de caña   la niña se volvería.

CMP, S2.9. Larache. Manrique de Lara. 1916.

Entrar quiere el mes de mayo,   entrar quiere antes que un día,
2   cuando las rosas y flores   amostran sus maravillas,
       cuando la señora infanta   a parir que ya se quería (?).
4   De los sus ojos lloraba,   de la su boca decía:
       —Adiós, adiós, aguas claras,   adiós, adiós, aguas frías;
6   adiós, siervos y siervas,   los que a mí mucho servían;
       adiós, adiós, mis doncellas,   las que conmigo dormían;
8   adiós, adiós, mis vergeles,   la gloria que yo tenía.
       Si te pregunta mi padre,   dile que el amor me lleva,
10   dile que el amor me lleva   a Francia la bien guarida.—
       En treinta y cinco navíos   la niña se embarcaría.

12   Con el ruido de los mares   el niña se vencería;
      con el cantar de los franceses   la niña se recordaría.
14   —Por tu vida, el escribano,   préstame tu plumería,
      para escribir una carta   a Francia la bien guarida,
16   para dársela a mi padre,   el que a mí mucho quería.—
      En la halda de don Luardo   un infante nacería,
18   y en un barquito de concha   la niña se volvería.

CMP, S2.10. Alcazarquivir. Manrique de Lara. 1916.

      Entrar quiere el mes de mayo   y el de abril antes que un día,
2   cuando las rosas y flores   amostran sus alegrías,
      cuando la querida infanta,   querida ya se espartía.
4   De los sus ojos lloraba,   de la su boca dezía:
      —Adiós, adiós, aguas claras,   y adiós, adiós, aguas frías,
6   y adiós, mis ricos vergeles,   las glorias que yo tenía,
      y adiós, mis ricas donzellas,   las que conmigo durmían.
8   Si mi padre os preguntare,   el que a mí mucho quería,
      dizilde que el amor me lleva,   que la culpa non es mía,
10   que para el amor y la muerte   naide lo pone a porfía.—
      En treinta y cinco navíos   la reina se embarcaría.
12   Con el cantar de los franceses   la niña se vencería;
      con el ruido de las mares   la niña recordaría.
14   —Adiós, adiós, aguas claras,   adiós, adiós, aguas frías;
      adiós, mis ricos vergeles,   las glorias que yo tenía.
16   —No lloréis, reina Elena,   no lloréis, alma mía.
      Si ricas casas dexates,   mejores las hallaríais;
18   si ricos vergeles dexateis,   mejores los hallaríais;
      si padre y madre dexateis,   suegro y suegra hallaríais.

Variante: 12b arrecordaría.

CMP, S2.11. Alcazarquivir. Manrique de Lara. 1916.

      Entrar quiere el mes de mayo,   por ver si antes que un día,
2   cuando las rosas y flores   amostran sus alegrías,
      cuando la querida infanta   ya se sale, ya se iba.
4   De los sus ojos lloraba,   de la su boca dicía:
      —Adiós, adiós, aguas claras,   adiós, adiós, aguas frías,
6   y adiós, mis ricas donzellas,   las que conmigo durmían.
      Si mi padre os preguntare,   el que a mí mucho quería,
8   dizelde que el amor me lleva   y la culpa que no es mía.—
      En treinta y cinco navíos   la niña se embarcaría.
10   Con el ruido del agua   el sueño la vencería;
      con el cantar de los frailes,   la niña se expertaría.

12   Se levantó con un pavor atan grande. [. . . . .]
        —Si padre y madre dejates,   suegro y suegra hallarías;
14   si ricas donzellas dejates,   mejores las hallarías;
        si alhajas y bienes dejates,   mejor los encontrarías;
16   si hermanos y primos dejates,   novio con bienes encontrarías.—
        En meatad de aquellas mares   un infante pariría.
18   En un barquito de cañas   la niña retornaría.
        La mujer y la gallina   por andar se perdería.

Appendix C

O Hortelão das Flores

Versions from Covilhã (Beira Baixa) and Mangualde (Beira Alta). In version *A*, the editor failed to indicate that verse 33 belongs to the princess, as if Don Duardos were the one to ask her for a glass of water, and attributed verse 35 to the princess, even though those words are spoken by the hero. I corrected this. In version *B*, the words that begin with verse 27, like the previous four verses, belong to the princess, but I divided them into two in order to show that verses 27–29 constitute a second speech, spoken the day after.

A.

	—Não venho por te ver, nem por te dar valor,
2	venho por erguer olhos e a vista no sol pôr.
	Falar quero à princesa, o amor me traz rendido;
4	a ti peço conselho, velha do tempo antigo.
	—Vista traje mudado, cante em seu bandolim,
6	boquinha de cristal, faces de serafim.
	—Um bom conselho, velha, me deste para mim!
8	Não farão de mim caso se me virem assim.
	Com Deus te fica, velha, mais a tua porfia;
10	mas se eu a render, velha, tens tença cada dia.
	Eu vou bater o mato, caçar altenaria,
12	mas, se ela me escapar, em ti me vingaria.
	—Abri lá essas portas, ó hortelão das flores!
14	Venha [*sic*] em traje mudado falar aos meus amores.
	—Senhor, podeis entrar, que tendes sempre acerto;

16	senhor, sois D. Duarte, que bem vos reconheço.
	—Oh que varandas altas com cem palmos de alteza!
18	Diz, velho de bom tempo, se ali vem a princesa.
	—Para as varandas altas, para tomar a fresca,
20	costuma vir sozinha quasi sempre a princesa.
	—Se ela te perguntar quem é o estrangeiro,
22	dize que é um teu filho vindo lá doutro reino.
	Que varandas tão altas, que jardim bem plantado!
24	Soubera o que hoje sei, que o tinha passeado.
	—Ó regador dos cravos, venha para mais perto,
26	conversar a princesa com prazer discreto.
	Ó regador dos cravos, venha para o mirante,
28	olhar para a princesa com olhos de diamante.
	—Mandaram-me cá vir? Não sei se é verdade.
30	—Tão verdade não fora, espelho belo e claro.
	—Tendes-me aqui, senhora, mandai como a vassalo;
32	já estive em noite escura, agora é dia claro.
	—Dai-me, que tenho sede, um pucarinho de água.
34	—Aqui vos mato a sede, espelho belo e claro.
	A mim não há quem mate a sede continuada.
36	—Vem cá falar comigo amanhã de madrugada.
	Aluga uma burrinha, que o não saiba ninguém,
38	que eu quero para sempre ir daqui para além.
	—Como a levarei, senhora, com quem ireis daqui?
40	Filho de um corta-carne, que apregoa aqui!
	—Não se me dá que o sejas ou que apregoe aqui.
42	—Aluguei a burrinha, vá-se despedir.
	—Adeus, ó fontes claras e poços de água fria;
44	eu já não ouço aqui rouxinóis ao meio-dia.
	Se meu pai perguntar quem é que me queria,
46	dizei que a desgraça não é a que me guia.
	—Cala-te, Madalena, lágrimas de peregrina!
48	Nos reinos estrangeiros melhor água haveria.
	Também há claras fontes, poços de água fria,
50	e canta o rouxinol à hora do meio-dia.
	—Pareces D. Duarte! Oh que fortuna a minha!
52	Tornemos ao palácio, a dizê-lo à rainha.
	Rainha e mãe, senhora, humildo-me ao castigo;
54	aqui está D. Duarte, que vem por meu marido.
	Rainha e mãe, senhora, que pena me acompanha
56	de não achar meu pai, senhor de toda a Espanha.
	Rainha e mãe, senhora, humildo-me com dor;
58	não tem a quem pôr culpa, é mui cego o amor.

(Covilhã; Braga 1906–9, 1: 426–28)

B.

—Venho pedir-te conselho,   velha dos tempos antigos:
2   quero falar à princesa,   quero que case comigo.
—Conselho, conselho,   que conselho lhe hei-de dar?
4   Vista-se em trajo de pastor,   vá à porta do pomar.
—Se nesse trajo me virem,   não farão caso de mim.
6   —Farão, senhor, farão,   tem cara de graça real,
olhinhos de marfim   e a boquinha dum rubim.
8   —Abre-me a porta, jardim,   hortelão das belas flores,
que eu venho em trajo mudado   p'ra falar aos meus amores.
10   —Venha ver, ó minha mãe,   este nosso hortelão,
que ele tem olhos de marfim,   mas ele prega-os no chão.
12   —Chama-mo cá, minha filha,   chama-mo cá p'ra mais perto,
[. . . . .]   que ele me parece ser discreto.
14   —Dai-me uma pinguinha d'água,   que estou morrendo à sede.
—Aí te apago a sede,   açucena bela e clara.
16   Minha sede não se apaga,   pois ela é tão continuada!
—Amanhã de manhã, cedo,   amanhã, de madrugada,
18   traga-me uma burrinha   muito bem aparelhada.
[. . . . .]   Que o não saiba ninguém:
20   que eu quero ir consigo,   estrangeirinha, p'r'i além.
—Sendo vós filha d'el-rei,   que nunca pagou à justiça,
22   eu filho do corta-carnes,   como pode ser assim?
—Amanhã de manhã, cedo,   amanhã, de madrugada,
24   traga-me uma burrinha   muito bem aparelhada.
[. . . . .]   Que o não saiba ninguém:
26   que eu quero ir consigo,   estrangeirinha, p'r'i além.
—Se meu pai perguntar   pela D. Aboladoura,
28   dizei-lhe que amores me levam,   a culpa não é só minha,
que irei com um pastor de gado   para maior perdição minha.
30   —Abala, abala, Aboladoura,   deixa teus bens à profia,
que entre Inglaterra   águas claras havia;
32   também há salas douradas,   d'ouro fino ou cutia (?);
também há belas senhoras   para a vossa companhia.

(Mangualde; VRP, no. 275)

Appendix D

El falso hortelano

Sephardic versions from the Menéndez Pidal Archive, collected by M. L. Wagner and Manuel Manrique de Lara in Salonika and Larissa (Greece) between 1908 and 1911, and edited here for the first time thanks to the permission of Diego Catalán. CMP (see the bibliography) refers to Samuel G. Armistead's classification of the Judeo-Spanish materials in the archive. I have been unable to see one version (CMP, R8.1), which is a manuscript from Sarajevo in Roman letters.

CMP, R8.2. Salónica. M. L. Wagner. 1908.

	—Andando por estas mares, naveguí por la fortuna:
2	me echaron en tierras ajenas ande non me conocían,
	ande non cantava gallo, ni menos gallina,
4	ande bramean leones y la leona respondía,
	ande crece la naranja y el limón y la cidra.
6	Siendo hija de quien so, me casaron con un diano;
	mozo ni es de un güertelano de la mi güerta.
8	Julián, falso y trahidor, y causante de los mis males,
	entrates en mi vergel y me engañates.
10	¿Qué dirán damas de mí, las que a mí me conocían,
	las que con mí se conhortavan, muchas amigas?
12	Julián, Julián, vamos de aquí, acogites la flor de mí;
	[. . . . .] la cogites a grano a grano.
14	Con tu hablas, muy delicado, a mí engañates.
	Julián, vamos de aquí y de este güerto sin provecho;
16	lluvias caigan de los cielos y mos amojen.

251

CMP, R8.3. Salónica. De la col. ms. del gran Rabino Isaac Bohor Amaradjí. 1860. Manrique de Lara. 1911.

—Andando por estas mares,   encontré con la fortuna:
2   caí en tierras ajenas   onde non me conocían,
onde no cantaba gallo,   ni menos canta gallina,
4   onde bramean leones,   la leona le respondía,
onde crece la naranja   y el limón y la cidra,
6   onde hay rudas menudas,   guadrián de criaturas.
¡Ah, Julián, falso y traidor,   causante de los mis males!
8   Me truxites en estas tierras   y me engañates.
¡Ah, Julián, vamos de aquí,   de este huerto sin provecho!
10   Lluvia caiga de los cielos   y vos amoje.
Los grandes truenos de los cielos   vos estropajen.

CMP, R8.4. Salónica. Ms. de Elisa de Botton, niña de 14 años. Manrique de Lara. 1911.

—Andando por estos mares,   naveguí con la fortuna:
2   kayí en tierras agenas   onde non me conossía,
onde non cantava gayo   ni menos canta gayna,
4   onde bramean leones,   la leona respondía,
onde cresse rouda minouda   que es guardia de las paridas,
6   onde caye la nieve a colmo   y el sol la deretía,
onde cresse la narandja   y el limón i la cidra.
8   ¡Ah, que dirían damas de mí,   las que a mí me conocía,
las que con mí se conortavan,   moutchas donzeas!
10   Juliana, vamos de aquí;   sin provecho louvia cayia
de los cielos i non la amoja.   Yo non la puedo más yevar,
12   [. . . . .]   ni al emperador servirlo,
que ya le crissió la barva,   y se le acourtó el vestido.
14   Entrates en mi vergil   y ouna tadre de enverano,
arrancates la flor de mí,   la acoupites a grano a grano.
16   Con tou avlar delicado   me engañiates.
Ciendo ija de quien sos,   me casaron con oun milano;
18   [. . . . .]   hijo es del ortelano
de la mi uerta.

CMP, R8.5. Salónica. Manrique de Lara. 1911.

—Yo andando por estas mares,   naveguando la fortuna:
2   cayera en tierras ayenas   ande non me conocían,
ande non cantaban gallos,   ni menos cantan gallinas,
4   ande bramean leones,   leonas les respondían,
ande crecen lirios y rosas   y alhabaca y violetas,

6	ande crece ruda menuda, guadria de criaturas.
	Yo andando por estas mares, andando para Firenza,
8	sentí armar grandes fiestas y a las armas.
	¡Ah, sentí ricos cantares, sus luengas perfilezas!
10	Yo andando por un camino para Firenza.
	Siendo hija de quien so, me casaron con un villano;
12	hijo es de un hortelano de la mi güerta.
	¿Qué dirán damas de mí, las que a mí me conocían?
14	Con mí se aconsejaban grandes y chicas.
	¡Ah, Julián, falso y traditor, causante de los mis males!
16	Entratex en mi chadir y me engañatex.
	¡Ah, Julián, vamos de aquí, de este huerto sin provecho!
18	Lluvia caiga de los cielos y que te amoxe.
	Ya no puedo ir en pies, ni al emperador servir,
20	que me creció la barriga y se me acortó el vestir.

CMP, R8.6. Larissa. Manrique de Lara. Jerusalén 1911.

	—Andando por altas mares, navegando con la fortuna:
2	caí en tierras ajenas onde no me conocían,
	onde no cantaba gallo, ni menos canta gallina,
4	onde no bramean leones y ni la leona arrespondía,
	onde cae la nieve a copos y el sol la derretía.
6	Julián, falso y traidor, causante de los mis males,
	entratex en el jadire en la horicas de tadre.
8	[. . . . .] Mañanica de enverano
	acogitex la flor de mí, la acogitex a grano a grano.
10	Con tu hablar delicado me engañatex.
	¿Qué dirán damas de mí, las que a mí me conhortaban,
12	las que de mí se conhortaban, muchas donzellas?
	Siendo hija de quien so, me casaron con un llano;
14	hijo es de un hortelano del mi huerto.
	Julián, vamos de aquí, de este vergel sin provecho;
16	lluvia caiga de los cielos y mos amoge.

Variantes: 1b combatiendo c.—11b me conocían.

Notes

Introduction

1. For a useful introduction to the study of myths and legends, see Jan Harold Brunvand 1968, 79–102.

2. Samuel G. Armistead is the leading expert on the relations between Hispanic and pan-European balladry. In his catalog of the Judeo-Spanish ballads at the Menéndez Pidal Archive in Madrid (CMP), he identified 51 text-types with numerous pan-European analogs; in our catalog of Portuguese and Brazilian balladry (RPI), he identified 46 text-types. See also Armistead 1970, 1976, 1978, and 1979; and Armistead and Israel J. Katz 1977.

3. Juan Timoneda's tale collections include *El patrañuelo* (1567), *El buen aviso y portacuentos* (1564), and *El sobremesa y alivio de caminantes* (1569). The most readily available edition of *El patrañuelo* was published by Rafael Ferreres in 1971. Juliá Martínez (1947), María Pilar Cuartero, and Maxime Chevalier (1990) have edited the other two works.

4. John E. Keller's motif-index of medieval Spanish *exempla* (1949) has been updated and considerably expanded by Harriet Goldberg (1998). See also Edward J. Neugaard's motif-index of medieval Catalan folktales (1993). Regarding the folktale in the first picaresque novel, the *Lazarillo de Tormes*, see Fernando Lázaro Carreter 1969 and María Rosa Lida de Malkiel 1976. The amount of work that Maxime Chevalier has dedicated to the role of the folktale in Golden Age Spanish literature is too extensive to be detailed here (see, e.g., Chevalier 1975, 1978, 1982, and 1983; see also Soons 1976). J. Wesley Childers (1948) and Childers and John R. Reynolds's indexes of folk motifs in the works of Juan Timoneda (1978) are very useful. For an excellent survey of the folktales in *Don Quijote*, see Mac E. Barrick 1976. For the source for the first madman story that Cervantes uses in his prologue to

part 2 in order to chastise Alonso Fernández de Avellaneda for daring to write a continuation to part 1, see Manuel da Costa Fontes 1992, 92–95.

5. Since the bibliography on the subject is too extensive to be included here, I will list only a few examples. José Gella Iturriaga has studied the use of proverbs in "444 refranes de *La Celestina*" (1977), "Los refranes de *La Lozana andaluza*" (1978a), two picaresque novels (1979), and the titles of Lope de Vega's plays (1978b). George S. Lancashire (1905) and Elías Olmos Canalda (1940) have studied the use of proverbs in *Don Quijote*.

6. See José Leite de Vasconcellos 1882; Marie Aliete Dores Galhoz 1960 and 1987.

7. See his splendid *Las dos sirenas y otros estudios de literatura tradicional* (1995b), in which he brings together some of his numerous studies on folk literature.

8. Personal communication. Dr. Pedrosa, who has developed a detailed, still unpublished field guide in order to assist other investigators with their fieldwork, will soon publish some of his findings.

9. Essentially, Armistead's catalog of the Judeo-Spanish ballads in the Menéndez Pidal Archive (CMP) may be regarded as a catalog of Judeo-Spanish balladry as well. There are catalogs for three regions of Spain: Galicia (Valenciano et al. 1998), Asturias (Busto Cortina 1989), and León (Catalán et al. 1991). Flor Salazar catalogs late ballads in her *Romancero vulgar y nuevo* (1999). So far, the *CGR: Catálogo general del Romancero*, prepared by Diego Catalán et al. (1982–88), which covers all the Hispanic traditions, classifies 82 ballads based on the Spanish epic, historical ballads, and Moriscos ballads. For the Portuguese and Brazilian traditions, see RPI.

10. For epic-ballad relationships, the three volumes that Armistead and Joseph H. Silverman have dedicated so far to the folk literature of the Sephardic Jews (Yoná and Armistead and Silverman 1986 and 1994) are indispensable. The authors will dedicate three additional volumes to Carolingian ballads. See also Armistead 1979–80 and 1981.

11. Bráulio do Nascimento's monumental Brazilian index, which also covers much of the tale tradition of Portugal, is at an advanced stage of preparation. Isabel Cardigos has begun to work on a separate Portuguese index.

12. Chapter 1 is based on "*Puputiriru*: Uma Rara Anedota Popular Portuguesa de Origem Medieval," *RLNS* No. 10 (1989): 25–40 and "A Portuguese Folk Story and Its Early Congeners," *HR* 58 (1990): 73–88. Chapter 2 reproduces, with minor changes, "On Alfonso X's 'Interrupted' Encounter with a *soldadeira*," *REH* 31 (1997): 93–101. Chapter 3 reproduces, also with minor changes, "Martínez de Toledo's 'Nightmare' and the Courtly and Oral Traditions," *Oral Tradition and Hispanic Literature. Essays in Honor of Samuel G. Armistead*, ed. Mishael M. Caspi (New York: Garland, 1995),

189–216. Chapter 4 conflates and updates "Celestina's *hilado* and Related Symbols," *Celestinesca* 8.1 (1984): 3–13, "Celestina's *hilado* and Related Symbols: A Supplement," *Celestinesca* 9.1 (1985): 33–38, and the first part of "Fernando de Rojas, Cervantes, and Two Portuguese Folk Tales," *Hispanic Medieval Studies in Honor of Samuel G. Armistead*, eds. E. Michael Gerli and Harvey L. Sharrer (Madison, Wisconsin: HSMS, 1992), 85–96. Chapter 5 adapts, with minor modifications, "*El idólatra de María*: An Anti-Christian Jewish Ballad?" *RPh* 48 (1994–95): 255–64. Chapter 6, which has been completely rewritten, was first published as "*Barca Bela* in the Portuguese Oral Tradition," *RPh* 37 (1983–84): 282–92. Chapters 7–8 are based on "*D. Duardos* in the Portuguese Oral Tradition," *RPh* 30 (1976–77): 589–608, "*Lizarda*: A Rare Vicentine Ballad in California," *RPh* 32 (1978–79): 308–14, and "Novas Versões Transmontanas de *Flérida*," *RLNS* No. 2 (1981): 17–29; the sections dedicated to the Sephardic and Spanish versions of *Flérida* and the Sephardic *El falso hortelano* are new. I would like to thank the publishers of these studies for their permission to use them in this book.

1. Puputiriru: *An Eastern Folktale from the* Disciplina clericalis

1. The fieldwork in New England was made possible by a fellowship from the National Endowment for the Humanities (1978); the folktales were transcribed and partially edited thanks to a Guggenheim fellowship (1984–85).

2. Mr. Silveira lived with a daughter and her family. Most of the interviews were conducted in her house, but he also recorded some stories at the home of my uncle, José Machado Fontes, who used to live in Taunton. It was there that Mr. Silveira recorded *Puputiriru*, with me, my uncle, my wife, Maria-João Câmara, and my aunt Patrocínio as an audience.

3. For the sake of completeness, and to show the difference between Mr. Silveira's detailed narrative style and the style of another storyteller, I have included a full transcription of *Puputiriru* and the only other Portuguese version that exists in appendix A. Mr. Silveira's version will also be included in my book *O Conto Popular Português na América do Norte, 2: Nova Inglaterra* (in preparation).

4. This distinction, of course, was a recurrent topic in medieval and Renaissance literature. For a medieval example, see *Elena y María*, a thirteenth-century debate in which Elena praises the virtues of her lover, a poor knight (arms), and María replies by extolling the attributes of the clergyman (letters) whom she loves (R. Menéndez Pidal 1965–66, 1: 288–92). For a Renaissance example, see Don Quijote's discourse on arms and letters, which he proffers at the inn before the characters involved in the Captive's Tale (Cervantes 1978, 1: 465–71).

5. There is a vestige of the travel motif, however; the captain is a naval officer and, at one point, the soldier, who is really a sailor, says that his ship is about to leave.

6. For a thorough and perceptive study of the metaphors in this song, see Louise O. Vasvari 1983. For additional bibliography, see Samuel G. Armistead 1992, 87n11; Francisco Márquez Villanueva 1988, 249–50n10; Vasvari 1983, 304n16.

7. The parallel translation was also done by Armistead. For bibliography on similar popular lyrics, see 87–88n12.

8. Pietro Toldo believed that Rabelais had borrowed from Troyes (1895, 98) and, at one time, Henri Clouzot thought that it was the other way around (1909, 385–86). Although Gaston Paris observed in 1912 that both authors merely used one of the anonymous stories that circulated "de bouche en bouche" (from mouth to mouth; 641n1), L. Sainéan (1930, 128n1) and Marcel de Grève (1953, 75 and n4) continued to speak of the possible influence of Rabelais on *Le Grand parangon*, with the reservation that the problem still needed further study. The hypothesis that both Rabelais and Nicolas de Troyes could have based themselves on Philippe de Vigneulles's earlier version has also been discussed. Charles H. Livingston dismisses such a possibility (1965, 33), but Marcel Françon feels that "Rabelais s'est adressé à Philippe de Vigneulles" (1973, 78). Other critics do not seem to have recognized that Rabelais was using a folktale. While agreeing that Panurge's reply was traditional during the fifteenth century, Marcel Schwob stated that it was a well-known proverb (1904, 141 12). In Raymond Lebègue's opinion, Pantagruel's saw merely causes his two interlocutors to parody him according to a well-established medieval tradition: "Epistémon le parodie sur le mode gastronomique . . . et Panurge sur le mode érotique" (1952, 196). At one time, R. L. Frautschi related the sayings of Rabelais and Nicolas de Troyes's protagonists to the versified *souhaits* that used the formula "il n'est que" throughout the sixteenth century (1961, 348–50).

9. Classified in J. Wesley Childers 1948 as H659.18*: *(A) Which shade is best? (B) Which view is best? (C) Which noise is best?* Winner: (A) bed canopy; (B) sight of a pretty woman; (C) noise of a mattress (see also Childers and Reynolds 1978, 407).

10. Cf. the following Egyptian story: "A sheik, a soldier, and a peasant meet in a prostitute's house and decide to find out which one is the strongest. The winner will be the one who is able to reach the greatest number of orgasms with her. The soldier goes first, then the peasant. When the sheik takes his turn, the prostitute tries to cheat him, claiming that he is counting too much. Undisturbed, the sheik would merely say: 'Let's start over again.' The prostitute is finally forced to give up, exhausted. Tired of waiting, the soldier and the peasant, who were in a room below, go to find out what had happened, and see the sheik coming down the stairs, mastur-

bating, for he was still unsatisfied. They buy him a lamb as reward, but the three eat it together." The two stories have much in common. There are three protagonists who represent three different professions, and one of them, the sheik, besides being a religious figure in Islam, also happens to win (cf. the monk in the French versions). The travel motif is implicit since, although the three men do not travel together, they meet at the prostitute's house (cf. Vigneulles's version, where the three groups meet at an inn). The decision of the protagonists to determine which one is the strongest is roughly equivalent to the best saying or reply in the European story. The prostitute, of course, corresponds to the French and Spanish innkeepers, as well as to the Portuguese prostitute. Finally, the winner gets a free meal (cf. Troyes), even though this had not been agreed upon previously. Despite striking similarities, the absence of the crucial three sayings or replies in the Egyptian narrative does not allow us to conclude that the second form of the story under scrutiny came from the Middle East, but there is a good possibility that it did. I am grateful to Halim El-Dabh for the Egyptian version which I have summarized; according to Professor El-Dabh, a similar story is also told in Iran.

11. Since the narrative style of this version differs so much from Mr. Silveira's, I have also included the full text in appendix A, thus enabling readers to compare both versions directly.

12. This version has been influenced by the relatively great number of folktales in which the princess's hand is won, often as the result of a wager (see Aarne and Thompson 1973, 284–90 [nos. 850–62]).

13. Note, however, the similarities with the Egyptian story in n. 10.

14. Américo Castro 1963, 194–200. In Portugal, the term *homens de negócio* (businesspeople, merchants) was practically synonymous with *gente de nação* (converts and their descendants; see Saraiva 1985, 127–40).

2. *On Alfonso X's 'Interrupted' Encounter with a* soldadeira

1. Sebastián de Covarrubias put it as follows in his *Tesoro de la lengua castellana o española* (1611): "La Iglesia Católica le dio nombre de *sexta feria*, y en ella hacemos remembranza de la pasión y muerte de nuestro Redentor Jesu Cristo, y con más particularidad el día del Viernes Santo. Los viernes, por esta razón, son días de penitencia, y nos abstenemos de comer carne y grosura, y fuera de los religiosos, muchos seglares devotos añaden el ayuno" (1994, s.v. *viernes* [966a]) (The Catholic Church called it *the sixth day*; on that day we remember the Passion and death of our Redeemer, Jesus Christ, and even more so on Good Friday. For this reason, Fridays are days of penance. Everyone abstains from meat and fat. Those bound by religious vows also fast, and many devout laymen follow their example.)

2. An excellent example of abstinence from both sex and meat during Lent, of course, is the battle between Don Carnal and Doña Cuaresma in Juan Ruiz's *Libro de buen amor* (cc. 1067–1209).

3. In a revised edition (1970), which was recently reprinted (1995), Manuel Rodrigues Lapa changed "covon" (2) to "conon," "Tol-te, arloton" (3) to "Tolhede-a, ladron," and modified his reconstructed reading of verses 4–5 ("ora d'alguen mi fornigar, u prendeu") to "sazon de vós mi viltardes, u prende." These changes do not really affect the meaning of the poem. Beginning with verse 8, however, Rodrigues Lapa attributes the remainder of the poem to the poet, rather than to the prostitute, as he had done before, changing "vós" (8) to "voz" and "coitada" (23) to "coitado" in order to make the text fit his new interpretation. This is wrong. As we shall see, the verses in question are spoken by the prostitute, not by the poet.

4. See, for example, Javier Herrero 1986; María Eugenia Lacarra 1990, 45–50; 1996; Ian Macpherson 1985; Paula Olinger 1985; Stephen Reckert 1970; Louise O. Vasvari 1988–89; and Keith Whinnom's influential and pathfinding book (1981).

5. The foot was more commonly associated with the penis (see Garci-Gómez 1989) and the hand with the vagina (see Allaigre 1980, 107–8 and 119, n65), but the foot could also represent the vagina (see Kossoff 1971).

6. For a synopsis of definitions, critical views, history, contemporary theories, and bibliography on metaphor, see Alex Preminger et al. 1993, 760–66.

7. For the reverse, that is, the transformation of secular poetry *a lo divino*, see Bruce W. Wardropper 1958; John Crosbie 1989; and Francisco Javier Sánchez Martínez 1995, 1996.

8. Not all modern readers are equally squeamish, however. While in Spain, visitors from Latin America and other countries are often shocked by the manner in which some people, without meaning to blaspheme, casually utter unthinkable, sacrilegious oaths involving Christ, the Virgin, and the sacraments. People used to such language, of course, would find nothing shocking in Alfonso's poem. I would like to thank Aníbal Biglieri for bringing this to my attention.

3. Martínez de Toledo's "Nightmare" and the Courtly and Oral Traditions

1. See, for example, Egla Morales Blouin 1981; John G. Cummins 1977; Daniel Devoto 1974b; 1974c; Alan Deyermond 1979; Paula Olinger 1985; Stephen Reckert 1970; Reckert and Helder Macedo n.d. Margit Frenk's monumental, profusely documented *Corpus de la antigua lírica po-*

pular hispánica (siglos XV a XVII) (1987) will no doubt facilitate many more such studies.

2. It must be noted here that, with the scholarly thoroughness to which they have accustomed us, Samuel G. Armistead and Joseph H. Silverman have always included detailed discussions of various motifs, including sexual symbols and metaphors, in their ballad studies. See, for example, their lengthy, profusely documented footnotes on the apple (Yoná 149–50, nn. 5–6), the hunt (Yoná 245–46, n6), hawks and doves (Yoná 247–51, n7), as well as their discussion of sexual metaphors and agricultural activities (1979, 109–11; 1982b, 110–17).

3. Louise O. Vasvari 1983; 1983–84; 1986–87; 1988–89; 1989; 1990a; 1990b; 1990–91; 1992a; 1992b; 1995a; 1995b.

4. Matthew Bailey 1989; Angus Mackay 1989; Ian Macpherson 1985; Jane Yvonne Tillier 1985.

5. Rosario Ferré 1983; Manuel da Costa Fontes 1984; 1985; 1990–91; 1992; 1993a; E. Michael Gerli 1983; Otis Handy 1983; María Eugenia Lacarra 1990, 45–50; 1996; Javier Herrero 1984; 1986; F. M. Weinberg 1971; Jack Weiner 1969; Geoffrey West 1979.

6. Claude Allaigre 1980; Costa Fontes 1993b; 1994b; 1998b; "The Idea of Exile."

7. Manuel Ferrer Chivite 1983; B. Bussell Thompson and J. K. Walsh 1988; Harry Sieber 1978, 45–58.

8. For Persian, Chinese, Japanese, and Indian parallels of some of the metaphors found in the Galician-Portuguese *cantigas de amigo*, see Reckert and Macedo n.d., 99, 208, 230. As Vasvari states, "because the psycholinguistic principles of metaphoric creation seem to be universal, it is possible and valid to collect corroborative documentation from diverse languages and periods" (1988–89, 8–9).

9. All quotations are from Gerli's 1981 edition.

10. Since the palinode is brief (304–6), I will omit page numbers in the citations that follow.

11. See Keith Whinnom 1979, 13–14; Pedro M. Cátedra 1989; and Mary Frances Wack 1990. The expression *mal de amores* still endures in the modern pan-Hispanic *Conde Claros insomne* (Sleepless Count Claros; see CMP, B11) and *El testamento del enamorado* (The Lover's Testament; CMP, K12).

12. For a succinct, abundantly documented summary of religious parody in Spain, see Daniel Eisenberg 1976, 164—65.

13. According to Colbert I. Nepaulsingh, these words also indicate that "the author had begun the work and was contemplating whether or not to

continue it" (1979–80, 343). Since it was the *Corbacho* itself that caused the ladies to be angry with the archpriest, however, it would seem that the book was already completed. Alfonso Martínez de Toledo is asking his friends whether he ought to stand by his work ("proseguir lo comiençado"), or attempt to regain favor with the ladies ("o nuevamente buscar paz y buena concordia"). The later, of course, implied that he would have to recant.

14. The original is studied in Ian Macpherson 1985, 60–62.

15. Miguel Garci-Gómez explains the phenomenon as follows: "En los textos aquí citados de Berceo y del cancionero, salta a la vista que es la hembra, en aparente inversión de papeles, la que pisa. Tal inversión, si la miramos desde una perspectiva psicoanalítica, no supone un gran problema tratándose de un producto de ficción. En la mitología, por ejemplo, es a veces la hembra la que monta el macho" (In the texts from Berceo and the songbooks cited here, it is clear that, in what amounts to a reversal of roles, the female is the one who does the stepping. Since we are dealing with fiction, this reversal does not constitute a great problem when examined from a psychoanalytical perspective. In mythology, for example, at times the female is the one who mounts the male; 1989, 21). See also A. David Kossoff's fundamental study (1971).

16. I am quoting an unedited version from Sítio da Torre, Gaula, Madeira Island, recited by Maria Rodrigues Aguiar, 72 years old, on 21 July 1990. It was collected by my wife, Maria-João Câmara Fontes. For additional versions of this extremely rare ballad, see Pere Ferré et al. 1982, nos. 1, 2, 246–48, 250, 254; Suzanne II. Petersen et al. 1982, 2.1; Joanne B. Purcell 1987, 2.1–2.6. Purcell 1976b summarizes the results of her dissertation on this ballad (1976a). I have also studied the ballad in question recently (1996). For the metaphoric value of *fuso* (spindle), see Pierre Alzieu, Robert Jammes, and Yvan Lissorgues 1984, nos. 45.14, 143.6–7.

17. See Costa Fontes 1998a.

18. Version of João Coelho de Melo, about sixty-two years old, born in Doze Ribeiras, Terceira, Azores; Mr. Melo had immigrated to California in 1967.

19. Nepaulsingh conveniently gathers all of those allusions (1979–80, 343–44). Marcella Ciceri also believes that the palinode was written by someone other than Alfonso Martínez de Toledo (her ed. of 1975, 2: 17), but, unfortunately, I was not able to consult directly her edition and study, which I cite through Gerli's review (1976b, 405).

20. In another poem, Encina asks a lady who had given him a few "bread crumbs" for the whole "loaf" (see Márquez 1988, 250–51).

21. Erich Von Richthofen 1941, 451; I am quoting Gerli's translation (1976a, 47).

22. It is possible to argue that Martínez de Toledo was imitating the ironic palinodes found in contemporary misogynistic works (see Gerli 1976a, 34; Whitbourn 1970, 62), but, since there was a retraction in his main model, it is more probable that he also follows it here.

4. Knitting and Sewing Metaphors and a Maiden's Honor in La Celestina

1. Samuel G. Armistead's bibliography is so vast that, at the very least, it would take an extensive article-length study to illustrate this important aspect of his work. For now, see Armistead 1979–80, 174–77, where the crucial importance of the oral tradition is forcefully and profusely documented with many examples. For a brief overview of the extensive fieldwork, editorial activity, and major critical studies that he has undertaken in collaboration with Joseph H. Silverman and Israel J. Katz, see Armistead and Silverman 1986, 3–26; Manuel da Costa Fontes and Katz 1995; and Manuel da Costa Fontes, "Samuel G. Armistead and Sephardic Balladry."

2. They will be included in my *O Conto Popular Português na América do Norte: Canadá* (in preparation). Regarding my fieldwork in Canada, see Can and Costa Fontes 1989–90.

3. On Bocage, see Joaquim Ferreira n.d., 7–59; António José Saraiva and Óscar Lopes n.d., 663–70.

4. His classification of the Brazilian folktale is nearing completion. For a representative sample of his bibliography on the ballad, see RPI, p. 573. Bráulio do Nascimento also compiled an indispensable *Bibliografia do Folclore Brasileiro* (1971). He inspired the great amount of fieldwork undertaken in Brazil during the last few years, and it is to him that we owe the classification of several important tale collections (i.e., Alencar Pimentel 1995; Meira Trigueiro and Alencar Pimentel 1996) according to Antti Aarne and Stith Thompson's (1973) international system.

5. For an important survey of this type of folk literature, see Candace Slater 1982.

6. A metaphor is a word or phrase whose literal meaning replaces another in order to suggest a likeness between the two (i.e., a maiden's "honor" instead of her "virginity"); a euphemism is an innoffensive expression used instead of one that may offend (i.e., "weave," "knit," "stitch," "sew," "plough," "sail," and "nail" instead of "screw"). Since the words examined in this chapter usually partake of both qualities, I use the two terms interchangeably, without delving into hairsplitting distinctions.

7. Saint Appolonia is supposed to help with toothaches because her executioners beat out all of her teeth when she was martyred in Alexandria, during the reign of Decius (de Voragine 1993, 1: 286).

8. The reference to Calisto as "a flower born into the world" constitutes a comparison with Christ, and makes the heresy of Celestina's words even greater (Costa Fontes 1993a, 171–74).

9. According to two former acquaintances in my department, Melissa Ludvigsen and Bob Nocera, the expression is also current in the United States.

10. As María Eugenia Lacarra points out, "mujer honrada" (honorable woman) can also be understood as "prostituta instalada fuera del burdel" (prostitute installed elsewhere other than the brothel; 1996, 428).

11. The term *to plough* was already used with an identical meaning in ancient Greece. In Sophocles's *Antigone*, when Ismene asks Creon if he plans to kill his son's betrothed, he replies: "Oh, there are other furrows for his plough" (1957, 1: 1.569). J. N. Adams also gives Latin examples from Plautus (1982, 154). For a discussion and bibliography on sexual metaphors and various agricultural activities in several European traditions, see Armistead and Silverman 1979, 109–111; 1982b, 110–17.

12. As shown by Harry Sieber 1978, 52–53 and by other scholars, as well as by the poem that follows, shoes were often associated with the female genitalia.

13. Since Cañizares deletes the word *mal*, he is also stating that Lorenza's mother has already died.

14. Together with the *chapines* (shoes) used by the ladies who appear in Alfonso Martínez de Toledo's nightmare at the end of the *Corbacho* in order to punish him for having treated them so harshly in his book, these metaphoric *ruecas* lend a new meaning to his comical retraction (see chap. 3).

15. See Pierre Alzieu, Robert Jammes, and Yvan Lissorgues 1984, 300 (nos. 6–7), and the notes to those poetic riddles on p. 304.

16. *Apud* Cervantes 1962, 4: 199n6 (Rodríguez Marín's ed.). Note also the two variants recorded by Gonzalo Correas in 1627: "Cada puta *hile* y devane y coma, y el rufián pape o aspe, y devane" (Let each slut *spin* her yarn and reel and eat, and let each rogue swallow, spool, or reel; Correas 1924, 99*b*); "Cuando la puta *hila*, y el rufián devana, y el escribano pregunta cuántos son del mes, con mal andan todos tres" (When the slut *spins* her yarn, the rogue reels, and the clerk asks what is the day of the month, all three are sick 138*a*).

17. Some critics postulated that Melibea was a *conversa* of Jewish ancestry; for bibliography, see Joseph T. Snow 1985, nos. 57, 105–6, 123, 195, 211, 306, 349, 684, and 833. According to Julio Rodríguez-Puértolas (1972a), the *converso* was Calisto.

5. El idólatra de María: *An Anti-Christian Jewish Ballad?*

1. The term "Eastern" is used to differentiate these Sephardim from their "Western" counterparts, who settled especially in Morocco. For bibliography on *El idólatra*, see Diego Catalán 1970, 270–77; Yoná 144; Samuel G. Armistead and Joseph H. Silverman 1979, 31; CMP, U2; RPI, U38.

2. In an interesting version from the Canary Islands, the mariner begs not to be thrown into the ocean, but rather on a nearby beach:

6   —Aquí, todos mis amigos,   que se me ha acercado el hora,
       no me boten a la mar   donde los pejes me coman,
8   tírenme en aquella playa   donde combaten las olas,
       donde me llore mi padre,   mi madre y mi gente toda.
(Catalán et al. 1969, no. 148)

("Help me here, all my friends, for my hour has come. Don't throw me into the sea, where the fish will eat me; throw me on that beach besieged by the waves, where my father will mourn me, my mother, and all my people.")

This seems to constitute a vestige of the custom of throwing a sinner into the sea in order to placate a storm (see Yoná 143n13).

3. As E. Michael Gerli indicates, "La imagen de *peregrinatio vitae* . . . informa toda la Introducción de la obra" (The image of *peregrinatio vitae* . . . pervades the introduction to that work; 1985, 9).

4. Abbreviations: CMG = Casto Sampedro y Folgar 1942; CPC = Diego Catalán 1970; FM = Catalán et al. 1969; Val = Ana Valenciano et al. 1998; VRP = José Leite de Vasconcellos 1958–60.

Sources: 1 FM 147.1 (I changed the name of the protagonist, "Saninés," to "el capitán"); 2 FM 150.2; 3a FM 151.3a; 3b: FM 150.3b; 4 CPC, p. 271, v. 1; 5 FM 149.4; 6 FM 148.5 ("Saninés" changed to "el capitán"); 7 CMG 271.7 (I changed the order in 7a, which read, "Virgen del Puerto, valedme"); 8 FM 147.7; 9a FM 601.8a; 9b CPC, p. 271, v. 6b; 10–12 FM 40.17–19; 13 Translated from VRP 616.7 ("Palavras não eram ditas, / o navio saiu da ola"); 14 Translated from VRP 616.8 ("Louvada sejais, ó Virgem, / ó Virgem Nossa Senhora"); 15 Val 89.10 (I changed "naipes" to "dados"); 16a Val 89.11a; 16b Translated from the synthetic Catalan version in CPC, p. 277, v. 12b ("reclams reina i senyora"). CPC lists the main variants in the Sephardic (271–73), Canary Islands (275), Galician (276), and Catalan traditions (277). There are no variants listed after the synthetic Portuguese version (277), probably because the four known Portuguese versions differ very little from each other.

5. Saninés (Catalán et al. 1969, nos. 147–51), San Ginés (601), San Inés (602), Doña Inés (361, 410), Genebra (Alves 1934, 573; VRP, no. 616), Seginebra (Tavares 1903–5, no. 8), Siselinos (Valenciano et al. 1998, no. 89),

Marcelino (Sampedro y Folgar 1942, no. 271), Don Luís (Milá y Fontanals 1882, no. 34A1), la Delgazina (Armistead and Silverman 1979, no. A2).

6. Moshe Attias (1961) prints these verses in 8-syllable lines; they correspond to verses 25–34 in his edition.

7. The Jews also collaborated in the creation of the *Romancero* but, so far as I know, the only certain example is *El sacrifício de Isaac* (RPI, E2; CMP, E5), a ballad with numerous midrashic motifs that were very unlikely to have been known among Christians (see Barugel 1990). For a study of the Crypto-Jewish Portuguese versions of this ballad, see Manuel da Costa Fontes 1994a.

6. *Gil Vicente's* Remando Vão Remadores *and* Barca Bela

1. Cf. Cal, no. 126; Manuel da Costa Fontes 1989–90, no. 22; NI, nos. 127–28; SJ, nos. 189–90; TM, nos. 1239, 1241–42.

2. Those festivities seem to have been started in the thirteenth century by Isabel of Aragon, wife of King Dinis; except for the Azores, they have practically disappeared everywhere. The sponsor, known as *imperador*, changes from year to year, and there are local *irmandades* (brotherhoods) to help with the festivities, which involve the donation of one or two heads of cattle. Their meat is distributed among the poor, together with loaves of bread. The Portuguese immigrants in California and New England have perpetuated this tradition. For abundant bibliography on these festivities, see Benjamim Enes Pereira 1965, nos. 1521–49.

3. Cf. Can, no. 272; Urbano Canuto Soares 1914, 146; Maria Aliete Dores Galhoz 1987–88, no. 451; P.e Manuel Juvenal Pita Ferreira 1956, 104.

4. Cf. Dores Galhoz 1987–88, no. 742; Rodney Gallop 1937, no. 105; A. Gomes Pereira 1906, 236; M. Inácio Pestana 1978, 24; Manuel Rodrigues Lapa 1929, 275n.

5. The only *desatino* (folly) here belongs to the informant who provided this version. Other versions place the appearance of the star after the visit to Herod, describing it as follows: "Os três reis, como eram santos, / uma estrela os guiou; // no meio duma cabana / a estrela ali pousou" (Being holy, the Three Kings were guided by a star; the star landed on the middle of a hut; TM, no. 999); "Mas os três reis eram santos, / jornada foram seguindo; // pôs Deus no céu uma estrela / para os ir dirigindo" (But the Three Kings were holy; their journey they continued, and God put in Heaven a star to guide them; NI, no. 180).

6. = Pires de Lima 1947–51, 3: 255–56; a second variant, on p. 216, is reprinted in Pires de Lima and Carneiro n.d., 16.; cf. Teófilo Braga 1869, no. 63.

7. Augusto César Pires de Lima 1942, 166; Gomes Pereira 1906, 236; António Tomás Pires 1882, nos. 26–29; 1902–10, nos. 204–9.

8. Cf. Braga 1906–9, 2: 498–99; Can, nos. 276, 282; SJ, no. 194.

9. Read *cálix*.

10. Cf. Dores Galhoz 1987–88, no. 550 [= Dias Costa 1961, 328]; Can, no. 583.

11. I heard it during a folk festival that included a *chegança* (type of dramatized folk dance) in January 1997, in Sergipe (in the city of Laranjeiras, I believe).

12. Here the Ship of Faith is guided by Christ, but, as we saw in *El idólatra de María* (chap. 5), as Patroness of Sailors, His Mother was also accorded that role (Pelikan 1978, 162).

13. Cf. Can, nos. 269–71.

14. Cf. Can, nos. 272–73; Dores Galhoz 1987–88, no. 451; Pita Ferreira 1956, 104.

15. Reprinted in Braga 1906–9, 2: 423; Armando Cortes-Rodrigues 1987, 580; Víctor Eugénio Hardung 1877, 2: 174–75.

16. Sources: NI, no. 125 (vv. 1–4); Can, no. 276 (5–6); Can, no. 267 (7–8).

17. I used these verses in a previous reconstruction, in which I also failed to take the parallelistic beginning into account (1983–84, 285).

18. Sources: Pedro da Silveira 1961, 483 (vv. 9–10); NI, no. 125 (11–12; I eliminated the word *já* in 12*b* because it was unnecessary, rendering the verse hypermetric); P.ᵉ José Luís Fraga 1963, 15 (13–14); Braga 1869, no. 63 (15–17); Silveira 1961, 176 (18–19).

19. The Sephardic *El infante cautivo* (The Captive Prince; CMP, H16) and *El cautiverio del príncipe Francisco* (The Captivity of Prince Francisco; CMP, H17) could be related to *Arnaldos*. For a further discussion see Samuel G. Armistead and Joseph H. Silverman 1976–77.

20. Listed in *Primavera* as a variant; the text has *que*.

21. Cf. William H. González 1994, nos. 70.1–6.

22. Cf. R. Menéndez Pidal 1958b, 29.

23. Cf. Juan Menéndez Pidal 1986, no. 93; González 1994, nos. 56.1–3.

24. Cf. González 1994, no. 9.2; Ana Valenciano et al. 1998, no. 142.

25. The poem may have made its way to India, however. Part 2 of what appears to be a version of *A Nau Catrineta* (The Good Ship Catherine; RPI, X1), sung by Anna Liberata de Sousa, an Indian woman whose grandpar-

ents had converted to Christianity, may represent a native adaptation of
Barca Bela. This poem, which describes a holy ship that carries the Sacra-
ment, praying beads, the Twelve Apostles, prophets, all the saints, and
Jesus of Nazareth, concludes as follows:

5.   The ship comes to our doors—
      Who brings it home?
      Our Saviour.
      Our Saviour bless the ship, and bring it safely home.
                              (Frere 1868, 219; rpt. Taylor 1952–53, 305)

26. = Horacio Jorge Becco 1960, 71; cf. Juan Alfonso Carrizo 1926, 33
(nos. 3*b–c*). For five recent Argentinian versions (consisting only of the first
two verses), see Gloria Chicote and Miguel A. García 1996, 50–53.

27. See Manuel da Costa Fontes 1998b. Gil Vicente himself uses this
image in his appropriately entitled *Nau de Amores* (Ship of Love; 1979,
288–97).

28. Margit Frenk 1987 has two additional poems with the same *incipit*: "Por la mar abajo / ban los mis ojos: / quiérome ir con ellos, / no baian
solos" (no. 177B); "Polo mar abaxo / se vão os meus olhos: / quero-me ir com
eles, / que não se vayão solos" (no. 177C) (The following translation applies
to both examples: Down the sea go the eyes of my beloved; I want to go with
them so they won't be lonely.)

29. This ballad is reprinted in Christ. Fr. Bellerman 1864, no. 1, and in
Braga 1906–9, 3: 22.

30. As we shall see in the chapter that follows, that was not the case
with Vicente's *Flérida*, which was written in Spanish.

31. Both were reprinted in Leo Spitzer 1962, 87–103. Spitzer reacted
against R. Menéndez Pidal's opinion that the short version found in the
Cancionero de romances impreso en Amberes sin año was poetically superior
to the longer one (discovered among the Moroccan Sephardim), which turns
the poem into a "sencillo romance de aventuras y reconocimientos, hermoso,
sí, pero que no tiene nada de extraordinario" (simple ballad of adventure
and recognition [of the missing hero], a pretty poem without anything ex-
traordinary; R. Menéndez Pidal 1958c, 64). For a third opinion, see Paul
Bénichou 1968a, 208–12.

32. See the series of articles by Francisco Caravaca (1968, 1969, 1970,
1971, 1972, 1973); Michelle Débax 1983; J. F. G. Gornall 1983; A. G. Hauf
1972; K. Huber 1968; Didier T. Jaén 1976; G. Grant MacCurdy 1983; H. A.
Rennert 1893, 549–50; Julio Rodríguez-Puértolas 1976, 126–27; Aquilino
Suárez Pallasá 1975.

33. The preservation of the only Portuguese versions of the extremely
rare *As Queixas de Ximena* (*Las quejas de Jimena*; RPI, A6; CMP, A3) may

also be attributed to its incorporation, as an *alvorada* (dawn song), into the various songs included in those festivities in the Azores (Braga 1906–9, 2: 248–49; 1911–13, 2: 56–57). The parallelistic songs from the Algarve also used to be sung in honor of the Holy Ghost (Guerreiro Gascon 1922, 274–85). In the county of Miranda do Douro, also in Trás-os-Montes, the group of folk dancers that dances with "sticks," the *pauliteiros*, has preserved several other types of lyrics that can be traced to the sixteenth century (Costa Fontes 1991–92, 358–59).

7. The Oral Transmission of Flérida

1. Juan Luis Alborg 1970–96, 1: 699–702; Eugenio Asensio 1970; Pere Ferré 1982–83; Margit Frenk 1987, 1165 (lists numerous references to Gil Vicente in her monumental *Corpus* of the early popular lyric); José Manuel Pedrosa 1995a; Stephen Reckert 1977b; Jorge de Sena 1963; Constantine C. Stathatos 1980, nos. 227, 249, 276, 290, 328, 334, 376A, 404, 433, 434B, 450, 609–15; Manuel Viegas Guerreiro 1978, 58–62, 65–66; 1981.

2. See Marcelino Menéndez Pelayo 1961, 1: 417–21. Thomas R. Hart published two of the chapters that inspired Vicente (1981, 78–88).

3. Various factors, including radio, television, the mechanization of agriculture, and the quick urbanization of the countryside are contributing to the rapid disappearance of the ballad tradition, but it is still possible to find informants.

4. See Reckert's splendid "Problemática textual de *Don Duardos*" (1977c).

5. This edition of the play was reprinted separately, in *folhas volantes* (Lisbon, 1647 and 1720). These reprintings, of course, are of no interest in the reconstruction of Vicente's original, but Carolina Michaëlis de Vasconcelos used the one from 1720 (1934, 121, 124).

6. C. Colin Smith 1964 (2nd ed. 1996); Giuseppe Di Stefano 1973 (2nd ed. 1993); Mercedes Díaz Roig 1981; Michelle Débax 1982; Paloma Díaz-Mas 1994.

7. They are reprinted by Israel S. Révah (1952, 116–23) and also by Reckert, who places them in parallel columns, in pages divided into two halves, thus allowing the four versions to be compared simultaneously (1977c, 446–61).

8. The other three changes I made are very minor. Révah capitalizes the months (1) and the words Ventura (10*b*), Amor (12*a*, 33*a*), and Muerte (33*a*); I do not. He spells *quando* (4*a*, 25*a*) and *quanto* (6*a*, 32*a*) with a "c"; I retained the sixteenth-century spelling. I also changed *vo* to *voy* (14*a*).

9. All the citations are from Hart's edition of the *Tragicomedia de Don Duardos*.

10. Samuel G. Armistead classified them in CMP as S2.1–11.

11. As its name indicates, the archive was started by Ramón Menéndez Pidal (1869–1968), who discovered the Castilian tradition in 1900 with his wife, Doña María Goyri, during their honeymoon (R. Menéndez Pidal 1953, 2: 291–92). Don Ramón continued to expand his holdings with the help of many collaborators throughout his long, extraordinarily productive life, but the archive was not created until 1954. Its present director, Diego Catalán, is Don Ramón's grandson. Beginning in 1974, Catalán organized four massive group fieldwork projects throughout Spain, which have increased the holdings of the archive tremendously. Some of the participants came from Portugal and were inspired to undertake massive subsequent expeditions in their own country (Catalán 1989, 13–32). Every serious scholar of Hispanic balladry is deeply indebted to Don Ramón and to his successors.

12. R. Menéndez Pidal 1958d, no. 105, is a partial edition of CMP, S2.1, and was reprinted in Manuel Alvar 1971, no. 104.

13. In the Portuguese versions of *Veneno de Moriana* (Moriana's Poison), the poisoned hero often requests: "—Venha papel, venha tinta, / venha também um escrivão; // quero deixar por notícia / o pago qu'as mulheres dão" (Bring me paper; bring me ink; bring me a clerk as well; I want to leave notice of the payment that women give; TM, no. 513). In *O Conde Alarcos* (RPI, L1; CMP, L1), the count's wife, who faces death because the king wants her husband to get rid of her in order to marry his daughter, requests as she is about to be killed: "Dá-me além aquele tinteiro / mais aquela escravaninha; / quero escrever a meus pais / a sorte desta sua filha" ("Bring me that ink pot, together with that writing set; I want to write my parents about the fate of this daughter of theirs"; Maria Aliete Dores Galhoz 1987–88, no. 179). This version is from the Algarve, and there is a similar request in some Brazilian versions: "Dá-me lá papel e tinta, / toda a minha escrivania; / quero escrever a meu pai / a morte que eu morreria" ("Bring me paper and ink, my whole writing set; I want to write my father about the death I shall die"; Galvão 1993, 53).

14. At the beginning of the play, Don Duardos asks the emperor for permission to challenge his son, Primaleón, for having killed Periquín, whom Gridonia loved. When Don Duardos and Primaleón, who was present, begin to fight, the emperor asks Flérida to separate them (1968, 161–63).

15. The classic work regarding this aspect of popular balladry is Paul Bénichou 1968b.

16. For the version in *El patrañuelo*, see Juan Timoneda 1971, 200–208 [no. 21]; Juan Miguel del Fuego wrote in the eighteenth century a version entitled *La peregrina dotora* (1760). Luis Estepa published recently a version from 1847 (1995–98, 560–68). For an earlier, medieval Spanish

version of the story (*Fermoso cuento de una santa enperatrís que ovo en Roma & de su castidat*), see Anita Benaim de Lasry 1982: 175–226.

17. See RPI, L9. It was popularized by Baltasar Dias, a blind poet from Madeira to whom King John III granted in 1539 exclusive rights to such works (see Dias 1985). António Machado Guerreiro and Dores Galhoz published in facsimile the oldest surviving edition, from 1649 (1989, 46–69).

18. Reprinted in Teófilo Braga 1906–9, 1: 442–43; Armando Cortes-Rodrigues 1987, 323–24; Víctor Eugénio Hardung 1877, 1: 12–15; George Young 1916, 30 (facing trans. on p. 31).

19. Braga's Azorean collection began to be put together on the island of São Jorge by João Teixeira Soares de Sousa, with the intention of helping Almeida Garrett, who had discovered the Portuguese ballad tradition in 1823 or 1824 (see Dias Marques 1988–92), being the first one to discover the modern tradition on the Iberian Peninsula as well. Because Almeida Garrett died in 1854, Teixeira Soares began to collaborate with Teófilo Braga instead (Braga 1869, v). In a letter of 24 September 1868, he excitedly announced the discovery of *Flérida* to Braga, explaining that he had heard it from a girl who assisted him with his fieldwork, and that he intended to go to the village of Rosais in order to hear it directly from Maria Vitorina, the informant who had taught it to her: "Tenciono ir a Rosais ouvi-lo da própria boca da senhora Maria Vitorina, mulher de José Silva Soares, abastado lavrador do lugar, que mo remeteu de boca por uma rapariga que muito me tem ajudado nestas coisas. Declarou ela que o aprendera em sua mocidade, contando hoje sessenta e tantos anos" (I intend to go to Rosais to hear it from the mouth of Maria Vitorina herself. She is the wife of José Soares, a wealthy farmer there. She sent it to me, by word of mouth, through a girl who has helped me much in these endeavors. She stated that she had learned it in her youth, and she is now sixty and some odd years old; Braga 1869, 449).

20. VRP 279 = Leite de Vasconcellos 1886, no. 10 and Braga 1906–9, 1: 445–46. VRP 280 = Pinto-Correia 1984, 344.

21. As already indicated (n. 9), I cite Hart's edition of the *Tragicomedia*.

22. The only instance in which the *incipits* of the Portuguese and Spanish ballad coincide, we recall, is an exception.

23. Verse 4, which announces the time of departure, could belong either to *Canta, Mouro* or *Flérida*.

24. For other examples of this contamination, see the bibliography in RPI, C2.

25. This term, which was frequently applied to Moors during the sixteenth and seventeenth centuries, is often used in other ballads (RPI, 2: 527, s.v. *perro*).

26. Ferré et al. 1987, no. 6; António Tomás Pires 1986, no. 12.

27. Ana Maria Martins and Pere Ferré 1989. nos. 2, 4, 6–8; Tomás Pires 1986, no. 13.

28. Since sailing was a metaphor for lovemaking (see Costa Fontes 1998b), the nightingale that sings aboard the ship all day and night long is probably metaphoric as well.

8. *Three New Ballads Derived from* Don Duardos

1. Reprinted in Víctor Eugénio Hardung 1877, 1: 264–66.

2. Reprinted in João David Pinto-Correia 1984, 343–44.

3. As my good friend Samuel G. Armistead pointed out to me on the telephone, this suggests that the ballad was originally hexasyllabic, and that *B* was gradually assimilated into the heptasyllabic form that prevails in such poems.

4. "In balladry, disguise—usually, and more logically, in girl's clothing—is a frequent adjunct to seduction" (Yoná 279; for a copious bibliography, see n. 6).

5. The expression *trabajar como un moro* means "to work very hard."

6. The hunt of love is very frequent in balladry. See Yoná 245–51 nn6–7; Rogers 1980, 6–40.

7. No. 104 is reprinted in Pinto-Correia 1984, 345.

8. Also published in Armando Cortes-Rodrigues 1987, 316–17. Although Pedro da Silveira's text is dated 1986, it appeared after the publication of Cortes-Rodrigues's collection. In the offprint that he sent me, Silveira noted that he had given a copy to Cortes-Rodrigues in 1945, and that the author had altered the text considerably.

9. As my good friend Jackson da Silva Lima pointed out (1991, 119–20), when I studied *Lizarda* in 1978–79 (and also in 1976–77), I did not know about the existence of these three Brazilian versions.

10. There is a similar *incipit* in the *a lo divino* adaptations of *Las almenas de Toro* (The Battlements of Toro) that turn the princess into the Virgin Mary; see RPI, S6: "Oh que linda rosa branca / naquele claro se passeia" (Oh, what a pretty white rose strolls in that clearing).

11. As I point out in RPI, 1: 155, *Não me Enterrem em Sagrado* does not exist as a separate text-type in the Luso-Brazilian tradition, and its appearance in contamination with other ballads is very frequent.

12. Some versions modify the ballad in order to avoid the repelling father-daughter incest theme (Dias Marques 1996).

13. 21*b* was copied by Binyamin Bekar Yosef in two broadsides, the *Sefēr renanôt* (Jerusalem, 1908) and the *Bukyeto de romansas* (Istanbul, 1926). Samuel G. Armistead, Joseph H. Silverman, and Iacob M. Hassán pointed out that the second reprinting includes variants of two verses that are apparently traditional (1981, 45–46). The authors edited both broadsides, including the poem in question (52–53, 56–57).

14. As Armistead and Silverman indicate, this version agrees essentially with the one reprinted by Yosef in his *Bukyeto de romansas* (Yoná 277n2).

15. According to Armistead and Silverman, this text seems to have been adapted from one of Yoná's versions (Yoná 277n2).

16. This three-verse *incipit* does not necessarily belong to *El falso hortelano* because, as we shall see, the opening verses are formulaic, appearing in several additional ballads and, as the author indicates, the third verse (Un día estando en la pexca, / pexcando mi estrellería; One day I was fishing, fishing for my fate ["stars"]) is from *La muerte del duque de Gandía* (The Death of the Duke of Gandía; CMP, C12).

17. I have been unable to see CMP, R8.1, a ms. from Sarajevo in Roman characters.

18. Reprinted in Marcelino Menéndez Pelayo 1945, 9: no. 16, and Rodolfo Gil 1911, 29–30.

19. Since this *incipit* is formulaic, it could also belong to another ballad.

20. For example, regarding the Portuguese in the United States, see Francisco Cota Fagundes 1974; Leo Pap 1949.

21. "Todo olor fuerte es bueno, assí como poleo, ruda, axiensos, humo de plumas de perdiz, de romero, de moxquete, de enciençо. Recebido con mucha dilingencia, aprovecha y afloxa el dolor y buelve poco a poco la madre a su lugar. Pero otra cosa hallava yo siempre mejor que todas, y ésta no te quiero dezir, pues tan santa te me hazes" (All strong smells are good, such as pennyroyal, rue, wormwood, smoke of partridge feathers, rosemary, musk rose, and incense. Taken frequently, these smells help to reduce the pain and put the uterus back in place little by little. There was another thing I always found better than anything else, but I do not want to tell you, because you are acting so holy; Rojas 1987, 203).

22. "Majada con vinagre y aplicada a la frente y sienes, o dada o oler, despierta los endormecidos de letargia. Las hojas de la ruda, metidas dentro de un higo con media nuez mondada y con sal, son evidente remedio contra la pestilencia y contra todo veneno, y se usa ordinariamente en los países de Flandes en tiempo de peste. Solíanla comer los pintores antiguamente a menudo, porque aguza mucho a la vista" (Ground with vinegar and applied to the forehead and temples, or smelled, it awakens people who are drowsy from their lethargy. When placed in a fig with half a peeled nut and salt, rue

leaves are a sure remedy against foul smells and all poisons, and people in the Low Countries use it regularly in times of plague. In ancient times painters ate it frequently, because it sharpens the eyesight very much; Sebastián de Covarrubias 1994, 872).

23. To these seven ballads, add now *El favorito de la reina acusado* (The Queen's Favorite Accused; CMP, H24.1), *El Huerco y el navegante* (Death and the Mariner; CMP, V3.1–2), and *Tiempo es el caballero* (It's Time to Leave; CMP, R2). The last ballad provides the verses with which, in two versions, Flérida complains:

> Ya no puedo ir en pies,   ni al emperador servir,
> 20   que me creció la barriga   y se me acortó el vestir. (CMP, R8.5)

(I can no longer walk or serve the emperor, for my belly has grown and my dress has become shorter.)

The second version constitutes, no doubt, a surprising corruption of the verses just cited:

> 12   [. . . . .]   ni al emperador servirlo,
> que ya le crissió la barva,   y se le acourtó el vestido.   (CMP, R8.4)

([. . .] or serve the emperor, for his beard has grown and his clothes have become shorter.)

24. The interpretation that follows, of course, is based on the synthetic version presented at the beginning of this section, for it is the one that best reflects how the ballad exists in the modern tradition.

Appendix A

1. Because the prostitute will ask three questions later, the informant became momentarily confused with a cumulative tale, *As Doze Palavras Ditas e Retornadas*, which Antti Aarne and Stith Thompson 1973 classify as type 2010.

Abbreviations

AMed	=	*Anuario Medieval*, Jamaica, New York.
ACCP	=	*Arquivos do Centro Cultural Português*, Paris.
AETPP	=	*Anuário para o Estudo das Tradições Populares Portuguesas*, Oporto, Portugal.
BAR	=	*Bulletin de l'Association des Amis de Rabelais et de la Devinière*, Tours, France.
BAAEE	=	Biblioteca de Autores Españoles, Madrid.
BBMP	=	*Boletín de la Biblioteca Menéndez Pelayo*, Santander, Spain.
BF	=	*Boletim de Filologia*, Lisbon.
BFIF	=	*Bulletin Folklorique d'Île de France*, Paris.
BHR	=	*Bibliothèque d'Humanisme et Renaissance. Travaux et documents*, Geneva.
BHS	=	*Bulletin of Hispanic Studies*, Liverpool.
BHTP	=	*Bulletin d'Histoire du Théâtre Portugais*, Lisbon.
BIBLB	=	*Boletim Internacional de Bibliografia Luso-Brasileira*, Lisbon.
BICC	=	*Thesaurus: Boletín del Instituto Caro y Cuervo*, Bogotá, Colombia.
BIHIT	=	*Boletim do Instituto Histórico da Ilha Terceira*, Angra do Heroísmo, Azores, Portugal.
BNCH	=	*Boletim do Núcleo Cultural da Horta*, Horta, Azores, Portugal.
BRAE	=	*Boletín de la Real Academia Española*, Madrid.
Brigantia	=	*Brigantia. Revista de Cultura*, Bragança, Portugal.
Celestinesca	=	*Celestinesca*, East Lansing, Michigan.
Corónica	=	*La Corónica*, Williamsburg, Virginia.

CSIC	= Consejo Superior de Investigaciones Científicas, Madrid.
CSMP	= Cátedra-Seminario Menéndez Pidal, Madrid.
ELO	= *Estudos de Literatura Oral*, Faro, Portugal.
EUC	= *Estudis Universitaris Catalans*, Barcelona.
FAnd	= *El Folk-lore Andaluz*, Seville.
FNAT	= Fundação Nacional para a Alegria no Trabalho, Lisbon.
Hispania	= *Hispania*, American Association of Teachers of Spanish and Portuguese, Washington, D.C.
HR	= *Hispanic Review*, Philadelphia.
HSMS	= The Hispanic Seminary of Medieval Studies, Madison, Wisconsin.
ICP	= Instituto de Cultura Portuguesa, Lisbon.
IMP	= Instituto Menéndez Pidal, Madrid.
INIC	= Instituto Nacional de Investigação Científica, Lisbon.
JAF	= *Journal of American Folklore*, American Folklore Society, Bowling Green, Ohio.
JFR	= *Journal of Folklore Research*, Bloomington, Indiana.
JHP	= *Journal of Hispanic Philology*, Hammond, Indiana.
JILS	= *Journal of Interdisciplinary Literary Studies*, Lincoln, Nebraska.
JMRS	= *Journal of Medieval and Renaissance Studies*, Durham, North Carolina.
JVF	= *Jahrbuch für Volksliedforschung*, Berlin.
KRQ	= *Kentucky Romance Quarterly*, Lexington, Kentucky.
La Torre	= *La Torre*, Río Piedras, Puerto Rico.
LBR	= *Luso-Brazilian Review*, Madison, Wisconsin.
ManQ	= *Manchester Quarterly*, Manchester, England.
MLN	= *Modern Language Notes*, Baltimore, Maryland.
MLR	= *Modern Language Review*, Exeter, England.
NRFH	= *Nueva Revista de Filología Hispánica*, México, D.F.

Olifant	=	*Olifant*, Société Rencesvals, Charlottesville, Virginia.
PhQ	=	*Philological Quarterly*, Iowa City.
PLL	=	*Papers of Language & Literature*, Edwardsville, Illinois.
PMLA	=	*Publications of the Modern Language Association of America*, New York.
QP	=	*Quaderni Portoghesi*, Rome.
RABM	=	*Revista de Archivos, Bibliotecas y Museos*, Madrid.
RAMSP	=	*Revista do Arquivo Municipal*, São Paulo, Brazil.
RBFo	=	*Revista Brasileira de Folclore*, Brasília, Brazil.
RCEH	=	*Revista Canadiense de Estudios Hispánicos*, Toronto.
RdB	=	*Revista do Brasil*, n.p.
RDM	=	*Revue des Deux Mondes*, Paris.
RDTP	=	*Revista de Dialectología y Tradiciones Populares*, Madrid.
REH	=	*Revista de Estudios Hispánicos*, St. Louis, Missouri.
REJ	=	*Revue des Etudes Juives*, Paris.
RER	=	*Revue des Etudes Rabelaisiennes*, Paris.
RF	=	*Romanische Forschungen*, Köln (Cologne), Germany.
RHi	=	*Revue Hispanique*, Paris.
RL	=	*Revista Lusitana*, Oporto and Lisbon.
RLNS	=	*Revista Lusitana (Nova Série)*, Lisbon.
Ro	=	*Romania*, Paris.
Románica	=	*Románica*, La Plata, Argentina.
RPh	=	*Romance Philology*, Berkeley, California.
RQ	=	*Romance Quarterly*, Lexington, Kentucky.
RSS	=	*Revue du Seizième Siècle*, Paris.
RUC	=	*Revista da Universidade de Coimbra*, Coimbra, Portugal.
SMP	=	Seminario Menéndez Pidal, Madrid.
SMV	=	*Studi Mediolatini e Volgari*, Bologna.
UCPMPh	=	University of California Publications in Modern Philology, Berkeley.
Vértice	=	*Vértice. Revista de Cultura e Arte*, Coimbra, Portugal.

VR = *Vox Romanica: Annales Helvetici Explorandis Linguis Romanicis Destinati*, Berne, Switzerland.

YIFMC = *Yearbook of the International Folk Music Council*, Kingston, Ontario.

ZRPh = *Zeitschrift für Romanische Philologie*, Tübingen, Germany.

Works Cited

Aarne, Antti, and Stith Thompson. 1973. *The Types of the Folktale*. 2nd ed. Folklore Fellows Communications, no. 184. Helsinki: Academia Scientiarum Fennica.

Adams, J. N. 1982. *The Latin Sexual Vocabulary*. Baltimore, Maryland: The Johns Hopkins UP.

Afonso X, o Sábio. 1959–72 [ca. 1282]. *Cantigas de Santa Maria*. Ed. Walter Mettman. Acta Universitatis Conimbrigensis. 4 vols. Coimbra, Portugal: Universidade.

Alborg, Juan Luis. 1970–96. *Historia de la literatura española*. 2nd ed. 5 vols. Madrid: Gredos.

Alencar Pimentel, Altimar. 1978. *Barca da Paraíba*. Rio de Janeiro: Ministério de Educação e Cultura.

———. 1995. *Estórias de Luzia Teresa*. Vol. 1. Brasília, Brazil: Thesaurus.

Alfonso, Pedro. 1980 [after 1106]. *Disciplina clericalis*. Introduction and notes by María Jesús Lacarra. Trans. Esperanza Ducay. Nueva Biblioteca de Autores Aragoneses. Zaragoza, Spain: Guara.

Allaigre, Claude. 1980. *Sémantique et littérature: le "Retrato de la Loçana Andaluza" de Francisco Delicado*. Grenoble, France: Ministère des Universités.

Almeida Garrett, João Baptista de. 1963 [1843–51]. *Romanceiro*. 3 vols. Ed. Fernando de Castro Pires de Lima. Lisbon: FNAT.

Alonso, Dámaso. 1958. "Canciones portuguesas de Gil Vicente." *De los siglos oscuros al de oro (Notas y artículos a través de 700 años de letras españolas)*. Madrid: Gredos. 153–57.

279

Alonso Hernández, J. L., ed. 1983. *Literatura y folklore: Problemas de Inter-textualidad (Actas del 2.° Symposium Internacional del Departamento de Español de la Universidad de Groningen 28, 29 y 30 de octubre de 1981)*. Salamanca, Spain: Universidad de Groningen-Universidad de Salamanca.

Alvar, Manuel. 1971. *Poesía tradicional de los judíos españoles*. 2nd ed. México: Porrúa.

Alvarenga, Oneyda. 1946. *Melodias Registradas por Meios Não-Mecânicos*. Vol. 1. São Paulo, Brazil: Arquivo Folclórico da Discoteca Pública Municipal.

Alves, P.ᵉ Francisco Manuel. 1934. "Cancioneiro Popular Bragançano." *Memórias Arqueológico-Históricas do Distrito de Bragança. Arqueologia, Etnografia e Arte*. Vol. 10. Oporto, Portugal: Tip. da Empresa Guedes. 347–585.

Alzieu, Pierre, Robert Jammes, and Yvan Lissorgues. 1984. *Poesía erótica del Siglo de Oro*. Barcelona: Crítica.

Anahory-Librowicz, Oro. 1988. *Cancionero séphardi du Québec*. Vol. 1. Montréal: Fonds FCAR, Collège du Vieux Montréal.

Aragão Pinto, Maria Angélica. 1990. "Deilão. Estudo Linguístico e Etnográfico." *Brigantia* 10.1–2 (Jan.–June): 3–30.

Armistead, Samuel G. 1970. "The Importance of Hispanic Balladry to International Ballad Research." Vol. 3. *Arbeitstagung über Fragen des Typenindex der europäischen Volksballaden*. Berlin: Deutsches Volks-liedarchiv. 48–52.

———. 1976. "The Portuguese *Romanceiro* in Its European Context." *Portuguese and Brazilian Oral Traditions in Verse Form / As Tradições Orais Portuguesas e Brasileiras em Verso*. Eds. Joanne B. Purcell et al. Los Angeles: U of Southern California P. 178–200.

———. 1978. "The Menéndez Pidal Collection of Judeo-Spanish Ballads and Its Importance for Pan-European Ballad Research." *Ballads and Ballad Research: Selected Papers of the International Conference on Nordic and Anglo-American Ballad Research*. Ed. Patricia Conroy. Seattle: U of Washington P. 205–9.

———. 1979. "Judeo-Spanish and Pan-European Balladry." *JVF* 24: 127–38.

———. 1979–80. "Neo-Individualism and the *Romancero*." *RPh* 33: 172–81.

———. 1981. "Epic and Ballad: A Traditionalist Perspective." *Olifant* 8: 376–88.

———. 1992. *The Spanish Tradition in Louisiana*. Vol. 1. *Isleño Folkliterature*. Newark, Delaware: Juan de la Cuesta.

Armistead, Samuel G.: See also CMP.

Armistead, Samuel G. et al. 1998. *Cancioneiro Tradicional de Trás-os-Montes*. Madison, Wisconsin: HSMS.

Armistead, Samuel G., and Israel J. Katz. 1977. "The New Edition of *Danmarks gamle Folkeviser*." *YIFMC* 9: 88–95.

Armistead, Samuel G., and Joseph H. Silverman. 1976–77. "Another Ballad Publication of Yacob Abraham Yoná." *Corónica* 5.2: 110–12.

———. 1977. *Romances judeo-españoles de Tánger recogidos por Zarita Nahón*. (with the collaboration of Oro Anahory Librowicz). Madrid: CSMP.

———. 1979. *Tres calas en el Romancero sefardí (Rodas, Jerusalén, Estados Unidos)*. Prologue by Ramón Menéndez Pidal. Partial trans. by Iacob M. Hassán and Selma L. Margaretten. Musical transcriptions and study by Israel J. Katz. Madrid: Castalia.

———. 1981a. "El antiguo *Romancero sefardí*: Citas de romances en himnarios hebreos (siglos XVI–XIX)." *NRFH* 30: 453–512.

———. 1981b. *Judeo-Spanish Ballads from New York Collected by Maír José Benardete*. Berkeley-Los Angeles: U of California P.

———. 1982a. "El substrato cristiano del Romancero sefardí." *En torno al Romancero sefardí (Hispanismo y balcanismo de la tradición judeo-española)*. Madrid: SMP. 127–48. First published as "Christian Elements and De-Christianization in the Sephardic *Romancero*." *Collected Studies in Honour of Américo Castro's Eightieth Year*. Ed. Marcel P. Hornik. Oxford: Lincombe Lodge Research Library, 1965. 21–38.

———. 1982b. *En torno al Romancero sefardí (hispanismo y balcanismo de la tradición judeo-española)*. With an ethnomusicological study by Israel J. Katz. Madrid: SMP.

———. 1986. *Judeo-Spanish Ballads from Oral Tradition*. Vol. 1. *Epic Ballads*. Musical transcriptions and studies by Israel J. Katz. Folk Literature of the Sephardic Jews, no. 2. Berkeley–Los Angeles: U of California P.

———. 1994. *Judeo-Spanish Ballads from Oral Tradition*. Vol. 2. *Carolingian Ballads (1): Roncesvalles*. Musical transcriptions and studies by Israel J. Katz. Folk Literature of the Sephardic Jews, no. 3. Berkeley–Los Angeles: U of California P.

Armistead, Samuel G., and Joseph H. Silverman: See also Yoná.

Armistead, Samuel G., Joseph H. Silverman, and Iacob M. Hassán. 1981. *Seis romancerillos de cordel sefardíes*. Madrid: Castalia.

Asensio, Eugenio. 1970. "Gil Vicente y las cantigas paralelísticas 'restauradas': ¿Folklore o poesía original?" *Poética y realidad en el cancionero peninsular de la Edad Media*. 2nd ed. Madrid: Gredos. 134–76.

Askins, Arthur L.-F. 1991. "Notes on Pre-1536 Portuguese Theatrical Chapbooks." *Estudos Portugueses. Homenagem a Luciana Stegagno Picchio*. Eds. Eugenio Asensio et al. Lisbon: Difel. 301–9.

Attias, Moshe. 1961. *Romancero sefaradí: Romanzas y cantes populares en judeo-español*. 2nd ed. Jerusalem: Instituto Ben-Zewi, Universidad Hebrea.

Baena, Juan Alfonso de. 1966 [ca. 1444]. *Cancionero de Juan Alfonso de Baena*. Ed. José María Azáceta. Clásicos Hispánicos. 3 vols. Madrid: CSIC.

Bailey, Matthew. 1989. "Lexical Ambiguity in Four Poems of Juan del Encina." *RQ* 36: 431–43.

Barreto, Luiz Antonio. 1996. *Sem Fé, sem Lei, sem Rei*. Aracaju, Sergipe, Brazil: Sociedade Editorial de Sergipe.

Barrick, Mac E. 1976. "The Form and Function of Folktales in *Don Quijote*." *JMRS* 6: 101–38.

Barroso, Gustavo. 1949. *Ao Som da Viola*. Corrected and enlarged edition. Rio de Janeiro: Imprensa Nacional.

Barugel, Alberto. 1990. *The "Sacrifice of Isaac" in Spanish and Sephardic Balladry*. American University Studies, no. 2: Romance Languages and Literatures, no. 116. New York: Peter Lang.

Baum, Paul Franklin. 1917. "The Three Dreams or 'Dream-Bread' Story." *JAF* 30: 378–410.

Becco, Horacio Jorge. 1960. *Cancionero tradicional argentino*. Buenos Aires: Librería Hachette.

Bellerman, Christ. Fr. 1864. *Portugiesische Volkslieder und Romanzen*. Leipzig, Germany: Wilhelm Engelmann.

Benaim de Lasry, Anita. 1982. *"Carlos Maynes" and "La enperatrís de Roma." Critical Edition and Study of Two Medieval Spanish Romances*. Newark, Delaware: Juan de la Cuesta.

Bénichou, Paul. 1968a. *Romancero judeo-español de Marruecos*. Madrid: Castalia.

———. 1968b. *Creación poética en el romancero tradicional*. Madrid: Gredos.

Benmayor, Rina. 1979. *Romances judeo-españoles de Oriente: Nueva recolección*. Madrid: CSMP-Gredos.

Berceo, Gonzalo de. 1985 [ca. 1252]. *Milagros de Nuestra Señora*. Ed. E. Michael Gerli. Madrid: Cátedra.

Blouin, Egla Morales. 1981. *El ciervo y la fuente. Mito y folklore del agua en la lírica tradicional*. Studia Humanitas. Madrid: José Porrúa Turanzas.

Boggs, Ralph Steele. 1930. *Index of Spanish Folktales*. Folklore Fellows Communications, no. 90. Helsinki: Academia Scientiarum Fennica.

Botkin, B. A. 1944. *A Treasury of American Folklore*. New York: Crown Publishers.

———. 1957. *A Treasury of American Anecdotes*. New York: Random.

Bottigheimer, Ruth B. 1993. Review of *Folklore and Literature. Rival Siblings*, by Bruce A. Rosenberg. *JAF* 106: 361–62.

Braga, Teófilo. 1869. *Cantos Populares do Arquipélago Açoriano*. Oporto, Portugal: Livraria Nacional. Facsimile, with a preface by José de Almeida Pavão Jr. Ponta Delgada, Azores, Portugal: Universidade dos Açores, 1982.

———. 1906–9. *Romanceiro Geral Português*. 2nd ed. 3 vols. Lisbon: Manuel Gomes (1–2); J. A. Rodrigues (3). Facsimile, with an introduction by Pere Ferré. Lisbon: Vega, 1982 (vol. 1; the others do not bear a date).

———. 1911–13. *Cancioneiro Popular Português*. 2nd ed. 2 vols. Lisbon: J. A. Rodrigues.

Brault, Gerald J. 1963. *"Celestine": A Critical Edition of the First French Translation (1527) of the Spanish Classic "La Celestina" with an Introduction and Notes*. Detroit: Wayne State UP.

Brunvand, Jan Harold. 1968. *The Study of American Folklore. An Introduction*. New York: Norton.

Busto Cortina, Juan. 1989. *Catálogo-índice de romances asturianos*. [Oviedo, Spain]: Principado de Asturias, Consejería de Educación, Cultura, Deportes y Juventud.

Cabal, Constantino. 1931. *Las costumbres asturianas, su significación y sus orígenes*. Madrid: Talleres Voluntad.

Cal = Costa Fontes, Manuel da. *Romanceiro Português dos Estados Unidos*. Vol. 2. *Califórnia*. Preface by Samuel G. Armistead and Joseph H. Silverman. Acta Universitatis Conimbrigensis. Coimbra, Portugal: Universidade, 1983.

Câmara Cascudo, Luís da. 1922. "Jesus Cristo no Sertão." *RdB* No. 77: 245–47.

———. 1952. *História da Literatura Brasileira*. Vol. 6. *Literatura Oral*. Rio de Janeiro: José Olympio.

———. 1955. *Trinta "Estórias" Brasileiras*. Lisbon, Portugal: Portucalense Editora.

———. N.d. *Contos Tradicionais do Brasil (Folclore)*. Colecção Prestígio. Rio de Janeiro: Edições de Ouro.

Camarena, Julio, and Maxime Chevalier. 1995. *Catálogo tipológico del cuento folklórico español. Cuentos maravillosos*. Madrid: Gredos.

———. 1997. *Catálogo tipológico del cuento folklórico español. Cuentos de animales*. Madrid: Gredos.

Can = Costa Fontes, Manuel da. *Romanceiro Português do Canadá*. Preface by Samuel G. Armistead and Joseph H. Silverman. Acta Universitatis Conimbrigensis. Coimbra, Portugal: Universidade, 1979.

Cancionero de Estúñiga. 1987 [ca. 1460]. Ed. Nicasio Salvador Miguel. Madrid: Alhambra.

Canuto Soares, Urbano. 1914. "Subsídios para o Cancioneiro do Arquipélago da Madeira: Tradições e Vocábulos do Arquipélago da Madeira." *RL* 17: 135–58.

Capellanus, Andreas. 1960 [1180s]. *The Art of Courtly Love*. With introduction, translation, and notes by John Jay Parry. New York: Columbia UP, 1990.

Caravaca, Francisco. 1968. "El romance del conde Arnaldos en el cancionero manuscrito de Londres." *La Torre* 16: 69–102.

———. 1969. "El romance del conde Arnaldos en el *Cancionero de romances de Amberes*, s.a." *BBMP* 45: 47–89.

———. 1970. "El romance del *Conde Arnaldos* en textos posteriores al del *Cancionero de romances de Amberes*, s.a." *BBMP* 46: 3–70.

———. 1971. "Hermenéutica del 'Romance del conde Arnaldos': Ensayo de interpretación." *BBMP* 47: 191–319.

———. 1972. "Tres apéndices al estudio del 'Romance del conde Arnaldos'." *BBMP* 48: 143–200.

———. 1973. "Tres nuevas aportaciones al estudio del romance del conde Arnaldos." *BBMP* 49: 183–228.

Carrizo, Juan Alfonso. 1926. *Antiguos cantos populares argentinos (Cancionero de Catamarca)*. Buenos Aires: Silla Hermanos.

———. 1939. *Cantares Tradicionales del Tucumán (antología)*. Buenos Aires: A. Baiocco.

Caspi, Mishael M., ed. 1995. *Oral Tradition and Hispanic Literature. Essays in Honor of Samuel G. Armistead*. The Albert Bates Lord Studies in Oral Tradition, no. 15. New York: Garland.

Castillo, Hernando del. 1520 [1511]. *Cancionero general*. Toledo. Reprinted with the permission of the Hispanic Society of America. New York: Kraus Reprint Corporation, 1967.

Castillo, María Rosa. 1967. *Leyendas épicas españolas de la Edad Media*. Prologue by Enrique Moreno Báez. 3rd ed. Odres Nuevos. Madrid: Castalia.

Castro, Américo. 1963. *De la edad conflictiva*. 2nd ed. Madrid: Taurus.

———. 1965. *"La Celestina" como contienda literaria (castas y casticismos)*. Madrid: Revista de Occidente.

Catalán, Diego. 1970. *Por campos del Romancero. Estudios sobre la tradición oral moderna*. Madrid. Gredos.

———. 1989. *Romancero e historiografía medieval. Dos campos de investigación del Seminario "Menéndez Pidal"*. Madrid: Fundación Areces-Fundación Ramón Menéndez Pidal.

Catalán, Diego, in collaboration with María Jesús López de Vergara et al. 1969. *La flor de la marañuela: Romancero general de las Islas Canarias*. 2 vols. Madrid: CSMP-Gredos.

Catalán, Diego et al. 1982–88. *CGR: Catálogo general del romancero. El romancero pan-hispánico: Catálogo general descriptivo*. 4 vols. Madrid: SMP.

Catalán, Diego et al. 1991. *Romancero General de León: Antología 1899–1989*. 2 vols. Madrid: SMP–Diputación Provincial de León.

Cátedra, Pedro M. 1989. *Amor y pedagogía en la Edad Media*. Salamanca, Spain: Universidad de Salamanca.

Cervantes Saavedra, Miguel de. 1962 [1605; 1615]. *El ingenioso hidalgo don Quijote de la Mancha*. Ed. Francisco Rodríguez Marín. 9th ed. 8 vols. Clásicos Castellanos. Madrid: Espasa-Calpe.

———. 1976 [1615]. *El viejo celoso. Entremeses*. Ed. Eugenio Asensio. Madrid: Castalia. 203–19.

———. 1978. *El ingenioso hidalgo don Quijote de la Mancha*. Ed. Luis Andrés Murillo. 2 vols. Madrid: Castalia.

Chevalier, Maxime. 1975. *Cuentecillos tradicionales en la España del Siglo de Oro*. Madrid: Gredos.

———. 1978. *Folklore y literatura: El cuento oral en el Siglo de Oro*. Barcelona: Crítica.

———. 1982. *Cuentos españoles de los siglos XVI y XVII*. Madrid: Taurus.

———. 1983. *Cuentos folklóricos en la España del Siglo de Oro*. Barcelona: Crítica.

Chicote, Gloria, and Miguel A. García. 1996. *Romances. Poesía oral de la provincia de Buenos Aires*. La Plata, Argentina: Universidad Nacional de La Plata, Facultad de Humanidades y Ciencias de la Educación.

Childers, J. Wesley. 1948. *Motif-Index of the "Cuentos" of Juan Timoneda*. Indiana U Publications, Folklore Series, no. 5. Bloomington: Indiana UP.

Childers, J. Wesley, and John R. Reynolds. 1978. "A Guide to the Motif-Index of Timoneda's Prose Fiction." *KRQ* 25: 399–412.

Cid, Jesús Antonio. 1993. "El romancero oral en Asturias. Materiales de Josefina Cela y E. Martínez Torner: Inventario, índices, antología." *RDTP* 48: 175–245.

Cirlot, J.E. 1971. *A Dictionary of Symbols*. Trans. Jack Sage. 2nd ed. New York: Dorset P, 1991.

C[louzot], H[enri]. 1909. "Un lecteur du IIe livre en 1535." *RER* 7: 385–86.

———. 1915. "Pour le commentaire de Rabelais." *RSS* 3: 287–88.

CMP = Samuel G. Armistead, in collaboration with Selma Margaretten, Paloma Montero, and Ana Valenciano. Musical transcriptions edited by Israel J. Katz. *El romancero judeo-español en el Archivo Menéndez Pidal (Catálogo-índice de romances y canciones)*. 3 vols. Madrid: CSMP, 1978.

Cohen, J.M., trans. 1966. *"La Celestina": The Spanish Bawd*. New York-London: New York UP and U of London P.

Correas, Gonzalo. 1924. *Vocabulario de refranes y frases proverbiales*. Madrid: RABM.

Cortes-Rodrigues, Armando. 1987. *Romanceiro Popular Açoriano*. Ed. J. Almeida Pavão. Preface by Pere Ferré. Ponta Delgada, Azores, Portugal: Instituto Cultural.

Costa Fontes, Manuel da. 1976–77. "*D. Duardos* in the Portuguese Oral Tradition." *RPh* 30: 589–608.

———. 1978–79. "*Lizarda*: A Rare Vicentine Ballad in California." *RPh* 32: 308–14.

———. 1981. "Novas Versões Transmontanas de *Flérida*." *RLNS* No. 2: 17–29.

———. 1983–84. "*Barca Bela* in the Portuguese Oral Tradition." *RPh* 37: 282–92.

———. 1984. "Celestina's *hilado* and Related Symbols." *Celestinesca* 8.1: 3–13.

——. 1985. "Celestina's *hilado* and Related Symbols: A Supplement." *Celestinesca* 9.1: 33–38.

——. 1988. "The Idea of 'limpieza' in *La Celestina*." *Hispanic Studies in Honor of Joseph H. Silverman*. Ed. Joseph V. Ricapito. Newark, Delaware: Juan de la Cuesta. 23–35.

——. 1989. "*Puputiriru*: Uma Rara Anedota Popular Portuguesa de Origem Medieval." *RLNS* No. 10: 25–40.

——. 1989–90. "Portuguese Ballads from Canada: A Supplement." *Corónica* 18.2: 51–68.

——. 1990. "A Portuguese Folk Story and Its Early Congeners." *HR* 58: 73–88.

——. 1990–91. "Celestina as an Antithesis of the Virgin Mary." *JHP* 14: 7–41.

——. 1991–92. Review of *Corpus de la antigua lírica popular hispánica (siglos XV a XVII)*, by Margit Frenk. *RPh* 45: 355–61.

——. 1992. "Fernando de Rojas, Cervantes, and Two Portuguese Folk Stories." *Medieval, Literary, Linguistic, and Folklore Studies in Honor of Samuel G. Armistead*. Eds. Michael Gerli and Harvey L. Sharrer. Madison, Wisconsin: HSMS. 85–96.

——. 1993a. "Adam and Eve Imagery in *Celestina*: A Reinterpretation." *JHP* 17.2–3: 155–90.

——. 1993b. "Anti-Trinitarianism and the Virgin Birth in *La Lozana andaluza*." *Hispania* 76: 197–203.

——. 1994a. "Between Oral and Written Transmission: *O Sacrifício de Isaac* in the Portuguese Oral Tradition." *JFR* 31: 57–96.

——. 1994b. "The Holy Trinity in *La Lozana andaluza*." *HR* 62: 249–66.

——. 1994–95. "*El idólatra de María*: An Anti-Christian Jewish Ballad?" *RPh* 48: 255–64.

——. 1995a. "Female Empowerment and Witchcraft in *Celestina*." *Celestinesca* 19.1–2: 93–104.

——. 1995b. "Martínez de Toledo's 'Nightmare' and the Courtly and Oral Traditions." *Oral Tradition and Hispanic Literature. Essays in Honor of Samuel G. Armistead*. Ed. Mishael M. Caspi. 189–216.

——. 1996. "The Ballad *A Morte do Rei D. Fernando* and the *Cantar de la muerte del rey don Fernando y cerco de Zamora*." *AMed* 8: 108–51.

——. 1997. "On Alfonso X's 'Interrupted' Encounter with a *soldadeira*." *REH* 31: 93–101.

———. 1998a. "Early Motifs and Metaphors in a Portuguese Traditional Poem: A *Fonte do Salgueirinho.*" *LBR* 35 (1998): 11–23.

———. 1998b. "The Art of 'Sailing' in *La Lozana andaluza.*" *HR* 66: 433–45.

———. MS. "Samuel G. Armistead and Sephardic Balladry." Proceedings of the Howard Gilman International Colloquium: The Spanish-Jewish Cultural Interaction, Harvard University, Cambridge, Massachusetts, 1 December 1995 (in press).

———. MS. "The Idea of Exile in *La Lozana andaluza*: An Allegorical Reading." *Jewish Culture and the Hispanic World: Essays in Honor of Joseph H. Silverman.* Eds. S. G. Armistead, M. Baumgarten, and M. M. Caspi. Newark, Delaware: Juan de la Cuesta.

Costa Fontes, Manuel da: See also Cal, Can, NI, RPI, SJ, TM.

Costa Fontes, Manuel da, and Israel J. Katz. 1995. "Introduction." *Oral Tradition and Hispanic Literature. Essays in Honor of Samuel G. Armistead.* Ed. Mishael M. Caspi. 3–14.

Cota Fagundes, Francisco. 1974. "O Falar Luso-Americano: Um Índice de Aculturação." *Report: First Symposium on Portuguese Presence in California.* San Francisco-San Leandro: Centro Cultural Cabrilho, UCLA, UPEC Cultural Center, and Luso-American Education Foundation. 8–17.

Covarrubias, Sebastián de. 1994 [1611]. *Tesoro de la lengua castellana o española.* Ed. C. R. Maldonado, revised by Manuel Camarero. Nueva Biblioteca de Erudición y Crítica, no. 7. Madrid: Castalia.

Crosbie, John. 1989. *"A lo divino" Lyric Poetry: An Alternative View.* Durham, England: University of Durham.

Cummins, John G. 1977. *The Spanish Traditional Lyric.* Oxford: Pergamon P.

Danon, Abraham. 1896. "Recueil de romances judéo-espagnoles chantées en Turquie avec traduction française, introduction et notes." *REJ* 32: 102–23, 263–75; 33: 122–39, 255–68.

Débax, Michelle. 1982. *Romancero.* Madrid: Alhambra.

———. 1983. "Relectura del romance del *Infante Arnaldos* atribuido a Juan Rodríguez del Padrón: Intratextualidad e intertextualidad." *Literatura y folklore.* Ed. José Luis Alonso Hernández. 199–216.

Delicado, Francisco. 1985 [1528]. *Retrato de La Lozana Andaluza.* Ed. Claude Allaigre. Madrid: Cátedra.

De Voragine, Jacobus. 1993 [ca. 1260]. *The Golden Legend. Readings on the Saints.* Trans. William Granger Ryan. 2 vols. Princeton, New Jersey: Princeton UP.

Devoto, Daniel. 1974a. *Textos y contextos. Estudios sobre la tradición*. Madrid: Gredos.

———. 1974b. "Pisó yerba enconada." *Textos y contextos*. 11–46.

———. 1974c. "Una mata de albahaca." *Textos y contextos*. 395–414.

Deyermond, Alan. 1972. "Folk Motifs in the Medieval Spanish Epic." *PhQ* 51: 36–53.

———. 1977. "Hilado-Cordón-Cadena: Symbolic Equivalence in *La Celestina*." *Celestinesca* 1.1: 6–12.

———. 1978. "Symbolic Equivalence in *La Celestina*: A Postscript." *Celestinesca* 2.1: 25–30.

———. 1979. "Pero Meogo's Stags and Fountains: Symbol and Anecdote in the Traditional Lyric." *RPh* 33: 265–83.

———. 1980. *Historia de la literatura española. La Edad Media*. 7th ed. Barcelona: Ariel.

———. 1995. *La literatura perdida de la Edad Media castellana. Catálogo y estudio, 1: Épica y romances*. Obras de Referencia, no. 7. Salamanca: Universidad.

Dias, Baltasar. 1985. *Autos, Romances, e Trovas*. Ed. Alberto Figueira Gomes. Lisbon: Imprensa Nacional–Casa da Moeda.

Dias Costa, Maria Rosa. 1961. *Murteira, uma Povoação do Concelho de Loures: Etnografia, Linguagem, Folclore*. Lisbon: Junta Distrital de Lisboa.

Dias Marques, José Joaquim. 1984–87. "Romances dos Concelhos de Bragança e de Vinhais." *Brigantia* 4.4 (Oct.–Dec. 1984): 527–50; 5.1 (Jan.–Mar. 1985): 43–62; 7.1–2 (Jan.–June 1987): 3–26.

———. 1988–92. "Nota Sobre o Início da Recolha do Romanceiro da Tradição Oral Moderna." *BF* 32: 71–82.

———. 1996. "'E Acabou Tudo em Bem'. Sobre uma Versão Algarvia do Romance de *Delgadinha*." *ELO* No. 2: 157–76.

Dias Marques, José Joaquim, and Maria Angélica Reis da Silva. 1984–87. "Para o Romanceiro Português." *RLNS* No. 5: 73–133; No. 8: 105–76.

Díaz-Mas, Paloma. 1994. *Romancero*. Preliminary study by Samuel G. Armistead. Biblioteca Clásica, no. 8. Barcelona: Crítica.

Díaz-Plaja, Guillermo. 1934. *Aportación al cancionero judeo-español del Mediterráneo oriental*. Santander, Spain: Publicaciones de la Sociedad de Menéndez y Pelayo.

Díaz Roig, Mercedes. 1981. *El romancero viejo*. Madrid: Cátedra.

Di Stefano, Giuseppe. 1972. "Aggiunte e postille al *Dicc. de pliegos sueltos poéticos* di A. Rodríguez-Moñino." *SMV* 20: 141–68.

———. 1973. *El romancero: Estudio, notas y comentario de texto.* 2nd ed. Madrid: Taurus, 1993.

Dores Galhoz, Maria Aliete. 1960. "Chansons parallélistiques dans la tradition de l'Algarve: Genres, structure, langage." *BF* 19: 5–10 (= *Actas do IX Colóquio Internacional de Linguística Românica da Universidade de Lisboa*, vol. 2).

———. 1987. "Une note de plus pour l'étude du petit corpus de chansons parallélistiques de Marmalete." *Littérature orale traditionelle populaire: Actes du colloque (Paris, 20–22 novembre 1986).* Paris: Fondation Calouste Gulbenkian, Centre Culturel Portugais. 39–58.

———. 1987–88. *Romanceiro Popular Português.* 2 vols. Lisbon: INIC.

Dougherty, Frank. 1977. "Romances tradicionales de Santander." *BICC* 32: 242–72.

Dunn, Peter. 1975. "Pleberio's World." *PMLA* 91: 406–19.

Durán, Agustín. 1945 [1828–32]. *Romancero general o Colección de romances Castellanos anteriores al siglo XVIII.* 2 vols. BAAEE, nos. 10, 16. Madrid: Atlas.

Eisenberg, Daniel. 1976. "Two Problems of Identification in a Parody of Juan de Mena." *Oelschäger Festschrift.* [Chapel Hill]: Estudios de Hispanófila. 153–70.

Encina, Juan del. 1977. *Poesía lírica y cancionero musical.* Eds. R. O. Jones and Carolyn R. Lee. Madrid: Castalia.

Enes Pereira, Benjamim. 1965. *Bibliografia Analítica de Etnografia Portuguesa.* Lisbon: Instituto de Alta Cultura, Centro de Estudos de Etnologia Peninsular.

Estepa, Luis. 1995–98. *La colección madrileña de romances de ciego que pertenció a don Luis Usoz y Río.* Madrid: Ministerio de Educación y Cultura, Biblioteca Nacional—Comunidad de Madrid, Consejería de Educación y Cultura.

Fernandes, Waldemar Iglesias. 1970. "Algumas Estórias Populares Colhidas em Sorocaba (São Paulo)." *RAMSP* No. 181: 183–231.

Fernandes Trancoso, Gonçalo. 1974. *Contos e Histórias de Proveito & Exemplo (Texto Integral Conforme a Edição de Lisboa, de 1624).* Ed. João Palma-Ferreira. Lisbon: Imprensa Nacional-Casa da Moeda.

Ferré, Pere. 1982–83. "El romance *El reguñir, yo regañar* en el *Auto de la Sibila Casandra* de Gil Vicente." *RLNS* No. 3: 55–67.

Ferré, Pere et al. 1982. *Romances Tradicionais*. [Funchal, Madeira, Portugal]: Câmara Municipal.

Ferré, Pere et al. 1987. *Romanceiro Tradicional do Distrito de Castelo Branco*. Vol. 1. Lisbon: Estar.

Ferré, Rosario. 1983. "Celestina en el tejido de la *cupiditas*." *Celestinesca* 7.1: 3–16.

Ferreira, Joaquim. n.d. *Líricas e Sátiras de Bocage: Introdução e Notas*. Oporto, Portugal: Domingos Barreira.

Ferrer Chivite, Manuel. 1983. "Lazarillo de Tormes y sus zapatos: una interpretación del Tratado IV a través de la literatura y el folklore." *Literatura y folklore*. Ed. J. L. Alonso Hernández. 243–69.

Fialho, Adam [pseud. of Manoel d'Almeida Filho]. s.d. *O Costureiro de Honra*. São Paulo, Brazil: Editora Luzeiro.

Fraga, P.ᵉ José Luís de. 1963. *Cantares Açorianos*. Offprint from *Atlântida*. Angra do Heroísmo, Azores, Portugal: União Gráfica Angrense.

Françon, Marcel. 1973. "Rabelais et le thème des trois questions." *BAR* 3.2: 77–78.

———, and Richard Frautschi. 1957. "Sur des variantes de Pantagruel." *BFIF* 20: 1052–53.

Frautschi, R. L. 1961. "Nicolas de Troyes and the Presumed Borrowings from Pantagruel." *MLN* 22: 345–50.

Frenk, Margit. 1971. *Entre folklore y literatura: Lírica hispánica antigua*. Jornadas, no. 68. México, D.F.: El Colegio de México.

———. 1978. *Estudios sobre lírica antigua*. Madrid: Castalia.

———. 1987. *Corpus de la antigua lírica popular hispánica (siglos XV a XVII)*. Madrid: Castalia.

———. 1992. *Corpus de la antigua lírica popular hispánica. Suplemento*. Madrid: Castalia.

Frere, Mary. 1868. *Old Deccan Days, or Hindoo Fairy Legends Current in Southern India*. London: John Murray, Albermarle Street.

Fuego, Juan Miguel del. 1760. *La peregrina dotora*. Madrid, n.p.

Gallop, Rodney. 1937. *Cantares do Povo Português*. Trans. António Emílio de Campos. Lisbon: Instituto para a Alta Cultura.

Galvão, Hélio. 1993. *Romanceiro. Pesquisa e Estudo*. Introduction and notes by Deífulo Gurgel. Natal: Universidade Federal do Rio Grande do Norte.

Garci-Gómez, Miguel. 1989. "La abadesa embargada por el pie." *RDTP* 44: 7–26.

Garza Cuarón, Beatriz, and Yvette Jiménez de Báez, eds. 1992. *Estudios de folklore y literatura dedicados a Mercedes Díaz Roig*. Estudios de Lingüística y Literatura, no. 20. México, D.F.: El Colegio de México.

Gella Iturriaga, José. 1977. "444 refranes de *La Celestina*." *"La Celestina" y su contorno social. Actas del I Congreso Internacional sobre "La Celestina"*. Ed. Manuel Criado de Val. Barcelona: Borrás. 245–68.

——. 1978a. "Los refranes de *La Lozana andaluza*." *Libro-Homenaje a Antonio Pérez Gómez*. Vol. 1. Cieza: "La fonte que mana y corre." 255–68.

——. 1978b. "Los títulos de las obras de Lope de Vega y el refranero." *RDTP* 34: 137–68.

——. 1979. "El refranero en la novela picaresca y los refranes del *Lazarillo de Tormes* y de *La pícara Justina*." *La picaresca: Orígenes, textos y estructuras. Actas del I Congreso Internacional sobre la Picaresca organizado por el Patronato "Arcipreste de Hita."* Ed. Manuel Criado de Val. Madrid: Fundación Universitaria Española. 231–55.

Gerli, E. Michael. 1976a. *Alfonso Martínez de Toledo*. Twayne World Authors Series, no. 398. Boston: Twayne.

——. 1976b. Review of A. Martínez de Toledo, *Arcipreste de Talavera*. Ed. Marcella Ciceri. *NRFH* 25: 403–5.

——. 1977. "The Burial Place and Probable Date of Death of Alfonso Martínez de Toledo." *JHP* 1: 231–38.

——. 1981. "La 'religión de amor' y el antifeminismo en las letras castellanas del Siglo XV." *HR* 49: 65–86.

——. 1983. "Calisto's Hawk and the Images of a Medieval Tradition." *Ro* 104 (1983): 83–101.

——. 1985. "La tipología bíblica y la introducción a los *Milagros de Nuestra Señora*." *BHS* 62: 7–14.

Gil, Rodolfo. 1911. *Romancero judeo-español*. Madrid: Imprenta Alemana.

Goldberg, Harriet. 1998. *Motif-Index of Medieval Spanish Folk Narratives*. Tempe, Arizona: Medieval & Renaissance Texts & Studies.

Gomes Pereira, A. 1906. "Tradições Populares e Linguagem de Vila Real." *RL* 9: 229–58.

——. 1911. "Tradições Populares do Porto, I: Romances." *RL* 14: 125–44.

González, William H. 1994. *Romancero religioso de tradición oral*. Preface by Samuel G. Armistead. Madrid: Eypasa.

Gornall, J. F. G. 1983. "*Conde Arnaldos*: Another Look at Its History." *KRQ* 30: 141–47.

Gottlieb, Bill et al. 1995. *New Choices in Natural Healing*. Emmaus, Pennsylvania: Rodale P.

Grève, Marcel de. 1953. "Les contemporains de Rabelais découvrirent-ils la 'substantificque mouelle'?" *François Rabelais: Ouvrage publié pour le quatrième centenaire de sa mort 1553–1953*. Geneva: Droz; Lille, France: Giard.

Guerreiro Gascon, José A. 1922. "Festas e Costumes de Monchique." *RL* 24: 274–85.

Haboucha, Reginetta. 1992. *Types and Motifs of the Judeo-Spanish Folktales*. Garland Folklore Library, no. 6. New York: Garland.

Handy, Otis. 1983. "The Rhetorical and Psychological Defloration of Melibea." *Celestinesca* 7.1: 17–27.

Hansen, Terrence L. 1957. *The Types of the Folktale in Cuba, Puerto Rico, the Dominican Republic, and Spanish South America*. Folklore Studies, no. 8. Berkeley: U of California P.

Hardung, Víctor Eugénio. 1877. *Romanceiro Português*. 2 vols. Leipzig, Germany: F. A. Brockhaus.

Hart, Thomas R. 1957. "*El conde Arnaldos* and the Medieval Scriptural Tradition." *MLN* 72: 281–85.

———. 1981. *Gil Vicente, "Casandra," and "Don Duardos."* London: Grant and Cutler-Tamesis Books.

Hauf, A. G. 1972. "La seducción de Gentil en el 'Canigó' de Verdaguer y el romance de 'El infante Arnaldos'." *RDTP* 28: 55–84.

Hauf, A. G., and J. M. Aguirre. 1969. "El simbolismo mágico-erótico de *El infante Arnaldos*." *RF* 81: 89–118.

Herrero, Javier. 1984. "Celestina's Craft: The Devil in the Skein." *BHS* 61: 343–51.

———. 1986. "The Stubborn Text: Calisto's Toothache and Melibea's Girdle." *Literature among Discourses: The Spanish Golden Age*. Eds. Wlad Godzich and Nicholas Spadaccini. Minneapolis: U of Minnesota P. 132–47, 166–68 (notes).

Holder, R.W. 1995. *A Dictionary of Euphemisms*. Oxford: Oxford UP.

Huber, K. 1968. "Romance del conde Arnaldos." *VR* 27: 138–60.

Infantes, Víctor. 1982. "Notas sobre una edición desconocida de la *Tragicomedia de Don Duardos* (Sevilla, Bartolomé Pérez, 1530)." *ACCP* 17: 663–701.

Jaén, Didier T. 1976. "El 'Romance del conde Arnaldos': ¿Balada mística?" *Hispania* 59: 435–41.

Jones, Joseph R., and Kenneth Douglas, eds. 1981. *Miguel de Cervantes, "Don Quixote." The Ormsby Translation, Revised Backgrounds and Sources Criticism.* New York-London: Norton.

Kasprzyk, Krystyna. 1963. *Nicolas de Troyes et le genre narratif en France au XVIᵉ siècle.* Paris: Klincksieck.

Keller, John Esten. 1949. *Motif-Index of Mediaeval Spanish Exempla.* Knoxville: The U of Tennessee P.

———, and Joseph R. Jones. 1969. *"The Scholar's Guide," A Translation of the "Disciplina Clericalis" of Pedro Alfonso.* Toronto: Pontifical Institute of Medieval Studies.

Kish, Kathleen V. 1973. *An Edition of the First Italian Translation of the "Celestina."* Chapel Hill: The U of North Carolina P.

Kossoff, A. David. 1971. "El pie desnudo: Cervantes y Lope." *Homenaje a William L. Fichter. Estudios sobre el teatro antiguo hispánico y otros ensayos.* Eds. A. David Kossoff and José Amor y Vásquez. Madrid: Castalia. 381–86.

Lacarra, María Eugenia. 1990. *Cómo leer "La Celestina."* Madrid: Júcar.

———. 1992. "El fenómeno de la prostitución y sus conexiones con *La Celestina.*" *Historias y ficciones. Coloquio sobre la literatura del siglo XV.* Eds. R. Bertrán, J. L. Canet, and J. L. Sirera. Valencia, Spain: Universidad. 267–78.

———. 1993. "La evolución de la prostitución en la Castilla del siglo XV y la mancebía de Salamanca en tiempos de Fernando de Rojas." *Fernando de Rojas and "Celestina": Approaching the Fifth Centenary.* Eds. Ivy A. Corfis and Joseph T. Snow. Madison, Wisconsin: HSMS. 33–78.

———. 1995. "Introducción." Fernando de Rojas. *La Celestina.* Ed. María Eugenia Lacarra. 2nd ed. Madison, Wisconsin: HSMS. v–lxvi.

———. 1996. "Sobre los 'dichos lascivos y rientes' en *Celestina.*" *Nunca fue pena mayor. (Estudios de literatura española en homenaje a Brian Dutton).* Eds. Ana María Collera and Victoriano Roncero López. Cuenca: Universidad de Castilla-La Mancha. 419–33.

Lacarra, María de Jesús. 1989. *Cuentos de la Edad Media.* Odres Nuevos. Madrid: Castalia.

Lancashire, George S. 1905. "The Proverbs of *Don Quijote.*" *ManQ* 24: 284–90.

Larrea Palacín, Arcadio de. 1952. *Romances de Tetuán.* 2 vols. Madrid: CSIC.

Lázaro Carreter, Fernando. 1969. "Construcción y sentido del *Lazarillo de Tormes." Ábaco. Estudios Sobre Literatura Española*. Vol. 1. [Ed. Antonio Rodríguez-Moñino.] Madrid: Castalia. 45–134.

Lebègue, Raymond. 1952. "Rabelais et la parodie." *BHR* 14: 193–204.

Legman, G. 1962. "Misconceptions in Erotic Folklore." *JAF* 75: 200–208.

Leite de Vasconcellos, José. 1882. "Antiga Poesia Popular Portuguesa." *AETPP* 1: 19–24. Rpt. in his *Opúsculos*. Vol. 7. *Etnologia (Parte II)*. Lisbon: Imprensa Nacional, 1938. 736–45.

———. 1886. *Romanceiro Português*. Biblioteca do Povo e das Escolas, no. 121. Lisbon: David Corazzi.

———. 1963–66. *Contos Populares e Lendas*. Coordinated by Alda da Silva Soromenho and Paulo Caratão Soromenho. 2 vols. Acta Universitatis Conimbrigensis. Coimbra, Portugal: Universidade.

———. 1975–83. *Cancioneiro Popular Português*. Ed. Maria Arminda Zaluar Nunes. 3 vols. Acta Universitatis Conimbrigensis. Coimbra, Portugal: Universidade.

Leite de Vasconcellos, José: See also VRP.

Levy, Isaac Jack. 1959. *Sephardic Ballads and Songs in the United States: New Variants and Additions*. M.A. Thesis. Iowa City: U of Iowa.

Lida de Malkiel, María Rosa. 1976. "Función del cuento popular en el *Lazarillo de Tormes." El cuento popular y otros ensayos*. Buenos Aires: Losada. 107–22.

Lindley Cintra, Luís Filipe. 1967. "Notas à Margem do *Romanceiro* de Almeida Garrett." *BIBLB* 8: 105–35.

Liu, Benjamin. 1995. "Obscenidad y transgresión en una cantiga de escarnio." *Erotismo en las letras hispánicas*. Eds. L. López-Baralt and F. Márquez Villanueva. 203–17.

Livingston, Charles H. 1965. "A propos de 'Pantagruel' II, Ch. XVII, un conte de Philippe de Vigneulles." *BHR* 27: 30–36.

Lockhart, John Gibson. 1823. *Ancient Spanish Ballads, Historical and Romantic*. London. I cite from the Nickerbocker Press's ed. New York and London: Putnam, n.d.

Lopes, António. 1967. *Presença do Romanceiro. Versões Maranhenses*. Rio de Janeiro: Editora Civilização Brasileira.

López-Baralt, Luce, and Francisco Márquez Villanueva, eds. 1995. *Erotismo en las letras hispánicas*. México: Centro de Estudios Lingüísticos y Literarios.

López Pinciano, Alonso. 1953 [1596]. *Filosofía antigua poética.* 3 vols. Madrid: CSIC.

Mabbe, James. 1894. *Celestina; or the Tragicke-Comedy of Calisto and Melibea.* Englished from the Spanish by James Mabbe, anno 1631. With an introduction by James Fitzmaurice Kelly. London; rpt. New York: AMS P, 1967.

MacCurdy, G. Grant. 1983. "La visión simbólica del *Conde Arnaldos.*" *Estudios sobre el Siglo de Oro en homenaje a Raymond R. MacCurdy.* Eds. Angel González, Tamara Holzapfel, and Alfred Rodríguez. Albuquerque: U of New Mexico P. 301–12.

Machado Ávila, Manuel. 1948. "Cantigas dos Foliões da Ilha Graciosa." *BIHIT* 6: 290–94.

Mackay, Angus. 1989. "Courtly Love and Lust in Lioja." *The Age of the Catholic Monarchs, 1474–1516. Literary Studies in Memory of Keith Whinnom.* Eds. Alan Deyermond and Ian Macpherson. Liverpool: Liverpool UP. 83–94.

Macpherson, Ian. 1985. "Secret Language in the *Cancioneros:* Some Courtly Codes." *BHS* 62: 51–63.

Machado Guerreiro, António, and Maria Aliete Dores Galhoz. 1989. "Imperatriz Porcina no Romance e no Teatro." *RLNS* No 10: 41–84.

Mal Lara, Juan de. 1996 [1568]. *Philosophía vulgar.* In *Obras completas.* Vol. 1. Ed. Manuel Bernal Rodríguez. Madrid: Biblioteca Castro.

Márquez Villanueva, Francisco. 1988. "Pan 'pudendum muliebris' y *Los españoles en Flandes.*" *Hispanic Studies in Honor of Joseph H. Silverman.* Ed. Joseph V. Ricapito. Newark, Delaware: Juan de la Cuesta. 247–69.

Martínez de Toledo, Alfonso. 1949 [1438]. *Corbacho, o Reprobación del amor mundano.* Ed. Martín de Riquer. Barcelona: Selecciones Bibliófilas.

———. 1955. *Arcipreste de Talavera.* Ed. Mario Penna. Turin: Rosenberg and Sellier.

———. 1975. *Arcipreste de Talavera.* Ed. Marcella Ciceri. 2 vols. Modena, Italy: Società Tipografica Editrice Modenese.

———. 1981. *Arcipreste de Talavera o Corbacho.* Ed. Michael Gerli. 2nd ed. Madrid: Cátedra.

Martínez Ruiz, Juan. 1963. "Poesía sefardí de carácter tradicional (Alcazarquivir)." *AO* 13: 79–215.

Martins, Ana Maria, and Pere Ferré. [1989.] *Romanceiro Tradicional do Distrito de Beja.* Vol. 1. Santiago do Cacém, Portugal–Madrid: Real Sociedade Arqueológica Lusitana–SMP.

Meira Trigueiro, Osvaldo, and Altimar de Alencar Pimentel. 1996. *Contos Populares Brasileiros. Paraíba.* Recife, Brazil: Fundação Joaquim Nabuco, Editora Massangana.

Menéndez Pelayo, Marcelino. 1945. "Apéndice y suplemento a la *Primavera y flor de romances* de Wolf e Hofmann." *Antología de poetas líricos castellanos*, no. 9. Edición Nacional de las Obras Completas de Menéndez Pelayo, no. 25. Santander: CSIC.

———. 1961. *Orígenes de la novela.* 2nd ed. 4 vols. Edición Nacional de las Obras Completas de Menéndez Pelayo, nos. 13–16. Madrid: CSIC.

Menéndez Pidal, Juan. 1986 [1885]. *Poesía popular: Colección de los viejos romances que se cantan por los asturianos en la danza prima, esfoyazas y filandones.* Madrid: Hijos de J.A. García. 2nd ed., in facsimile, ed. Jesús Antonio Cid. Madrid–Gijón: SMP–Gredos–GH Editores.

Menéndez Pidal, Ramón. 1933. "Los 'Estudos sobre o Romanceiro peninsular' de Doña Carolina." *RUC* 11: 493–500.

———. 1953. *Romancero hispánico (hispano-portugués, americano y sefardí).* 2 vols. Madrid: Espasa-Calpe.

———. 1958a. *Los romances de América y otros estudios.* Austral, no. 55. 6th ed. Madrid: Espasa-Calpe.

———. 1958b. "Los romances tradicionales en América." *Los romances de América y otros estudios.* 13–51.

———. 1958c. "Poesía popular y poesía tradicional en la literatura española." *Los romances de América y otros estudios.* 52–87.

———. 1958d. "Romancero judíoespañol." *Los romances de América y otros estudios.* 114–79.

———. 1965–66. *Crestomatía del español medieval.* Completed and revised by Rafael Lapesa and María Soledad de Andrés. 2 vols. Madrid: Universidad de Madrid-Facultad de Filosofía y Letras, SMP.

Michaëlis de Vasconcelos, Carolina. 1934. *Estudos sobre o Romanceiro Peninsular: Romances Velhos em Portugal.* 2nd ed. Coimbra, Portugal: Imprensa da Universidade.

Milá y Fontanals, Manuel. 1882. *Romancerillo catalán: Canciones tradicionales.* Barcelona: Verdaguer.

Molho, Michael. 1960. *Literatura sefardita de Oriente.* Madrid: CSIC.

Monteiro, José. 1943. "Introdução ao Cancioneiro da Beira Baixa." *RL* 38: 143–95.

Nascimento, Bráulio do. 1971. *Bibliografia do Folclore Brasileiro.* Rio de Janeiro: Biblioteca Nacional.

Nepaulsingh, Colbert I. 1979–80. "Talavera's Images, and the Structure of the *Corbacho." RCEH* 4: 329–49.

Neugaard, Edward J. 1993. *Motif-Index of Medieval Catalan Folktales.* Medieval and Renaissance Texts and Studies, no. 96. Binghamton, New York: Center for Medieval and Renaissance Studies, State U of New York.

NI = Costa Fontes, Manuel da. *Romanceiro Português dos Estados Unidos.* Vol. 1. *Nova Inglaterra.* Preface by Samuel G. Armistead and Joseph H. Silverman. Acta Universitatis Conimbrigensis. Coimbra, Portugal: Universidade, 1980.

Nucio, Martín. 1945 [ca. 1548]. *Cancionero de romances impreso en Amberes sin año.* Ed. Ramón Menéndez Pidal. Madrid: CSIC.

———. 1967. *Cancionero de romances (Anvers, 1550).* Ed. Antonio Rodríguez-Moñino. Madrid: Castalia.

O'Kane, Eleanor S. 1959. *Refranes y frases proverbiales españolas de la Edad Media.* BRAE, Anejo 2. Madrid: Real Academia Eespañola.

Olinger, Paula. 1985. *Images of Transformation in Traditional Hispanic Poetry.* Newark, Delaware: Juan de la Cuesta.

O Livro da 3.ª Classe. 1958. 4th ed. Lisbon: Ministério de Educação Nacional.

Olmos Canalda, Elías. 1940. *Los refranes del Quijote.* Valencia, n.p.*

Pap, Leo. 1949. *Portuguese-American Speech; An Outline of Speech Conditions among Portuguese Immigrants in New England and Elsewhere in the United States.* New York: Kings Crown P (Columbia U).

Paris, Gaston. 1912. *Mélanges de littérature française du Moyen Âge.* Ed. Mario Roques. Princeton: Princeton U Library; rpt. New York: Burt Franklin, 1971.

Partridge, Eric. 1968. *Shakespeare's Bawdy: A Literary & Psychological Essay and a Comprehensive Glossary.* London: Routledge & Kegan Paul, 1947; revised and enlarged, 1968.

Payer, Pierre J. 1984. *Sex and the Penitentials. The Development of a Sexual Code (550–1150).* Toronto: U of Toronto P.

Pedrosa, José Manuel. 1994–95. "Una colección de romances rarísimos recogidos en Villasumil de Ancares (León)." *Corónica* 23.2: 64–73.

———. 1995a. "Correspondencias folclóricas españolas de la *Farsa de Inês Pereira* de Gil Vicente." *ELO* No. 1: 137–43.

———. 1995b. *Las dos sirenas y otros estudios de literatura tradicional.* Madrid: Siglo Veintiuno.

Pelikan, Jaroslav. 1978. *The Growth of Medieval Theology (600–1300).* The

Christian Tradition: A History of the Development of Doctrine, no. 3. Chicago & London: The U of Chicago P.

Pereira, Eduardo C.N. 1989–90. *Ilhas de Zargo*. 4th ed. 3 vols. Funchal, Madeira, Portugal: Câmara Municipal.

Pereira da Costa, Francisco Augusto. 1908. *Folclore Pernambucano*. Rio de Janeiro: Livraria J. Leite.

Pestana, M. Inácio. 1978. *Etnologia do Natal Alentejano*. Portalegre, Portugal: Edição da Assembleia Distrital.

Petersen, Suzanne H. et al. 1982. *Voces nuevas del romancero castellano-leonés*. AIER (Archivo Internacional Electrónico del Romancero), nos. 1–2. Madrid: SMP.

Pimentel, Alberto. 1899. *História do Culto de Nossa Senhora em Portugal*. Lisbon: Guimarães, Libanio & C.ª.

Pinheiro Torres, Alexandre. 1977. *Antologia da Poesia Trovadoresca Galego-Portuguesa*. Oporto, Portugal: Lello & Irmão.

Pinto-Correia, João David. 1984. *Romanceiro Tradicional Português*. Lisbon: Comunicação.

Pires de Lima, Augusto César. 1915. "Tradições Populares de Santo Tirso." *RL* 18: 183–204.

———. 1942. *A Poesia Religiosa na Literatura Popular Portuguesa*. Oporto, Portugal: Domingos Barreira.

———. 1947–51. *Estudos Etnográficos, Filológicos e Históricos*. 4 vols. Oporto, Portugal: Edição da Junta de Província do Douro Litoral.

———, and Alexandre Lima Carneiro. n.d. *Romanceiro para o Povo e para as Escolas*. Oporto, Portugal: Domingos Barreira. New ed., entitled *Romanceiro Popular Português para o Povo e Para as Escolas*. Oporto, Portugal: Domingos Barreira, 1984.

Pita Ferreira, P.ᵉ Manuel Juvenal. 1956. *O Natal na Madeira (Estudo Folclórico)*. Funchal, Madeira, Portugal: Edição da Junta do Distrito Autónomo.

Pliegos poéticos del s. XVI de la Biblioteca de Catalunya. 1976. 2 vols. Ed. José Manuel Blecua. Madrid: Joyas Bibliográficas.

Pliegos poéticos góticos. 1957–61. Introduction by José Antonio García Noblejas. 6 vols. Madrid: Joyas Bibliográficas.

Poema de Mío Cid. 1968 [ca. 1140]. Ed. Ramón Menéndez Pidal. 12th ed. Clásicos Castellanos, no. 201. Madrid: Espasa-Calpe.

Preminger, Alex et al., eds. 1993. *The New Princeton Encyclopedia of Poetry and Poetics*. Princeton: Princeton UP.

Primavera = Wolf, Fernando J., and Conrado Hofmann. [1856]. *Primavera y flor de romances*. Ed. Marcelino Menéndez Pelayo, *Antología de poetas líricos castellanos*, no. 8. Edición Nacional de las Obras Completas de Menéndez Pelayo, no. 24. Santander: CSIC, 1945.

Purcell, Joanne B. 1976a. "The *Cantar de la muerte del rey don Fernando* in Modern Oral Tradition: Its Relationship to Sixteenth-Century Romances and Medieval Chronicles." Diss. U of California, Los Angeles.

———. 1976b. "Recently Collected Ballad Fragments on the Death of Don Fernando I." *Portuguese and Brazilian Oral Traditions in Verse Form*. Eds. Joanne B. Purcell et al. Los Angeles: U of Southern California P. 158–67.

———. 1987. *Novo Romanceiro Português das Ilhas Atlânticas*. Vol. 1. Eds. Isabel Rodríguez García and João A. das Pedras Saramago. Fuentes para el Estudio del Romancero: Serie Luso-Brasileira, no. 4. Madrid: SMP-Universidad Complutense.

Quevedo, Francisco de. 1988 [ca. 1604]. *La vida del buscón llamado don Pablos*. Ed. James Iffland. Newark, Delaware: Juan de la Cuesta.

Rabelais, François. 1912–22 [1532]. *Pantagruel*. In *Oeuvres*. 4 vols. Eds. Abel Lefranc et al. Vol. 4. Paris: Edouard Champion.

Reckert, Stephen. 1970. *Lyra minima. Structure and Symbol in Iberian Traditional Verse*. London: Grosvenor P.

———. 1977a. *Gil Vicente: Espíritu y letra*. Vol. 1. *Estudios*. Madrid: Gredos.

———. 1977b. "La lírica vicentina: Estructura y estilo." *Gil Vicente: Espíritu y letra*. Vol. 1. *Estudios*. 135–70.

———. 1977c. "La problemática textual de *Don Duardos*." *Gil Vicente: Espíritu y letra*. Vol. 1. *Estudios*. 236–469.

———, and Helder Macedo. n.d. *Do Cancioneiro de Amigo*. Documenta Poética, no. 3. 2nd ed. Lisbon: Assírio e Alvim (1st ed. 1976).

Rennert, H.A. 1893. "Lieder des Juan Rodríguez del Padrón," *ZRPh* 17: 544–58.

Révah, Israel S. 1952. "Édition critique du 'romance' de don Duardos et Flérida." *BHTP* 3: 107–39.

Richthofen, Erich Von. 1941. "Alfonso Martínez de Toledo und Sein *Arcipreste de Talavera*, ein kastiliches Prosawerk des 15. Jahrhunderts." *ZRPh* 61: 417–537.

Robe, Stanley L. 1973. *Index of Mexican Folktales*. Folklore Studies, no. 26. Berkeley: U of California P.

Rodrigues de Azevedo, Álvaro. 1880. *Romanceiro do Arquipélago da Madeira*. Funchal: "Voz do Povo."

Rodrigues Lapa, Manuel. 1929. *Das Origens da Poesia Lírica em Portugal na Idade Média*. Lisbon: Seara Nova.

———. 1965. *Cantigas d'escarnho e de mal dizer. Dos cancioneiros medievais galego-portugueses*. Vigo, Spain: Galaxia. 2nd ed., revised: 1970. Reprinted: Lisbon, 1995.

Rodríguez-Moñino, Antonio. 1973. *Manual bibliográfico de cancioneros y romanceros impresos durante el siglo XVI*. Coordinated by Arthur L.-F. Askins. 2 vols. Madrid: Castalia.

———. 1997. *Nuevo Diccionario bibliográfico de pliegos sueltos poéticos (Siglo XVI)*. Corrected and updated by Arthur L.-F. Askins and Víctor Infantes. Madrid: Castalia.

Rodríguez-Puértolas, Julio. 1972a. "El linaje de Calisto." *De la Edad Media a la edad conflictiva: estudios de literatura española*. Madrid: Gredos. 209–16.

———. 1972b. "El romancero, historia de una frustración," *PhQ* 51: 85–104. Rpt. in his *Literatura, historia, alienación*. Barcelona: Labor Universitaria, 1976. 105–46.

Rogers, Edith. 1980. *The Perilous Hunt: Symbols in Hispanic and European Balladry*. Lexington: The UP of Kentucky.

Rojas, Fernando de. 1987 [1499]. *La Celestina*. Ed. Dorothy S. Severin. Madrid: Cátedra.

Rosenberg, Bruce A. 1991. *Folklore and Literature. Rival Siblings*. Knoxville: The U of Tennessee P.

RPI = Costa Fontes, Manuel da. *O Romanceiro Português e Brasileiro: Índice Temático e Bibliográfico (com uma bibliografia pan-hispânica e resumos de cada romance em inglês) / Portuguese and Brazilian Balladry: A Thematic and Bibliographic Index (with a Pan-Hispanic bibliography and English summaries for each text-type)*. Selection and commentary of the musical transcriptions by Israel J. Katz. Pan-European correlation by Samuel G. Armistead. Madison, Wisconsin: HSMS, 1997.

Ruiz, Juan. 1974 [1330; 1343]. *Libro de buen amor*. Ed. Jacques Joset. 2 vols. Clásicos Castellanos, nos. 14, 17. Madrid: Espasa-Calpe.

Sainéan, L. 1930. *L'influence et la réputation de Rabelais. Interprètes, lecteurs et imitateurs, un rabelaisien (Marnix de Sainte-Aldegonde)*. Paris: J. Gamber.

Salazar, Flor. 1999. *El Romancero vulgar y nuevo*. Madrid: Fundación Ramón Menéndez Pidal-Seminario Menéndez Pidal, Universidad Complutense.

Sampedro y Folgar, Casto, and José Figueira Valverde. 1942. *Cancionero musical de Galicia: Colección de la Sociedad Arqueológica de Pontevedra.* 2 vols. Madrid: El Museo de Pontevedra.

Sánchez Martínez, Francisco Javier. 1995. *Historia y crítica de la poesía lírica culta "a lo divino" en la España del Siglo de Oro.* Vol. 1. *Técnicas de divinización de textos líricos y otros fundamentos teóricos.* Alicante, Spain: F. J. Sánchez Martínez.

———. 1996. *Historia y crítica de la poesía lírica culta "a lo divino" en la España del Siglo de Oro, 3: De los orígenes a la divinización de la lírica de Garcilaso, con un estudio del centón poético "a lo divino" de Juan de Andosilla.* Murcia, Spain: F. J. Sánchez Martínez.

Santillana, Iñigo López de Mendoza, marqués de. 1987 [before 1458]. *Refranes de las viejas tras el fuego.* Ed. José Esteban. Madrid: s.n.

Santos Neves, Guilherme. [1963]. "O Romance da Barca Nova: Suas Variantes no Brasil." *Actas do Congresso Internacional de Etnografia Promovido pela Câmara Municipal de Santo Tirso de 10 a 18 de Julho de 1963.* Vol. 6. Lisbon: Junta de Investigação do Ultramar. 351–62.

Saraiva, António José. 1985. *Inquisição e Cristãos-Novos.* 5th ed. Lisbon: Estampa.

———, and Óscar Lopes. n.d. *História da Literatura Portuguesa.* 6th ed. Oporto, Portugal: Porto Editora.

Scholberg, Kenneth R. 1971. *Sátira e invectiva en la España medieval.* Madrid: Gredos.

Schwob, Marcel. 1904. "Notes pour le commentaire. Utrum chimera." *RER* 2: 135–42.

Sena, Jorge de. 1963. "Gil Vicente e o Romanceiro." *Estudos de História e Cultura (1.ª Série).* Lisbon: Revista de "Ocidente." 315–22.

Shakespeare, William. 1937. *The Passionate Pilgrim. Complete Works.* Roslyn, New York: Walter J. Black.

Shipley, George A. 1975. "Concerting Through Deceit: Unconventional Uses of Conventional Sickness Images in *La Celestina.*" *MLR* 70: 324–32.

Sieber, Harry. 1978. *Language and Society in "La vida del Lazarillo de Tormes."* Baltimore, Maryland: The Johns Hopkins UP.

Silva Lima, Jackson da. 1977. *O Folklore em Sergipe.* Vol. 1. *Romanceiro.* Rio de Janeiro–Brasília: Livraria Editora Cátedra–Instituto Nacional do Livro.

———. 1991. "Achegas ao Romanceiro Tradicional em Sergipe." *Estudos de Folclore em Homenagem a Manuel Diégues Junior.* Ed. Bráulio do Nascimento. Maceió, Brazil: Comissão Nacional de Folclore. 119–47.

Silveira, Pedro da. 1961. "Materiais para um Romanceiro da Ilha das Flores." *BNCH* 2.3: 471–90.

———. 1986. "Catorze Trovas e um Conto Recolhidos na Ilha das Flores." *RLNS* No. 7: 103–23.

Silverman, Joseph H. 1979. "La contaminación como arte en un romance sefardí de Tánger." *El romancero hoy: Nuevas fronteras, 2.º Coloquio Internacional, University of California, Davis*. Eds. Antonio Sánchez Romeralo, Diego Catalán, and Samuel G. Armistead. Madrid: CSMP–U of California–Gredos. 29–37.

Singleton, Mack Hendricks, trans. 1975. *Celestina, A Play in Twenty-One Acts Attributed to Fernando de Rojas*. 5th printing. Madison: The U of Wisconsin P.

SJ = Costa Fontes, Manuel da. *Romanceiro da Ilha de S. Jorge*. Preface by Samuel G. Armistead and Joseph H. Silverman. Musical transcriptions by Halim El-Dabh. Acta Universitatis Conimbrigensis. Coimbra, Portugal: Universidade, 1983.

Slater, Candace. 1982. *Stories on a String. The Brazilian "Literatura de Cordel."* Berkeley–Los Angeles: U of California P.

Smith, C. Colin. 1964. *Spanish Ballads*. Oxford: Pergamon P. 2nd ed., London: Bristol Classical P, 1996.

Snow, Joseph T. 1985. *Celestina by Fernando de Rojas: An Annotated Bibliography of World Interest 1930–1985*. Madison, Wisconsin: HSMS.

———. 1990. "The Satirical Poetry of Alfonso X: A Look at Its Relationship to the *Cantigas de Santa María*." *Alfonso X of Castile, The Learned King (1221–1284): An International Symposium, Harvard University, 17 November 1984*. Eds. Francisco Márquez Villanueva and Carlos Alberto Vega. Harvard Studies in Romance Languages, no. 43. Cambridge, Massachusetts: Department of Romance Languages and Literatures of HU. 110–31.

Soons, Alan. 1976. *Haz y envés del cuento risible en el Siglo de Oro. Estudio y antología*. London: Tamesis.

Sophocles. 1957. *Antigone. The Complete Greek Tragedies. Sophocles*. Trans. Elizabeth Wykoff. Eds. David Grene and Richmond Lattimore. Vol. 1. 3rd ed. Chicago: The U of Chicago P.

Soromenho, Alda da Silva, and Paulo Caratão Soromenho, eds. 1984–86. *Contos Populares Portugueses (Inéditos)*. 2 vols. Lisbon: Centro de Estudos Geográficos, INIC.

Spitzer, Leo. 1955. "The Folkloristic Pre-Stage of the Spanish *Romance* 'Conde Arnaldos'." *HR* 23: 173–87.

————. 1956. "Annex to *HR*, 23, 173–87 ('Conde Arnaldos')." *HR* 24: 64–66.

————. 1962. *Sobre antigua poesía española*. Buenos Aires: Universidad.

Stathatos, Constantine C. 1980. *A Gil Vicente Bibliography (1940–1975)*. Preface by Thomas R. Hart. London: Grant and Cutler.*

Suárez Pallasá, Aquilino. 1975. "Romance del *Conde Arnaldos*: Interpretación de sus formas simbólicas." *Románica* 8: 135–80.

Tavares, José Augusto. 1903–6. "Romanceiro Transmontano (da Tradição Popular)." *RL* 8: 71–80; 9: 277–323.

Taylor, Archer. 1952–53. "*A nao Caterineta* in India." *RPh* 6: 304–05.

Thompson, B. Bussell, and J. K. Walsh. 1988. "The Mercedarian's Shoes (Perambulations on the fourth *tratado* of *Lazarillo de Tormes*." *MLN* 103: 440–48.

Thompson, Stith. 1946. *The Folktale*. New York: Holt.

————. 1955–58. *Motif-Index of Folk-Literature*. 6 vols. Bloomington, Indiana: Indiana UP.

Tillier, Jane Yvonne. 1985. "Passion Poetry in the *cancioneros*." *BHS* 62: 65–78.

Timoneda, Juan. 1911 [1564]. *El buen aviso y portacuentos*. Ed. Rudolph Schevill. *RHi* 24: 171–254.

————. 1947. *El buen aviso y portacuentos*. *Obras*. Ed. Juliá Martínez. 3 vols. Madrid: Sociedad de Bibliófilos Españoles. 1: 273–379.

————. 1963. *Rosa de amores*. *Rosas de romances (Valencia, 1573)*. Eds. Antonio Rodríguez-Moñino and Daniel Devoto. Valencia, Spain: Castalia.

————. 1971 [1567]. *El patrañuelo*. Ed. Rafael Ferreres. Madrid: Castalia.

————. 1990 [1564; 1569]. *Buen aviso y portacuentos; El sobremesa y alivio de caminantes*. *Cuentos de Joan Aragonés*. Eds. M.ª Pilar Cuartero and Maxime Chevalier. Clásicos Castellanos Nueva Serie, no. 19. Madrid: Espasa-Calpe.

TM = Costa Fontes, Manuel da. *Romanceiro da Província de Trás-os-Montes (Distrito de Bragança)*. Collected in collaboration with Maria-João Câmara Fontes. Preface by Samuel G. Armistead and Joseph H. Silverman. Musical transcriptions by Israel J. Katz. 2 vols. Acta Universitatis Conimbrigensis. Coimbra, Portugal: Universidade, 1987.

Toldo, Pietro. 1895. *Contributo allo studi della novella francese del XV e XVI secolo considerata specialmente nelle sue attinenze con la letteratura italiana*. Rome: Ermanno Loescher.

Tomás Pires, António. 1882. "Poesia Popular Portuguesa: Cantigas de Natal Recolhidas da Tradição Oral na Província do Alentejo." *FAnd* 1.10: 406–10.

———. 1902–10. *Cantos Populares Recolhidos da Tradição Oral*. 4 vols. Elvas, Portugal: Tipografia Progresso.

———. 1986. *Lendas e Romances*. Ed. Pere Ferré. Lisbon: Presença.

Torres, António. 1922. *Prós & Contras*. Rio de Janeiro: Castilho.

Trapero, Maximiano, in collaboration with Elena Hernández Casañas. 1987. *Romancero de la Isla de La Gomera*. [Las Palmas, Spain]: Cabildo Insular de la Gomera.

———. 1990. *Romancero de Gran Canaria*. Vol. 2. Musical transcriptions and commentary by Lothar Siemens Hernández. [Las Palmas, Spain]: Cabildo Insular de Gran Canaria.

———. 1991. *Romancero de Fuerteventura*. Musical transcriptions and commentary by Lothar Siemens Hernández. [Las Palmas, Spain]: La Caja de Ahorros de Canarias.

Troyes, Nicolas de. 1970 [ca. 1536]. *Le Grand Parangon des nouvelles nouvelles (choix)*. Ed. Krystyna Kasprzyk. Paris: Didier.

Valenciano, Ana et al. 1998. *Os romances tradicionais de Galicia. Catálogo exemplificado dos seus temas*. Romanceiro Xeral de Galicia, no. 1. Madrid-Santiago de Compostela: Publicacións do Centro de Investigacións Lingüísticas e Literarias Ramón Piñeiro-Fundación Ramón Menéndez Pidal.

Vasvari, Louise O. 1983. "La semiología de la connotación. Lectura polisémica de 'Cruz cruzada panadera'." *NRFH* 32: 299–324.

———. 1983–84. "An Example of 'parodia sacra' in the *Libro de Buen Amor*: 'quoniam' 'pudenda'." *Corónica* 12: 195–203.

———. 1986–87. "Erotic Polysemy in the *Libro de Buen Amor*: A Propos Monique de Lope's *Traditions populaires et textualité*." *Corónica* 15: 127–34.

———. 1988–89. "Vegetal-Genital Onomastics in the *Libro de Buen Amor*." *RPh* 42: 1–29.

———. 1989. "The Two Lazy Suitors in the 'Libro de Buen Amor': Popular Tradition and Literary Game of Love." *AMed* 1: 181–205.

———. 1990a. "A Tale of 'Tailing' in the *Libro de Buen Amor*." *JILS* 2: 13–41.

———. 1990b. " 'Chica cosa es dos nuezes': Lost Sexual Humor in the *Libro del Arcipreste*." *REH* 24: 1–22.

———. 1990–91. "The Battle of Flesh and Lent in the 'Libro del Arçipreste': Gastro-Genital Rites of Reversal." *Corónica* 20: 1–15.

———. 1992a. "Pitas Pajas: Popular Phonosymbolism." *REH* 26: 135–62.

———. 1992b. "Why Is Doña Endrina a Widow? Traditional Culture and Textuality in the *Libro de Buen Amor*." *Upon My Husband's Death: Widows in the Literature and Histories of Medieval Europe*. Ed. Louise Mirrer. Ann Arbor: The U of Michigan P. 259–87.

———. 1995a. "El hijo del molinero: Para la polisemia popular del *Libro del Arcipreste*." *Erotismo en las letras hispánicas*. Eds. L. López-Baralt and F. Márquez Villanueva. 461–77.

———. 1995b. "Múltiple transparencia semántica de los nombres de la alcahueta en el *Libro del Arcipreste*." *Medioevo y Literatura. Actas del V Congreso de la Asociación Hispánica de Literatura Medieval*. Ed. Juan Paredes. Granada: Universidad, 1995. 453–63.

Vicente, Gil. 1968 [ca. 1525]. *Tragicomedia de Don Duardos. Obras dramáticas castellanas*. Ed. Thomas R. Hart. Clásicos Castellanos, no. 156. Madrid: Espasa-Calpe. 161–227.

———. 1979 [ca. 1515]. *Auto da Barca do Purgatório. Obras Completas*. Ed. Álvaro Júlio da Costa Pimpão. Oporto, Portugal: Livraria Civilização. 78–87.

Vicuña Cifuentes, Julio. 1912. *Romances populares y vulgares recogidos de la tradición oral chilena*. Santiago de Chile: Imprenta Barcelona.

Viegas Guerreiro, Manuel. 1978. *Para a História da Literatura Popular Portuguesa*. Biblioteca Breve, no. 19. Lisbon: ICP.

———. 1981. "Gil Vicente e os Motivos Populares: Um Conto na Farsa de Inês Pereira." *RLNS* No. 2: 31–60.

Vigneulles, Philippe de. 1972 [1515]. *Les Cent nouvelles nouvelles*. Ed. Charles H. Livingston, in collaboration with Françoise R. Livingston and Robert H. Ivy Jr. Geneva: Droz.

VRP = Leite de Vasconcellos, José. *Romanceiro Português*. 2 vols. Acta Universitatis Conimbrigensis. Coimbra, Portugal: Universidade, 1958–1960.

Wack, Mary Frances. 1990. *Lovesickness in the Middle Ages. The Viaticum and Its Commentaries*. Philadelphia: U of Pennsylvania P.

Wallensköld, A. 1907. "Le conte de la femme chaste convoitée par son beau-frère." *Acta Societatis Scientiarum Fennicae* 34: 1–95.

Wardropper, Bruce W. 1958. *Historia de la poesía lírica a lo divino en la cristiandad occidental*. Madrid: Revista de Occidente.

Webber, Ruth House. 1951. *Formulistic Diction in the Spanish Ballad*. UCPMPh, no. 34. Berkeley-Los Angeles: U of California P.

Weinberg, F. M. 1971. "Aspects of Symbolism in *La Celestina*." *MLN* 86: 136–53.

Weiner, Jack. 1969. "Adam and Eve Imagery in *La Celestina*." *PLL* 5: 389–96.

West, Geoffrey. 1979. "The Unseemliness of Calisto's Toothache." *Celestinesca* 3.1: 3–10.

Whinnom, Keith. 1979. "Introducción crítica." Diego de San Pedro, *Obras completas*. Vol. 2. *Cárcel de amor*. Madrid: Castalia. 7–76.

———. 1981. *La poesía amatoria de la época de los Reyes Católicos*. Durham, England: U of Durham P.

Whitbourn, Christine J. 1970. *The "Arcipreste de Talavera" and the Literature of Love*. Occasional Papers in Modern Languages, no. 7. Hull, England: The U of Lull P.

Wolf, Fernando J., and Conrado Hofmann: See *Primavera*.

Xavier Alcoforado, Doralice Fernandes, and Maria del Rosário Suárez Albán. 1996. *Romanceiro Ibérico na Bahia*. Salvador, Bahia: Livraria Universitária.

Yoná = Armistead, Samuel G., and Joseph H. Silverman. *The Judeo-Spanish Ballad Chapbooks of Yacob Abraham Yoná*. Folk Literature of the Sephardic Jews, no. 1. Berkeley–Los Angeles: U of California P, 1971.

Young, George. 1916. *Portugal: An Anthology*. Oxford: Clarendon UP.

---

*There is a second edition of Olmos Canalda's *Los refranes del Quijote* (Madrid, 1998), but I have not seen it. Constantine Stathatos has published a new *Gil Vicente Bibliography (1975–1995)* (Bethlehem, Pennsylvania: Lehigh UP; London: Associated U Presses, 1997), which, unfortunately, I was unable to use.

Index of Ballads, Popular Songs, and Folktales

The slashes separate Portuguese ballad titles from their Spanish equivalents. When applicable, ballad titles are followed by their classification in Samuel G. Armistead's Sephardic catalog (CMP) and our Portuguese and Brazilian catalog (RPI). Folktales are correlated with Aarne and Thompson's index (AT).

Index of Euphemisms and Metaphors

Index of Subjects and Proper Names

317